Space Packed

The Architecture of Alfred Neumann

Rafi Segal

PARK BOOKS

Imprint

Author: Rafi Segal
Design: Ben Fehrman-Lee
Editing and Proofreading: Bronwen Saunders
Typeface: Mercator by Dick Dooijes (1959), and Ben Fehrman-Lee (2016)

Lithography, printing, and binding by DZA Druckerei zu Altenburg GmbH, Altenburg

Park Books AG
Niederdorfstrasse 54
8001 Zurich
Switzerland

www.park-books.com

ISBN 978-3-03860-055-8

Introduction
6

Towards a Humanized Unit of Space
18

Theory and Practice
38

Architecture is Creation of Patterns
58

The Battle for Architecture
82

Buildings and Designs (1922–1968)
98

Appendix
322

Excerpts from the Writings of Alfred Neumann
MΦ System: The Humanization of Space
Morphologic Architecture
Architecture as Ornament
Irrational Factors in Building Industrialization

Chronology
Photographs and Drawings
Index
Acknowledgments

Introduction

Alfred Neumann's death in 1968 came as a surprise to many. It was premature, according to Zvi Hecker, his former student, apprentice, and collaborator, who lamented that Neumann was just then beginning to develop "totally new ideas in architecture."[1] Neumann's late years of active practice in Israel during the 1960s had yielded an intriguing collection of buildings and designs that by then was at last garnering extensive international recognition. Like his teaching at the Technion-Israel Institute of Technology during those years, Neumann's design work carried the notion of a new architectural language: radical, original, and vibrant.

"We were all shocked to hear of Professor Alfred Neumann's death during the printing of this issue," wrote Moshe Safdie, renowned Israeli-Canadian architect and creator of the Habitat 67 housing project in Montreal, in the foreword of the November 1968 issue of the journal *Architecture Canada*. "One of the great men of architecture is no longer with us [...] Neumann through his buildings showed a compassion for the indigenous environment and the depth and potential of his 'morphological architecture,'"[2] he continued. Neumann's unique interpretation of local context was just one aspect of his broader innovative approach to architecture. "Irrational factors in Building Industrialization," Neumann's essay featured in that same issue of *Architecture Canada*, in which he alluded to problems of industrial building production and outlined the emergent role of the computer in future design and building, provides further insight into his prescient outlook. In his condolence letter to Neumann's wife, Naomi, Moshe Safdie wrote: "For me, he was the only architect with whose work I felt total affinity. This I felt even before I met him and more so when I got to know him."[3] Safdie was just one of the many young architects impacted by Neumann who went on to have illustrious careers.

In a 1969 *New York Times* article, Ada Louise Huxtable situated Neumann as the leading figure of a theory and practice that yielded one of the most unique architectural works of the time: "The father of the space-packing theory was Alfred Neumann," she wrote, "an archetypal European intellectual and architectural polemicist." She then proceeded to assess Neumann's work as being of debatable experimental value, but argued that his space-packing approach nevertheless indicated "a progressive fertility of ideas that can open eventual avenues to solutions of problems from housing to environment," and that it had produced "some of the most stunning, unsung half successes anywhere in the world."[4] Huxtable was not the only critic who found it difficult to categorize Neumann's work. Many, including Maria Bottero and Peter Cook,[5] labeled his projects "experimental," although Neumann himself never regarded his work as such.[6]

Sixty-eight years of age at the time of his death, Neumann was an accomplished, exceptionally well-read, creatively mature architect. He was engaged in research, theory, and teaching, and brought to his work a professional and life experience both rich and diverse. He was so highly respected within the international community that the leading French journal of the time, *L'architecture d'aujourd'hui*, published his obituary in the 1969 June-July issue alongside an obituary of Walter Gropius, one of the most influential modern architects of the twentieth century, giving each man an equal full-page spread. Gropius and Neumann had also known each other personally: They met at various international meetings of CIAM (Congres Internationaux d'Architecture Moderne),[7] at which Neumann represented first Czechoslovakia and later the State of Israel. Gropius spoke highly of Neumann, and praised the theory of proportion that he developed in the early 1950s:

> The EM-PHI System (The Humanization of Space) by Alfred Newman represents, in my opinion, an important contribution to the whole field of design, planning, architecture, and industrial design. It is the first attempt I know to create a modular system which comprehends the whole range of possibilities of proportion [...] The only system akin to the new investigations of Alfred Neumann is Le Corbusier's *Modulor* [...] Mr. Neumann goes beyond this system and gives it an all-embracing mechanical background.[8]

Le Corbusier, the prominent architect and author of what is perhaps the most famous modernist proportion theory, the *Modulor*, also cited Neumann's theory: "Alfred Neumann of Jerusalem is well acquainted with the whole question. He believes in the value Φ. He has created a beautiful term: 'Humanization of Space.'"[9] Neumann would go on to develop the idea of a humanized unit of space throughout his design practice in the 1960s, and would apply his proportion theory to architecture in a completely new way.

Moving between theory and practice, teaching and painting, Neumann was a rare example of someone who was both an inspirational professor and a skillful, thoughtful designer. He was a critical and independent thinker who continuously engaged in learning, questioned conventions, and sought to place the creative act of architecture within the broadest context of human and natural phenomena. As one of his former students, Israel Goodovitch, recalled, "Neumann was such an original and captivating thinker, we were always curious to hear his opinion on any matter."[10]

I first heard of Alfred Neumann in the late 1980s during my first year of architecture studies at the Technion-Israel Institute of Technology's Department of Architecture and Town Planning, where Neumann had taught as a professor, and over which he had presided as dean during the 1950s. His name was mentioned by some of my older instructors in design studio, and again in a required course on architectural morphology, which Neumann himself had introduced into the curriculum and which was still being taught by one of his former teaching assistants. I did not particularly enjoy the architectural morphology course, which to me seemed overly technical, narrow-minded and dated, so was not surprised when, years later, while conducting the research for this book, I discovered letters penned by Neumann in which he expressed his utter dissatisfaction with how this course had been taught by his successors. After my fourth year of studies, I became more closely acquainted with Neumann's work in Israel when I started working for one of his former students and collaborators, Zvi Hecker.

My eight years of work with Zvi Hecker had an immense influence on my understanding of, and approach to, architecture. From a practical perspective, I learned to approach design through the use of geometric modules as a means of subdividing space, and to think of architectural design as a balance between the overall form of a building and the units or parts out of which it is assembled. Conceptually, I formulated a position on the place of architecture within society and cultural production at large. Although Hecker rarely spoke of Neumann during my years with him, in the process of working on this book it became clear to me just how much I had been exposed to Neumann's thinking through him.

After working with Zvi Hecker, I established my own practice in Tel Aviv in 2000. A few years later, I moved with my family to the United States to pursue a PhD at Princeton University. During my first year of study at Princeton, in a seminar on post-World-War II architectural theory taught by Prof. Christine Boyer, I encountered Neumann's name again when studying 1950s discourse on proportion theories. I realized that behind the name that had remained so vague for many years there lay much more to be explored. I thereupon decided to dedicate my time at Princeton to studying further the architecture of Alfred Neumann.

This book is the first collection of Alfred Neumann's work. It explores his projects, writings, and teachings in the context of both Israel's local architectural scene of the 1960s, his most active years, and the international architectural discourse of the time. It investigates and analyzes his central ideas, principles, and designs, and examines them in relation to contemporaneous developments within the discipline. Tracing and documenting Neumann's built and unbuilt projects from his early years in Europe through his unique accomplishments in Israel in the 1960s, this study presents a significant collection of projects that expands the repertoire of modern architecture and underscores its role as a form of innovation and novel artistic expression.

In examining Neumann's work I have identified his space-packing approach as a method of architectural thinking and design. The interest in space packing—a type of patterned thinking—as a mode of understanding, measuring, and controlling architectural and urban space extends well beyond 1960s architecture as it shares many of the ideas and preoccupations of contemporary practice. A study of how Neumann interpreted and applied spatial thinking to different scales of an architectural project based on an examination of his designs and writings can contribute to contemporary architectural discourse by expanding the theoretical basis underlying the current interest in form-generating methods. My interest is not in these methods for their own sake, however, but rather, as will be shown through the chapters of this book, in the way they carry and express a system of values.

This book also offers insight into Neumann's creative process and how abstract concepts and ideas are concretized and take shape in built form in architecture generally. As we shall see, while Neumann developed theoretical principles and concepts in advance of generating his groundbreaking designs, he arrived at his method or "theory of design"—the process of space packing—only through the practice of architecture. In other words, his space-packing approach emerged through the process of developing a project for construction, translating a drawing into a building, preparing construction documents, resolving issues of structure and other building systems, addressing features of scale, natural light, and climate, and responding to the opportunities and limitations of the program and the site. All architects will perhaps be familiar with how a certain design logic emerges from what is otherwise an often messy, intuitive, circuitous process of creation.

As much as an examination of Neumann opens a window onto an era when conventions of modernism were challenged, his story is also about an architect's struggle for artistic creativity within a society that demanded conformity to mainstream architectural conventions. Highlighting the conflicts embedded in the profession, this study raises longstanding questions about the role of the architect in modern democratic society. Is the architect to serve society by providing it with what it expects—often, the familiar and the known—or is his or her task to explore and propose new forms and expressions? Can architecture be an art in the sense that it wields creative freedom with respect to the form of a building? Should it aspire to critique and innovate on the basis of existing forms and typologies, or should it merely follow the call to serve the tastes and preferences of the client or public? Furthermore, what kind of role does society play in promoting the creative re-interpretation and reshaping of architecture, particularly of publicly funded buildings? Neumann's life and career certainly offer a fruitful case study for exploring these questions.

Life and contribution

Neumann was born in 1900 to a Jewish family in Vienna. He spent his early years there, until his family relocated to Brno in 1910. In Brno his father established a cabinetry and furniture workshop, where in his youth Neumann spent a lot of time working and developing various skills—among them drafting and furniture design—that would help him later on in his architectural career. Around this time, Neumann also cultivated an interest in mathematics and philosophy.

In 1914, Neumann commenced his formal education in architecture at the Deutsche Baugewerbeschule (German Building Trades School) in Brno. His studies were interrupted by the outbreak of the

First World War, and in 1918, the final year of the war, Neumann served in the Austro-Hungarian army. Czechoslovakia gained independence in October of that year and the war ended soon after. Neumann was permitted to return to Brno, where he was a student at the Deutsche Technische Hochschule (German Technical University) until 1922. He also continued to help his father design furniture.

On completing his studies in Brno, Neumann moved to Vienna to study under the eminent modernist architect Peter Behrens at the Vienna Academy of Fine Arts. Neumann's talents were evident from the early stages of his studies, and he received the Behrens Award for the work he accomplished during his second year at the academy. In Neumann's diploma, Behrens wrote: "Without doubt, one may expect a lot from his future artistic development [...] he belongs to my most capable students."[11] In 1925, Neumann completed his studies at the Vienna Academy of Fine Arts and moved to Paris. There, he worked initially for Charles Siclis, and then for the great modernist architect and pioneer of reinforced-concrete construction, Auguste Perret, at his Atelier du Palais de Bois. In Paris Neumann became acquainted with several artists and architects, such as the photographer Man Ray. From 1926 to 1927, he was in Berlin, where he worked for Peter Behrens on various projects, including social housing developments in Vienna and Zagreb, and department stores in Frankfurt am Main and Magdeburg. By 1928, he had been drawn back to Paris, the hub of the avant-garde movement at the time, where he returned to work for Perret. Here, Neumann also met several other architects, such as Jacques Guiauchain and Pierre Forestier, with whom he collaborated on some projects of the late 1920s and early 1930s. In 1931, Neumann joined the avant-garde artist group Cercle et Carre, and began working for the architectural office of Jean Ginsberg.

From 1932 to 1934, Neumann divided his time between Paris and Brno. In 1934, he moved to Cape Town where he worked for the firm Kalenbach, Kennedy, and Furnes. On returning to Europe in 1936 he settled in Brno. Hitler was already consolidating power by then, and by 1938 had set his sights on occupying Czechoslovakia; German forces invaded the country the following year. Neumann tried to flee Europe before World War II broke out, but was unsuccessful. He went into hiding first in Brno and then in Prague, but was captured by Nazi soldiers in early 1945 and deported to Theresienstadt concentration camp. He was fortunate to survive the war, which ended in May of that year.

After the war, Neumann returned to Brno and found work at the Provincial Research Institute, where he designed urban plans for the Moravia region of Czechoslovakia. He presented this work at CIAM 6, the sixth meeting of the Congrès Internationaux d'Architecture Moderne held in Bridgewater, England, in 1947, where he was part of the Czech delegation. His time with the Institute was short-lived, however, as it was dissolved in 1948, shortly after the Communist Party of Czechoslovakia staged a coup d'etat and seized power. In 1949, Neumann left Czechoslovakia and emigrated to Israel, opening a new chapter in his life. There, he first found work as a regional planner for various districts of Jerusalem and Haifa, but soon was hired as a professor in the Faculty of Architecture and Town Planning at the Technion-Israel Institute of Technology, becoming dean in 1953.

Neumann developed his theory of proportion in Israel during the 1950s. Published in 1956 in a pamphlet titled *The EM-PHI System: The Humanization of Space*, Neumann's theory reflected a desire to "humanize" architecture—to create spaces and buildings that were better suited to human users—by determining a unit of measure that could make for better design. Neumann's theory was based on two measures, the meter and the value Φ, hence the name. Throughout the 1950s, Neumann corresponded with Le Corbusier, Walter Gropius, Sigfried Giedion, Wells Coates, Matila C. Ghyka, and others about his ideas on human scale and proportions. HIs theory contributed to the broader postwar discourse on the use of proportions in architecture. Architectural proportions, along with the concept of using a unit of measure as a design tool, are explored in the first chapter. Neumann's own proportion system would later lead him to translate a linear unit of measure into a unit of space with the aim of scaling three-dimensionally composed architectural space to the human body. His theory of the humanization of space reflects his preoccupation with space as a concept to be further explored, developed, and defined in architectural thought and practice. Chapter 1 illustrates how this concept set the stage for Neumann's later work, which is explored in the rest of the book.

In 1959, Neumann established an architectural practice in Tel Aviv in partnership with two of his former students, Zvi Hecker and Eldar Sharon. In the course of the 1960s, Neumann and his young collaborators produced a body of work that combined and synthesized ideas and influences drawn from his education, professional experience, and theoretical work. He developed an approach to form generation that challenged what was then the predominant way in which buildings were conceived and shaped. During the 1950s and early 1960s, Israel had experienced an immense building boom, which had seen the International Style of modern architecture proliferate and had given rise to several generic, orthogonal slab buildings, many of which were hastily erected to fill the steep postwar demand for housing without much attention to location or site. Neumann was critical of this architecture, haphazardly filling the landscape all across the country. Rather than blindly following European architectural trends, Neumann sought instead to develop a new architectural expression of polyhedral, non-orthogonal geometries that could relate to the local climatic, natural lighting, and topographical conditions. Instead of appropriating the European modernist aesthetic, Neumann took inspiration from the geometries of the Islamic and vernacular architectural traditions of the region at large (of Arab, Ottoman, and Persian origin). His use of polyhedral geometries and his method of space packing, as we shall see in the second chapter, were not ideas and expressions determined *a priori* to be implemented later in his designs, but were rather developed and shaped *through* the process of design. By examining the designs for a few key projects, such as the Bat Yam Town Hall and the Dubiner Apartment House, chapter 2 offers an insight into how these ideas were developed.

Considered in the context of international architectural discourse of the 1950s and 1960s, Neumann's work reflects a paradigm shift in architectural practice and theory, away from conceiving buildings as isolated "objects" and toward construing them instead as "patterns." The building-as-object approach, exemplified by the "modernist slab," involved conceiving buildings as enclosed, isolated structures in an undifferentiated setting, while the building-as-pattern approach, perhaps emblematized by the mat building, construed them rather as potentially limitless, interconnected spaces branching out into the environments surrounding them. Rather than ushering in this shift, Neumann's space-packing method nuanced it, offering a means of bridging the gap between pattern and object, part and whole, two-dimensional area-covering scheme and spatial "packing" system. As we shall see in chapter 3, it yielded what I call the "patterned-object" approach to architecture, whose aim was to cultivate a more fruitful rapport between a building and its environment, while retaining the building's integrity as a discernible, freestanding architectural object. Rather than conceiving a building as a single large form, Neumann regarded it as a structure created through the spatial assembly of smaller repeated, stacked, and interconnected units. His space-packing approach to architecture stood at the core of his work and guided the development of his designs. Its centrality to Neumann's methods illustrates how he regarded architecture as a form of spatial thinking.

Space packing was more than an operative device deployed to facilitate the design of a building, however; it was also a concept in architectural morphology, a field of study that Neumann helped to develop which examines how architectural forms change over time. Space packing specifically describes a theory according to which human settlements exhibit a tendency to aggregate over time. As civilizations developed, primitive individual cells gradually merged together to form larger grouped settlements, leading eventually to entire cities. But Neumann's work with space packing and architectural morphology, much of which remained unpublished, was less concerned with deploying pattern-making to create urban fabrics than with creating new types of architectural spaces and building envelopes. This approach to patterns transformed the building's envelope into a kind of spatial filter that functioned as its structure, and also performed environmentally in terms of reducing heat intake, enhancing natural ventilation, and diffusing natural light.

While Neumann's projects garnered more international recognition than any other body of work undertaken in Israel at the time, within the country itself his work met with much skepticism and critique from both professional and public circles. As we shall see in the fourth and final chapter, Neumann's break with convention exacted a heavy price: The unusual appearance of his designs turned every project into a struggle, in the course of which he and his collaborators were continually re-evaluated, questioned, and called on to justify and explain their designs. Neumann was not new to this situation: He was already regarded as an outsider, and he was not part of the established milieu of Israeli architects who received a steady stream of jobs. For most of his life he did not belong to any movement, group, or place—perhaps more by circumstance than by choice, or a combination of both.

The final blow to Neumann's work came with the alignment of two historical events: the Danciger Building controversy, which will be described in detail in chapter 4, and the dramatic cultural and political changes that swept through Israeli society after 1967. Following Israel's victory in the Six Day War, which led to the conquest and unification of Jerusalem, nationalism accelerated and along with it the search for an architecture of national identity. Israel's post-1967 identity was marked by new projects that imitated the historic stone architecture of Jerusalem, spelling the emergence of Israeli postmodernism. This post-1967 stone architecture offered the younger generation of Israeli-born architects a means of defining a "national" architecture that was rooted in its geographical location and based on the historic image of Jerusalem, rather than appropriating the abstract geometric modernism associated with the international scene. Neumann's architecture, or rather what it came to represent, was nevertheless irrelevant in relation to these new objectives.

Beyond the context of Israeli architecture, Neumann's work offers an insight into the alternatives to 1960s mainstream modernism. While it adhered to modern principles of design such as abstraction, geometric emphasis, the elimination of ornament, fidelity to and exposure of materials, the expression of structural logic, and the alignment of an architectural work with a broader sociocultural agenda, it did not follow the compositional and formal approaches of the predominant International Style of modernism current at the time. When Neumann was active in the mid-twentieth century, modernism was a widespread architectural movement, widely hailed as a "new style of architecture" that broke away from the past. This rhetoric, which painted modernism as a new movement for a new era, inaugurated and objectified a novel, totalizing vision of radically new conditions of human life in disjunction with the past. Its aim was a cultural tabula rasa, and its proponents endeavored to rethink the fundamentals of architecture. Until modernism disassociated itself from history, however, it was understood as a means of combining traditional principles of architecture with new building techniques. Neumann, who was educated by the first generation of modernists in Brno and Vienna, was an adherent of these earlier ideals of modernism. A closer reading of the principles guiding his work reveals the influence of early modern masters, particularly of Adolf Loos and Auguste Perret, as well as French architecture and art of the early twentieth century.

Auguste Perret was an influential and prominent teacher and practitioner who advanced an approach to architecture that assured historical continuity while utilizing contemporary construction materials and techniques. Perret argued openly for an essential linking of innovation and tradition, a bond that guided the design of architecture and both grounded it in history and oriented it toward the future. He was not the only one: Several other early twentieth-century pioneers of modern architecture, such as Peter Behrens and Gunnar Asplund who developed their work outside the more radical avant-garde movement, forged a form of modernism that sought to unify tradition and innovation and to implement classical principles with a new architectural expression.[12] Perret's approach propagated within the Palais de Bois[13] informed Neumann's own rational approach to architecture, which had been nurtured by his early years of study in Brno—a prominent center of early twentieth-century modernism and home to an established functionalist school of thought.[14] From Perret, Neumann learned to innovate on the way buildings were structurally composed, to modulate the façades of buildings to foster a sense of human scale (employing proportion as a design tool), and to use concrete as a new building material, exploiting its properties to enhance the overall design expression. Perret also inculcated in Neumann the notion that the architect, by producing a refined and precise expression of a structurally "honest," well-crafted building, offers society a contribution akin to that of a work of art.

Perret's understanding of the role of the architect was informed, as it was for several other French artists and architects, by the writings of Paul Valéry, an eminent early twentieth-century author, poet, and cultural critic.[15] In his renowned *Eupalinos, The Architect* (1921),[16] Valéry posited an analogy between building and language, explaining that architecture is to building what poetry is to language. Valéry asserted that in new construction, as in language, different degrees of expression could co-exist at the same time and within the same medium. While most buildings are "mute," that is, they are constructed simply to serve a specific purpose, in some exceptional cases, they reach a poetic level of expression and "sing"; only then can they be considered works of architecture.[17] Valéry's analogy between building and language is also instructive in that by distinguishing between a building's content (its function or program) and its form, it suggests a conceptual divide between "what is said" and "how it is said." This distinction between form and content, between expression and the substance or function being expressed, dismantles the later modernist fixation on form and function as inseparably tied together.

According to Valéry, the poet strives for new expression since that is the nature of the creative act, its guiding force, and the raison d'être of all artistic endeavor. The search for the new is inherent in the act of artistic creation and stems from the individual's inner need for expression. Valéry argued that novelty in art does not require external justification, such as a perceived need to respond to changes in the external world. Every era, after all, is marked by change, whereas the human condition—people's desires and needs—have remained relatively constant through the ages. The architect's task, then, like the poet's, is not to emphasize what has changed in the world but rather to respond to enduring realities: that is, to encapsulate unchanging human conditions, desires, and needs, and to express them in a new way. That is how poetry, in his words, "extends time."

Neumann was quite familiar with the writings of Valéry. He quoted from *Eupalinos* in the introduction to his *EM-PHI System* and opened his major essay, "Morphologic Architecture" (1963), with a discussion of the analogy between architecture and poetry. In his words,

> The built human environment, seen as a whole in its geographical distribution and historical process has almost nothing to do with art. To use an analogy—of all the spoken or written communication material very little represents poetry. It is obvious that in building a certain latent potential of art can be freed, but such a case represents more the exception than the rule.[18]

Neumann does not explain exactly how this "latent potential of art" is to be released, but like Valéry, he maintains that as a creative act, architecture aspires to reach a poetic level of expression. Following Valéry, Neumann's search for a new architectural expression, like Perret's, was not based on the concept that modernity had changed life in a radical way. To his mind, the architect's role, like that of the artist, was to provide society with new expressions of enduring physical and psychological human needs and desires. In architecture, according to Neumann, this constituted a search for new spatial patterns and forms, since space was the factor that differentiated architecture from the other visual arts.

"Morphologic Architecture" offers further insight into Neumann's ideas on architecture during the 1960s. In the article, he postulates the possibility of approaching architecture as a kind of science by analyzing space in a morphological way. "A science of architecture," Neumann writes, "like any other science should describe the different phenomena by a common lawfulness. But until now, styles and periods of style have remained isolated phenomena." Neumann suggests that a "morphology of design" might be analogous to morphology in biology, and thus serve as a basis for a science of architecture. The underlying idea here is that what he calls architecture's "common lawfulness," that is, certain salient features or laws, can explain changes in architectural form over time. Defining such principles and laws would enable architecture to be understood as a single continuous phenomenon. The essay in its entirety moves between the scientific and artistic aspects of architecture, and poses some pressing questions: How is the architecture of the modern era to be understood as a combination of both science and art? How might this synthesis occur? At what point does science give over to art, or vice versa, and how does this shift take place?

Thinking of architecture—especially Neumann's—as a paired process of abstraction and creation can, I believe, help to illuminate these questions. Abstraction in this context refers to a rational, analytical operation that seeks to deduce common laws and principles from the diverse architectural forms of various historical stylistic traditions. The process of abstraction involves defining these principles in abstract terms using mathematics and geometry. Neumann's relationship to tradition was not based on any need or desire to establish a direct and mimetic visual link with history. He was not interested in referencing historical precedent in literal, formal terms. The process of abstraction involved looking at the past in an analytical, scientific manner, rather than simply mirroring the specific appearances of older motifs.[19] Morphological analysis can be seen as one means of abstracting, analyzing, and categorizing spaces as cells and groupings, which will be described in more detail in chapter 3.

The act of creation as the exploration of new forms and modes of expression, on the other hand, refers to the artistic act of synthesizing impressions, ideas, intuition, and abstract principles to produce a work of art or architecture. It is, in other words, the artistic drive to find new ways of using the "abstractions" described above. By invoking the paired concepts of abstraction and creation, I do not mean to suggest that they are, or ought to be, an overarching approach to design; my intention is rather to help explain how Neumann, and other modern architects, believed that both tradition and new expression could be addressed within a single project.

On examining Neumann's work, it becomes apparent that lying behind the unusual shapes and geometries of his designs is often a simple floor plan based on solid, established, architectural typologies, lines of symmetry, and conventional organizational principles. The complexity of Neumann's architecture lies in the interface between interior and exterior. His approach transformed the conventional planar surface of the modernist envelope into a thick, three-dimensional envelope. This "thick" space occupies a significant part of the building's habitable spaces, for while oscillating between inside and outside, it in fact belongs to both at once, as well as constituting an element in its own right. This thick, spatially packed envelope is thus both a place to occupy and a threshold space that configures movement routes and spatial sequences, creates a diversity of relationships between interior and exterior, and acts as a filter that controls natural light as it enters the interior.

Neumann's architecture attempts to balance this plural condition. Its inception relies on an understanding of climate and light and the belief that the relationship between inside and outside is a sociocultural value, a projection of how a specific society or culture understands its place within the environment that it occupies. The degree to which our buildings stand as isolated objects that are more or less indifferent to their surroundings, or the extent to which they interact with them, is a cultural question. The way we build reflects our attitude toward the environment as much as toward one another.

Architecture is never an isolated endeavor, but always takes place within a defined context. A building has a program, a physical site, a client, and a budget. It is conceived in a specific reality of time and space. Its construction is dependent on the alignment of many factors, most importantly on the successful human relationships that join forces in a collective endeavor. Starting from the inception of a design, in which the architect is directly engaged, is the long and ever-expanding process of translation—from concept to sketch, from sketch to plan, from plan to structure, and so on—which gradually involves more and more people as ideas are transfigured into buildings. While this process can lead to innovative design, the broader reception of architecture is nevertheless more often than not informed by old habits and a desire for the familiar. Although resistance to new ideas in architecture varies from culture to culture, original work is not necessarily considered a virtue in every period and place. In the context of Israeli culture, new forms and sculptural buildings such as Neumann's were doomed to be rejected eventually, regardless of their functional or utilitarian performance. Neumann's designs today are anomalies, just as they were then: unique exceptions to the norm. Some might even refer to their construction as being "accidental," but in that case a product of accidents that pose important, looming questions about how we understand architecture.

1 In his obituary of Alfred Neumann published in *L'architecture d'aujourd'hui* in 1969, Zvi Hecker wrote: "Like all great artists that leave behind their misunderstood ideas and unachieved work, Alfred Neumann died prematurely. It is not only that in a relatively late period of his life, he began to develop totally new ideas in architecture, his death prevented his creativity from reaching its highest peak." Zvi Hecker, "Alfred Neumann, 1900–1968," *L'architecture d'aujourd'hui*, no. 144 (June–July 1969), p. 7. Author's translation from French.

2 See Moshe Safdie's preface to Neumann's essay, "Irrational Factors in Building Industrialization," *Architecture Canada* (November 1968), p. 37.

3 The letter is from Neumann's personal archives held by Eva-Marie Neumann and is not dated, although the envelope is postmarked November 18, 1968.

4 Ada Louise Huxtable, "Tinker Toy City Hall in Israel is 'Space Packed,'" *The New York Times*, June 5, 1969, p. 49.

5 See Peter Cook, *Experimental Architecture* (London: Studio Vista, 1970).

6 Zodiac editor Maria Bottero introduced the contents of no. 16 as "some accounts of a number of contemporary architectural experiments (Neumann & Hecker, Stirling, De Carlo, Vittoria), among which we would stress that of Neumann and Hecker as being a particularly significant first step towards the practical and theoretical formation of new spatial and architectural languages." Maria Bottero, editor, *Zodiac*, 16 (1966), p. 237.

7 The Congrès internationaux d'architecture modern (CIAM) or International Congresses of Modern Architecture was an organization that hosted events and congresses for the purpose of fostering discussion and debate about, and propagating knowledge of, the modern movement in architecture. Eleven congresses were held in various cities across Europe in the period 1929–1959. Each meeting focused on a different theme of modern architecture, such as the "Functional City," (CIAM Athens), the "Heart of the City," and "Dwelling and Recovery."

8 Letter from Walter Gropius, January 7, 1953. The letter later appeared in the introduction to the booklet *EM-PHI System*, published in 1956.

9 Le Corbusier, *Modulor 2*, translated by Peter De Francia and Anna Bostock, (Cambridge, MA: Harvard University Press, 1958, second edition, first edition 1955). Le Corbusier mentions Neumann in pp. 86–88, and on p. 87 presents an excerpt from the *EM-PHI System* tables.

10 Author's conversation with Israel Goodovitch, July 30, 2005.

11 The original German text, signed by Peter Behrens, of July 3, 1925, reads as follows: "Es ist ohne Zweifel, dass man von seiner weiteren kunstlerischen Entwicklung viel Gutes erwarten darf und ich stelle ihm gerne das Zeugnis aus, dass er zu meinen befahigsten Schülern zählt. Ich habe seine Arbeit im zweiten Jahr mit dem Behrenspreis ausgezeichnet." Translated into English by Ingeborg Rocker.

12 Karla Britton, *Auguste Perret* (New York: Phaidon Press, 2001), pp. 14–15. Similar ideas are also expressed in: Kenneth Frampton's "On Classical and Modern Themes in the Architecture of Mies van der Rohe and Auguste Perret," *Classical Tradition and the Modern Movement*, 2nd International Alvar Aalto Symposium (Finland: Finnish Association of Architects, Museum of Finnish Architecture, Alvar Aalto Museum, 1982), pp. 20–41; Elias Cornell, "The Modernist and History," from the same publication, pp. 8–21. See also Peter Collins, *Concrete—The Vision of a New Architecture* (Montreal, London: McGill-Queen's University Press, 2004 second edition, first published by Faber and Faber in 1959), particularly the foreword to the second edition by Kenneth Frampton and the introduction by Réjean Legault.

13 Neumann's participation in Perret's Atelier du Palais between 1923 and 1928 was confirmed by Joseph Abram in a letter to the author dated January 31, 2005. Abram presented a list of approximately forty students who attended the atelier in those years, including Pierre Forestier, Ernö Goldfinger, Bertold Lubetkin, and Paul Nelson. Pierre Forestier later formed a partnership with Neumann in Paris. Abram mentioned in his letter that Forestier admired Neumann and stayed in touch with him over the years. "Forestier avait une grande admiration pour Neumann avec qui il avait garde des contacts assez longtemps." Joseph Abram's letter to the author of January 31, 2005. Joseph Abram, *Perret et l'Ecole du classicism structurel* (1910–1960), (Nancy: École d'architecture de Nancy, 1985). Charles Jencks's "Evolutionary Tree 1920–70," which maps the six major movements within modern architecture, categorizes Neumann as belonging to the "Rational School," and places him on the logical branch alongside Jean Prouvé and Arup. See Charles Jencks, *Modern Movements in Architecture* (New York, England: Penguin Books, 1986, first published 1973), p. 28.

14 For further reading on the Brno school of the early twentieth century, see Vladimir Šlapeta, *The Brno Functionalist* (Helsinki, Jyväskylä: Museum of Finnish Architecture, Alvar Aalto Museum, exhibition catalogue, 1983).

15 Perret clearly stated that the architect should be seen as a poet and architecture understood as a combination of science and poetry. See Auguste Perret, "Architecture: Science et Poésie," *La Construction Moderne*, XLVIII/2 (October 1932), pp. 2–3.

16 Karla Britton (see note 12), p. 8.

17 "Tell me (since you are so sensible to the effects of architecture), have you not noticed, in walking about this city, that among the buildings with which it is peopled, certain are mute; others speak; and others, finally—and they are the most rare—*sing*?" Paul Valéry, "Eupalinos or The Architect," from *Dialogues*, translated by William McCausland Stewart, (Princeton: Princeton University Press, 1956) p. 83. Originally published as "Eupalinos ou l'Architecte" in Louis Süe and André Mare (eds.), *Architectures*, (Paris, 1921).

18 "Morphologic Architecture," see Appendix.

19 I will later show how this approach leads to a reading of architectural history that understands architecture as a development of certain systems and pattern types that evolved independently of style.

1 Towards a Humanized Unit of Space

Humanizing architecture and the city

The atrocities of World War II—the exposure of genocides on an unimaginable scale and the horrors of atomic warfare—struck the world with a dark reality. The war seemed to have demonstrated the dispensability of human life in a world that had lost its sense of what it meant to be human. Many began to cast doubt on the rationalist philosophy that had supported the scientific and technological advancements of the prewar years. It seemed more important than ever to refocus attention on the human, and human values were given pride of place across scientific, technological, and artistic endeavors in hopes of recovering the dignity of humankind. This call to place the human being at the center of cultural activity had a profound impact on architectural discourse.

The terror of Hiroshima and the active role played by science in atomic warfare led to the scientific community being accused of acting irresponsibly and lacking concern for humanity. More than ever, science was considered disconnected from human concerns—a perception reflected on an intellectual level by the gulf that had opened up between it and the humanities. Essays from the early 1950s, such as Jacob Bronowski's "Science and Human Values" and Erwin Schrödinger's "Science and Humanism," attempted to reconcile the sciences with an unflinching commitment to human values.[1] Bronowski and Schrödinger believed that it was important to supplement science with other bodies of knowledge in order to deflect its limitations and expand its areas of interest.

Schrödinger argued that to understand the nature of science, it was necessary to have a better understanding of human nature itself, which could be obtained through the study of history. He stressed the importance of unified knowledge, declaring that the only way to arrive at a complete world picture or "world in common" was to intertwine non-scientific and scientific findings. Accordingly, science in itself could not truly relate to, or explain, the way we feel pain, delight, beauty and ugliness, good or bad, and "why and how an old song moves us to tears."[2]

The philosophical writings of the postwar years reflect a desire to re-establish the human as the center of intellectual thought. This tendency informs an array of works, among them Ernst Cassirer's *An Essay on Man: An Introduction to a Philosophy of Human Culture* (written in 1944, published in 1953), Erich Kahler's *Man the Measure: A New Approach to History* (first appeared in 1943, later revised in 1956), Ralph Barton Perry's *The Humanity of Man* (1956), and even Jean Paul Sartre's book *Existentialism Is a Humanism* (1946), written to defend existentialism against claims that it snubbed humanism.[3]

The interest in humanism also took root in postwar architectural discourse, which likewise reflected a renewed focus on human values in architecture on the scale both of the individual building and of the entire city. After the war, the scope and magnitude of urban destruction became apparent. The widely circulated images of cities in ruins from all corners of Europe raised questions as to how they should be reconstructed. The city planning principles then in currency were those formulated by the Modern Movement in architecture during the interwar years, specifically those defined in the early CIAM conferences of the 1930s. These were the principles responsible for the Athens Charter that promoted the "functional city": an approach to urban planning in which the city was to be partitioned into function-based zones. Enthusiasm for this approach waned after the war, when it came to be viewed as overly rational and lacking in regard for notions of community and personhood. Architects began instead to focus their attention on the place of the human subject in architecture and the city, and so went off in search of architectural ideas and principles from history that expressed a special concern with or sensitivity to humanity. For many of them, the greatest challenge lay not in identifying earlier expressions of a human-sensitive approach to design, but rather in finding ways to articulate this sensitivity through the language of modern architecture, without mimicking the formal styles of the past.

The post-World War II notion of reinstalling human interests at the center of architectural production was first raised at CIAM 6 in Bridgewater, England, in 1947. Although as a congress it aimed to reaffirm functionalism, CIAM 6 also stressed the importance of expressing spiritual and emotional values in architecture and urban planning. Alfred Neumann participated in CIAM 6 as a member of the Czech delegation, and there presented the urban plans for the Moravian region that he had been working on since the end of the war on the staff of the Czech regional planning office in Brno.

The discussion of the "humanization of cities"—a term coined by Sigfried Giedion—featured most prominently, however, at CIAM 8 of 1951 in Hoddeston, England. This congress explored the urban core—"the heart of the city"—as a site that could be designed to recover a sense of community. At CIAM 8, the "heart of the city" was defined as "the element that makes a community a community, and not merely an aggregate of individuals."[4] The metaphor of the "heart" was meant to connote a conceptual shift away from treating the city as a machine and toward envisioning it as a living organism. For Giedion, this entailed reimagining the city by designing it for a different user, for "another type of man who will take part in activities and be himself both spectator and actor."[5] For humankind to be restored to the status of active participants, it would be necessary to re-awaken the emotional experience of brotherhood and solidarity and to create places within the city where this could be expressed. The core of the city represented a place where, as Giedion expressed it, an "intimate relationship between man and man, individual and community can be re-established."[6] The humanization of urban life was a reaction against mechanization and bureaucracy, which, according to Giedion, had taken root in the early twentieth century in the preoccupation with, and purification of, the single-family dwelling, the apartment building, and the multifamily dwelling. The interest in reinvigorating the city center can thus be understood as an attempt to recover a sense of the communal, which for Giedion was the core of the humanistic project.[7]

As humanism entered postwar architectural discourse through these and other inquiries into the future of the city, architects became particularly interested in examining how systems of proportion might play a role in engendering more humane buildings and spaces.[8] In fact, it was through the theory and practice of proportions that humanism as a design principle found concrete articulation on an architectural scale.

Post-World War II discourse on proportion

The discussion and influence of proportion theories entered post-World War II architectural discourse through two seminal publications: Rudolf Wittkower's *Architectural Principles in the Age of Humanism* (1949) and Le Corbusier's *Modulor* (1950), both of which were instrumental in drawing attention to issues of humanism in architecture. Architectural periodicals of the early 1950s made frequent mention of these texts, bringing them to the public's attention and setting in motion a dialogue between them that accelerated the influence of their parallel ideas among practicing architects and writers. Published reviews and articles on these works related them to the wider interest of humanistic values in architecture. Both were regarded as attempts to "humanize" architecture by reintroducing the human body as a measure for the dimensions and proportions applied in the design of buildings, and by providing a historical precedent for architecture based on systems of proportion. Promoting a proportion system for architecture also helped institute an aesthetic system which was "acceptable to the scientifically minded establishment,"[9] and which went hand in hand with post–World War II social policies of the welfare state.

Wittkower, an art historian, composed a scholarly work that examined proportion systems in Renaissance architecture. His study of design traditions impelled post-World War II modern architects to seek recourse to historical materials that in recent years had been absent from architectural discourse. Although he avoided making direct reference to contemporary architectural practice, his ability to speak in abstract terms made his work appealing and influential among architects.

Le Corbusier's *Modulor* was written more like a how-to book that introduced a working tool of design. The eponymous Modulor, an anthropometric scale, served as a means of incorporating proportions and human dimensions into architectural practice and the building industry in general. The Modulor system was also intended to address practical problems that arose from mass production and standardization, such as the need to reconcile two different units of measure, the imperial and metric systems.

Wittkower's and Le Corbusier's works complemented one other, bringing together scholarly and professional approaches, history and technology, and theory and practice. Wittkower provided the historical justification for the use of a system of proportion, while Le Corbusier developed the argument for its practical need in the profession at that time. The appearance of these works led to several debates and discussions on proportion, modular systems, universal methods and design principles, and the general quality of modern design. Since it is within this specific context that Alfred Neumann developed his own theory of proportion, further exploration of both Wittkower's and Le Corbusier's work is necessary to a better understanding of what Neumann contributed to this discourse, and how these ideas on proportion were to influence his designs and buildings.

Rudolf Wittkower's *Architectural Principles* presented three main preoccupations of Renaissance architects:

1 A belief in a hierarchical order among the various categories of building, with each category possessing its own inner logic and placing unique demands on an architect's ingenuity. The central concern was with the planning of churches, whose designs had to express, both as a whole and in their details, symbols of eternal validity.
2 The role of tradition, particularly in how to employ ancient theory and practice in support of contemporary requirements.
3 Proportion as the system which, used both practically and symbolically, enabled buildings to be conceived as manifestations of the mathematical harmony of the universe.

Architecture in the Renaissance was regarded as capable of visually expressing the structures by which the universe is governed. Its construction followed a systematic, objective method. As Wittkower explains:

> The conviction that architecture is a science, and that each part of a building, inside as well as outside, has to be integrated into one and the same system of mathematical ratios, may be called the basic axiom of Renaissance architects. We have already seen that the architect is by no means free to apply to a building a system of ratios of his own choosing, that the ratios have to comply with conceptions of a higher order and that a building should mirror the proportions of the human body; a demand that became universally accepted on Vitruvius' authority.[10]

Wittkower argues that the Renaissance proportion system emphasized the geometric relationships derived from the numerical ratios between whole numbers. He explains in detail how Renaissance architects combined the ancient harmonic mean (of the Pythagorean school) with Plato's belief in the common cosmic and harmonic order contained in numbers. Wittkower further articulates an important distinction between the way proportions were used in various building types, distinguishing between the designs of villas and of churches. He explains how in Palladio's villas, the ratios are not necessarily all harmonic throughout the entire building, the proportions of one room rather being systematically linked to the proportions of the one next to it. Thus, in Palladio's designs of villas, the ratio—the equation that expresses a proportional relation between two elements—manifests itself in the sizes of adjacent rooms. The demand for a more comprehensive and inclusive use of proportion in which "all parts should correspond to the whole and to each other" was generally adhered to in churches, however.[11] Wittkower uses the example of Alberti's program for an ideal church to illustrate a structure that can incorporate both number ratios and harmonic relations, encompassing the ideal proportions of a human body in terms of dimension, ratio, and the relationship between the parts and the whole.

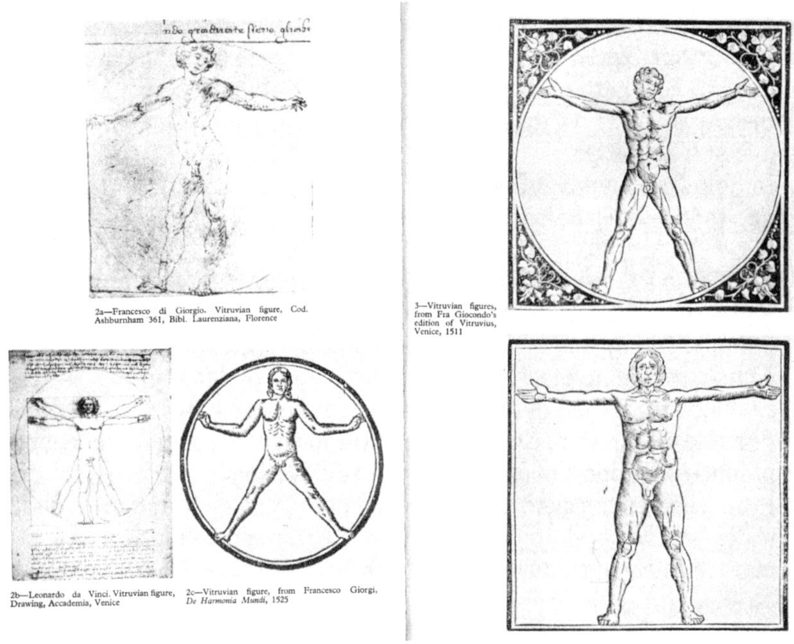

Renaissance theories of proportion; the human body in harmony with perfect geometry

In her analysis of Wittkower's *Principles*, Alina Payne points out that his ability to trace these relationships in plan and section and to closely observe the different uses of proportion rests largely on his focus on syntax. Apart from examining broad compositional strategies, Payne describes Wittkower's reading of architectural form as constructed out of an "available classic kit of parts" acting as structural elements for the overall form. He recognizes the importance of placement relationships between the constituent parts, and investigates the rules that control these relationships. Payne concludes that the link between syntax and science via mathematics allowed Wittkower "to situate Renaissance formal practices within the objective rationale rather than subjective realm."[12] It was this "objective rationale" that enabled Wittkower's work to expand beyond historical study and to impact the contemporary architectural discourse of the early 1950s.

Le Corbusier's Modulor was far from Renaissance notions of the ideally proportioned, perfect figure. Rather than approximating the analytical, objective, and detailed figure of the "Vitruvian man" with outstretched limbs inscribed within equilateral geometric forms, the Modulor man was depicted as a hastily sketched diagram that was suggestive but not precise. With one arm raised, the Modulor man's fluid body contour was set beside the two geometric constructs of the proportion system. The Modulor indicated measurements for parts of the body not by analyzing the harmonic relationship between the parts and the whole, but in terms of the dimensions derived from the different positions assumed by the body in space while engaging in various activities. Le Corbusier's innovation, as Peter Collin has noted, consisted in combining "two modules in one, module of measurement and module of scale."[13] The modules of measurement are the actual dimensions used to design building parts, such as sizes for doors, window partitions, and ceiling heights, while the modules of scale are the ratios and relationships between the dimensions, mainly between lengths and heights. For example a module of measurement will prescribe the actual length of a window, while the module of scale will indicate a width dimension that proportionally matches that length.

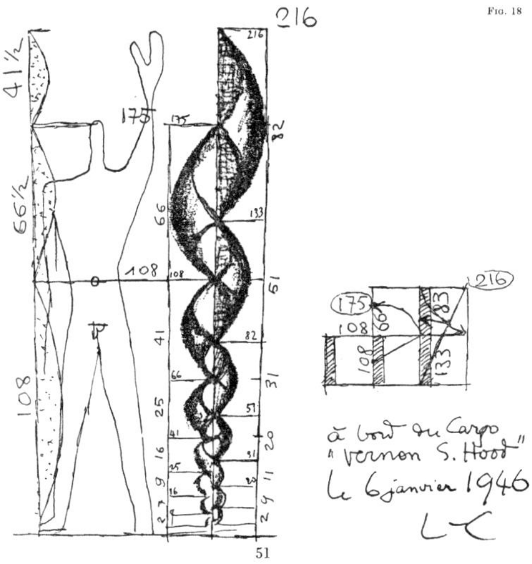

Le Corbusier's early sketch of Modulor man

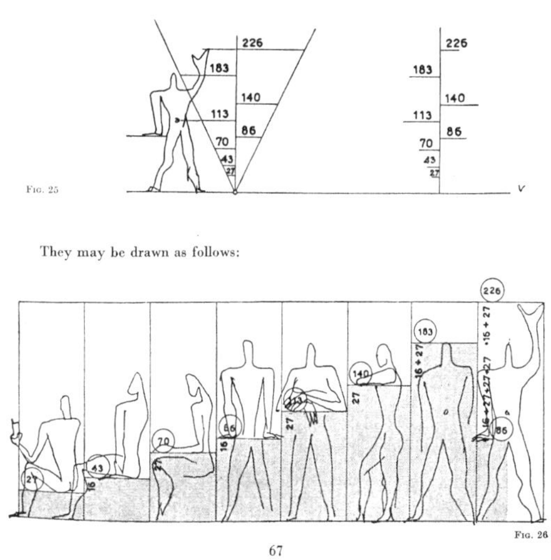

The Modulor system: activities and body positions in relation to dimensions

If we arrange the sketches and drawings that Le Corbusier produced while developing the Modulor chronologically, we see the sequence of geometric operations in relation to the human body that appeared as the system was conceived. The basic starting point was the height of the figure, measured both from the foot to the head, and from the foot to the top of a raised arm. Le Corbusier aimed to confine these two measures within a rectangle that could also incorporate the Golden Section. The height of this rectangle was then divided into a Fibonacci sequence, which is a set of numbers, each of which is equal to the sum of its two preceding numbers, such as: 1, 1, 2, 3, 5, 8, 13, 21, and so on. Le Corbusier used two such series, which he called the red and the blue series. Each series provided the necessary dimensions applicable to the Modulor man's different body parts while enacting various poses, such as sitting, standing, and lying down.

The ratio between each of the numbers in the Fibonacci series is very close in value to what mathematicians term Φ (phi), or the Golden Section. When Le Corbusier was searching for a geometric ratio that could combine the two dimensions obtained by measuring from the foot to the top of the head and from the foot to the end of the raised arm, all the other features of the body were overlooked. In several sketches, for example, the other, unraised arm was disregarded, often not drawn at all. Modulor man, unlike "Vitruvian man," did not need his full body to define a relationship with geometry and proportion. Modulor man's other arm, for example, was set in place only after the series was worked out and some kind of height measurement was found to be useful for another arm position. The Modulor was not about using body proportions as an ideal form from which to derive perfect measures, but rather about imagining how different postures and parts of the body could comply with the Golden Section.

Le Corbusier adopted the Golden Section (phi) in his Modulor system not only because of historical precedent; his use of it was also inspired by several contemporary writings and investigations, most notably Matila Ghyka's *The Geometry of Art and Life*.[14] Le Corbusier was also familiar with Alfred Neumann's studies and his use of phi with the metric system.[15]

As I mentioned earlier, Le Corbusier envisioned the Modulor in part with the aim of providing a practical solution for linking the metric and imperial systems of measurement, and as a means of standardizing dimensions to make mass production more efficient. He argued that if the world was to be united, then its measuring systems must be, too. In terms of practicality, however, the Modulor was not a convincing tool for bridging this difference. Rudolf Arnheim demonstrated the difficulties of transitioning between centimeters and inches, units that are not multiples of each other, and other critics were also skeptical of Le Corbusier's Modulor, and doubted whether it could be practically applied beyond Le Corbusier's own architectural projects, presented in the sequel publication, *Modulor 2.*

Le Corbusier and Wittkower both understood proportion to function on two levels. The first, in which proportion expressed a higher order and relationship between nature, God, and humanity, was symbolic. The second, in which proportion was used as a practical working tool in the design and construction of buildings, was concrete and operational. Both of these functions—the symbolic and the practical—were achieved through the use of geometry. Discussing the symbolic role of proportion, Le Corbusier argued that the logical structure of nature was demonstrated through the use of the Modulor. Geometry, accordingly, is what reveals and translates the similar ratios found in nature, the human body and the manmade world of artifacts and buildings. Architecture's symbolic role, he said, stemmed from the assumption that meanings of a "higher order" could be expressed through geometry.[16] As Alina Payne explains, "architecture takes a leading role amongst the arts in materializing a *Weltanschauung* rooted in (the) mathematical conception of the universe: science (cosmology), simultaneously absorbed and transcended, receives visible expression in architectural form."[17]

In an operational sense, proportional geometry served as a working tool which, through the drawing of guidelines (regulating lines), established the proportions of plans, elevations, and sections of buildings. It also defined proportions in other scales of planning and design: from building detailing and window partitioning to the design of large urban plans. This is unquestionably evident not only in the work of Palladio and the treatise of Alberti, as Wittkower suggested, but also in Le Corbusier's use of the Modulor in the Unité d'habitation and in the urban layout and design of Chandigarh, the capital of the Indian state of Punjab.

Both Palladio and Le Corbusier used proportion systems through what I would call the "planar method," meaning that the proportions manifest themselves primarily on a plane: either horizontally (as in the floor plan) or vertically (as in the section or elevation), while the third dimension, in other words the depth or height of the plane, was achieved by extruding mainly the horizontal, but at times the vertical, dimensions into the same space. In the planar method, plan and section are treated as separate entities or surfaces of operation, each independently set in proportion by the same method and measurements and treated as a total composition in its own right. This method of setting things in proportion was made possible through what Le Corbusier called "regulating lines": guidelines marked on the drawing to ensure that the elements are correctly sized relative to each other, a technique often used in painting. This use of proportion differs substantially from Alfred Neumann's approach, as will be shown later.

Le Corbusier's example of regulating lines as a means to outline architectural proportions

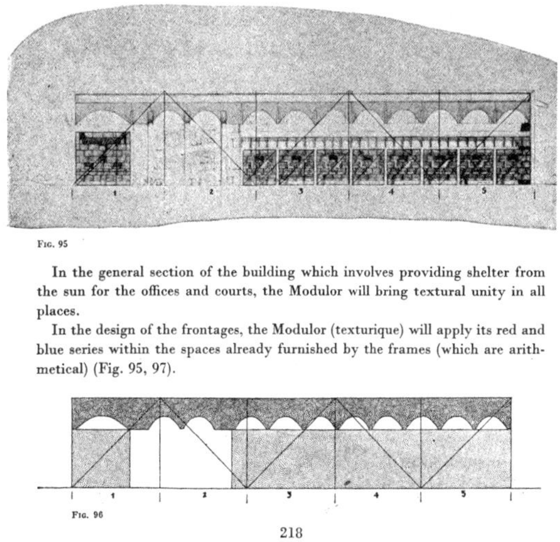

Regulating lines are used to determine the Modulor system proportions of the High Court elevation in Chandigrah

The post-World War II discussion of proportions in architecture had an impact on architectural theory and practice well into the 1960s. Influential critic Reyner Banham, for example, evaluated the proportion systems introduced by Wittkower and Le Corbusier as tools that theoretically enabled the architect to close the gap between technology and tradition and between historical and contemporary architecture.[18] Banham also claimed that there was an inherent contradiction in implementing proportion in design. While on the one hand, using a proportion system seemed to demand of the architect an extended knowledge and understanding of his cultural function and social responsibilities, on the other, it supposedly narrowed his view and specialized his practice by providing an expedient shortcut for the act of design. The question of whether or not architects should use theories of proportion in their designs was hotly debated in the 1950s. Banham further linked proportions to a wider discussion that he himself instigated, through the pages of the British journal *Architectural Review*, on the theme of the architect as "Universal Man," or "*l'uomo universale*," familiar to us from the Renaissance.[19] The definition of the Renaissance architect as *l'uomo universale* assumed that the architect held a major role in creating architecture which, by adopting an objective, rational approach that included social as well as artistic and aesthetic qualities, could bridge science and art. The Universal Man represented the possibility of combining different bodies of meaning and knowledge in one architectural product.

This holds true for Le Corbusier's definition of Universal Man as well. Le Corbusier extended the links recently forged between science and art to the realm of industrialization with its prefabricated construction techniques and elements of mass production, to which the modern architect—as Universal Man—could bring beauty, pleasurable dimensions, and a true expression of materials. Furthermore, in Le Corbusier's view, the architect must aspire to connect architecture with the natural world by using geometric proportions to reveal the structures embedded in the forces of nature—an axis, a rule, a means by which to define and relate the manmade to the natural world. He explained, "the straight line that marries the axis of fundamental laws must be found: biology, nature, cosmos. Unbending straight line like the horizon of the sea."[20] Le Corbusier's search for the connective straight line reflects the desire to unify: to bring laws and phenomena into balance, to seek an equilibrium which, through geometry, will set the elements of the natural and built worlds in harmony as part of a larger universal structure. For Wittkower, who depicted the architect as "an all-round humanist with an encyclopedic knowledge, and immense productivity,"[21] the modern *l'uomo universale* architect possessed not just a large body of knowledge, but also an acute social and cultural awareness of his role, as his generation regained the social responsibility of expressing cultural values.

Progress, in the form of applied scientific research, knowledge, and information, flooded the postwar period. Many people expected that this surge of data would be taken up in architecture and urban planning, too. Yet this desire for extended, but practical, knowledge was, in the end, unattainable. The amount of information that could be regarded relevant to the design of buildings and cities was simply too voluminous for any single architect to absorb. Acknowledgment of this dilemma raised many questions concerning the limits, responsibilities, scope, and capabilities of the architectural profession generally. The revaluation of the architect's professional position unavoidably led to a discussion of the objectives and demands placed on the architect's education. What should an architectural education entail, or, more generally, what knowledge was the architect expected to master?[22]

Alfred Neumann's theory of proportion: L'Humanisation de l'espace

The EM-PHI System—Humanization of Space by Alfred Neumann represented an important contribution to the entire field of design, planning, architecture, and industrial design. It was the first attempt

> to create a modular system that comprehended the whole range of possibilities of proportion; the only system akin to Neumann's was Le Corbusier's Modulor, which was conceived intuitively. Neumann went beyond this system and gave it an all-embracing mechanical background.

This quote from a 1953 review by Walter Gropius prefaced Neumann's booklet titled *L'Humanisation de l'espace, le système mΦ* (published in 1956 as part of Editions Architecture d'Aujourd'hui's Collection Espace series).[23] What was to be Neumann's only published book combined a dense, concise, part philosophical, part mathematical text on the idea of space in contemporary culture with a series of mathematical tables and exercises in arithmetic and geometry that explored numerical and geometric relations. The few images included in the EM-PHI booklet—black and white reproductions of paintings by Leonardo Da Vinci and Giorgione, which were analyzed by tracing lines on them—did not present anything new, or even support Neumann's main argument about humanizing space in contemporary life. Rather, they demonstrated only that Neumann's own proportion system could be applied to analyze artistic masterpieces of the Renaissance and uncover the proportional thinking underlying them.

Neumann's book had two main aims. The first was to unfold a theory of proportion through a series of tables, graphs, and equations whose purpose was to provide a scale, or a series of measurements and dimensions, for the design of architecture and other human artifacts. The second was to discuss the concept of "humanized space," the problem of space in contemporary life, and the need to humanize space as a general cultural idea. Neumann's thesis was a rational, abstracted approach to proportion systems. It lacked the symbolic aspect that Wittkower, and to some degree Le Corbusier, assigned to systems of proportion.

Neumann worked on his thesis for several years before he finally managed to have it published in 1956.[24] He stated that several of his findings were based on studies and measurements of furniture and interior fittings that he had conducted himself during the late 1920s while working on furniture designs for his father's cabinetmaking and joinery business in Brno.[25] Neumann developed the logic of his system without attempting to tie it to building or design practice. It was abstractly conceived, comprising a reference chart, guidebook, a series of scales, and numerical tables that expressed the mathematical logic and extent of his system. There was no explicit guidance on how to implement the system. The numerical tables and geometric drawings are copious, even excessive, and their numbers overwhelming. This was not only due to Neumann's insistence on methodically following the rationale of his system to its full extent and on being loyal to the mathematical operations it demanded; it was also due to the fact that he was not engaged with design practice at the time he developed it. Unlike *Modulor*, which presented some of Le Corbusier's designs based on his proportion system, Neumann's EM-PHI booklet, at the time of its publication, was merely a theoretical exploration of a potential practical tool without any concrete examples of its application. Neumann was relying solely on the rationale of mathematics and the persuasiveness of his theoretical argument. The degree to which the system was applicable was not a criterion for its validation. It was only in the years to follow that

Neumann utilized the EM-PHI system in his architectural practice, as he continued to do throughout the 1960s.

Description of the EM-PHI system of proportion

What is the EM-PHI (MΦ) system? What was its role in design? How is it similar to, or different from, other theories of proportion that appeared around the same time?

The EM-PHI system, as its name suggests, is based on two factors: M (EM), which represents the meter, the basic unit of measurement of the metric system, and Φ (PHI), which represents the Golden Number, also known as the Golden Ratio, the Golden Mean, or the Golden Section.[26] Neumann subscribed to the view that the Golden Section represented a unique proportional ratio distinguished from others by its preponderance in nature and pleasing perceptual effects.[27] Neumann deduced that since this ratio governs natural creation, it should also appear in the environment and objects that humans create. "It has long been known that the proportion of most shapes of organic growth, particularly the proportion of man, is related to the Golden Section," he wrote. "The manmade human environment, as tools, furniture, utensils, is a prolongation and projection of the human body. Consequently it is bound to follow its proportional and dimensional structure."[28]

The EM-PHI system applied the meter to the Golden Ratio to produce a series of numerical grids that all corresponded and related to each other by an equation that expressed the Golden Ratio: a/b = b/a + b. There are both algebraic and geometric methods of approaching this formula. If applying the meter unit (b = 1), the equation will be 0.618/1 = 1/1.618, which includes 1.618, known as the Golden Number. Taking these two values as a departure point, 1.00 (meter) and 1.618 (Golden Number = Φ = PHI), which produce a ratio of the Golden Section, a mathematical series is derived that follows the basic equation of the Golden Section. As discovered by the Ancient Greeks, Renaissance architects, and Le Corbusier, Neumann saw that these Golden Section series were almost aligned with the proportional relations between the numbers in a Fibonacci series. In Neumann's system, the Fibonacci sequence is appropriated onto the values 1.00 and 1.618 as the first two numbers in a single mathematical series, but then further extrapolated to produce multiple series. To explain: The values 1.00 and 1.618 are the first two numbers to appear in the central vertical column—the Φ column (under the value of Φ series) in the main table of the EM-PHI system. This central column is made up of the following values: 1.00, 1.618, 2.618 (1.00 + 1.618), 4.236 (1.618 + 2.618), 6.854 (2.618 + 4.236), and so on, both by addition: 1.00 + 1.618 (growing as you move downward), and by subtraction: 1.618 – 1.00 = 0.618, 1.00 – 0.618 = 0.382, 0.618 – 0.382 = 0.236, and so on (decreasing as you move upward), hence constructing a Fibonacci series. An additional column (to the right of this central one) is created by the simple addition of two intermittent values of the central column: 1.618 + 0.618 (1.618 – 1.00 = 0.618) = 2.236, which equals √5. This value becomes part of another Fibonacci series following the same logic of addition and subtraction, thus creating a column parallel to the Φ column, titled √5, since at its center stands the value 2.236, which equals √5. The operation of adding and subtracting intermittent values continues to produce more parallel columns on either side of the central Φ column. Thus, a table of columns and rows is achieved, providing an extensive series of numbers, measurements, and dimensions that all derive from the Golden Ratio in the metric scale and from the same method of addition and subtraction. The result is a system of Fibonacci series that forms a geometric series progressing by 5 (in the addition direction, to the right: 5, 5√5, 5^2, 5^2√5, and so on, and likewise to the left, in the subtraction direction). Since each column can be considered a √5 of its preceding one, every value in the table is also divisible by 2 and by 5 (of course), and thus also by 10 (2 × 5 = 10). The table could therefore be set in relation to the decimal system, which is the system of the meter, allowing the decimal point to be moved to the right or left, while maintaining the relation between the values (see EM-PHI system tables in Appendix). This operation extends the system to cover several other dimensions. This is how the EM-PHI system resolves the lack of intermediate values between the growing "jumps" of a Fibonacci series.

La GSΦ multiplicative. Table numérique II.

SΦ $(\sqrt{5})^{-3}$	SΦ $(\sqrt{5})^{-2}$	SΦ $(\sqrt{5})^{-1}$	SΦ $(\sqrt{5})^{0}$	SΦ $(\sqrt{5})^{1}$	SΦ $(\sqrt{5})^{2}$	SΦ $(\sqrt{5})^{3}$	SΦ $(\sqrt{5})^{4}$	SΦ $(\sqrt{5})^{5}$	SΦ $(\sqrt{5})^{6}$
...	...	...	...	...	...	...	...	...	...
0,005	0,010	0,025	0,056	0,124	0.284	0,620	1,400	3,100	7,000
0,008	0,018	0,040	0,090	0,202	0,450	1,010	2,250	5,050	11,250
0,013	0,029	0,065	0,146	0,326	0,730	1,630	3,650	8,150	18,250
0,021	0,047	0,105	0,236	0,528	1,180	2,640	5,900	13,200	29,500
0,034	0,076	0,170	0,382	0,854	1,910	4,270	9,550	21,350	47,750
0,055	0,123	0,276	**0,618**	1,382	3,090	6,910	15,450	34,550	77,250
0,088	0,200	0,447	**1,000**	2,236	5,000	11,180	25,000	55,900	125,000
0,144	0,323	0,723	**1,618**	3,618	8,090	18,090	40,450	90,450	202,250
0,234	0,523	1,170	**2,618**	5,854	13,090	29,270	65,450	146,350	327,250
0,378	0,847	1,894	4,236	9,472	21,180	47,360	105,900	236,800	529,500
0,613	1,370	3,065	6,854	15,326	34,270	76,630	171,350	383,150	856,750
0,992	2,218	4,959	11,090	24,798	55,450	123,990	277,250	619,950	1386,250
1,605	3,588	8,024	17,944	40,944	89,720	200,620	448,600	1003,100	2243,000
2,598	5,807	12,984	29,034	64,922	145,170	324,610	725,850	1623,050	3629,250
...	...	...	...	...	...	...	...	...	...

Table numérique III. Valeurs décuplées de la table II.

10 SΦ $(\sqrt{5})^{-3}$	10 SΦ $(\sqrt{5})^{-2}$	10 SΦ $(\sqrt{5})^{-1}$	10 SΦ $(\sqrt{5})^{0}$	10 SΦ $(\sqrt{5})^{1}$	10 SΦ $(\sqrt{5})^{2}$	10 SΦ $(\sqrt{5})^{3}$	10 SΦ $(\sqrt{5})^{1}$
...	...	...	...	...	...	...	...
0,081	0,180	0,408	0,904	2,050	4,500	10,100	22,500
0,130	0,292	0,652	1,460	3,260	7,300	16,300	36,500
0,211	0,472	1,056	2,360	5,280	11,800	26,400	59,000
0,341	0,764	1,708	3,280	8,540	19,100	42,700	95,500
0,552	1,236	2,764	**6,180**	13,820	30,900	69,100	154,500
0,894	2,000	4,472	**10,000**	22,360	50,000	111,800	250,000
1,446	3,236	7,236	**16,180**	36,180	80,900	180,900	404,500
2,340	5,236	11,708	**26,180**	58,540	130,900	292,700	654,500
3,788	8,472	19,944	42,360	94,720	211,800	.473,600	1059,000
6,130	13,708	30,652	68,540	153,260	342,700	766,300	1713,500
9,918	22,180	51,596	110,900	247,980	554,500	1239,900	2772,500
6,048	35,880	83,248	179,440	401,240	897,200	2006,200	4486,000
5,956	58,060	134,844	290,340	649,220	1451,700	3246,100	7258,500
1,944	93,940	219,092	469,780	1050,460	2348,900	5252,300	11744,500
	...	...	...	...	...	...	...

25

A table of proportions from Neumann's EM-PHI system

The EM-PHI system differs from both Le Corbusier's Modulor and Renaissance proportion theories by being abstract, and by not relying on the physical shape and dimensions of the human body, either as a whole or in part, to express and represent the proportion system. Rather than drawing on the human figure to derive a set of human dimensions, Neumann presumed the meter itself to have an inherent, albeit indirect, relation to the body. According to this understanding, the meter—even though it does not describe the dimension of any one part of the human body in particular, nor can be deduced from analyzing relations between body parts—which has been used since Antiquity, is considered to have an affinity with the human body. This contravenes the common presumption that the meter is an abstract invention of the French Enlightenment. As Neumann explained: "There has to be found an objective measuring system which will provide for individual diversity of dimensions without losing its structural unity." Neumann found that many human measures are very close to the meter dimension, even though the meter itself hardly ever appears directly. Thus, he suggested that any objective dimensioning system to be established should be based on the meter, "to reunite the geometrical with the anthropometrical Golden Section system."[30]

Neumann commented on Le Corbusier's Modulor by stating that it presented only a partial solution, one particular case within the larger framework of a more general system. He believed that Le Corbusier's decision to base measurements on a man with his arm raised was arbitrary, as was Le Corbusier's choice of a "standard" man, which seemed more reminiscent of the ancient notion of the canon rather than an objective system of measurement proposed for universal use, as is also evident in the Modulor's exclusion of the dimensions of women.

Not until years after the EM-PHI system was published did Neumann begin to incorporate his proportional system in his own designs. There, he used it in a fashion very different from the way in which both the Modulor and Renaissance proportion systems were employed. His approach differed both in the conception of part-to-whole relationships and in the process and method of implementation. As we saw earlier, Renaissance proportion systems, and Le Corbusier's after them, were planar and compositional, while Neumann's was aggregative, spatial, and constructional. The former employed planar, two-dimensional guidelines and regulating lines (*lines regulare*) to divide either a vertical plane (when composing a façade), or a horizontal plane (when organizing the parts of a plan), while Neumann used EM-PHI dimensions to define a volumetric spatial unit that could be repeated and clustered into a kind of three-dimensional spatial pattern to construct the form of the building. By this logic, if each of these spatial units related to the human body, then the whole did as well, by virtue of their repetition. Neumann's "volumetric units," stacked and assembled to form the building as a whole, generated and articulated architectural form in a radically different way from what architects generally refer to as the "formal-compositional approach" proposed through Le Corbusier's regulating lines and method of planar composition.[31] In Neumann's system, plans and façades were not separate planes of operation to be proportioned or composed as elements of their own, but rather an outcome of a larger whole, a result of the system of spatial assembly.

Neumann's EM-PHI theory introduced two essential ideas that guided his later work. The first was a system of proportion that aimed to provide a set of dimensions and relationships to be used in the design of buildings, and the second was a conception of architecture that foregrounded space as the major generator of built form. This conception of space was first defined in the EM-PHI system booklet, and years later was further articulated through terms such as "morphologic architecture," a history of architecture as spatial evolution, and "space packing," a principle explaining the composition and structure of built form. These ideas will be discussed in the following chapters.

Architecture as theory of space

> Our time is characterized by a pluralistic conception of space. Between the abstract spaces of the atomic and cosmic which we can conceive in mathematical symbols only, there is our everyday space into which the other spaces precipitate, shaped into statistical physical "laws" and organic life. From a human point of view this space is as unfinished and has to get transformed to fit human needs.
> —Alfred Neumann, letter to Wells Coates, dated April 20, 1953.[32]

Space is an abstract concept. It can refer to diverse physical and imaginary conditions. Various fields of knowledge conceive and define space according to its place and use within a given field, and strive to define it in precise terms that will allow its applicability as part of a set of concepts within that discipline. To extend the implication Neumann makes in the quote above, the sciences construe space such that it may be utilized as a workable concept within the scientific method, as part of a scientific theory. Thus space is prescribed within an equation that sets it in relation to other concepts such as time and mass, for example, whose definitions differ greatly among biology, chemistry, mathematics, and other fields. Physics deals with cosmic or atomic space; mathematics, through different geometries, deals with multidimensional space; and microbiology, as a further example, draws a distinction between inner-cellular and extra-cellular space.

Neumann believed that architecture as a field should also seek to define space in the most precise way that best served its overall goals, and in a way which made it an applicable and workable concept. In the last part of the above quote, he states that the space intended for human, everyday use has yet to be fixed and formed to address human needs. In this sense, space is problematic, for it is not predefined or ready-made, but rather needs to be shaped. As he sees it, the main objective of architecture is to serve human beings by transforming and modeling everyday space to fit the requirements of human habitats. As such, the act of design can be described as being primarily an act of humanizing space, that is, defining space in physical, concrete ways to fit human needs. The questions that arise are these: How can space be transformed to fit human habitats? And, what are those human needs that are to guide the shaping of space, from both a physical and psychological point of view?

The primacy of space as a concept in architectural discourse follows a tradition of spatial thinking that emerged in late nineteenth-century writings, most prominently through August Schmarsow's theory of *Raumgestaltung*. August Schmarsow (1853–1936) understood space as a fundamental characteristic of architecture.[33] He defined the creation of space as the translation of the area imagined by the human mind into material terms. Accordingly, architectural space was derived from the human spatial imagination and from personal sensory-physical experience. The basis of Schmarsow's spatial theory was the human body and the development and role of space in an individual's conscience. He saw architecture as constructed by the imposition of order upon space. Schmarsow believed that the task of creating space belonged solely to architecture and was the discipline's most significant characteristic in comparison with the other arts.[34] He further asserted that spatial thinking, or "spatial intuition," as he called it, had its own evolution, starting from unconscious impulses in primitive societies to sophisticated mathematical calculations in the modern era.[35]

In the twentieth century, two main factors extraneous to architecture influenced the discussion of space and spatial thinking in architecture. The first, coming out of modern psychology, were studies in perception as a key element in how humans understand and experience the world, and thus the space they move through and inhabit. Ideas about perception necessarily gave prominence to the human body, opening questions about the movement of the body in space and the ways in which space is perceived by the senses and affects human emotions. The emphasis on architecture as responsible for the creation and design of interior spaces was also part of a larger discussion that attempted to identify more precisely architecture's unique qualities in order to distinguish it from the other plastic arts. Architecture was singled out as the art of creating man-made spaces that were inhabited and thus experienced.

The other important influence on the conception of space in twentieth-century architecture was derived from science. New ideas on space emerged in the early part of the century following the work of Henri Poincaré and Albert Einstein on the relativity of space. These ideas were extremely important to future architects and writers, especially to people like Sigfried Giedion, who in his seminal work, *Space, Time, and Architecture*, incorporated an interpretation of Einstein's theories as a guiding principle in explaining the spatial qualities of modern architecture. Science played a major role in shaping the modern mind and culture. Thanks to the growing popularity of science between the wars, Einstein's theories became well known, even if not fully understood and often over simplified. The common notion was that modern life and culture were characterized by a new understanding of space-time, and that developments in science would not remain only within the realm of science, but would influence other cultural fields, including art and architecture.[36]

Far from the Aristotelian or Newtonian understanding of "neutral" space, modern science understood space as an active "substance." In modern science, space was an active, workable concept in and of itself, a factor that could be defined in precise mathematical terms. It had transmuted from what Jacob Bronowski refers to as a phenomenon to a scientific concept, which allowed it to partake in the scientific process. According to Bronowski, this transition is characteristic of scientific thinking in general, which examines phenomena, a set of appearances, in an attempt to organize them into laws. As Bronowski explains, a knot can be identified at the center of the laws, "a point which several laws cross; a symbol which gives unity to the laws themselves." He continues with an example: "Mass, time, magnetic moment, the unconscious; we have grown up with these symbolic concepts, so that we are startled to be told that man had once to create them for himself. He has indeed, and he has; for mass is not an intuition in the muscle, and time is not bought ready-made at the watchmaker's."[37] The act of creating laws or concepts feeds the scientific method that then establishes relationships between these concepts to form a scientific theory. This is what happened in the twentieth century with space: It became a concept of modern science, defined and set in relation to other concepts. These new ideas of space circulated beyond scientific circles into the larger cultural milieu, and were discussed in several works throughout different periods of the twentieth century. The treatment of space as a central architectural theme was taken further in the middle of the twentieth century. It was then, building on some of Schmarsow's spatial ideas, that Sigfried Giedion and Bruno Zevi published their books, *Space, Time and Architecture* (1941), and *Architecture as Space* (1948), respectively. Both described architecture as spatial theory, postulating space as the main preoccupation of architectural creation.

Giedion's *Space, Time and Architecture* is likely the best-known work that approaches architecture as spatial theory. Its central idea is that in the modern age, a new conception of space developed and became the fundamental principle of modern architecture, and the basis for its syntax. The purpose of Giedion's book, as stated in the introduction, was to "reveal the hidden unity within the apparent chaos and confusion," and so to expose the growth of a new tradition. This new tradition was an architecture based on a new spatial conception. Influenced by Heinrich Wolfflin and Jacob Burckhardt, Giedion understood that as a historian, his role was to reveal and grasp the spirit of an epoch and to show how this spirit could be traced in the different activities and creations of an era.[38] He believed a culture could be analyzed from within its present moment, rather than only from a historical perspective. It is the *zeitgeist*—the "spirit of the age" that unifies diverse cultural realms—which guides human tendencies and activity within each historical period and which, he believed, impacts all aspects of human activity, even though we are not always conscious of its influence. Giedion followed the logic that if the *zeitgeist* is evident in certain aspects of artistic or scientific endeavor, then it must inevitably appear in architecture. Furthermore, he maintained that the *zeitgeist* of his own era was closely tied to a new conception of space, which was destined to influence architecture. Giedion also proclaimed that architecture, during the first two decades of the twentieth century, gained an "objective means of organizing space in ways that gave form to contemporary feelings."[39] Art, including architecture, belonged to that field of human creation that expresses the emotional connections between man and his world. Although Giedion's text can be criticized and challenged in several ways, it is important for our purposes to understand its role in legitimizing the preoccupation with space as an architectural concept.

In *Architecture as Space*, Bruno Zevi argued for an "organic culture" that would establish continuity between past times and modernism.[40] He claimed that this continuity had for some time been impossible because the criteria for evaluating contemporary architecture and that of past centuries differed.[41] Although many understood modern architecture to mark a radical break from the past, Zevi argued that it was merely the most recent stage in a natural continuum. He also claimed that a satisfactory history of architecture had not yet been written, mainly because historians of architecture had not yet become accustomed to thinking in terms of space, nor were they able to apply a coherent method of studying buildings from a spatial point of view. According to Zevi, space became concrete reality only in architecture, and was thus architecture's unique characteristic. "Everyone who has thought even casually about the subject," he wrote, "knows that the specific property of architecture—the feature distinguishing it from all other forms of art—consists in its working with a three-dimensional vocabulary which includes man."[42]

Humanization of space

Neumann coined the phrase the "humanization of space" in 1952. It was the title of a letter he wrote to Giedion and alluded to the phrase "humanization of the city" as a theme that Giedion had introduced in response to post-World War II discussions on the restitution of the core of the city. While Neumann's concept of "humanization" also bears a strong connection to Zevi's motto of humanizing architecture through scientific thought as a rational consequence of modernism's preoccupation with space, Zevi in fact barely elaborated on this idea—aside from associating scientific thought with the role of psychological factors in the creation of space.

In addition to Neumann's use of the phrase "humanization of space" in the title of his proportion theory and in numerous letters, it also crops up in 1957 in Hebrew—as "*hahumanizatzia shel hachalal*"—in Jewish philosopher Martin Buber's foreword to the Hebrew translation of Bruno Zevi's *Architecture as Space*.[43] Zevi's book was the first architectural book to be translated into modern Hebrew and appeared in the same year as its English translation, nine years after it was first published in Italian. Buber's foreword was initially written in Hebrew, and appears only in this Hebrew edition. It is interesting to note that Zevi's book was retitled in Hebrew as *Behalala shel Adrichalut* (*Within the Space of Architecture*), while the earlier Italian title was *Saper Vedere l'Architettura* (*Architecture as Space: How to look at Architecture*).[44] Buber had been living and teaching in Jerusalem since 1938. He was a prominent public figure in the Jewish intellectual circle and it is likely that Neumann met him and exchanged ideas with him while living in Jerusalem during the 1950s. Neumann's *L'Humanisation de l'espace, le système mΦ* was published in French in 1956, but as mentioned above, he had been using the term throughout the early 1950s. Buber borrows the term for the opening assertion of his text: "The fundamental principle of architecture is nothing but the humanization of space."[45] He then goes on to describe ancient man's constant efforts to infuse space with a friendly spirit "for himself and for his gods; homes of solid and heroic cubes [...]"[46] Buber does not, however, go on to explain exactly what he means by the "humanization of space."

For Neumann, the "humanization of space" was a recurring concept to be explored, abstracted, and reinterpreted. It was not a static idea, nor one with a predefined mode of expression; nor was it a style, but rather an idea about how to conceive and organize space. Humanization is a rational workable concept, a design principle that deals with scale, proportion and spatial relationships. It is a process intended to aid the designer in the process of fitting and shaping space, proportioning it, and establishing physical and material relationships within it. Neumann was neither concerned with, nor interested in, the "humanized expression," whether of the human body or of humanism's stylistic associations in architecture; his concern was rather with the concept of space, devoid of any predetermined form, building program, or size, and with the action of "humanizing," of making something tangible in scale with the human body. His argument is a logical, deductive one aimed toward developing a methodological approach to design. Neumann claimed that design, like any other scientific activity, should aspire to be guided by well-defined principles that are set in sequence and thus constitute a method. As will be explained later, this approach does not, however, negate the role of the individual designer and individual expression.

In accordance with humanistic philosophy, Neumann believed that humanism could not remain an abstract concept, but must be applied to material things. The process of humanization thus served to concretize space. It transformed space from an abstract concept into a material phenomenon, lending it scale and dimensions, expressing it tangibly. The most direct manifestation of the process of humanization in architecture was effected through a system of proportion that Neumann deduced to prove geometric relationships between dimensions. But Neumann's later work can be seen to extend this prescriptive set of dimensions to include other principles of design that were much less quantifiable, among them the layout and sequence of spaces within the building, the gradual transition between exterior and interior, the relationship between building and ground, the relationship between structure and envelope, and the filters and control of natural light. All were factors that determined the way one arrived at, and moved through, space, and will be discussed in detail in the following chapters. The concept of humanization thus implicates all the sensual aspects of *experiencing* space.

Neumann's spatial theory notably followed Schmarsow's ideas in two respects. Like Schmarsow, Neumann assumed first that space was the primary medium through which to understand and think of architecture, and secondly, that an understanding of the human body was the basis for designing architectural space.[47]

Neumann cited the symmetry, number, and repetition of parts of the body in support of the physiognomic qualities of the decimal system that he used in the EM-PHI system. The numbers 2, 5, and 10, which structure the metric system, represent the mathematical basis for the EM-PHI system and are inherently related to the body with its pairing of parts and the symmetry reflected in the number 2: hands, legs, eyes, ears, etc. and 5 as the number of fingers or toes, with the pairing of 5 producing 10, and so forth. Neumann therefore regarded the metric system to be "anthropometric." Associating the metric system with the proportions and dimensions of the human body was at odds with the conventional wisdom of the 1950s, however, which regarded the French metric system as an abstract system of measurement, unlike the English foot, which bore a direct relation to the body.

Neumann's rational approach aimed to establish objective criteria through which architecture could be analyzed and categorized. Accordingly, space was that factor through which buildings were to be understood. Neumann's stance aligned with both Giedion's and Zevi's understanding of spatial thinking as a means of historical analysis and as a way of understanding the development of the built environment throughout the history of human civilization. The adoption of spatial thinking as a tool of historical analysis, however, was not Neumann's main concern, as it was Giedion's and Zevi's. Although Neumann's approach to architectural history is adumbrated in his writings and late research, specifically in "Morphologic Architecture" (1963) and "Architecture as Ornament" (1968), he was not interested in analyzing historical styles—such as Byzantine, Gothic, or Renaissance—in and of themselves, but instead sought to perform a pseudo-anthropological analysis of the development of human settlements in general. He therefore analyzed historical structures for the purpose of theorizing how architecture should be understood in modern times. Like Zevi, Neumann attempted to establish the continuity of modernism and the past, but he did so by augmenting the scope of what could be regarded as architectural history to include all forms of the built environment, and not only those few buildings that had been admitted to the canon of artistic masterpieces. Neumann's approach therefore involved reading the built environment in its totality, and in this respect, he was more aligned with the discipline of urban morphology, which deems all built forms to be permissible objects of study. Read as such, the features of early societies and pre-civilization man become a stage in the evolution of built forms and settlement typologies, of which modernism is only the most recent iteration. I will discuss this in more detail in the later chapters.

The two main components of Neumann's EM-PHI system—the set of dimensions and the general tendency toward humanizing space—come together, I would argue, in Neumann's design work of the 1960s. His architectural works, as I will describe in detail throughout the remainder of the book, were based on the insights he arrived at through his EM-PHI system. In the next chapter, we will look at some of Neumann's main projects to examine how his ideas of architectural space were put into practice.

1 See J. Bronowski, *Science and Human Values* (New York: Julian Messner, Inc., 1956), and Erwin Schrödinger, *Nature and the Greeks and Science and Humanism* (Cambridge: Cambridge University Press, 1951).

2 Schrödinger (see note 1), p. 97, see also pp. 93–98, pp. 108–13

3 Ernst Cassirer, *An Essay on Man: An Introduction to a Philosophy of Human Culture* (New Haven: Yale University Press, 1944); Erich Kahler, *Man the Measure: A New Approach to History* (New York: Pantheon Books, 1943); Ralph Barton Perry, *The Humanity of Man* (New York: George Braziller, 1956); and Jean Paul Sartre, *Existentialism and Humanism* (Paris: Éditions Nagel, 1946).

4 Sigfried Giedion, "The Heart of the City; a summing up," in J. Tyrwhitt, J. L. Sert, and E. N. Rogers (eds.), *CIAM 8, The Heart of the City, Towards the Humanization of Urban Life* (New York: Pellegrini and Cudahy, 1952), pp. 159–63, p. 160.

5 Ibid., pp. 160–61.

6 Ibid., p. 162.

7 One important event that informed the discussion at CIAM 8 was the 1948 symposium "In Search of a New Monumentality" organized by Gregor Paulsson, Henry-Russel Hitchcock, William Holford, Sigfried Giedion, Walter Gropius, Lúcio Costa, and Alfred Roth. The central concern of this symposium was that although modern architecture had successfully incorporated the functionalist approach and done away with historical styles, it still needed to address the non-utilitarian functions of buildings and cities in order to provide symbolic expressions of collective purpose and significance. This new mandate to which architecture was to aspire was termed "a new monumentality." It was not to be taken up in all buildings, but rather only in those for which the "community called for some kind of monumental gesture." (In this context, the word "monumental" refers to the representation of the collective.) One major idea motivating the new monumentality was that modern architecture should be accessible to the public: If modern architecture was to be sustained, then the public must see in it an expression of itself, in the form of a community.

8 The term "humanism" is often used in a very broad and general sense, and is most often associated with a historical period, specifically the Renaissance, referred to by Rudolf Wittkower and others as the "Age of Humanism." Within the context of postwar architectural discourse, I prefer to use the verb "to humanize" or the concept of "humanization," as used by Sigfried Giedion and Alfred Neumann to describe the act of making spaces attuned to humans' physiology, psychology, needs, and sensitivities. In 1950s architectural and urbanist discourse, humanization referred to the focus on the human factor in design, specifically the use of the human body as a measure for dimensions and scale in the design of buildings, and the idea of positing the human community as the guiding principle in urban planning and design. This aspiration found expression and manifested itself across all architectural scales, from the individual building, particularly in housing, to the larger urban scale, for example in the attempts made to recover the notion of public space or civic space for human use.

9 Eva-Marie Neumann, "Architecture Proportion in Britain 1945–1957," *Architecture History* no. 36 (1996), pp. 197–221, p. 197. Eva-Marie Neumann is the daughter of Naomi and Alfred Neumann.

10 Rudolf Wittkower, *Architecture Principles in the Age of Humanism* (New York: W.W. Norton, 1971) first published in 1949, p. 101.

11 Wittkower, p. 130.

12 Alina A. Payne, "Rudolf Wittkower and Architectural Principles in the Age of Modernism," *JSAH* 53, September 1994, pp. 322–42, p. 328. It is this objective rationale that appealed to the postwar modern architect, who discovered in Renaissance practices a strong methodological approach to design based on objective abstract principles that could guide the design, yet still leave room for subjective expression.

13 Peter Collins, "Modulor," *The Architectural Review*, 116, no. 691 (July 1954), pp. 5–8, p. 7.

14 Matila Ghyka, *The Geometry of Art and Life* (New York: Sheed and Ward, 1946).

15 Le Corbusier mentions Neumann and presents a table from his EM-PHI system in his *Modulor 2*, p. 87. Le Corbusier, *Modulor 2* (1955), translated by Peter De Francia and Anna Bostock, (Cambridge, Harvard University Press, 1958). *Modulor 2* was preceded by *The Modulor, a Harmonious Measure to the Human Scale Universally Applicable to Architecture and Mechanics*, translated by Peter De Francia and Anna Bostock, (Cambridge, MA: Harvard University Press, 1954, second edition).

16 "According to Vitruvius, whose treatise reflects Greek ideas, Renaissance theory and practice pronounced axiomatically that the proportions of architecture must echo those of the human body. This ancient theory lent itself to being incorporated into a Christian conception of the world. The Bible tells us that Man was created in the image of God. It logically follows that Man's proportions are perfect. The next axiom appears unavoidable: man-made objects, such as architectural structures, can only be attuned to universal harmony if they follow man's proportions." Rudolf Wittkower, "Le Corbusier's Modulor," in Palazzolo Carlo and Vio Riccardo (eds.), *In the Footsteps of Le Corbusier*, (New York: Rizzoli, 1991), pp. 11–19, p. 13. This article was first presented as a conference paper at Columbia University, New York 1961.

17 Payne (see note 12), p. 328.

18 See his writings for *Architectural Review*, particularly the "stock-taking" articles of the 1960s.

19 Reyner Banham, "Architecture after 1960," *The Architectural Review*, 127, no. 756 (February 1960), pp. 91–93. The ideas are repeated in "1960: The Future of Universal Man—Symposium with Anthony Cox, Gordon Graham, John Page, and Lawrence Alloway," *The Architectural Review*, 127, no. 758 (April 1960), pp. 253–60, and "Where Are You Universal Man, Now That We Need You...?" *RIBA Journal*, 83 (July 1976), p. 295.

20 Jacques Lucan, "The Search for the Absolute," in Palazzolo Carlo and Vio Riccardo (eds.), *In the Footsteps of Le Corbusier* (see note 16), pp. 197–207, p. 207.
21 Wittkower (see note 10), p. 57.
22 Some of these questions were debated in a 1957 RIBA (Royal Institute of British Architects) conference at which Charles Eames motioned "That systems of proportion make good design easier and bad design more difficult." The title paraphrased Albert Einstein's comment made a decade earlier on Le Corbusier's Modulor, namely that it "is a scale of proportions which makes the bad difficult and the good easy." After almost a decade of fascination with proportion, the architectural community, particularly in Britain, arrived at the conclusion that proportional systems were misguided attempts to provide universal guidelines to aid in the design of buildings. The supporters of proportion systems argued that they provided a set of principles intended to facilitate one aspect of their professional duties: that of securing proper dimensions and formal relations, which in turn freed the architect to tackle other factors such as social sciences, environmental studies, human engineering, mechanical systems, program analysis, project management, and so forth. Peter Smithson, one of the speakers at the RIBA debate, argued the opposite. He dismissed the significance of, and any future need for, proportional systems applied to architecture, stating that their use could not result in any architecture of cultural significance. Even though Alison and Peter Smithson, at the beginning of their architectural careers, had seemed enthusiastic about Wittkower's and Le Corbusier's ideas on proportion, by this time they had moved away from any interest in these systems and had established a different notion of human values in architecture. Proportion for the Smithsons was not understood in terms of its use in conveying symbolic meanings, nor as an operative tool by which architecture could be related to man, on the one hand, and to the universe or nature on the other. Beyond rejection of any system of general principles, their "humane" approach was to be found not necessarily in history, but, more significantly, outside it, as their definition of New Brutalism found its closest affinities not in a past architectural style or tradition but in peasant dwellings and "as found" architecture—what they believed to be "poetry without rhetoric"—as a direct statement of a way of life. The Smithsons' approach called for the integration of mundane considerations into design, and envisioned the city as a space allowing freedom of movement and choice, in other words as a "true" human value, which would provide the individual with different degrees of contact and an overabundance of in-between spaces. The 1957 RIBA debate concluded in a vote, with most speakers agreeing not to adopt a universal modular system, but to leave the use of proportion as a matter of subjective and personal choice.
23 Extracts from this booklet are reproduced in Alfred Neumann, *L'Humanisation de l'espace: le système mΦ* (Boulogne, Seine: Collection Espace; Editions Architecture d'Aujourd'hui, 1956).
24 The correspondence on the EM-PHI system between Alfred Neumann and Monica Pidgeon, Richard P. Lohse, Sigfried Giedion, Matila Ghyka, Well Coates, and José Luis Sert dating from 1951 to 1953 is held at the RIBA Archives, acc. 361: "File of correspondence relating to attempts by architect Alfred Neumann (1900–1968) to publish a system of modular coordination and architectural proportion, called system mΦ, based on the Golden Section."
25 In a draft article dated December 3, 1951 commenting on Le Corbusier's Modulor and summarizing his own EM-PHI system, Neumann writes: "Starting from that principle when researching the dimensions and proportions of furniture in 1927, I found a rational division allowing for a good approximation of the Golden Section. In order to arrive at a common measure for the correct dimensioning of containers, I had undertaken a great deal of measurements of household objects [...] I had executed some furniture models showing a good utilization of space."
26 The Golden Mean, the Golden Ratio, and the Golden Section are all synonyms for the same concept—a mathematical ratio of such unique qualities that it has fascinated us for centuries.
27 Much ink has been spilled on the Golden Section, and while a thorough discussion of it exceeds the scope of this book, suffice it to say that this mathematical ratio has been both studied and implemented in the arts since Antiquity.
28 From an undated draft paper by Neumann describing the EM-PHI system.
29 From a three-page draft article by Neumann describing the EM-PHI system, dated December 3 1951.
30 Ibid.
31 The method of planar composition re-appeared later, in the 1970s, and was endorsed and used by Peter Eisenman, Richard Meier, Michael Graves, Charles Gwathmey, and John Hejduk, a group later known as the "New York Five."
32 This letter was one of many in which Neumann attempted to promote the publication of his theory of proportion (from the personal archives of Alfred Neumann).
33 Mitchell W. Schwarzer, "The Emergence of Architectural Space: August Schmarsow's Theory of 'Raumgestaltung,'" *Assemblage*, 15 (August 1991), pp. 48–61.
34 Architecture's relationship to the other arts, the differences and parallels between them, forms part of late nineteenth-century art history discourse and is to be found in several German writers of the time, such as Adolf Hildebrand, *The Problem of Form in Painting and Sculpture* (New York: Garland, 1978. Reprint of the 1932 English translation by Max Meyer and Robert Morris Ogden; first published in German in 1893).
35 Architecture as spatial theory lingered on into the early twentieth century through works such as Gustav Platz's history of modern architecture, *Die Baukunst der neuesten Zeit* of 1930, and R.M. Schindler's "Space Architecture" of 1934.
36 According to Arthur Molella, "[Giedion] viewed scientific concepts as expressive of key ideas underlying contemporary art," Arthur Molella, "Science Moderne: Sigfried Giedion's Space, Time and Architecture and Mechanization Takes Command," *Technology and Culture*, 43 (April 2002), pp. 374–89, p. 376.
37 Jacob Bronowski, *Science and Human Values* (New York: Harper & Row Publishers, 1956), p. 35.
38 Sigfried Giedion, *Space,Time and Architecture, The Growth of a New Tradition* (Cambridge, MA: Harvard University Press, 1954, [third edition] first edition 1941). In the introduction, Giedion acknowledges that it was from Wolfflin that he adopted the idea of the historian grasping the spirit of an epoch and from Burckhardt the notion that this underlying spirit can be detected in the different activities and creations of the period. Giedion, pp. 2–5.
39 Ibid., p. 26.
40 Bruno Zevi, *Architecture as Space—How to Look at Architecture*, translated by Milton Gendel, edited by Joseph A. Barry (New York: Horizon Press, 1957).
41 "It has become evident that organic culture cannot, in dealing with the past and specifically with architectural history, use two standards of judgment, one for modern and the other for traditional architecture," Zevi (see note 40), p. 17.
42 Zevi (see note 40), p. 22.
43 This is the only place that I have found the term in Hebrew.
44 Bruno Zevi, *Behalalah shel Adrichalut*, translated from Italian by Haim Verdi (*Saper Vedere l'Architecttura*) (Jerusalem: Bialik, 1957). Noted by Judi Loach and Raquel Rapaport in "Buber on (Looking at) Architecture," *The Journal of Architecture*, 5 (Summer 2000), pp. 189–91, an article devoted to this short foreword by Martin Buber. With the retitling of the book, Zevi also decided to rewrite his introduction specifically for the Hebrew edition.
45 Loach and Rapaport (see note 44), p. 190.
46 Loach and Rapaport (see note 44), p. 190.
47 As Mitchell W. Schwarzer concludes of Schmarsow's approach: "The first step towards spatial consciousness thus leads from bodily sensations to an awareness of the space and form of our own body as circumscribed by the space around it. [...] our own physiognomy, the symmetrical pairing of our two hands or eyes, forms the principle of the dimension of length," from Schwarzer (see note 33), p. 54.

2 Theory and Practice

In 1949, Alfred Neumann arrived in Israel to start a new life. Vladimir Slapeta, who has studied the transformations in Czechoslovakian architecture that took place following the Communist takeover of 1948, contends that Neumann, like other architects, saw no future for himself in Czechoslovakia, and was intent on fleeing the new Communist regime.[1] Zvi Hecker, on the other hand, had the strong impression that Neumann arrived in Israel of his own volition, seeing an opportunity to contribute to, and actively partake in, the building of the new state. Neumann's decision to move to Israel was most likely a combination of these factors.

By 1950, Neumann was living in Jerusalem and working for the Jerusalem Planning Department. Rehoven Abram, a Jerusalem-based architect who became acquainted with Neumann there, wrote a compelling letter to the Technion-Israel Institute of Technology suggesting that they approach Neumann and invite him to teach, believing that he would "greatly contribute to higher education in the field of architecture."[2] Neumann began teaching at the level of assistant professor in the Technion's Faculty of Architecture and Town Planning in 1952, but at the same time kept up his search for academic opportunities abroad, mainly in France and the United States. Students and faculty at the Technion regarded Neumann as an eccentric outsider. His former students there, all of whom held him in high esteem, remember his foreign, "European" appearance—his dress, manners, knowledge, and style of speech—which stood out in the Technion's architecture department of the 1950s.

Zvi Hecker first studied under Alfred Neumann in 1952. "It was during my third year of studies at the Technion," Hecker recalls. "We heard rumors that our second semester studio teacher was a Czech architect who had just joined the faculty. Given that our first semester teacher was also Czech—a dull and uninspiring instructor—we had very low expectations of this 'next Czech.' But after one meeting with Prof. Neumann, I realized he was completely different, and that we were fortunate to be in the presence of a brilliant man."[3] Eitan Kaufmann, another of Neumann's students in those years, remembers him as the first teacher he had encountered at the Technion who knew Le Corbusier personally and even referred to him as "Corbu."

Many regarded Neumann's pedagogy and conduct in the design studio as unusual. His manner was frequently criticized by other teachers and left students perplexed. As the Israeli architect Israel Goodovitch, another of Neumann's former pupils, recalls, "The first day of class we gathered around the table, then Prof. Neumann began talking of Beckett's *Waiting for Godot*, and after that he went on to discuss Sartre, and Wittgenstein—we had no idea what he was talking about. None of us had read these works, which had not yet been translated into Hebrew, and in some cases were not even to be found in English in those days, at least not in Haifa. Everyone was baffled, asking, 'What does this have to do with our project assignment?' Only later did I understand that it was all about architecture; but he had addressed us in a way that no one had ever spoken to us before."[4] Goodovitch also recalls Neumann's explanation of a studio project to design a fair: "It has to be portable, moveable, storable, and attractive," he remembers Neumann saying. "It has to represent contemporary technical progress. Please remember it's like a woman's evening dress: you pay a fortune and put in the best material—for just one evening, for just a single show. Are you aware that fashion designers are now trying to introduce a paper evening dress that looks just like a real one, and survives exactly one evening? Cost equals time equals value," he continued. Goodovitch and his peers were incredulous: "To this free program he [Neumann] did not add a single word of explanation. What kind of fair? Where is it to be located? How many pavilions or buildings will it consist of? What is the budget? He went back to his room leaving the students shocked and puzzled."[5]

As far as architectural education goes, especially that provided by a technical university, Neumann's teaching methods certainly broke with convention. This was especially true in the context of Israel in the 1950s, which had a growing need for professionally trained architects who were expected to have gained practical knowledge and technical expertise while in school. The objective of architectural education at the Technion at that time was to train students to tackle the hands-on task of building to service the demands of the growing state.

Despite Neumann's idiosyncratic pedagogical methods, the faculty must have appreciated his breadth of knowledge and experience, because in 1953 he was promoted from assistant professor to Dean of the Faculty of Architecture and Town Planning, a position he retained until 1958.

Modern architecture in Israel: The International Style as mainstream

The establishment of the state of Israel in 1948 ushered in a dramatic change in the scale, pace, and character of building there. The new state immediately took control of most of the land in the country and initiated development on a vast scale. The growing waves of immigrant Jews—many of them refugees still traumatized by war and unsure of the state's future existence—fueled an urgent and rapid construction campaign. During these years, building not only met practical needs, but also functioned symbolically, as an assurance that the new Jewish state would endure. As more and more immigrants arrived in the new nation, a government ministry was formed to launch a building campaign to oversee the construction of towns, neighborhoods, infrastructure, and public buildings. As a small, new country with a rapidly growing population, Israel had a demand for new buildings that far exceeded the pace of construction. The Israeli government was faced with the immense challenge of building a state that sought to belong to the international community as one nation among many, while at the same time establishing a firm hold on the land through construction. Building became a national project. The evacuation of Palestinians and the destruction of Palestinian villages and towns following the 1948 War of Independence reflected the desire to annex Palestine. In fact, beyond providing housing for the mass of immigrants, construction also had a larger sociopolitical role: By evenly distributing the population to establish a Jewish presence in all parts of the country, it helped to stabilize the politically uncertain state, which was in conflict with its neighbors. To forge Israel's cultural affiliation with the West, many Israeli architects emulated European architectural styles. One benefit of following European idioms was that Israeli architects could work with an established kit of parts, which in turn enabled them to move from design to construction more rapidly—a boon when new building was in high demand. Mainstream Israeli architecture thus favored the International Style, or what was generally referred to as functionalism.

The propagation of modern architecture in Israel after 1948 may be seen as a natural extension of the situation in Palestine earlier on, where, as I will soon describe, modernism was already the prevalent architectural style associated with the existing Jewish presence there. Israel sought to create for itself a new form of cultural expression, which would identify it as a society that associated itself much more with Europe than with its hostile Arab neighbors. And architecture would come to its aid.

Prestate modern architecture in Palestine (1917–1948)

During the 1920s and 1930s, when Palestine was under the British mandate, architects and engineers educated in Europe immigrated to Palestine and brought modern architecture to the Jewish communities (*yishuv*) living there. Throughout the late 1930s and 1940s, Tel Aviv, in those years the commercial-economic center of the *yishuv*, was dominated by privately built, modern residential buildings that were later referred to as "Bauhaus style." Small-scale developers and builders often built three- and four-story town houses and apartment buildings, at times living in one apartment while renting out the others. Built with keen attention to detail and good-quality construction and building finishes, the style was in fact less dogmatic than the modern architecture coming out of the Bauhaus School during those years. Tel Aviv "Bauhaus style" was also more adaptable to the climate and building technologies available, and on a pleasing human scale. This was a result of a consistent architectural language of simple geometric volumes, well-proportioned openings, and whitewashed stucco facades—elements which fostered the myth of the "White City," as Tel Aviv later became known.

"White City" architecture; various residential buildings from the 1930s, mostly designed by immigrant European-trained architects

The European-educated immigrant Jewish architects working in Palestine were not yet building in the service of an Israeli state or for an institutionalized public body. Thus, apart from some large-scale buildings commissioned by public organizations, such as workers' unions or the *kibbutzim*,[6] most construction was on a small scale, and it was of a fairly high quality.

Many of the architects who trained in Europe and worked in Palestine during the 1930s and 1940s viewed it as a place outside the so-called "civilized world," far removed from the cultural setting that they had experienced in their native countries. Whether they came to Israel to escape riots and anti-Semitic persecution in Europe, or were drawn there by the utopian zest of the Zionist movement, or both, most were enthusiastic about the opportunity to build the Jewish homeland. At any rate, the Levant, as the region at the eastern end of the Mediterranean was still called, was regarded by these young émigrés as an exotic place in which to start afresh. With some imagination, optimism, and endurance, the hot, underdeveloped, and all too often conflicted place called Palestine seemed to offer more possibilities under its clear blue skies and bright sunshine than old, gray Europe did. Modern architecture's aspiration to break with the past and create a new society could not have found a better context in which to flourish than in 1930s Tel Aviv. Here, architects could implement a new language of architecture, but also have the freedom to respond to the challenges posed by the particular conditions of climate, material availability, and other issues. The lack of air conditioning, for example—a modern convenience which only became available in Israel after 1948—meant that architects had to learn to incorporate other features, such as balconies, façade apertures, overhangs, and parasol elements to mitigate the oppressive heat. These features, adhering to simple orthogonal geometric compositions, were often cast in concrete, washed in white stucco, and carefully integrated into the architecture.

Nourished by the myth of a "White City" rising from the sand, and unencumbered by any need to respond to an existing urban context, the "Bauhaus style" architecture in Tel Aviv became a symbol of a new society in the making. Purified, clean, confident, and devoid of ornament, it was European in manner yet appropriate to the local climate and light. It was also an architecture which, in the words of Sharon Rotbard, was also ideally suited to "white out" and suppress the presence of neighboring, "black" Jaffa.[7] Even in prestate Israel, modern architecture emerged not only in the city but in rural areas, too, gradually becoming the dominant style everywhere.

In the 1950s, Israel's preoccupation with the pressing problem of how to house the masses and with building technologies developed in Europe and America facilitated the construction of housing for the large immigrant waves arriving in the country. The modernist nation-building project of planning and designing a country in its totality gained momentum with the commissioning, and later the presentation, of a state-wide master plan. After the War of Independence ended in March of 1949, Israeli Prime Minister David Ben-Gurion hired Arieh Sharon (who headed one of the most established, well-connected, and influential architectural firms in the country, and was also the father of Eldar Sharon, who would later become Neumann's student and professional partner) to formulate both regional and country-wide master plans that would serve as a blueprint for the building of the nation.[8] These plans established guidelines and planning principles that reflected the political aspirations of the Israeli nation.[9] The waves of new construction were beyond what anyone could have imagined for a young country of that size. Novice architects, mostly graduates from the Technion-Israel Institute of Technology, just out of school and with little experience, had the opportunity to design and build on all scales, from public buildings to entire neighborhoods. Several architectural competitions were also organized during those years and they, too, presented design opportunities for young professionals.

Architectural practice

In 1959, Zvi Hecker, a talented young architect who had studied architecture in the 1950s in Cracow, Poland, and then at the Technion in Israel, along with his former classmate from the Technion, Eldar Sharon, won the national competition for the design of a town hall for the new city of Bat Yam. Hecker and Sharon were both former students of Neumann, and they decided to invite him to join them when working on the design. It was Hecker who initiated the invitation. "I felt that Neumann should be given the opportunity to build in Israel," he explained. "Eldar was an easy-going guy, he didn't mind, especially since both of us admired Neumann."[10] Having Neumann involved as a more experienced architect, not to mention a professor at the Technion, was a factor in securing the commission for the project, and in assuring the client that Hecker and Sharon's inexperience would not be an obstacle to the execution of the building.

Early 1950s slab housing haphazardly constructed across the country regardless of topographic conditions: in Yad Eliyahu, a neighborhood of Tel Aviv (left) and in Haifa (right)

The combination of the older, established professor, who had designed and built in the past, but who had been disconnected from practice since the late 1930s, with the young talent and ambitions of two of his former students, fresh out of school, yielded a dynamic and productive team. Neumann's approach to architectural practice at that point in his life seems to have been less opportunistic, less inclined to "get a design built at all costs," and hence unwilling to compromise the project's architectural and artistic quality. Since he himself was not a young professional under pressure to establish his credentials, he did not consider himself bound by client expectations for a certain kind of architectural style and felt free to explore new ideas.

Challenging conventions and rethinking architecture came to Neumann as a natural extension of his inventive teaching style and thought-provoking ideas, which as former students both Hecker and Sharon were familiar with. As young, ambitious architects they embraced this different approach, although Hecker was more receptive to it than Sharon.

As the three began to work together on the Bat Yam Town Hall, other opportunities for collaboration opened up through different personal connections and design competitions. The partnership Neumann-Hecker-Sharon therefore set up shop in a small space on the ground floor of a residential building in Tel Aviv owned by the family of Hecker's wife. Over the next few years, Neumann-Hecker-Sharon became a peculiar and interesting partnership which produced an extraordinary body of work that gained international recognition without precedent in Israeli history. Their designs were by far the most publicized works of Israeli architecture in international professional journals and magazines dating from that time. This was immensely significant in the context of 1960s Israel, which was a small, young, provincial country without any substantial architectural tradition or previous contributions to the international architectural scene. Neumann-Hecker-Sharon's work was characterized as radical, and at times experimental and avant-garde. Their projects aroused interest abroad, but were received with skepticism and critique within Israel, first on the part of a few influential and established local architects and later also from the broader public.

Bat Yam Town Hall and Civic Center, 1959–63

Bat Yam, which in Hebrew means "daughter of the sea," is a small city that was established in the early 1950s along the Mediterranean coast just south of Tel Aviv. Later in the decade, the town decided to construct a new town hall, for which it designated a site within an already built-up area of the city. On joining his former students Hecker and Sharon, Neumann proposed that they should look for an alternative site outside the built-up area but within the bounds of the city's future extension. He suggested that the new town hall be a catalyst for urban growth and draw development to the neighborhoods surrounding it. City officials agreed with Neumann's suggestion, and designated a long, rectangular city-owned site for the new building: It was an empty, sandy lot just three hundred meters from the Mediterranean, on the southern fringe of the developing city. Because both this site and its surrounding areas were empty, it also presented the architects with an opportunity to shape the area around the town hall. They therefore expanded their plan and provided a larger vision for the development of the whole area (fig. 12.1). They decided to design a large, rectilinear public square around the town hall with the aim of making it the new civic center of Bat Yam. This longitudinally shaped urban space, which followed the site lines of the lot, was intersected at one end by a boulevard leading to the sea. As an urban typology—in terms of the scale, proportion, and form of the urban space and its connection to the waterfront—Bat Yam's public square resembled Pompeii's historic main square and in its dimensions also bore a resemblance to the Piazza San Marco in Venice.

Neumann not only decided to increase the scope of the project to accommodate a large urban plan and civic space, but he also reworked the design that Hecker and Sharon submitted for the town hall building in the competition phase. Hecker and Sharon's competition entry had proposed an orthogonal building with an open atrium space at the center, and an inverted ziggurat form for the exterior massing. These two features of the early scheme remained present in the final building, but in the meantime had been completely redesigned by Neumann. Neumann's proposal envisaged a freestanding town hall building within a long rectangular public space surrounded by a three- to four-story continuous slab building with shops at ground level, and two to three floors of apartments and offices above. All entrances and access to the shops and the offices above them were to be positioned along an arcade along the inner perimeter of the building, which was an integral part of the design. The town hall itself was set at a forty-five-degree angle to the square, and marked the intersection of the boulevard leading from the square to the waterfront (fig. 12.12). Since the building's form was that of a three-story, inverted ziggurat, each of its floors extended beyond, and provided shade for, the one below it. The municipal offices were arranged along the periphery of each of the extended floor plans, while at the center of the building was a void that ran the height of all three floors, creating an atrium—a shaded, covered space that was open to the public and acted as an interior extension of the public square outside. Neumann-Hecker-Sharon envisioned the surrounding areas developing beyond this new civic center into a fairly dense, three-story housing fabric in line with the existing urban fabric, but with occasional taller buildings spread out at intervals. This ambitious design extended the original idea. It proposed not only a whole new urban space and image for the city, but also a radically different architectural expression of a public building and public space. To promote their design, the architects referenced the relation of Pompeii to Rome as analogous to the relation of Bat Yam to Tel Aviv. Bat Yam, although smaller and less central than Tel Aviv, was nevertheless encouraged to aspire, like Pompeii, to create its own urban character and identity (the reference to Pompeii was part of the published material describing the project).Throughout the process of designing and constructing the town hall, Neumann changed and modified the design, and ideas continued to surface even while the building was under construction. Hecker later recalled several instances when workers were asked to dismantle frameworks for concrete casts because Neumann had decided to change the design even after the construction documents had been approved and even after work on the building had commenced. While continuously modifying a design during its construction phase is typically considered unacceptable, it met with less resistance than feared because the city engineer responsible for overseeing the project was an architect who supported the design and who appreciated Neumann's evident commitment to its success. Hecker and Sharon's continuous presence on the site and motivation to have the project succeed, both on its own terms and in relation to Neumann's expectations, greatly contributed as well. Bat Yam Town Hall was the first major architectural work that Neumann had accomplished in over two decades. Its design became a kind of testing ground, a clean canvas on which he could express several of the ideas and principles that had filtered through from his research and teaching. The building expressed most of the ideas that Neumann would develop further in later designs. It was in this project, for example, that he began to work out his concept of space packing, the use of polyhedral geometry, and the implementation of his EM-PHI proportion system.

Changes to the design can be traced from the competition phase to the built design, where a more comprehensive architectural language developed. The early design (figs. 12.2, 12.3) presented the building's general *parti* (essential architectural idea, usually shown through a massing or solid-void diagram), which conveyed its two main components: the central interior atrium and the inverted ziggurat shape. It also subdivided the façades into modules to match the arrangement of the offices along the perimeter of the square plan. At this point, the building's façades were treated as two-dimensional planes, (figs. 12.3, 12.4), subdivided and modulated as a separate surface related to the inner organization of the plan by the rhythm of its openings. As the design developed, however, the elevation began to be conceived more as a volumetric assembly of rooms, as three-dimensional elements impacting both the shape of the interior spaces and the building's outer face. The structure of the building and the elevation design, in other words, came to be understood as one system rather than as two separate ones.

The breakthrough in the design process was the imposition of the 45-degree grid on the orthogonal, stepped-out massing of the building. This was first introduced through the building's roof plan, since the 45-degree shift worked better as a structural grid, reducing the distance to be spanned over the central interior space (figs. 12.7, 12.15). It was then adopted and extended to govern the structure of the whole building, eventually finding expression in the interior and exterior alike. Significantly, this 45-degree grid was conceived as a spatial structure, a three-dimensional frame which, based on its geometry, resembled a cuboctahedron where it met the orthogonal massing. While the idea of proportioning and subdividing the overall building mass into smaller, "humanized" elements existed before the 45-degree grid was implemented—as can be seen in one of the earlier models (fig. 12.4)—the 45-degree grid offered a new expression of an overarching pattern. Neumann's insistence on "thinking in space" led to the creation of the elevation as a spatial pattern of volumetric units (figs. 12.13, 12.24, 12.25). These were then set in proportion, following the tables of measurements defined by Neumann's EM-PHI system. As we saw in chapter 1, Neumann's proportional method posited that if the single spatial unit were set in proportion, that is, if it were "humanized" in scale, then creating the entire building by repeating this unit would set the whole in proportion. In the case of Bat Yam Town Hall, the unit was multiplied to form an aggregate close in size to the previously defined general building mass, which was then, in its turn, adjusted to match the modulation created by the aggregated, scaled volumetric units. The design was thus a process of continuous exchange between the dimensions of the unit and those of the overall building, of calibrating the one against the other. Since the building's form had to comprise a certain number of whole units, a balance between the two had to be achieved. The design fell into place when the various different building systems were unified: structure, openings, façade, volumetric subdivision, and façade articulation.

Neumann's space-packing approach was first developed in the context of the Bat Yam project outlined here, but the concept was still in its early stages and had yet to be fully articulated.[11] In this project, the purpose of the space-packing approach was not to generate form; it was rather applied spatially onto a massing not originally designed to accommodate it, specifically the form that Hecker and Sharon had proposed earlier on, during the competition phase. Neumann's revisions to the design established a means of subdividing the building mass into smaller elements, creating a new relationship between the parts and the whole. In other words, the space-packing approach with its lexicon of volumetric subdivision that Neumann developed for the Bat Yam project was subject to the constraints and limitations of a building already under construction. The massing and design of Bat Yam Town Hall's overall structure had already been fixed, indeed its foundations already poured, when Neumann decided to apply the space-packing approach to the building. The space-packing pattern as developed in the Bat Yam project, however, would in time evolve into an important means of unifying the spatial elements and systems of a given building, and soon became an integral aspect of Neumann's design process. While at first glance, Bat Yam Town Hall's unique façade appears to have a planar geometric pattern, a closer look reveals that its square forms, rotated through a 45-degree angle to the horizontal, are not components of a flat pattern. Rather, they are the multifaceted outer surfaces of composite volumetric elements, lined up and stacked to form the inner massing spaces of the building. The idea of the building as an accretion of volumetric units, or cells, is reinforced by the placement and geometry of the windows and the structure of the overhung ceilings (figs. 12.25, 12.28, 12.30, 12.32, 12.33), both clearly visible from outside and inside the building. In the interior, these units are realized through the structuring of the perimeter corridor that serves the offices; the office and corridor layout are a result of the same volumetric unit, which is "hollowed out" as it meets the central atrium space (fig. 12.33). Neumann's design of Bat Yam Town Hall was also significantly informed by attempts to manage the climatic conditions and natural light levels in Israel. At the time, many European-trained architects, especially ones based in colder climates, were captivated by the intense sunlight bathing the shores of the Mediterranean. Since the open façades, strip windows, and glass walls that were characteristic of the modernist movement in Europe left the interiors of their buildings too exposed to strong sunlight, they had to develop different ways of adapting their creations to warmer, sunnier conditions. The discovery of the "power of sunlight" led several architects to re-imagine the building envelope in terms of how light fell on the exterior, and how it was filtered through and directed into the interior. George Candilis and Shadrach Woods, for example, developed a series of deep balconies that they treated as another layer of the façade for their ATBAT project in Morocco. And it was while working on projects in the Mediterranean that Le Corbusier developed his *brise-soleil* (lit. "sun break") technique, which involved appending rows of either horizontal or vertical fins to the façades of a building in order to reduce and control the fierce daylight penetrating its interior. The *brise-soleil* went on to have an important influence on Israeli architecture of the 1950s, becoming one of the most common architectural elements of 1950s Israeli modernism. Nevertheless, while the *brise-soleil* functioned as an element applied post hoc to a building's façade—a separate system that was merely "added on"—in the Bat Yam project, Neumann devised a way to make light-mitigation an intrinsic feature of the building's structure. Both the overall massing of the projecting floors, which cast shadows on the floors below, and the articulation of the elevations as a kind of screen, functioned to minimize the building's heat intake and to diffuse natural light as it entered the interior (figs. 12.24, 12.25, 12.27).

The *brise-soleil* as a common architectural element of 1950s architecture in Israel

Bat Yam was Neumann's first attempt to express the idea of repeating volumetric units to create a whole, in which the units followed a pattern that corresponded with, and resulted from, their geometry. It was also his first attempt to arrange the units in a way that suited their geometric tendency to meet and cluster—something that I will describe in more detail in chapter 3. This was an idea that Neumann developed in his later work, and that found a purer expression in projects such as the El Al Terminal (project 21) and the Negev Synagogue (project 26). Bat Yam Town Hall became an icon of 1960s Israeli architecture. It was one of the four modern buildings in Israel to appear on a mailing stamp, and it was accorded extensive publicity and press coverage, both locally and internationally, even before its completion; yet at the same time it was also the subject of professional and public critique, which saw it as too much of a foreign intrusion into the city and which while expressing wonder, also questioned whether the architects were not too much invested in self-expression. Nevertheless, Bat Yam Town Hall was considered a radical design that drew many curious visitors from around the country.

Reinforced concrete was a broad presence in Israeli society in the 1950s and 1960s. Since Israel had natural resources such as limestone and sand, the base materials for cement, it was one of the most readily available materials for construction, But concrete was also culturally significant in Israel. As a durable building material, it symbolized the new Israeli society putting down permanent roots in the landscape. Concrete's solid, heavy presence signified a direct, immediate, and enduring hold on the land. "Supplementing the act of forestation and plowing, and as part of the 'conquering the desert,'" wrote Gideon Ofrat, concrete "in this sense is an erotic conquering of the earth."[12] The building material was even discussed and celebrated in poetry, literature, popular theatre, and music.

Stylistically, bare concrete gained prominence as a means of architectural expression in Israel only in the 1950s, mainly as a consequence of influences from abroad, such as Le Corbusier's postwar concrete works and the New Brutalism movement in England. The use of bare concrete is the defining aspect of Brutalism, a term derived from the French *béton brut*, meaning raw, or bare, concrete. Brutalism has many connotations, but appealed to the younger generation of Israeli architects on grounds of its rough and unmediated expression. This matched their image of the new Israel as an archaic presence with modern materials and means, recovering, in the words of Ram Karmi, "the erotic, native Canaanite dimension, which sings a song of praise to nakedness and youth, but especially to power: the power of the body in the image of bare concrete."[13] Bare concrete best reflected Israel's modernist aspiration to the truth of materials, and represented the crude, forceful, and passionate attachment of buildings to the land. It projected an image of the new Israeli—as opposed to the European—Jew: the Jew who had nothing to hide, but instead stood bare, proud, and strong in the reconquered ancient Promised Land. Under the fierce Israeli sun, the exposed bare concrete attained a sense of vitality, a sharpness and a definition that counteracted its heavy blurred grayness.

Neumann's use of bare concrete, however, did not seem to carry these intentions. For one, he moved away from the characteristic Brutalist use of rough, untreated concrete for a building's exterior finish and toward a more refined expression that emphasized the building's complex geometries. For Neumann, concrete's sculptural qualities enabled a purity of form, a crystalline expression of a building's geometry as one continuous construct. Neumann's handling of concrete can be seen in the Bat Yam project, particularly in the triangular planes of the roof structures that functioned as light and wind wells (fig. 12.26). Here, he attempted to achieve a refined texture by minimizing the thickness of the casts and by paying special attention to the precision of corners and edges. In this sense Neumann's use of concrete drew influence from Auguste Perret's elegant and refined work with bare concrete, which Neumann was familiar

Malqaf–the element that channels wind into chimneys (left), and four windcatchers (right), near Fahraj, Iranian Plateau

with through his work as a young apprentice at Perret's Atelier du Palais de Bois in the late 1930s.

In addition, while the concrete walls and panels of Brutalist-style buildings were cast with chamfered corners, Neumann refused to do this. The corners of his building had to be sharp and precise, even if "Israel Brutalism" appropriated the chamfered corner for aesthetic and practical purposes on a multitude of scales. (Contractors, incidentally, preferred to chamfer corners when casting concrete on site, since the insertion of a plastic triangle into the cast, which creates the chamfered corner, allows for a hastier disassembly of the formwork after the cast has dried.)

A further distinction between Neumann's use of concrete and its appearance in Israeli Brutalism pertained to color. While Brutalist architecture relied on concrete's direct and "truthful" expression for its material qualities and presence, Neumann chose instead to emphasize the geometries that shaped the sculptural spaces of his designs by coloring various faces. As Neumann's polyhedral structures became more complex in the course of his career, so did the space-packing scheme that brought the single units together, just as color became an increasingly important means of spatial differentiation. If all the units shared the same material and color, the idea of an overall form composed of stacked individual units was difficult to discern. They tended to be read as one continuous surface rather than as a conglomeration of several repetitive smaller elements. The use of different colors enhanced the surface pattern's rhythm, pace, and symmetry, and ultimately enhanced its sculptural dimensionality. The systematic coloring of the same side of a polyhedral unit throughout a building accentuated its spatial presence and strengthened the perception of repetitive units creating a larger whole. This can be seen very clearly in the Negev Synagogue (project 26), for which Neumann used a variety of colors, but never any that resembled the gray-white shades of raw concrete; he thus followed Adolf Loos's "principle of cladding," according to which a material can be painted any color except those that might be confused with its "natural" color.[14]

While Neumann in principle deployed color to enhance the sculptural qualities of his buildings, it operated in other ways as well. For one, it could convey symbolic meaning. For the façade of Bat Yam Town Hall, for example, Neumann employed a palette of red, blue, and gold—colors commonly found in traditional Byzantine and Islamic buildings—in order to evoke associations with the architectural heritage of the surrounding region. Color, moreover, could diffuse and reflect light differently than unpainted concrete, and thus could affect the strength and brightness of the light reflected into a building's interior. Despite Neumann's strategic use of color and the striking visual effects it produced, it was a controversial aspect of his architecture, as is borne out by the Danciger Building that he was asked to design for the Technion's Faculty of Mechanical Engineering on the new Haifa campus, as we shall see in chapter 4.

Dubiner Apartment House, Ramat Gan, 1961–65

Sam Dubiner was a wealthy Canadian entrepreneur who made his first fortune marketing the yo-yo in North America. As a committed Zionist, he immigrated to Israel in the 1950s and established a plastics company that produced boxes for packaging Jaffa oranges intended for export. It was a privately run company that proved to be very successful—until it ran into opposition from state-supported agricultural unions that did not want to rely on a private supplier to package a national export product. Dubiner was also an art collector and enthusiastic supporter of the Israeli art scene centered in Tel Aviv. In 1961, he opened a modern art gallery in Tel Aviv, the Gallery Israel, which became a central meeting place for artist, architects, and intellectuals.

Dubiner decided to build a villa for his family on land that he owned in Ramat Gan, a town on the outskirts of Tel Aviv. He consulted Israeli sculptor Itzhack Danziger, who recommended the firm Neumann-Hecker-Sharon for the job.[15] Dubiner initially intended to build a large detached, single-family house on the site, but Neumann proposed an apartment building, claiming that this was more appropriate within the context of the neighborhood, and that a single large villa would look like a mansion in Ramat Gan, a small town consisting mainly of apartment blocks and attached houses. A villa, in other words, would seem inordinately lavish, and would have the effect of socially isolating Dubiner and his family from the community. Dubiner, being a businessman, bought into the idea, realizing that he could provide each of his children with an apartment unit and also sell a few for profit. Neumann-Hecker-Sharon's proposed design for the apartment building exceeded the floor area ratio and zoning regulations allowed on the site at that time. Anxious to remain on good terms with the wealthy and influential Dubiner, the mayor of Ramat Gan nevertheless supported the variances and zoning changes to ensure that the project was approved.

The site was a steep, southwest-facing slope bounded at top and bottom by cul-de-sacs. Dubiner had spent hours there, learning the prevailing wind directions and passage of the sun, and hence was eager to have the architects develop a design that took these factors into consideration. Neumann's primary idea was to design a hillside building that could be entered from both the top and the bottom of the hill, creating a path that would run through the building and connect the two dead-end streets. His idea was to have all the apartments accessible from this path. The early models for the Dubiner Apartment House (fig. 17.14) studied the way in which connections to the apartments could be made while retaining a contiguous space for movement along the hill. Hecker recalls that this was a very difficult problem to solve since it created several access issues, which were resolved by creating entrance bridges to the apartments and by designing apartments much larger than was common in Israel at the time. A larger apartment area offered more options for locating the point of entry for the bridges leading to the apartments, while minimizing the total number of apartments and thus the number of bridges needed. The scheme took the form of an internal, stepped courtyard between the side of the hill and the building floors, which projected out from the hillside (figs. 17.4, 17.6, 17.15). The building contained seven stories that were stepped along and against the slope. The first three followed the retreating profile of the hill, whereas the upper stories were stepped in the opposite directing, projecting outward from the hill and forming an overhang above the central space created between these two sections (figs. 17.4, 17.35).

This condition meant that the original slope of the hillside could be maintained in certain areas; even more interestingly, however, it created an outdoor space that was partly covered, partly open to the sky, and defined by the common path climbing the hill. The stepped inner courtyard also created its own microclimate by channeling airflows and controlling sunlight, allowing shade in the summer and direct sunlight in the winter (figs. 17.30–33).

This cool, shady space along the hillside offered respite from the blazing sunlight outside; but its multiple paths, which crossed and intersected throughout the steep, irregularly shaped courtyard, also fostered a sense of disorientation. The result was unlike any building in Israel at the time. From the aesthetic, organizational, and unit-size aspect, the Dubiner House stood out. The placement of the bridges and access points within the building's interior, along the slope of the hill, meant that the parking areas had to be relegated to the space around the building's outer edges. The structure, moreover, did not contain an elevator or even an enclosed staircase, meaning that access to each apartment required walking. The building as a whole stood out for its magnitude; on completion, it was much larger than the smaller three-story building next to it. Its visual expression as an aggregate of units inspired some to nickname it "honeycomb housing" or an "Arab village," owing to its aggregation of smaller forms that were often associated with terraced vernacular architecture.

Perhaps because it was so unique, and because of the high costs of its larger apartments, the Dubiner Apartment House remained largely unoccupied for many years after its completion in 1964. Dubiner's family moved into the largest apartment on the top floor, and Zvi Hecker's family moved into one of the mid-level apartments; but the rest remained unoccupied. A few years later, as the city grew—and with it, the demand for larger apartments—the building became more desirable. Its unique, terraced courtyard and spaces, and especially the abundance of rooftop terraces attached to each unit, made it an attractive place to live in the densely growing city.[16]

Like Bat Yam Town Hall, the Dubiner Apartment House started from a general massing strategy (fig.17.13), and only later was it subdivided into a pattern of elongated prismatic hexagons. This idea emerged from the need to articulate and subdivide the volumes of each floor into individual apartments, and the apartments into smaller rooms. Neumann did not attempt to make the single room the unit of repetition that generated the pattern, but instead he imposed a pattern derived from the geometry of the building's overall shape. The pattern's primary role was to articulate the larger mass and to provide the structure as a whole with a scale, or a unit of measure. Each unit's dimensions and proportions were taken from the EM-PHI system. Although one unit was not necessarily equal to one room of the apartment, it did constitute a module within the overall underlying pattern that controlled the organization of the plan (figs.17.2–3, 17.9–10, 17.17). Larger spaces such as living rooms were made up of a few of these modules, while smaller spaces such as bathrooms occupied only part of them. The stepped massing meant that each apartment had a balcony formed by the roof of the floor below it, a feature well suited to Israel's climate. The hexagonal pattern expressed itself most clearly in the building's longitudinal elevation. From this view, the building's envelope is not a flat surface, but a saw-tooth texture of protruding and receding spaces created by alternating hexagonal prisms, in which the gap between two hexagonal units on one floor coincides with the hexagonal balcony of a unit on the floor below (figs.17.25, 17.27–28, 17.34). From the interior, the effect is one of a rhythmic sequence of interlocking balconies and interior spaces.

Alfred Neumann's space-packing system

Over the years that Neumann worked on these and other projects, space packing emerged as a design strategy and as a new architectural expression. Although space packing came to be associated with his later polyhedral structures, it seems to have originated in a series of geometrically orthogonal studies for dormitories and housing projects in the 1950s. These studies were later published under the title "Space-Packing Patterns" as a set of proposals for dormitories and housing prototypes. In his design for the dormitory projects of the 1950s (project 11), Neumann proposed stacking upright, I-beam-shaped wall dividers to create a building of partitioned units. Each successive row of I-beam-shaped dividers was offset from the one it rested on, forming a pattern of spatial units which, from the section cut, resemble the running bond pattern common in brickwork. The repetitive pattern of the section was supplemented by variations in floor-plan layouts, shown in several drawings and sketches. The arrangements of the dorm units can be altered and are not as constrained by the rigidity of the non-conventional building section as they might seem to be. The variations in plan aimed to show the flexibility in dorm layout, suggesting that fixed, predetermined patterns created in section do not necessarily dictate a single kind of arrangement in plan. Here, space packing, still in its early stages, treated plan and section as separate entities. The I-beam-shaped wall element was indeed three-dimensional, but it was an extruded form, and acted as a planar partition rather than as a volumetric unit.

Neumann wrote the following text to accompany this project:

> Architecture is essentially a system of juxtaposed or superposed horizontal areas. About half of them are human movement areas. Besides there is another type of area on different levels above the movement areas—the lifted floors—serving various purposes as: lying in bed, sitting on chairs or benches, working and eating at tables, storage of things in open or closed cupboards. The volume underneath the furniture not only remains useless but is also difficult to clean. But also the volume above the furniture is superfluous, therefore it is imperative to exploit that volume too. It is done in the simplest way by adding the lost volumes to the movement space above or underneath.

> Without reducing the usual height of movement space, one arrives at a space-packing pattern with a reduced building volume and an important reduction of the total building height. All furniture is built-in and the considerable cost of the acquisition and maintenance of furniture falls off.[17]

The intent of this project was to provide an efficiently arranged, compact space. Neumann's explanation does not discuss the construction advantages as much as the practical advantages of spaces economically designed to fit their functions. He describes a certain spatial and structural efficiency: the maximization of interior space by getting rid of all seemingly useless spaces, such as the superfluous spaces above furniture, and the structural composition of the whole building from a minimal number of repetitive standardized elements.

The main achievement of this project, considering how Neumann's work would later develop, was in tying a structural building component (in this case an I-shaped wall section element) to the space it generated. In this early version of space packing, Neumann's approach resembles the work of Joop van Stigt, a member of Dutch Forum, in the way it stacks patterns without clearly defined boundaries. Most of the drawings and models using this design were shown as open-ended fragments, rather than as parts comprising a building. Neumann's drawing of the overall layout of the dormitory buildings (figs. 11.8–9) features rectangular, slab-like buildings hemming an hexagonal open space—an arbitrary arrangement since the project never had a specific site. Unlike in Neumann's later work, the overall form of this project and the shape of its parts were not related. From the geometric point of view, the overall form did not confine the pattern. The unit of repetition could be extended sideways and up and down indefinitely, without submitting to a larger shape that fixed its limits of expansion. The project lacked the scalar part-to-whole relationship characteristic of Neumann's later work. It was more of a pattern, without yet being an object.

The inventiveness and originality of this project nevertheless merits closer attention. Both in its totality and in its detailing, it is a unique and original building section. Neumann's acute sensitivity to the arrangement and articulation of interior space, so evident in this project, may be explained by his early experience in his father's interior fittings workshop. When the family moved from Vienna to Brno in 1910, his father established an interior fittings company that was active throughout the 1920s and 1930s. After graduating from the German Building Trades School, and likely even before this, the young Alfred designed furniture, and other interior fittings, for the family business.[18] This work made him aware of how interior spaces are used, as it required him to examine the activities, dimensions, and movements of the human body in relation to the objects that serve our daily routines. The practice of furniture design, to a greater degree than building design, is more conducive to the notion of a spatially unified object, since the process of designing furniture, partly due to its small scale, permits a closer synthesis between the vertical and horizontal sections of an object. In building design, by contrast, the plan is often the generator for the whole—the horizontal base from which the vertical walls are extruded. The practice of furniture design trained Neumann to establish a closer rapport between the different parts of a designed object, since the transition between section and plan in furniture was more immediate and intuitively understood as belonging to one and the same thing. Applied on a large architectural scale, this mode of thinking could have a significant impact on the conception of spaces. Neumann later wrote: "When researching the dimensions and proportions of furniture in 1927, I found a rational division allowing for a good approximation of the Golden Section. In order to arrive at a common measure for the correct dimensioning of containers, I had undertaken a great deal of measurements of household objects."[19] Neumann described his execution of furniture models as a "good utilization of space."[20]

Interestingly, Neumann's dormitory project can be read as a synthesis of Adolf Loos's terraced housing proposals and Le Corbusier's Unité d'habitation section: It was a particularization of the prototypical Unité section on the one hand, and a generalization of Loos's localized and specific sectional conditions, as described by his *Raumplan*, on the other. It is a project that in architectural jargon would be referred to as having been derived from "sectional design," which simply means that the vertical section is the "site" where the architectural idea is worked through, or where the primary design operation can be identified.

The connection to Adolf Loos is not surprising. Neumann was well acquainted with Loos's work; his library contained Loos's writings; he himself had studied in Vienna, Loos's hometown, during the 1920s, and he referenced Loos on numerous occasions. Loos's writings on ornament were of special interest to Neumann, especially his famous essay, "Ornament and Crime," which was influential in formulating modern architects' approach to ornamentation. One of Neumann's last essays, "Architecture as Ornament," (written in 1968 and published in 1969, after his death) begins with a description of nineteenth-century ornament and analyzes Adolph Loos's statements on the relationship between ornament and modern architecture. Neumann then proceeds to explain how Loos's denunciation of the use of ornament in his time was based on a certain understanding of ornament's historical development and its projected future role in society. Loos believed in a historical trajectory on which ornament gradually diminished as human culture progressed, and that this would eventually lead to the disappearance of ornament from both architecture and manmade artifacts. Loos, according to Neumann, therefore saw no reason to artificially accelerate or perpetuate this evolutionary process, and he criticized those who interfered with ornament's "natural" course toward obsolescence. He rejected not only the Arts and Crafts movement, which had perpetuated historicist ornamentation, but he also resisted purists, such as the modernist avant-garde, who sought to accelerate the evolutionary process and purge ornament in a single blow. Rather than regarding ornament as a decorative add-on, Loos believed that the way in which materials are used and assembled to create certain patterns in building finishes could be considered ornamental (in the formal sense), and surpass merely decorative devices in terms of expression. Natural building materials, therefore, might qualify as ornamental by virtue of their arrangement on surfaces. Loos also argued that the way in which ornament was expressed in architecture, interior design, and artifacts changed over time, as ornament itself was constantly changing. In this sense, Loos's designs can be seen to offer an interpretation of how ornament should appear in architecture in his own time and in the culture of early twentieth-century Europe. According to Neumann, Loos felt misunderstood when his texts, adapted by Le Corbusier and the young modernists, were read only as a revolt against ornamentation. He even felt compelled to respond by publishing, in 1921, a series of essays, penned between 1897 and 1900, tellingly titled *Spoken into the Void*.

Neumann used Loos's reading of "ornamentation as an evolutionary process" as a point of departure for his own interpretation of ornament. Tying it into a broader morphological line of thinking, Neumann agreed that ornament should be seen as part of an evolutionary process and not eliminated altogether, but rather transformed. He suggested that ornament's dominant presence in architecture as two-dimensional patterning—primarily as an applied, decorative device—should be replaced with an intrinsic, three-dimensional expression, an expression in spatial form or building mass that would reflect the building's principle spatial organization. Ornament, whether two- or three-dimensional, was understood by Neumann to be generated by pattern making, which was a foundational operation in the creation of architecture.

In architecture, according to Neumann, three-dimensional pattern making was born of a broad, historical, morphological process of grouping. He described this process as the tendency of individual cells or units of single spaces, to gradually group together, over thousands of years of human development, into closer proximity, eventually merging and producing patterns. Since this grouping process in architecture was spatial, so the process of pattern making was spatial, leading Neumann to term this process "space packing." Each phase of its historical development can be read through the pattern generated by the relations among spaces created by the individual units that make up the overall form. This process is integral to the way in which architecture is conceived: first as a set of small spatial relations, such as an assembly of rooms in a house or building, then as a collection of houses or apartments giving rise to a larger building, and so on, eventually leading to neighborhoods and other larger urban configurations such as cities. Neumann described the development of the built environment as having originated in primitive forms of settlement composed of scattered individual huts, which over time grew both in size from single rooms to double rooms, and in the number of units per settlement. Thus, architecture gradually became more organized and ordered for purposes of social and practical proximity, accessibility, and efficiency. These groupings evolved and generated different forms that brought together a series of individual spaces to create a single entity, a larger form with several spaces and subdivisions within it. The process of grouping not only transformed the overall organization of the individual units, but it also altered the shapes and geometries of the units themselves. Adopting a broad, historical perspective, we can trace a general transformation from round, amorphic shapes, often found in very early settlements, to the orthogonal system, which appeared much later. As a historical, evolutionary process, space packing, or three-dimensional pattern making, was characterized by a general tendency toward a grouping of spaces and forms. Thus while scattered arrangements, such as settlements made up of scattered huts, persisted, other built-up areas, such as large single structures and dense urban environments, grew and developed. Neumann's theory of spatial grouping did not dismiss the existence of non-grouped settlements, just as by analogy, Darwinian evolution did not reject the continued existence of apes alongside humans.

The idea of grouping is thus a consistent principle that holds true for all scales of the built environment. This reading of the built environment establishes a direct, inseparable link between the conception and formation of the unit and the pattern that sets it in a larger order. Space packing can thus be viewed as an essential, inevitable feature of architectural creation.

The phenomenon of spatial grouping appears in nature, its geometrically most vivid manifestation being in the formation of crystals. With the aid of mathematics, mid-twentieth-century scientists began to study crystallography more carefully, mapping and defining the types of groupings or patterns that could be generated. They found that there were a limited number of possible mathematical operations that could produce patterns; that all these operations depended on utilizing symmetry, and that they could all be categorized into a fixed number of possibilities.

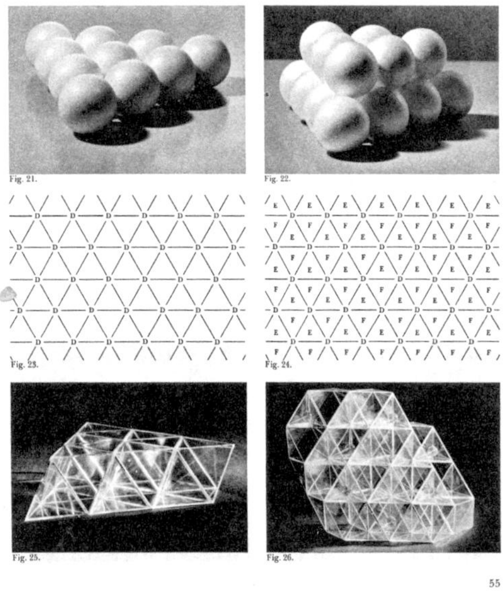

Buckminster Fuller, closest packing systems, 1950s

In terms of the utilization and efficiency of space, the concept of space packing is most strongly linked to the work of Buckminster Fuller in the 1950s. Although much has been written on Fuller's contribution to modern architectural thought, here I will confine myself to his study of "closest packing systems"[21] to illustrate how Neumann's work relates to it. Fuller examined packing and spatial efficiencies from a scientific point of view in order to quantify and geometrically describe models and patterns of organization. He was most interested in those structural and geometric systems that revealed the range of possible "closest packing" configurations, irrespective of their design expression or experiential qualities from the human perspective. The study was also intended to explore the construction of both megastructures and compact, moveable, self-sufficient units, as in the example of his geodesic domes. The main goal, as Fuller described it, was to investigate the most compact and efficient assembly of small, repetitive units and the possibilities for generating larger structures from them.

Neumann's interest in space packing differs substantially from Fuller's investigations. For Neumann, space packing was more than a strategy for design; it also comprised a conceptual framework for understanding the development and transformation of architectural form. We can thus define two levels on which space packing operates:

1 As an operative tool, it serves as a geometric strategy for generating shapes and spaces made up of a series of subdivisions. This is a working concept in the practice of architecture that produces what I refer to, in relation to Neumann's designs, as "patterned objects." Neumann first began implementing this approach using orthogonal geometries, and later developed it through the use of polyhedral geometries.
2 As a method of spatial analysis, it provides a way to analyze the historical development of built form as successive transformations, variations, and groupings of spaces, under the larger umbrella of architectural morphology.

Both of these ideas will be discussed in more detail in the following chapter.

1 Author's conversation with Vladimir Šlapeta in Finland, August 11, 2005.
2 Letter dated April 17, 1950 from the architect Rehoven Abram to the engineer S. Kapilanski of the Technion administration. Author's translation from Hebrew.
3 Author's conversation with Zvi Hecker in Berlin, July 15, 2005. Author's translation from Hebrew. This view is also evident in Arieh Fatran's mention of Alfred Neumann, Efrahim Freud, Dov Kwesler (eds.), *The Jews of Czechoslovak Origin in Israel* (Israel: mishrad ha'bitachon, 1998), pp. 377–81.
4 Author's conversation with Israel Goodovitch in Tel Aviv, July 30, 2005.
5 Israel M. Goodovitch, *Architecturology* (Tel Aviv: AD Publishing Co., 1967), p. 30.
6 Plural of Kibbutz, a form of communal settlement based on agricultural production and equal division of labor and profits developed by Jewish communities in Palestine in the early twentieth century.
7 Sharon Rotbard, *White City, Black City* (Tel Aviv: Babel, 2005).
8 Arieh Sharon studied at the Bauhaus.
9 For further reading see Zvi Efrat, "The Plan," Rafi Segal and Eyal Weizman (eds.), *A Civilian Occupation—The Politics of Israeli Architecture* (London, Tel Aviv: Verso, Babel, 2003), pp. 59–78.
10 Author's telephone conversation with Zvi Hecker on July 12, 2009.
11 An architectural idea rarely appears in its mature form within the first design that attempts to express it, but is more likely to develop over a series of works. Good design, one could argue, is the task of improving and perfecting a previous model, one step at a time.
12 Gideon Ofrat, "Eibur ha'beton ha'mezuyan," Osnat Rechter (ed.), *Yacov Recther Architect* (Tel Aviv: Hakibbutz Hameuchad, 2003), pp. 15–25, p. 15. Author's translation from Hebrew.
13 Ibid., p. 20.
14 "We must work in such a way that a confusion of material clad with its cladding is impossible. That means, for example, that wood may be painted any color except one—the color of wood." Adolf Loos, "The Principle of Cladding", *Spoken into the Void—Collected Essays 1897–1900*, translated by Jane O. Newman and John H. Smith (Cambridge, MA, London: MIT Press, 1982).
15 After his studies at the Technion, Hecker worked for a period as an assistant in Danziger's atelier and stayed in touch with him for many years.
16 Zvi Hecker's family has been living in that same apartment ever since—for over fifty years. Hecker's daughter and her family recently purchased the top-floor apartment originally occupied by Sam Dubiner, which Hecker redesigned in line with its original features.
17 From a letter to Andrea Brenta, dated September 6, 1966, from Neumann's personal archives, later published in *Zodiac*, 19 (1969).
18 Neumann was named as an architect on the company letterhead from the 1920s and his personal archives contain several drawings of diverse items of furniture, mostly built-in pieces (dating from the mid-1920s to the early 1930s) to be integrated into rooms or wall niches as an integral part of the interior.
19 Page 2 of Neumann's draft article describing the EM-PHI system, dated December 3, 1951.
20 Ibid.
21 R. Buckminster Fuller and Robert W. Marks, *The Dymaxion World of Buckminster Fuller*, (New York: Doubleday Anchor Books, 1973).

3 Architecture is Creation of Patterns

The emergence of pattern thinking in architecture

The move toward pattern thinking in architecture of the 1960s reflects a paradigm shift away from the prevailing notion that buildings are autonomous formal compositions—contained, self-referential, fixed objects—toward an understanding of them as systems and patterns. Designing buildings as patterns was more of an open-ended approach in which architecture was to be understood through its organizational qualities, namely as a system capable of interacting with other systems, and whose parts could be changeable and adaptable. This approach dealt with relationships among architectural elements, and expressed their interactions as patterns. Thinking in patterns could yield buildings that were better integrated into their urban contexts and that could better serve their purposes.

Much of post-World War II construction was guided by modernist functionalist principles, often applied hastily to the task of building on a large scale. The intended culmination of the functionalist approach to architecture was the "functional city," an urban model whose goals were outlined at CIAM 4, held in 1933 on a ship sailing from Marseilles to Athens, and which became emblematic of the rational approach to urban planning from the 1930s onward. According to this concept, the city was to be composed of different functional zones, including ones for dwelling, recreation, work, transportation, and historical preservation. These districts were to be separated and zoned according their functional, programmatic demands in order to yield the most efficient urban plan. Functionalist principles not only informed the reconstruction of European cities ravaged by World War II, but they were also taken up during the 1950s in several recently decolonized states in Africa and Asia that aspired to Western standards of living. On the scale of both the city and the individual building, the functionalist approach was widespread and far-reaching.

The architectural products of this formal approach, however—the dull, indistinguishable, and inadequate large-slab housing blocks built all over Europe in the 1950s—were often regarded as monotonous and boring, artistically incompetent and often also impractical. They were vehemently opposed by a younger generation of European architects, who critiqued functionalism not only because of its urban organization and aesthetic, but also from a sociopolitical position on the grounds that it reflected a modern architecture which, according to Alan Colquhoun, had become "conservative, professionalized and routinized."[1] Intellectuals, architects, and artists opposed the idea of housing people in functionalist buildings and neighborhoods, which very often seemed too rigid, overly controlled, and inhumane. Their vision of a more open and malleable sociopolitical condition resonated in those years with Karl Popper's call for an "open society,"[2] an idea that rejected "the absolute authority of the merely established and the merely traditional"[3] and that encouraged a break with over-determined systems that could not measure up to "standards of freedom and humanness."[4] Popper's ideas, which were intended to strengthen democracy, offered young intellectuals, architects, and artists a social, theoretical, and philosophical justification for promoting social change, and furnished an ideal notion, however abstract, of a free society. This younger generation of European architects active in the 1950s and 1960s thus envisioned a different kind of city: one that was not functionally segregated or arranged around a static core, but that rather allowed interconnections, change, and growth. To them, the pattern-thinking approach seemed a means of ensuring that flexibility was integral to any designed urban system.

Postwar reconstruction placed a host of new demands on architecture, and ultimately tested the limits of the functionalist approach. The urgent need to house the masses and to accommodate larger programs meant that building had to be done on an entirely new scale. It soon became clear that the existing modernist urban-architectural approach that dealt with buildings as individual, fixed entities was unsuitable for addressing this new issue of scale. The formal rules of functionalism, which had largely been developed through the design of relatively small buildings—villas, low-rise housing, and small public buildings—were now being used to tackle design on a much larger scale. In other words, functionalism became a style: The tasks and challenges of architecture had changed, but the solutions remained the same. The freestanding, autonomous, functionalist building was criticized for its inability to generate an urban fabric that could express the notion of community or allow it to develop. Another problem was that the autonomous building-as-object became easily replicable and was all too often implemented without reference to the particularities of site and context. As such, it was invested primarily in expressing singular formal characteristics among its parts rather than engaging with its urban environment. In search of new theoretical and practical premises on which to operate, architects saw the significance of patterns in scientific disciplines such as biology, cybernetics, systems and information theory, and the emerging field of computation. In their own field of architecture, they saw patterns as tools that could establish order in time and space, address the design problems posed by larger scales, and interface with more complex systems, such as cities.

During the 1950s, biologists began to examine cellular organization and biological patterns and discovered pattern making as an underlying concept of nature. Articles such as C. H. Waddington's "Biological Form and Pattern"[5] and the revised interest in D'Arcy Thompson's *Growth and Form* presented visualizations of patterns found in nature and explained their structural roles. Advances in biology also exposed new visual forms. Patterns previously invisible to the naked eye became available to human perception, and nature's hidden structures were revealed. The artist and art theorist György Kepes compiled aspects of this research, along with several visualizations of it, in his book, *The New Landscape in Art and Science*, which was part of a series that he edited during the 1950s. Kepes's work helped to expose a wider audience to the visual, almost artful, qualities of natural structures and processes, and highlighted pattern logic's intrinsic place in them.

Crystallography, the study of crystals and the process of crystallization that was advanced in England in the 1950s and 1960s, also exerted a strong influence on pattern thinking. Crystals are three-dimensional forms that are hidden from the naked eye and have to be rendered visible and analyzed. As a science which combines the study of nature, mathematics, and geometry under one disciplinary umbrella, crystallography further helped unveil nature's strategy of form making, which turned out to be based on the creation of abstract, geometric, spatial patterns. In an attempt to incorporate nature's own design strategy into the built world, architects looked to the patterns discovered in biological and crystallographic research as inspiration for their architectural creations. These patterns of nature were appreciated and adapted more for their structural and organizational qualities, however, than for their capacity to beautify designs. The intention within architecture was not necessarily to mimic biological or crystalline forms or patterns, but to adopt their structural organization as an approach to form making. Mathematics played a crucial role here, as it permitted architects to identify the rhythm, repetition, and symmetrical operations needed to generate and control a pattern and its units of repetition. Through mathematics, patterns could be traced and interpreted.

Buckminister Fuller, who was well known to architects in the post-World War II years and throughout the 1960s, and who was one of the most renowned scientist-engineer-architects of the period, synthesized different kinds of scientific knowledge, from biology and mathematics to material engineering and geometry. Fuller's work with pattern making steered architectural discourse toward issues of efficient spatial structures and units of mass production, and led designers to inquire into new possibilities for physical structures. For Fuller, patterns dealt with the behavior of a whole system and were inherently comprehensive and universal. Furthermore, he considered energy itself to be a type of regenerative patterning entity. "Energetic geometry," as he termed it, assumed that "the basic energy patterns in nature could be expressed by families of geometric 'solids' whose common metric is the tetrahedron."[6] Fuller's geodesic dome structure, for example, was understood as a physical instantiation of a larger pattern. In his 1950s study titled "Closest Packing

Systems," he explored the most efficient patterns for spatial arrangements in the packing of solids. The purpose of this study was to find a way to pack together the maximum number of elements with the minimum amount of "wasted" space between them. Fuller's work not only provided vivid proof that pattern thinking encompassed the total built environment, but it also showed how a reading of nature combined with scientific investigation and engineering could lead to the creation of new physical structures on multiple scales. While Neumann's work bears similarities with the geometries and concepts used by Fuller, his interpretation and use of pattern thinking differs significantly, as we shall see later in this chapter.

Buckminster Fuller, tensegrity system; minimum unit, maximum enclosure

Types of pattern thinking

Here I propose to distinguish between two different interpretations of pattern thinking in architecture, both of which had a significant place in the architectural discourse of the 1960s. One is the "pattern-as-language" approach, in which pattern thinking was understood as an abstract system or a design method that treated buildings as composites of patterns, assembled as if from a kit of parts. This approach is perhaps best represented by the work of the architect and architectural theorist, Christopher Alexander. The second approach, which is more relevant to our discussion, posits pattern as a concrete, visual, physical, and spatial structure for organizing, controlling, and subdividing built space. Here the idea of pattern as a system lends form to the building itself, often giving rise to architecture that visually and spatially expresses system as built form.

1 *Pattern as a "kit of parts"*

The conception of pattern as a language or "kit of parts" became well known through the work of the architect and design theorist Christopher Alexander and is often referred to as the "Berkeley School" of design. Patterns, according to Alexander, are archetypes in the sense of primary elements or conditions derived from repetitive occurrences that are diagrammatically recorded, categorized, and compiled in a system. This system becomes a kind of language made up of arrangements or sequences of archetypes, which describe a phenomenon in the form of diagrams and charts and can then be used to guide the architectural design process. This understanding of pattern follows Alexander's idea of a "generating system" as a kit of parts with combinatory rules "capable of generating many things."[7] In his concise and important article, "Systems Generating Systems," Alexander provided two meanings for the concept of system: 1) the idea of a system as a whole, or what Alexander calls a "holistic phenomenon which can only be understood as a product of interaction among parts,"[8] and 2) the idea of a generating system as a way to produce things. Pattern Language combines both of these understandings of system. Conceived as a kind of guide (pattern) book, it relies on interpreting wholes within the environment as a result of interactions between parts. These parts are themselves derived from the study of the human use of spaces, activities, habits, and customs, and from defining and naming them so that they can be included as elements within the kit.

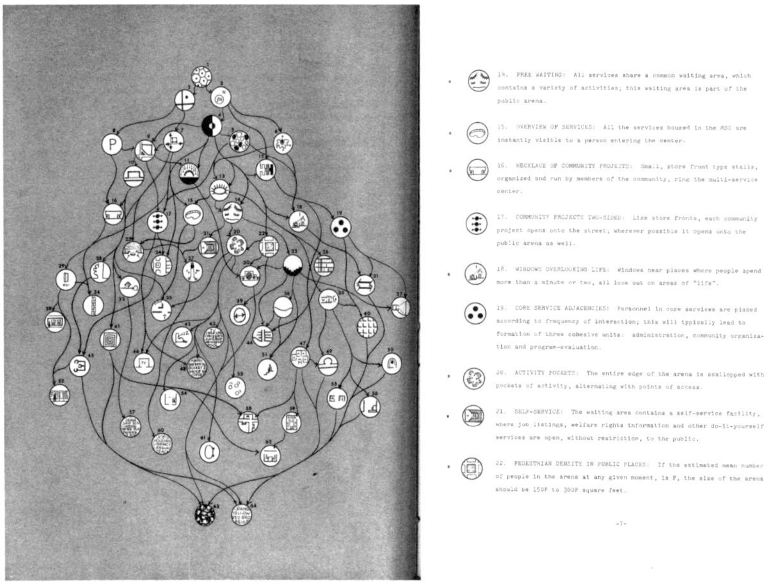

Early diagram explaining Christopher Alexander's pattern language as a "kit of parts"

Theoretically, the pattern-language approach did not favor, imply, or impose any particular aesthetic preference, architectural style, or expression as its outcome. In principle it dealt with specific visual and physical shapes of architecture not as forms in their own right, but rather as the spatial conditions they represented; the experiences and emotional sensations they created; the needs they fulfilled; and even as events in time. Patterns, in this case, defined as spatial conditions, could include "positive outdoor space," "house for a couple," "access to water," "ring road," "stair seats," and many more combinations of both physical architectural features (on all scales) and cognitive, physiological occurrences.

A Pattern Language, which became one of the twentieth century's best-selling architectural books, was a collective effort by Alexander and his colleagues, who envisioned it as a tool or "pattern book" to be used for the assembly of towns and buildings. Published in 1977, the book was the product of a much longer study that had begun years before. Its seeds were sown in Alexander's much earlier work, *Notes on the Synthesis of Form*, dating from 1964, and in various papers written, and studies conducted, in the late 1960s.[9]

By offering a systematic language derived from the ways in which the built environment is used, Alexander's approach did not need to prescribe a specific aesthetic or formal preference, although it did tend to present examples from vernacular architecture and common everyday space. *A Pattern Language* revolted against the high, formalist architecture that was popular at the time of its publication and advocated a more democratic design process. It rejected the notion that buildings should be conceived as works of art—that is, as built objects dominated by aesthetic qualities. Rather, according to Pattern Language, buildings should be approached as ad hoc assemblies, that is to say, as combinations of different elements of the correct dimensions and sequences. All that was necessary was that they include "patterns of language" or "phrases," that derived meaning from their placement, sequence, and relationship to both user and environment.

A Pattern Language framed design as a problem-solving process of assembling parts—not necessarily the physical parts of a building, but the conditions that create certain experiences for users. In this sense, it prioritized the user as the guiding agent in the design process, since the elements available to the architect in the assembly of a design were all derived from conditions already identified as positive or negative from the user's point of view.

As a design system, pattern language could be used across scales and for a variety of different tasks. It was thus an effective tool for the design of small rooms and large towns alike, and was no better suited to one form than to another. Alexander's pattern language could, moreover, help to generate either the most conventional architectural objects, buildings, and shapes, or the most unusual ones. As a system that could yield endless possibilities, pattern language could be used by anyone, for anything, at any time. It was the language of the everyday, for everyone, and for every plan. As will become clear, Neumann's understanding and use of pattern soon became far removed from Alexander's approach and more closely tied to another kind of pattern thinking in the architecture of his time: pattern as built or architectural form.

2 *Pattern as architectural form*

The notion of the building as a clearly defined, figural object was to be replaced by the notion of the building as pattern, an anti-object acting more as a field—an expandable structure, primarily organizational, made up of a sequence of repetitive elements.[10] While understanding buildings as objects posits architecture as an irreducible form or unit, the building-as-pattern approach construes it as a system in which the whole is made up of a repetition of smaller units. The way in which the units are assembled creates the overall shape. To express the expandable nature and formal adaptability of patterns, designs reflecting this approach produce forms with jagged or open edges rather than closed, contained forms, which instead connote the figurative and fixed contour lines of object buildings. The pattern conception did not necessitate clearly demarcated boundaries since what made it distinctive was its unit of repetition and not its overall form. After all, it is sufficient to observe just a part of a pattern to understand how it might continue. Looking at a floor created by a pattern

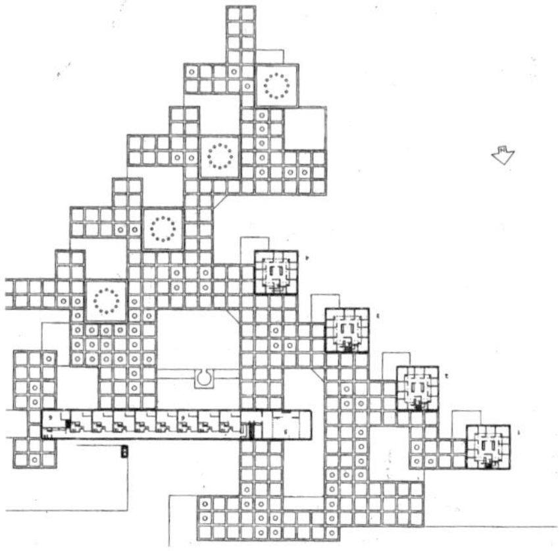

Aldo van Eyck, *Orphanage*, Amsterdam, 1960

of tiles, for example, we can easily imagine how the pattern looks in those areas of the floor that are hidden from sight. This kind of pattern thinking is most clearly tied to the structural-organizational qualities of unit repetition as infill within an overall structural frame.

This approach was advanced by the Metabolists and by members of Team 10, but chiefly, throughout the 1960s, through the pages of *Forum* magazine in the Netherlands, whose architect-editors came to be called the Dutch Forum group. Many works by these groups and other works that were similar in appearance were later deemed structuralist.[11] This interpretation was also advanced within the Israeli context through the work of Alfred Mansfeld, an established architect who worked in Israel in the 1950s and 1960s and taught at the Technion. Mansfeld's design for the Israel Museum in Jerusalem is often regarded as the peak achievement of structuralism in Israeli architecture. Mansfeld described his approach in an article titled "Design for Growth, Change and Uncertainty" and in the exhibition and catalogue *Structuralism in Architecture, Selected Works of Al Mansfeld and his Team*.[12]

Neumann's work in the early 1950s, especially his designs for dormitories (project 11) can be seen to fit in well with this approach to pattern thinking. This is clearly the context in which Neumann's work is most readily understood, even if his later work marks a departure from it.

Certain architects of the 1960s were preoccupied with the relationship between buildings and their urban environment, and the role of structure and infill as a strategy for urban change and growth. The Japanese architects later referred to as the Metabolism Movement were one such group. Their concerns were first articulated by Fumihiko Maki and Masato Ohtaka, whose "Group Form" article of 1960 promoted a master system of dynamic, open-ended structuring as a critique of the traditional fixed and closed plan. It also called for architecture to grasp the total picture of the environment and to deal with the problem of structure in urban society, modern cities having become characterized by conflict between institutions and individuals, and rapid and expansive transformation. According to Maki, this new condition necessitated an appropriate visual language, a "group form," rather than particular formal or compositional qualities. "Group form" ensures that the total image of a building is not altered even if certain parts or elements are taken out or others added. Maki developed these ideas in his text "Investigation into Collective Form" of 1964, and many of them were later summarized in Noriaki Kurokawa's *Metabolism in Architecture* of 1977.

In his 1966 article "Function, Structure and Symbol,"[13] Kenzo Tange took constant physical change in contemporary society into account and considered modern communication systems and information technology to be the main influences on spatial organization and transportation systems. According to Tange, modern architecture from 1920 to 1960 was characterized by a static relationship between function and space; each function was identified with a specific space, as was the method of planning that defined relationships between the functional unit and the city. He called this method the "functionalist approach," but did not necessarily dismiss it as wrong. On the contrary, he defended it as quite a useful approach for modernist architecture of the early twentieth century; but he also argued that the time had come for a change, since there were problems that the functional approach alone could not solve. Tange proposed to establish what he termed the "communication link" by connecting the separate functional units and creating a structure to physically and visually link and express communication activities and flows. "We can say," wrote Tange, "that the spatial organization is a network of energy and communication or a living organism, in which growth and change are incorporated as constant factors [...] Creating an architecture and a city may be called a process of making the communication network visible in space." "Making the communication network visible in space"[14] would produce a pattern, an extendable system or structure of connections in which pieces could be added or taken away—hence another interpretation of structure and infill.

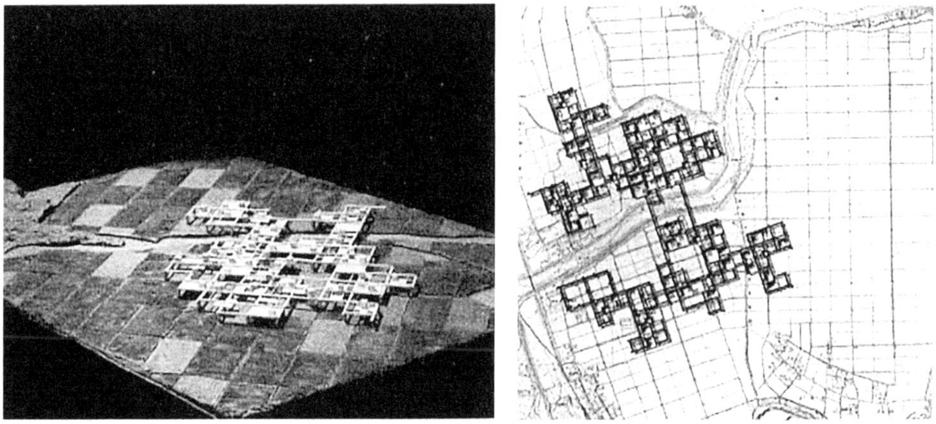

Kisho Kurokawa, Agricultural City, Aichi, Japan, 1960. Example of "pattern as building" on an urban scale

The pattern-as-architectural form approach also emerged in the United States around this time, but in a much less theoretical way than it appeared in the European and Japanese context, and furthermore neither socially nor politically engaged with questions regarding the city. The artist and art theorist György Kepes and architect Walter Netsch were two of the main figures to influence pattern thinking in the American context. Kepes's publication, *The New Landscape in Art and Science*, as we saw above, presented a collection of images derived from biological and natural patterns with the aim of demonstrating that our environment is in fact made up of patterns and systems rather than merely objects. Kepes's main interest was in the formal qualities of patterns as visual and spatial stimuli. The visual power and appeal of the patterns he presented supported his call for a synthesis of art and science by showing that science could uncover patterns found in nature, and that these, in turn, could influence art. Netsch, as one of the leading designers at SOM (Skidmore, Owings and Merrill Architects) during the 1950s and 1960s, incorporated an approach to design that he termed "field theory," which was, in his words, "a highly versatile approach to the geometric generation of architectonic structures intended to be uniquely suited to their purposes and environments."[15] What he later referred to as "field theory lattice studies" constituted a series of overlapping geometric patterns, drawn to form the generating basis for a building's form and structure. Netsch did not provide any theoretical motivation or detailed explanation of his field theory designs—aside from a desire to "break the box," as he put it, and to expand on the possibilities of using individual elements to create spatial fields.

One of the earliest and most prominent demonstrations of building as pattern, however, is found in the work of the Dutch Forum group of young Dutch architects, who found a collective voice in *Forum*, a magazine published throughout the 1960s. Alison Smithson later categorized much of their built work as "mat buildings,"[16] a typology that referred to buildings conceived as horizontal "mats" covering a substantially large area. Dutch Forum conceived buildings as open-ended, expandable entities. This was the result of a conscious attempt to conceptually and visually avoid making buildings that might seem like isolated objects and to focus instead on those that resemble systems of spaces and connections that can expand or change to better interact with the existing urban environment.

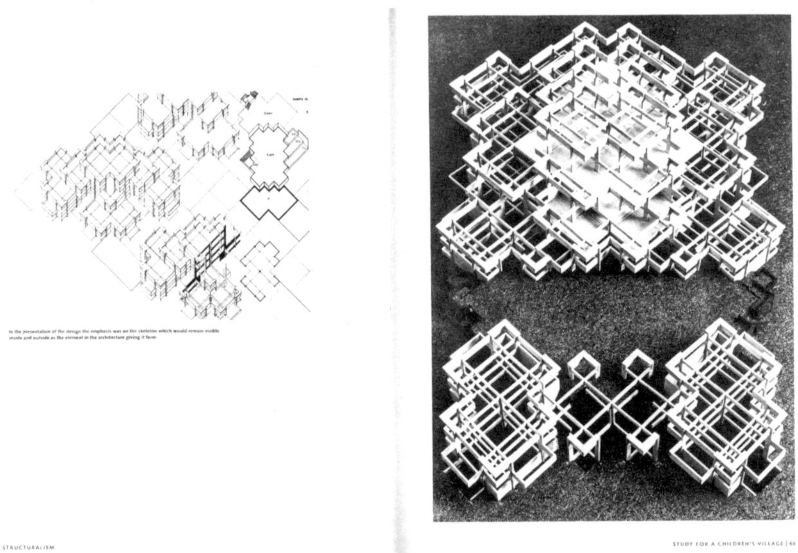

Joop van Stigt, member of the Dutch Forum group: study for a Children's Village, Netherlands, 1962

Dutch Forum's aspiration to a more humane style of modern architecture was guided by its belief that large-scale housing should provide the individual with a sense "that he is somebody living somewhere rather than nobody living nowhere."[17] The group of architects and designers who published their projects in *Forum*, namely Herman Hertzberger, Aldo Van Eyck, Jaap Bakema, Gert Boon, Orek Apon, Joop Harely, and Jurriaan Schrofer, followed in large part Aldo van Eyck's "configurative design" approach, which aimed to address modern architecture's key challenge of the time, that of dealing with large-scale mass housing in a humane way that fostered a sense of identity for its inhabitants.[18] The challenge was to define an individual unit that could be expressed within a larger grouping of units. To achieve this, Van Eyck's configurative design approach proposed replacing classical or modernist compositional principles with the logic of structural modules and an organizing system combined with programmatic indeterminacy. According to this conception, the overall built form was to result from the arrangement of the building's parts within an organizing system. The formal products of this approach resembled patterns, which could be not only extended, but also adapted to different conditions in their surroundings. Their flexible perimeters allowed them to expand and contract while offering a clearly visual and experiential logic of organization.

Pattern here played a dual role, both programmatically and formally. It challenged the notion of the fixed, closed form of a building, and at the same time questioned the idea that a building design had to be based solely on one preconceived program (often associated with a certain form). As Karin Jaschke notes, this made possible an architecture "devoid of functional, iconographic or typological pedigree, an architecture antithetical to the idea of architecture *parlante* and, in fact, an architecture reminiscent more of playing fields and game boards than of conventional buildings."[19] Aldo van Eyck associated this architecture with the idea of self-organization and invoked the *casbah organisé* discussed in the 1960s as a concept that shifted the role of organizer from the architect to the user. Architecture as "game board" described this condition well. The architecture in itself was not prescriptive, nor did it confine certain functions to certain spaces. Rather, it offered a field of opportunities based on spatial relationships—i.e. a pattern condition—rather than on a sequence or hierarchy of programs. The user activated the building and turned space into place, thereby imbuing the architecture with meaning.[20] Furthermore, the forms used for this approach were intentionally de-emphasized so as not to distract too much from the notion of building as a free, open game board or playground. The aim was to evoke a spatial field neutral enough to encourage the user to interact with it and to endow it with form. This was architecture that sought to provide opportunities for use and spaces for play, rather than an aesthetically appealing "object" to look at.

Throughout the 1960s, *Forum* and *Team 10 Primer* published studies on various primitive types of community-life settlements from archaic cultures. Their interest was piqued by a belief that examining societies from different times and places could help recover the permanent and timeless principles of human nature, which many felt that modern architecture had lost sight of.[21] These rediscovered primitive forms influenced the Dutch Forum group and others, too. The Dutch Forum group was interested in the visual appearance and physical nature of vernacular settlement patterns. In this respect it differed from Christopher Alexander's approach to patterns, which was less formal, and instead sought out the experiential qualities of certain timeless conditions. The image of the casbah, a traditional form of clustered settlement most commonly found in the hot climates of the Islamic world, for example, was used by both the Dutch Forum group and Christopher Alexander, but in very different ways. Alexander used it to represent one pattern among others of "positive outdoor space" (a condition that associated positive spatial traits with an outdoor space).[22] In *A Pattern Language*, for instance, he compares the image of the casbah with images of other urban typologies that also create positive outdoor space. He studies the casbah from the viewpoint of the kind of spatial experience it creates, focusing particularly on the spaces created for collective use. By contrast, the Dutch Forum group used the example of the casbah as a source of visual and organizational inspiration and as a form—or rather structure—capable of addressing the problem of quantity and scale within a single structure. For them, the casbah represented a more humane environment that incorporated both order and chaos, a balanced combination of single unit and overall structure. The group was inclined to romanticize vernacular architectural forms, however, and in reality the casbah rarely engendered the humane environment they claimed it did.

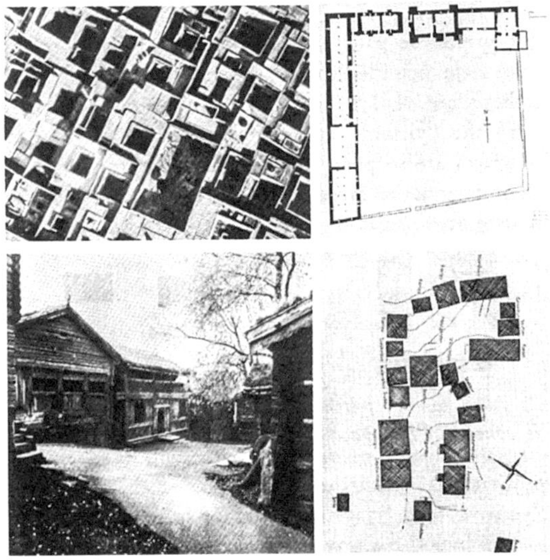

Christopher Alexander referenced the casbah in his publications as representing a pattern within the pattern language

The casbah referenced in the pages of *Forum* magazine as an important influence on the work of the Dutch Forum group

"Buildings as patterns" as practiced by the Dutch Forum group and their European contemporaries raised questions regarding the scale and size in which single buildings or structures should be conceived. Their work also addressed the relation of unit to whole, i.e. the individual dwelling unit in relation to the overall building, for example, which was an especially important factor in the context of the urgent post-World War II demand for housing on a vast scale.

The expressions "aesthetics of number," coined by Van Eyck, and "*le plus grand nombre*," coined by Michel Ecochard and adopted by Georges Candilis, a Team 10 cofounder, came to describe the practical and aesthetic problems posed by designing housing for the masses. Architecture not only had to devise a practicable means of providing large numbers of people with living space, but it also had to resolve the aesthetic and expressive problems that ensued from the creation of dwellings and recreational facilities for a large number of people. According to Van Eyck, "quantity cannot be humanized without the sensitive articulation of number," although it was unclear what, exactly, he meant by the "sensitive articulation of number." The humanization of quantity was a theme that had preoccupied Aldo van Eyck for several years, and was likely a factor behind the 1956 CIAM meeting in Dubrovnik, which discussed habitat in terms of clusters, mobility, growth, and change.[23]

The relation between unit and whole, between individual element and overall structure, was also a major concern in Herman Hertzberger's work. In the 1960s, Hertzberger, an active member of the Dutch Forum group, developed the concepts of "polyvalent form and individual interpretation" or "structure and infill" as an alternative to the functionalist understanding of form. Hertzberger's explanation of the transition from housing block to housing tissue questioned the formal rigidity of the existing organization of housing. He wanted to break away from the practice of designing housing blocks as contained and fixed "chests of drawers," which made the "springing up of a residential community" very difficult. He was instead in favor of clustered, loosely formed assemblies that could expand, engage with their surroundings, and encourage social interaction.[24] According to Hertzberger's conception, the units that are to be clustered and "loosely" arranged can be obtained from subdividing the large, conventional, monolithic housing block into smaller cellular units. His model therefore did not necessarily oppose the basic unit of habitation in form or function; it merely challenged its rigid arrangement. Hertzberger proposed a method by which architecture could transition from the closed and fixed to the open-ended and diffused. Arguing in the same vein, he reacted against the existing system by which buildings were organized. In an effort to redefine community, Hertzberger proposed that communal space within a domestic setting could be created by grouping individual cells without the overpowering presence of a single larger form, such as in Le Corbusier's *Unité d'habitation*.

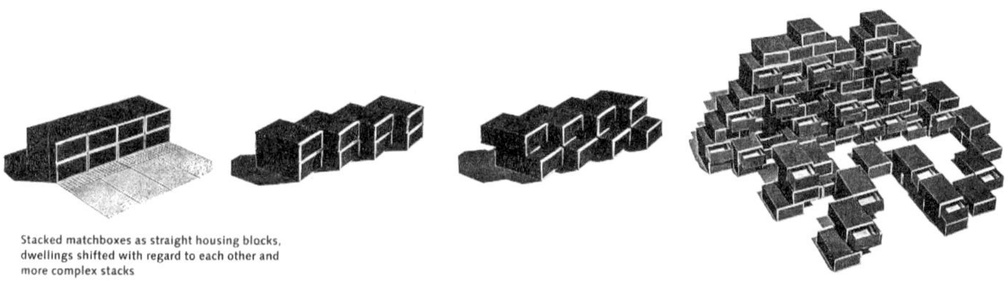

Herman Hertzberger, diagram of housing blocks grouped to form an "open structure"

This is not to suggest that pattern thinking in architecture completely disregarded the notion of the individual or the single. Rather, it aspired to strike a balance between the *individual* and the whole (the collective), in which the *individual* was the cell, while the whole was to be generated out of a pattern made up of many such cells.[25] "What we must look for in place of prototypes, which are collective interpretations of individual living patterns," wrote Hertzberger in 1963, "are prototypes which make individual interpretation of collective patterns possible; in other words, we must make houses alike in a particular way, such that everyone can bring into being his own interpretation of the collective pattern." The pattern, according to Hertzberger, must allow for personal interpretation and freedom of choice, which in turn presupposes greater flexibility and a redefinition of the relationship between function and form. This marks a departure from the assumption that forms have a preconceived, definitive function.

I raise the work of these architects and thinkers active in Europe, Japan, and North America during the 1950s and 1960s in order to show how the "building-as-pattern" approach to architecture was taken up simultaneously in different parts of the world as a challenge to the earlier "building-as-object" mode of thought. We can identify a paradigm shift in architectural discourse away from an interest in architecture as object and toward an understanding of architecture as a spatial system of interconnected parts, where the parts that make up the whole exist as separate elements held together by an overall structure. The building as object, a modernist conception, came to be seen as limited in its ability to interact with its surroundings. Those who advocated a building-as-pattern approach sought a new understanding of the role of the building within its environment, and in turn a new means of generating built form. This pattern thinking of the 1960s was the context in which Neumann's work emerged and in which, by offering his own interpretation and expression of building as pattern, he rethought the way buildings are assembled.

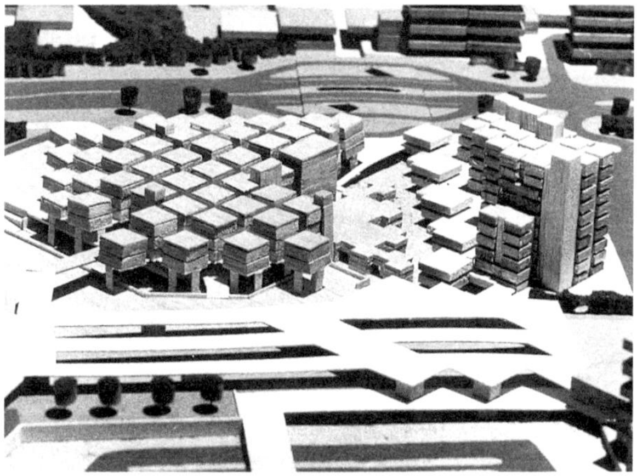

Herman Hertzberger, Central Beheer office building, Apeldoorn, Netherlands, 1968–72, completed (left) and model (right)

Neumann's approach and the building-as-pattern paradigm, as practiced by the Dutch Forum group and the Metabolists, both attempted to provide an answer to the anti-modernist critique of functionalism, albeit in different ways. Both offered a means of creating architecture independent of the modernist aesthetic link between function and form. The Dutch Forum group did this by treating architecture as a game board or playground, that is to say as a space that the user activates and thus appropriates and programs for his or her own use. In this case, function does not predetermine or restrict the form of the building. Rather, the form allows different functions and programs to occur, depending on how the space is activated. As a result, Dutch Forum projects sought primarily to express how the building's spaces and organization might encourage multiple uses, and fostered a condition that made it possible for a building's users to interpret its spaces in different ways. By contrast, Neumann's space-packing designs did not set out to enable maximum flexibility of use, nor was he interested in providing the user with a space for play or interpretation. His buildings performed through their interaction with climate, light, and site. The building acted as a spatial frame or envelope, rather than as an open-ended horizontal field of movement. This envelope was not closed or sealed, but was rather porous in nature, and acted as a kind of spatial filter between interior and exterior. Yet the envelope was not a planar surface or membrane, nor was it something that aspired to minimize the skin of the building. On the contrary, it attempted to create an intermediate, "third" space that would renegotiate the relation between inside and outside by becoming a spatial filter for light and human passage, while at the same time creating a habitable place of its own.

The patterned-object approach

Neumann's architecture of the 1960s—beginning with his design of Bat Yam Town Hall right up to his last built project, the Negev Synagogue (designed in 1967)—can be described as what I call a "patterned-object" approach. Almost all of the projects that Neumann designed and executed in those years shared a common formal strategy and design methodology. All of them were done in collaboration with Zvi Hecker, and some with Eldar Sharon as well.

The approach did not precede and guide the designs, but rather developed through them, taking shape from one project to the next. Bat Yam Town Hall, for example, which Neumann began work on at the start of this period in 1959, contained many of the design ideas and principles that would be further articulated in his later work. The six main principles of Neumann's patterned-object approach are outlined below.

1 *Patterns in architecture should have a physical limit, and can appear within the notion of "building as object"*

For Neumann, pattern thinking was not antithetical to the notion of the building as object, nor did it reflect a desire to rid architecture of its figurative, sculptural qualities, as it did for many of the Dutch Forum architects. Furthermore, Neumann did not use patterns for their inherent possibility of expansion. Instead, he avoided open-ended forms specifically in order to prevent additive continuations to his buildings' patterns, and opted instead for defined shapes with closed edges that suppressed the structure's potential to expand. In that sense, Neumann's architecture was very different from the work of the Dutch Forum group, Moshe Safdie, and other Israeli designers such as Israel Goodovitch, Al Mansfeld, and Leopold Gerstel (an engineer by training), all of whom emphasized the inherent expandability of their buildings as accretive, clustering arrangements.[26] In architecture, where humans are the subject, argued Neumann, patterns should not continue indefinitely as they do in mathematics, for example. When creating spaces that are to be inhabited and experienced by humans, the boundless pattern becomes frightening and inhuman. In his view, therefore, it was essential that pattern making in architecture be confined to definite limits and forms.

2 *The building as an assembly (stacking) of units rather than "structure and infill"*

Neumann's pattern thinking offered an alternative way of assembling units. His approach was not structuralist in the sense of Herman Hertzberger's "structure and infill," where the structure serves as an overall organizational armature, and the infill is inserted into it. Instead, for Neumann, the unit composed the structure, its spatial repetition and assembly creating the shape of the building. Whereas the structuralist approach attached the utmost importance to relationships—parts could be changed as long as the relationship between the parts and the whole was maintained—in Neumann's system, the units were irreplaceable. As the form, shape, and size of each unit in Neumann's designs were particular, no single unit could be replaced without altering the shape of, and the relations established by, the whole. The unit in Neumann's designs was both formally and dimensionally tied to the overall scale and shape of the building. Neumann's architecture was thus a result of its own logic of assembly, echoing architect Konrad Wachsmann's view that "buildings should develop indirectly, as a result of the multiplication of cells and elements."[27] In other words, Neumann believed that the overall form of a building should result from an assembly process predefined through the identification of its parts, causing the building's form to grow seemingly from within, rather than from the imposition of a predetermined form and its subsequent subdivision. According to this conception, buildings had the potential to express the operations involved in their creation. For Neumann, the form of the building had to follow and express the space-packing system that generated it. The size and shape of the unit of repetition, which was conceived spatially, were what determined the spatial pattern.

3 *The geometric specificity of the unit and formal relation between unit and pattern*

Another guiding factor in the development of Neumann's patterned-object approach was the desire to best express the spatial qualities of the packing that guided his buildings' designs. He aspired to perfect the clarity of the overall form composed of assembled units by eschewing those building elements that were external to the main system. As Neumann's design practice developed, so did the correlation between overall shape, pattern, and unit. Structure and form became increasingly synthesized and unified. This differed from the work of the Dutch Forum group and the Metabolists, for example, for whom the role of the unit was secondary to that of the overall structure, which, as I described earlier, they conceived as a master system or governing principle that dominated the unit. The specific shapes of the parts that comprised this whole acquire meaning based on the relationships they establish or enable within the overall structure. In much Dutch Forum and Metabolist work, the specific form of the unit is not intended to convey meaning due to its particular shape or formal traits. Neumann's work, by contrast, grew out of his thinking of both unit and whole at the same time, which is something that he achieved far more clearly in his later projects, such as the El Al Terminal (project 21), the synagogue project (project 22), Netanya City Hall (project 18), and the Negev Synagogue designed in 1967 (project 26).

In the work of Alfred Neumann, the unit has two roles: symbolic and formal. Symbolically, it is a humanizing element because it creates a unit of space that is sympathetic to the human body, being derived from dimensions and relationships that are considered amenable to human perception and physical dimensions. Formally, Neumann's insistence on using certain geometries, specifically polyhedral rather than orthogonal ones (marking a transition from mainstream modernism), also served

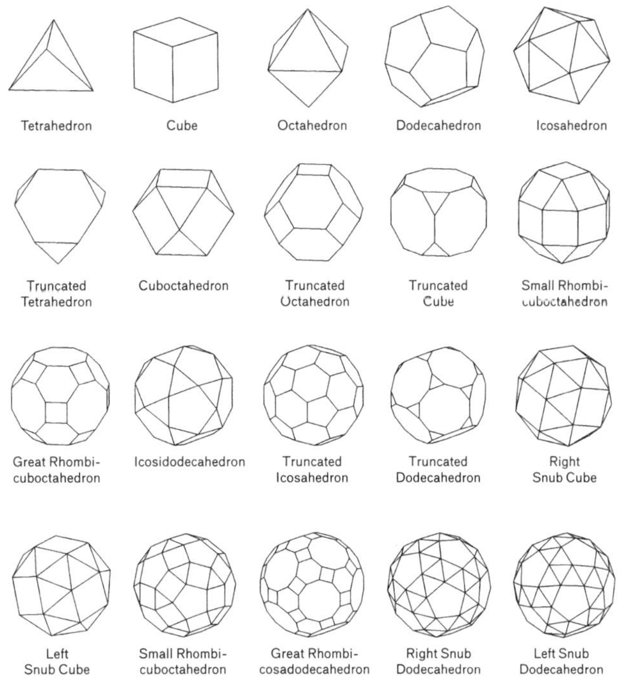

Platonic solids on top row, Archimedean solids on bottom three rows

as a critique of the overarching dominance of orthogonal architecture in Israel. His work offered an alternative to the prevailing International Style, while at the same time referencing traditional Islamic architecture, which featured similar polyhedral geometries.

4 *Pattern as a spatial operation—unifying plan and section*
In most of his projects, Neumann first established the overall massing before employing a pattern. Commencing with the building's general mass or volume allowed him to first examine the larger issues of scale that are encountered when designing buildings, such as the building's coverage or footprint, its orientation and interaction with its site, the areas required by the program, and more besides. Once a general sense of the building's massing had been established, Neumann subdivided it into smaller units, from which he then recreated the overall shape by packing them together. This design process understood the creation of architecture as a progression from the more abstract mass to the more developed and detailed elements that construct that mass. The size, shape, and proportion of the overall mass were in turn redefined by the multiplication of the single unit. The unit's size and proportions followed fixed dimensions, defined using Neumann's EM-PHI system.

Neumann's space-packing approach did not prioritize the plan as the primary generative device for creating the total built form. The plan was not extruded vertically to create space; instead, the overall building space was assembled from smaller spatial parts, like a three-dimensional puzzle made of three-dimensional pieces. His approach also differed from those modernist conventions of composition that treated the façade as a separate architectural element to be designed independently: Neumann's approach eliminated this notion entirely, and the façade became a result of the assembly. It was a spatial zone rather than a planar surface, distinct from the modernist conception of the façade as an independent plane and component of the composition.

This difference can be seen very clearly in the way the proportion system was used in the composition of the whole. Neumann's EM-PHI system served to define a single volumetric unit: a geometric solid, often confined to a limited range of sizes and multiplied to create a whole, in order, to use his words, to "set it in proportion." Since the whole was composed of repetitive units that were each sized according to a desirable proportion attuned to a human scale, it attained a desirable proportion itself. This differed from Le Corbusier's practice of using regulating lines to define the proportion of the whole building at once. The regulating line was more appropriate for dealing with planar conditions such as façades for example, where it became a tool for guiding the subdivision of a plane and determining the relationship between the dimensions of a wall, say, and those of the openings in it, windows, and other façade elements.

5 *Building as filter: Pattern making as a way to unify building systems and redefine the building envelope*

For Neumann, patterns were necessary as their specific architectural and spatial quality permitted a large mass to be subdivided into smaller units of space. These smaller units, when packed, allowed for a revision of the relationship between a building's structure and its envelope. Space packing was not only a method of generating an entire building in terms of scale and proportion, therefore, but it also became a way of unifying different building elements. Whereas factors such as a building's structure, the apertures created to let in daylight, thermal solutions, and systems of internal spatial division, for example, were often treated as independent, separate systems by International Style architects, Neumann was able to integrate these various considerations into one system by deploying a single spatial pattern to generate the design. Spatial patterning was used as a means of combining structure with spatial subdivisions, window openings, and thermal control elements such as overhangs and shading elements that were an integral part of the unit. The concrete faces of the units were structural load-bearing components that included openings as integral parts of their shape. The forms of Neumann's buildings also meant that their façades could provide their own shading. Spatial patterning became a way to transform the building envelope from a surface into a spatial, porous, filter-like element that interacted with its surroundings and provided a habitable space between interior and exterior.

6 *Non-programmatic function of the unit*

For Neumann, the unit did not correspond to a fixed, predetermined program. In his architecture, form and program were disassociated, and polyhedral shapes, as opposed to conventional orthogonal forms, were better suited to it since they did not evoke any existing building typologies or functions. Architectural "stacking" projects, such as Moshe Safdie's Habitat buildings of the late 1960s composed of box-like residential units, tied a specific programmatic role to the unit, since the Habitat boxes were designed as apartments. When the unit of assembly had a predetermined program, its shape was often valued in terms of how well it served its purpose. For Neumann, the individual unit was not assigned a specific program, nor was it shaped in response to the breakdown of the program into units. The unit was an intrinsic structural and spatial component of the whole building, whose functions and program could change.

This idea of architecture as made up of repetitive units was typical of 1950s and 1960s architectural discourse and practice. One can outline various approaches to the role and nature of the unit in the construction of buildings. In most cases, including the Dutch Forum group, the Japanese Metabolists, and Moshe Safdie's Habitat, the unit is conceived and shaped to satisfy a certain activity and use, and in that sense it can be referred to as programmatic. This is not the case with Neumann's patterned-object buildings, however.

The following table summarizes the differences between the "patterned-object" and "compositional" approach to generating form:

Building aspect/feature	Patterned-object approach	Compositional approach / International Style architecture
Proportion	EM-PHI system: volumetric, spatial, additive	Modulor/regulating lines (Le Corbusier, Colin Rowe), planar, divisible
Part/whole relationship	Agglomeration of units creates the whole	Unit equals whole
Scale	Scale derived by unit repetition	Scale expressed through asymmetrical composition of whole
Relation between building systems	Unification of building systems/elements into single building element	Separation of systems/elements; free-plan, free-façade
Cultural reference	Ottoman and Islamic traditions	European abstract modern art
Relation of building envelope to light and climate	Envelope as spatial filter (fenestration concealed)	Envelope as surface; cut-out and add-on elements

Morphologic architecture

> The possibility exists to conceive the whole man-made environment from a unifying point of view by applying morphological criteria. Scientific domains which have been developed up to now and which are predominantly of ecological nature, can easily be integrated into a morphological system, because they possess the value of selection factors only. A science of architecture, like any other science, should describe the different phenomena by a common lawfulness.[28]

The above statement appeared in Neumann's first published article, "Morphologic Architecture" of 1963, in which he critiqued those existing conventions in the study of architecture that focused, as in the study of art history, on selected masterpieces. Neumann argued that a selection—whether of artworks or of buildings—based on aesthetic appreciation cannot constitute scientific research. This would be analogous, he claimed, to botanists deciding to study only beautiful flowers: applying a predetermined selection criterion would inevitably result in all other plants, which were just as much a part of botanical studies, being neglected.

Neumann developed the term "morphologic architecture" to describe a scientific approach to the study of architecture. Morphology is defined as the study or classification of form, shape, structure, or arrangement. In a more general sense, it refers to the history of variation in form (the morphology of coins, for example, refers to the history of the changes that have taken place in the shape of coins). Neumann believed that the "common lawfulness" that he called for in the above quote could be extrapolated from the morphological study of architectural forms from prehistoric times to the present, analyzed and classified according to their transformations and characteristics.[29] Neumann believed that such a study would promote a broader and more objective understanding of architecture that encompassed the total built environment in all its different geographies, cultures, and historical processes.

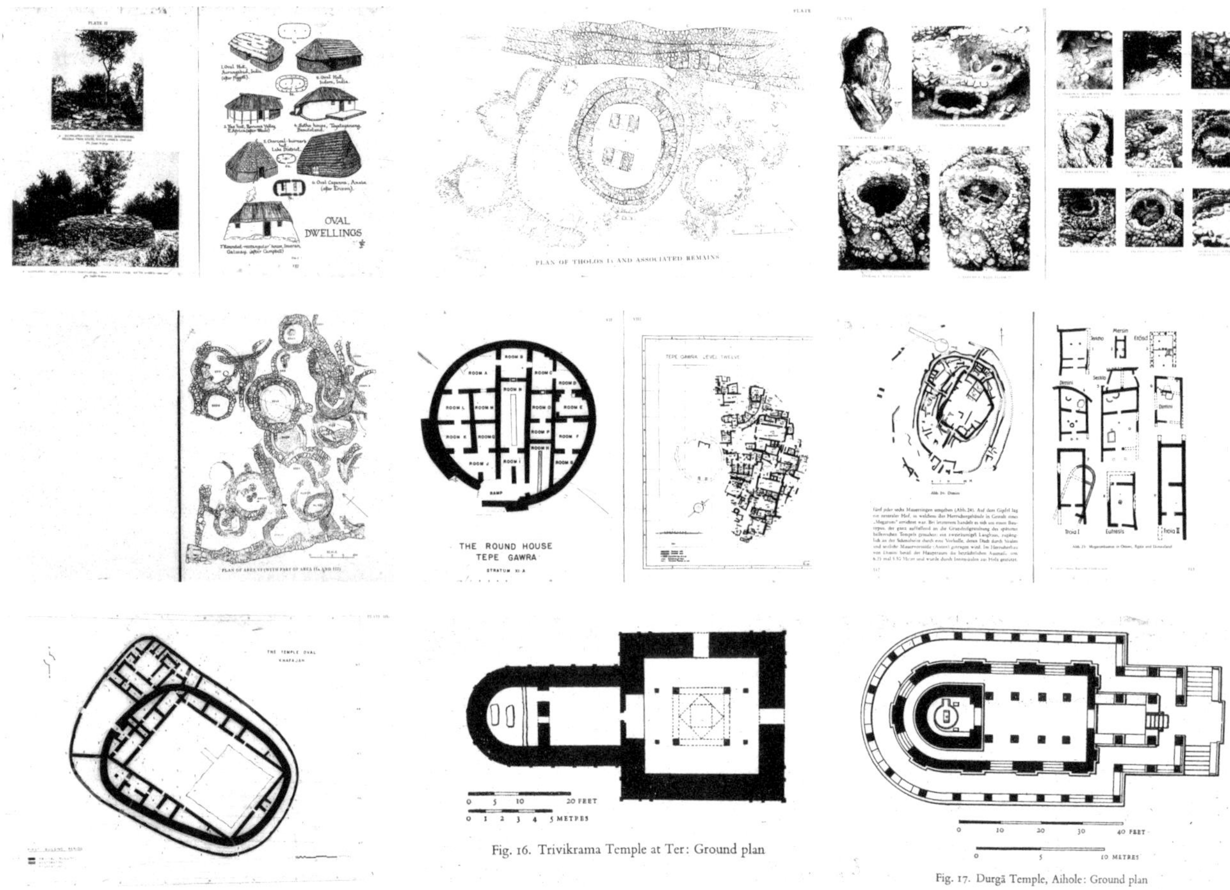

Sequence of slides describing morphological changes from circular to rectilinear forms of organization
Selected from slides that Neumann used to teach architectural morphology

While architecture had never been approached scientifically, except in certain aspects such as acoustics, light, and climate, Neumann claimed that it could, in fact, be investigated as a whole, much like any other phenomenon. Neumann also claimed that a scientific, morphological study of architecture should not have aesthetic appreciation as a criterion. If morphological research was to be considered scientific, it could not be guided by subjective preferences.

According to Neumann, the human environment is made up of "containers." The container in closest proximity to humans is clothing, the next closest a house.[30] Architecture can create containers that provide horizontal areas for diverse kinds of human movement, that can be described through both linear and rotational geometries. The basic container or cell of a room or a house, for example, can be augmented in two different ways: It can grow in size to create larger spaces, which can be achieved architecturally with large-span shells or vaults, such as the ones that constitute the main structural component in stadiums and large halls; alternatively, a spatial cell can aggregate with others just like it, as is the case with architectural typologies such as apartment buildings, hospitals, and schools.

In "Morphologic Architecture," Neumann presented his general theory of the major morphological processes that began with prehistoric dwelling units and settlement forms and evolved over time. During the pre-urban era, according to this theory, primitive housing types of various forms and materials and in different regions seem to have followed the same grouping phenomena. Early round-shaped huts (or cells) enclosed by walls with round openings were scattered individually at first, but with time began to move closer to each other and group together. Topological transformations took place and the round shapes, by aggregating over time, gradually mutated until the orthogonal grid emerged as a more efficient organizational geometry for grouping these cells. (Adjoining circular structures gives rise to unusable spaces between them, whereas an orthogonal geometry allows a series of squares to be arranged, one adjacent to the other, without any unused space between them.) What this theory claims is that the geometry and spatial organization of settlements evolved over time through a process of, or tendency toward, grouping. Orthogonal forms that originated with the development of agriculture, according to Neumann, spanned a long phase throughout history and human civilization. Modern society, he argued, had surpassed orthogonal typology by producing new kinds of forms and spaces, such as those found in planes, cars, and ships. A different understanding of space and form, guided by different criteria for shaping space, is now present. Architectural morphology, as a line of study, should therefore be open to the exploration of non-orthogonal, and other less conventional shapes and geometries. It does not, however, preclude the continued existence of orthogonal forms, in the same way that round forms and older settlement patterns continue to exist to this day.

In "Morphologic Architecture," Neumann avoided arriving at a single statement or conclusion. The essay reads more like a series of thoughts and reflections on the origins of architectural form. Aside from presenting a collection of ideas and questions to be further explored, Neumann's text attempts to contextualize and justify the contemporary use of polyhedral forms in architecture. This laid the groundwork for his own designs, many of which he inserted at the end of the essay through images and textual explanations.

The study of morphology in architecture began for Neumann during his time at the Technion. There he taught a course called "Architectural Morphology," in which he explored a rich variety of architectural forms and the geometric-volumetric relations between them. He continued his inquiry at the School of Architecture at Laval University in Quebec, where in 1965 he founded the graduate program in architecture. Between 1965 and 1968, he collected and studied a broad range of forms, from biological ones to different vernacular architectures worldwide. This research remained unfinished and unpublished; but the materials gathered include a large collection of slides of a variety of dwellings built by different species of animals. Although animals are usually thought of as being guided by instinct alone, what they build often proves to be highly rational. Bees, birds, desert rats, and a variety of insects produce extremely efficient structures with minimal floor area per task, using building materials determined by what is available in their environment. This, according to Neumann, was a valuable lesson for understanding how form originated.

By the time Neumann began to research morphology at Laval, the subject had already become the preoccupation of two major schools of thought.[31] The first was the Italian school, led first by Saverio Muratori, and later by his follower Gianfranco Caniggia. (Muratori's theories on urban morphology and typology, incidentally, also influenced *Tendenza*, a group of Italian and Swiss architects active in the late 1960s, whose members included Aldo Rossi, Giorgio Grassi, Massimo Scolari, and Ezio Bonfanti.) The second was the geographical school, led by M.R.G. (Michael Robert Gunter) Conzen, a geographer educated in pre-World War II Germany, who worked at the University of Birmingham, England. The geographical school of morphology, also called the Conzenian School, examined the relationships between historical geography and planning, concentrating on the larger processes of town formation and change.

Pierre Larochelle, one of Neumann's students in the masters program at Laval, continued to work on urban morphology after Neumann's death. According to him, Neumann's approach was informed neither by the geographical and urban-scale concerns of Conzen, nor by the urban studies approach of the Italians, but rather by an overall interest in processes of morphological change on diverse scales, from small artifacts and decorative arts and ornamentation to building, encompassing both the natural and the manmade. Neumann was interested, as Larochelle describes, not only in the mathematical-geometric expressions of these processes of change, but also in their psychological impact, in how humans attach themselves to certain forms.[32] That said, when the issue is the study of morphology in architecture, the Italian school is perhaps the one most similar to Neumann's thinking, which, whether due to lack of time or ability, he never organized as a conclusive or comprehensive theory, but rather left as scattered essays, lecture notes, collections of images, and other materials.

The Italian school of morphology

In the book, *Architectural Composition and Building Typology: Interpreting Basic Building*, which summed up several years of morphological research and thinking by the Italian school, Gianfranco Caniggia and Luigi Gian Maffei drew an analogy between "typological process" and "biological process."[33] They proposed understanding buildings as one of humankind's biological necessities, as organisms that could be described through their transformations over time. This approach aimed to bring the study of buildings and cities to bear on the relationship between humans and the natural environment, and to examine the development of the built environment in its broadest historical perspective, specifically over a period of thousands of years from prehistoric times to the present. Caniggia described the emergence of cities as part of a gradual process of development from rural to urban and from simple to complex urban types, and as a continuous process of adaptation to internal and external changes. Even though this process can be observed in endless examples throughout the world, it is best understood, according to Caniggia and Maffei, with reference to the compact city, such as the historic cities of Italy that the Italian school analyzed.

According to the Italian school of morphology, building, or what they termed "constructed space," which included built space and the open spaces adjoining it, emerged from two types of *coscienza* (or consciousness): spontaneous consciousness and critical consciousness. (Consciousness here refers to knowledge, or the capacity to realize, grasp, and assess facts.) Spontaneous consciousness was described as a non-mediated mode of architectural knowledge, one that does not require or involve choice, but is applied spontaneously and directly. Spontaneous building, as Caniggia describes it, is thus the "immediate, synthetic comprehension of what occurs to form a building product"[35]—in other words, a building guided by heritage and tradition that characterizes each culture at a given point in history. Critical consciousness, on the other hand, involves a conscious choice, not necessarily derived from past experience, but rather driven, in many cases, by uncertainty, that is, without any firmly established precedent. This condition is marked by a loss of spontaneity and reflects the problem of drawing specific, focused knowledge from a common heritage. Critical building is therefore associated with a conscious awareness of the practice of architecture as the artistic creation of individual expression.[36]

The Italian school of morphology maintained that the built environment is guided primarily by spontaneous consciousness. This variety of consciousness yields spontaneous, anonymous buildings of a kind often omitted from architectural history, thus excluding from history the majority of the built environment, which in fact may be the best register of the authentic forces shaping the world.[37] Because the history of architecture tends to focus on extraordinary instances and examples of new kinds, spontaneous buildings that emulate extant traditions and do not exhibit any remarkable differences from what came before them are often omitted as objects of study. Here we can clearly draw parallels with Neumann's aspiration to an all-inclusive study of architectural morphology: the study of architectural form over time that would reach beyond the conventional history of masterpiece works.

After the Italian school we re-encounter the term morphology in architecture during the 1970s and early 1980s, but this time in the context of the development of computer programs to mathematically describe and generate architectural forms and the geometries needed to create them. J. P. Steadman, William Mitchell, and Robin Liggett were among the pioneers here, and worked on computer-aided design with support from institutions such as the Martin Centre at the Cambridge School of Architecture, the School of Architecture and Urban Planning at UCLA, and the Centre for Configurational studies at the Open University.[38]

Steadman's view of architectural morphology differed from Neumann's. To Steadman, the aim of architectural morphology was not so much to better understand the historical development of how forms came about, but to expand the repertoire of possible forms that an architect could choose from. The choice of form in design is limited by what is geometrically and topologically possible; (a topological limitation, for example, might be the number of possible arrangements of rooms within a single floor area). The geometrical nature of a design task, according to Steadman, encompasses the following: geometric discipline, meaning the grid or other disciplinary constraint under which the plan is laid out; geometric elements, meaning the geometric forms from which the plan is made, namely rectangles or other room shapes; and the conditions by which the elements are packed, such as their proximity and overlap, which imposes dimensional constraints on form. Steadman's architectural morphology dealt primarily with the formal-organizational possibilities of the architectural plan in terms of its different geometric variations and arrangements. The computer was used to provide all the possible configurations that might result from each set of requirements and restrictions, from which the architects could then choose their preferred form. The study was conceived as a science of building by virtue of its mathematical, scientific method and its capacity to provide the architect with a set of possible plan arrangements to address a given design or programmatic task.[39] Steadman's morphology explored the variations of form at a given time and in response to a given task, whereas Neumann was interested in morphology as the historical development of form over time.

Neumann's morphologic architecture is often associated with a particular aesthetic approach rather than a mode of formal analysis. In several publications, and from conversations I have had with people familiar with Neumann's work, the term "morphologic architecture" evokes an architectural style of non-orthogonal (polyhedral) solids. This misinterpretation is most prevalent in Israel, perhaps because Neumann's original "Morphologic Architecture" article is seldom read in Israel (it was never published in Hebrew), but perhaps also because a misunderstanding of the subject was perpetuated in the teaching of Neumann's successors at the Technion, which for several decades was the only school in Israel to educate architects.[40] The term "Polyhedric Architecture," which appeared later, offered a better description of the formal nature of Neumann's work than did morphologic architecture.

1 Alan Colquhoun, "Postmodernism and Structuralism: A Retrospective Glance," *Assemblage*, 5 (February 1988), (Cambridge, MA: MIT Press, 1988), pp. 6–15.

2 Karl R. Popper, *The Open Society and Its Enemies* (London: Routledge and Kegan Paul, 1950), written in 1945.

3 Dante Germino, "Preliminary Reflections on the Open Society: Bergson, Popper, Voegelin," from Dante Germino and Klaus Von Beyme (eds.), *The Open Society in Theory and Practice* (The Hague: Martinus Nijhoff, 1974), pp. 1–25, quoting Popper on p. 13.

4 Dante Germino's analysis of Karl Popper's and Henri Bergson's notions of the "open society" identifies Popper's as possessing a horizontal openness, meaning an openness to critical thought and the experimental method of trial and error, which might be regarded more as anthropocentric humanism. This contrasts with Bergson's vertical openness and the opening of the "psyche toward the ground of Being," which is a theocentric humanism modeled on Plato's "god is the measure," Germino (see note 3), pp. 13–14.

5 Published in the *Journal of Architecture Association* in 1958.

6 Robert W. Marks, *The Dymaxion World of Buckminister Fuller* (New York: Reinhold Publishing Corporation, 1960), p. 13.

7 Christopher Alexander, "System Generating Systems," see note on p. 19 *Architecture Canada*, November 1968, pp. 39–44.

8 Ibid., p. 39.

9 Christopher Alexander, Sara Ishikawa, and Murray Silverstein, with Max Jacobson, Ingrid Fiksdahl-King, and Shlomo Angel, *A Pattern Language* (New York: Oxford University Press,1977). Earlier works by Alexander: *Christopher Alexander, Notes on the Synthesis of Form* (Cambridge, MA: Harvard University Press, 1964), in which Alexander begins to deal with variables in the design process and "The Patterns of Streets," *American Institute of Planners Journal*, 32 (September 1966), pp. 273–78, and Christopher Alexander, Sara Ishikawa, and Murray Silverstein, *A Pattern Language Which Generates Multi-Service Centers* (Berkeley, CA: Center for Environmental Structure, 1968).

10 The shift away from an interest in the creation of objects and toward an interest in system thinking can also be identified in 1960s art. Conceptual Art, Minimalism, or what Mel Bochner proposed as a "Serial Attitude," aspired to replace the notion of the work of art as an "object in space" with a project that would create something with space itself, whether inside or outside the art gallery. This movement against "the object" in art can be detected throughout the 1960s and is evident in approaches such as the repetition and serialism in the works of Sol LeWitt, Hanne Darboven, On Kawara, Mel Bochner, and others. LeWitt's work, "Paragraphs on Conceptual Art" (1967), describes how the artist selects the basic form and rules that are to govern the production of the work, and how this minimizes the need for further formal decisions. LeWitt, like others, aspired to create systems that would generate forms rather than relying on artists' individual and personal visions—or what he termed

"arbitrary and subjective" form-making processes. According to LeWitt, the work of art should be based on a set of relationships between its parts and elements rather than on a single fixed object or form. Mel Bochner's seriality reflected his interest in how order, as the constructive principle underlying the work, might be most directly expressed (see Mel Bochner, "A Serial Attitude," *Artforum*, VI, 4 [December 1967], pp. 28–34). Seriality was introduced as an organizational scheme or system that could produce several visual effects, as opposed to the creation of a single object or painterly image. Artists used seriality as a framework—a means of generating a pattern for the existential experience of space and time. Examples of this can be seen in Hanne Darboven's works that deal with numbers and marking calendar time, On Kawara's postcards, "I went," "I read," "I met," and Mel Bochner's use of the series as a means of re-investigating traditional forms of creating sculpture.

11 See Arnulf Lüchinger, *Structuralism in Architecture and Urban Planning* (Stuttgart: Karl Kramer Verlag, 1981), and Wim J. van Heuvel, *Structuralism in Dutch Architecture* (Rotterdam: Uitgeverij 010 Publishers, 1992).

12 Alfred Mansfeld, "Design for Growth, Change and Uncertainty," *Architecture in Israel* (Tel Aviv, 1978), pp. 14–26, 28–36.

13 In Udo Kultermann (ed.), Kenzo Tange, *Architecture and Urban Design 1946–1969*; (New York: Praeger Publishers,1970), pp. 240–45

14 Ibid., p. 241

15 Walter Netsch in an interview with Detlef Mertins, May 21, 2001, from *SOM Journal*, 1 (Stuttgart: Hatje Cantz Publishers, 2001), pp. 137–51, here p. 137.

16 Alison Smithson, "Mat Building," *Architectural Design* (September 1974), pp. 573–90.

17 Well-known Aldo van Eyck quote, here taken from Karin Jaschke, "Architecture as Artifice," *The Journal of Architecture*, 6 (Summer 2001), pp. 135–44, here p. 135.

18 Examples of these projects include proposals for the Prix de Rome of 1962 by Piet Blom and Jaap van Stigt, Herman Hertzberger's Centraal Beheer, and numerous other projects by Piet Blom, Jan Verhoeven, Jaap van Stigt, Frank van Klingeren, Henk Klunder, and others.

19 Jaschke (see note 17), p. 135.

20 Accordingly, in order to understand this approach to architecture (the Dutch Forum approach) it was necessary to observe the way in which the buildings were being used. Without users, the buildings looked empty and uncanny—like game boards without any playing pieces. It is thus no coincidence that much of Aldo van Eyck's work, for example, dealt with children as the best candidates for bringing "user-based architecture to life." Children's spontaneity and imagination, innocence and playfulness became most fitting for such architectural game boards, and easily enabled what Aldo van Eyck called "turning space into place." This reading is supported by Karin Jaschke (see note 17), pp. 135–44.

21 Aldo van Eyck: "Man, after all, has been accommodating himself physically in this world for thousands of years. His natural genius has neither increased nor decreased during that time. It is obvious that the full scope of this enormous environmental experience cannot be contained in the present unless we telescope the past, i.e. the entire human effort, into it." Quoted from Lüchinger (see note 11), p. 23.

22 Alexander, *A Pattern Language* (see note 9), p. 520.

23 Van Eyck summarized the 1956 CIAM presentations as follows: "There is a tendency to change from small cellular units of cluster, which are used additively, to the formation of a major structural element, increasing the scale in order to make it more comprehensible." From Lüchinger (see note 11), pp. 35–36. Lüchinger also quotes Van Eyck in 1966: "[T]he art of humanizing vast numbers hasn't advanced beyond the first vague preliminaries [...] no discipline available to us now can solve the social and form problems which vast numbers pose," p. 39.

24 "The character of the block disappears through a strongly plastic treatment and a new size makes its appearance, the size of the domestic cell as an element of scale, to be experienced visually and recognizable in the complete settlement," p. 52 from *Forum*, 8 (1961).

25 These are ideas that Herman Hertzberger described in "Flexibility and Polyvalency," from *Forum*, 7 (1967).

26 This basic difference in attitude was left unnoticed by Zvi Efrat's *The Israeli Project*, which situated Neumann's work among other cluster-oriented expandable designs, categorized under the broad and misleading term "habitat."

27 Principle number four of seven as presented in Konrad Wachsmann's "On Building in Our Time," in Joan Ockman (ed.), *Architecture Culture 1943–1968* (New York: Rizzoli, Columbia Books on Architecture, 1993) p. 267. See also Konrad Wachsmann, *The Turning Point of Building*, (1961). According to Zvi Hecker, Konrad Wachsmann accepted an invitation from Alfred Neumann to lecture at the Technion's Faculty of Architecture and Town Planning in 1959. On the similarities in Neumann's and Wachsmann's conception of the role of the artist, cf. Ockman, p. 269.

28 Alfred Neumann, "Morphologic Architecture," *RAIC Journal* (May 1963), pp. 40–47. "Morphologic Architecture" is the title of a major essay in which Neumann coined and explained the term. It was first published in the *RAIC Journal* as a transcript of a lecture given to the Ontario Association of Architects that same year. This article later appeared in *Zodiac*, 16 (1966) and extracts from it were published as short texts accompanying photos and drawings of his projects in several other publications. The full article is published here in the Appendix.

29 "Analogies with biological phenomena might contribute to a better understanding. Morphogenesis of design is analogous with morphogenesis of biology." From Neumann, "Morphologic Architecture," *RAIC Journal*, p. 41, or see Appendix.

30 Neumann's discussion of containers and tools was closely tied to Jean Piaget's structuralism and writings on cognitive development. Piaget described human development as a progression from the child's comprehension of objects in his hand to the perception of larger spaces external to the body. See Jean Piaget, *Structuralism*, translated and edited by Chaninah Maschler (London: Routedge and Kegan Paul, 1971). First published in French 1968.

31 From an interview with Pierre Larochelle, recorded by the author in Quebec City, Canada, June 1, 2005.

32 Ibid.

33 Gianfranco Caniggia and Gian Luigi Maffei, *Architectural Composition and Building Typology–Interpreting Basic Building*, translated by Susan Jane Fraser, revised by Karl Kropt and Brenda Scheer (Florence: Alinea, 2001).

34 Structuralism can be useful in understanding the twin concepts of spontaneous consciousness and critical consciousness, which are analogous to what linguists refer to as "*la parole*," meaning an intrinsic capability, and "*la langue*," meaning a constructed or learned system of signs that structures language.

35 Caniggia (see note 33), p. 44.

36 Caniggia criticizes the way in which the contemporary built environment is conceived and characterized by highly "personalized" and unrelated objects. This state of individualism results in a panorama of individual objects, apparently different, yet in fact creating a monotony of unrelated "monuments." This, according to Caniggia, reflects the capitalist mechanisms at work and the financial advantages of the individual over the community. Architects contribute to this phenomenon by promoting every building as a single, individual, unique expression, so that "even a shack in the midst of a thousand others [becomes] an emergence, a monument unto itself." Caniggia (see note 33), p. 34.

37 The interest in anonymous buildings can be seen as part of a twentieth-century tendency to write histories of anonymous things—whether inventions, artifacts, objects, or buildings—which are not attributable to any particular author or creator yet occupy an important part of modern life. Sigfried Giedion's *Mechanization Takes Command* (1954), which was influenced by Lewis Mumford's earlier work, *Technics and Civilization* (1934), is one of the best known of these attempts. Giedion described the development of anonymous things brought forth by mechanization—a phenomenon that by the 1950s was already dominating society. The anonymous also played an important role in Christopher Alexander's pattern-language approach, which collected and incorporated patterns, spatial conditions, and other phenomena, disregarding whether they appeared in well-known designs or in anonymous, vernacular buildings. In that sense, Alexander's pattern language can be seen as a system that goes beyond the distinction between buildings by architects (the profession of architectural design) and buildings by non-architects, or architecture without architects.

38 Several of these studies relied on sources found in the journal, *Environment and Planning B*, edited by Lionel March.

39 See preface to J. P. Steadman, *Architectural Morphology—An Introduction to the Geometry of Building Plans* (London: Pion Limited, 1983).

40 The course "Architectural Morphology" was later taught by Professor Avraham Wachman of the Technion, whom Neumann criticized for improperly using his research.

4 The Battle for Architecture

By the early 1960s, the leadership of the architectural community in Israel had changed. This gradual process began in the late 1950s, when the young architects of the Sabra generation (Israeli-born, as opposed to immigrant, Jews) became more established. Many Sabra had fought as soldiers in the 1948 Arab-Israeli war and had played an active part in the national struggle for independence. They therefore felt more confident about actively participating in, and leading, the local architectural scene, and gradually replaced the older generation of immigrant architects. The younger Sabra architects were interested in the international architectural scene and wanted to be part of it, although they ended up seeming parochial when they tried too hard to copy what was happening elsewhere in the world. In the context of the extensive building activity of the early 1960s, during which the functionalist architecture described in the previous chapters flourished, the younger Sabra architects were responsible for some of the most original design projects that Israel had ever seen. By the mid-1960s, many Israeli architects were in direct contact with professional periodicals from abroad, and were partaking in the larger architectural discourse.

A parallel process took place within Israel's art scene as Israeli artists became more exposed to influences from the international art world. Some began to travel more, attending workshops abroad, and on their return sharing their knowledge with their peers. Rafi Lavi, one of the leading Israeli artists of the time, remembers this gradual shift: "From the rupture of World War II, through the end of the British Mandate and the War of Independence, the depression period and the early visits of Israeli artists abroad, we were totally disconnected from what was going on in the world. From the mid-1950s this gap began to decrease."[1] Within the small Israeli art scene, international influences were so apparent that each could be traced to a specific artist who had returned home from abroad and there promoted the latest avant-garde. International influences thus began to permeate both the architecture and art worlds of early 1960s Israel. A vibrant local scene emerged made up of young creative people who sought to interact and exchange ideas within a larger circle. Young architects became more confident in their design ideas and enthusiastically promoted them to an international architectural audience.

Within this setting, Neumann-Hecker-Sharon's work counted as unique and radical, due primarily to its rigorous, non-orthogonal geometries and repetitive patterns. It was understood as an alternative to mainstream architecture and as a proposition of a new formal language. In international journals, publications, and reviews, the firm's work was labeled experimental, even though the architects themselves never used this term to describe it. On the contrary, Neumann, who penned their project descriptions and accompanying texts, often foregrounded the traditional architectural principles behind the designs, and highlighted how his work addressed the demands of both program and site. These written accounts were concise and explained the geometric character of the work in a didactic and technical manner, outlining the form of each building's basic unit and how its repetition and spatial arrangement resulted in the structure's overall massing.

In his book of the same name published in 1970, Peter Cook identified Alfred Neumann's work as the Israeli representative of "experimental architecture." Cook's book covered architectural projects, mainly from the 1960s, that had been published in *Architectural Design*.[2] He divided them into six different categories based on the architectural approach they exhibited, positioning Neumann's work as an example of the opportunistic approach, a rubric under which he classified designs that took advantage of a single material or form. Thus he argued that the Achziv Holiday Camp design (project 13), for instance, represented "an opportunistic use of material and such opportunism seems much closer to the idea of experiment than the mere theoretical use of special geometrics." This was an allusion to the straw structures as examples of the novel use of local, unconventional building materials.[3] Yet Cook's use of the term "experimental" to describe Neumann's work, as well as other works covered in his book, is confusing and misleading. His categories cut across geographic regions and nations, making experimental architecture seem like an international phenomenon, even though the experimental works he covers are described in terms of their particular relation to their respective country or geographic locale. Cook described the Achziv Holiday Camp, for example, as representing "a rawer, more sculpturesque and more obviously 'peasant' technology"[4] that was characteristic of architecture in Mediterranean regions, as opposed to experimental works in Switzerland or Germany, which were notable for their precise engineering details. He stated that he was searching for the psychology of each particular country, and that the "experimental" could be discovered by examining the idiosyncrasies of particular traditions.[5] Experimental approaches to architecture, according to Cook, were localized, and derived from the particular psychological condition specific to a place. In other words, he understood the experimental to occur within a particular place as a result of a certain kind of local thinking or set of conditions. Ironically, for Cook, experimental work was not unique and radical because it departed from local cultural conventions (which is what we often associate with the idea of the experimental), but was rather work driven by attempts to uncover affinities with the particular undercurrents of a place.

Maria Bottero also invoked the term "experimental" to describe Neumann's work in her editorial introduction to the 1966 issue of the journal *Zodiac*. She wrote that Neumann and Hecker's work stood out among a few contemporary architectural experiments as "being a particularly significant first step toward the practical and theoretical formation of new spatial and architectural languages."[6] For Bottero, the term "experimental" could describe any new architectural expression. In Neumann's case, novel architectural expression derived from the use of both polyhedral geometries and the space-packing method that guided the designs.

The New York Times architecture critic Ada Louise Huxtable described Neumann as the father of an Israeli school of design, which she claims led to Moshe Safdie's Habitat. She explained this in a *New York Times* article published after Neumann's death:

> Israel's best publicized export beyond Jaffa oranges is probably Habitat, the dramatic complex of box-like units by the architect Moshe Safdie that was the centerpiece of Montreal's Expo 67. In Israel, the school of design that led to Habitat has produced a small and strange collection of buildings of intriguing appearance and—like Habitat—of debatable experimental value. They are undoubtedly some of the most striking and provocative buildings to be seen today [...] All these buildings are based on a theory of three-dimensional geometric forms that attempt to find a building shape that would be established as a basic unit of construction that will give the most economical and efficient use of space. It is called a "space-packing" system by its inventors. The father of the space-packing theory was Alfred Neumann, an archetypal European intellectual and architectural polemicist, who emigrated from Germany [*sic*] to teach at the Technion where many students became his disciples.[7]

Huxtable's oversimplified reading perpetuated a recurrent misunderstanding which assigned all buildings formed by accreted units—however dissimilar from Safdie's Habitat Montreal project—to the same category, the category of "Habitat buildings." She failed to distinguish between the different architectural approaches of Neumann and Safdie, and did not distinguish between the distinct formal and compositional features of their designs, such as the relationship between part and whole, the way geometry was used, the relationship between a building's structure and envelope, its programmatic organization, and a building's edge conditions. Neumann's and Safdie's approaches differ in the following ways: Safdie's Habitat incorporates a unit of construction that I would term "programmatic," in that there is a correlation between a certain program and the shape, size, scale, and arrangement of the unit. In Safdie's Habitat, the apartment unit is a cuboid form that follows the arrangement of a set of rooms. In this case, the unit is conceived as functionally independent, self-supported by its own internal subdivision and organization. Moreover, it defines the way the program is arranged, and within the overall building it acts as infill in a supporting structure that provides a system of circulation and connections between individual units. The unit, in other words, "fixes" the organization of the program within the whole building. For Neumann, on the other hand, the unit did not contain the program within it. He intentionally avoided associating the unit with a predetermined program, but instead defined it by its scale qualities, geometry, and role in creating the building's envelope. The unit's dimensions were derived from Neumann's EM-PHI proportion system, and its shape had to conform to a larger pattern, which produced the overall building form.

Moshe Safdie, Habitat Montreal under construction, Montreal, 1967

Safdie's conception of Habitat as an expandable pattern of repetitive, interchangeable units is more closely affiliated with the approach of the Dutch Forum group, whose work was described in chapter 3, than with Neumann's space-packing method. Safdie's Habitat was conceived as an open structure, capable of expansion and growth. The habitation units form clusters, which are connected by a separate circulation system of bridges and vertical connections, all held together by a separate structural system. These different systems, although very much present in the design, were left out of the published photographs, which focused solely on the stacked apartment units. The Habitat boxes seem almost randomly arranged, like a hillside village that has developed organically over time. The iconic image of Safdie's Habitat project as a seemingly arbitrary stacking of volumes—an expression of random organization—is very different from Neumann's highly organized, structured, and contained patterns. While form-making (through the use of multiple geometries) was of central importance for Neumann, Safdie might be seen as a proponent of anti-form, as someone for whom the overall shape of the building was the least of his concerns.

In that sense, Neumann's designs follow conventional formal operations of symmetry and repetition, and often have simple building plans and repeated interiors. In their form and conception, his buildings were understood as closed objects that could neither grow nor expand and hence, I would argue, much less of a departure from conventional approaches to architectural design than Safdie's.

The excessive use of the term "experimental" in analyses of Neumann's projects of the 1960s is likely a result of contemporaries' breezy appreciation of, and attempts to categorize, Neumann's work without having to understand it fully. "Experimental," as shown in all the above citations, was considered synonymous with "new" and "original."[8] The international interest in Neumann's work, which is reflected in the large number of reviews it gained in the professional periodicals and magazines of the time, attests to a common acknowledgement of a body of work that was new and different more than anything else.

The Danciger Building controversy

Although some architectural critics of the time found Neumann's buildings a challenge to understand, their writings nevertheless had the positive effect of exposing his work to a broader audience. Other misapprehensions of his work from this time—most notably the failure of the Technion, his client in the mid-1960s, to understand and appreciate his design for its new laboratory building—did not end favorably for Neumann. The Mechanical Engineering building, also known as the Danciger Building, designed and constructed between 1963 and 1966, marked a shift in Neumann's career, ending his presence and continued work in Israel.

The Danciger Building was initially conceived as part of a larger design scheme that included four laboratory wings, an administration and staff wing, a teaching wing, and a boiler house. Together, these were to comprise the Faculty of Mechanical Engineering complex on the Technion's new campus on Mount Carmel. In 1956, as part of the widespread construction that was to take place on the new Technion campus, Technion President Yaakov Dori asked Alfred Neumann, at the time Dean of the Technion's Faculty of Architecture and Town Planning, to design the Faculty of Mechanical Engineering's first laboratory building, to be named after the Danciger family who donated the funds for the project.

The Technion sought to involve its architecture faculty in the design and construction of the new buildings on the Haifa campus. Before commencing the design work, Neumann was asked to cooperate with a committee assigned by the Technion to determine the program of the laboratory buildings. This process took several years, partly because the buildings were to be the first modern mechanical engineering laboratories in Israel, and partly because the economy was rather sluggish at the time, causing the project to be put on hold and the committee to defer its decisions. In the early 1960s, however, the building boom began to push many projects ahead, and in 1963, plans for the Danciger Building were submitted for evaluation to the Saunders Committee, the Technion committee appointed to work with the architects during the design process. This committee recommended certain changes, which Neumann and his collaborator Zvi Hecker incorporated into their design.[9] Soon after, the committee reached a consensus on the conditions of the project. They decided to construct the Danciger Building first, before the other components of the complex. The idea was to have a pilot project that could be evaluated so that any potential functional or design changes recommended could be implemented in the other buildings. All the Danciger plans were finalized by Neumann and Hecker according to the agreed specifications and were later approved for construction, which began in 1964.[10]

The site designated for the Faculty of Mechanical Engineering's new complex was rectangular and on a slight gradient, and the Danciger Building was to run across it as a long, linear building (figs. 19.1, 19.3, 19.7). The laboratory's program dictated the size, shape, and dimensions of its central halls. Because one of the halls was to house moveable machinery, it had to have an open plan without internal columns, supports, or divisions, requiring all load-bearing capabilities to be shifted onto the envelope instead. This idea of transferring the structural system to the building's perimeter envelope was one of the guiding principles of the design.

The earliest design of the building (fig. 19.4), dating from the late 1950s, envisioned a rather simple, conventional modernist slab building. Neumann's new space-packing approach, however, which started to be defined during the early 1960s, a few years after his initial 1956 proposal, led him to radically rethink the design. He replaced the conventional orthogonal design of his 1956 proposal with one composed of triangular slabs of concrete, standing upright and oriented in plan at alternating 45-degree angles. These he lined up end-to-end to create a jagged building envelope with narrow spaces between the triangular planes that allowed light to enter the building's interior. On the second level, the angles of the triangular planes were inverted so that the upper façade protruded outward where the lower façade receded inward, creating shade over parts of the wall and mitigating solar heat intake (figs. 19.12–13, 19.35). Neumann then decided to paint the faces of the façade's triangular elements in an alternating pattern of vivid blue and yellow. A lattice of ceiling beams oriented at 45 degrees to the right angle formed by the building's plan, much like the system implemented for the Bat Yam project, and resting on the upper edges of the first-floor triangular planes, completed the structural system (figs. 19.14–15, 19.17, 19.19).

The two main principles through which Neumann described the building were structural and climatic. Although both impacted the overall shape and performance of the building and its spaces, they were primarily expressed through the building's envelope. The project requirements determined the floor plan's dimensions, layout, and organization, but did not recommend any specifications for the envelope, which remained an element of the building that had not been regulated in advance by the Saunders Committee. By its nature, a building's envelope has two intrinsic conditions: external and internal. Externally, it defines a building's image, internally it controls how natural light enters the interior spaces, determines views from the interior, and impacts climatic performance. In the case of the Danciger Building, the envelope became a major bone of contention. Its outward appearance (an aesthetic issue rather than a utilitarian one) and the levels of natural daylight that it admitted into the building's interior became the two key issues around which the Danciger Building controversy revolved.

Would there be enough light in the interior? Would the cost of the proposed windows, as designed, fall within the budget? Would the façades painted yellow and blue improve the quality of natural light entering the interior? Could the building function properly? These were some of the questions and issues that triggered the controversy. The debate led to disputes that eventually found their way into the courthouse and into the press, and that between them pushed Neumann out of Israel for good.

During the process of design and construction, the Saunders Committee questioned certain design features and requested changes that the architects believed undermined the design's integrity. The disagreement at first concerned technical matters and questions regarding the amount of natural light that the building would admit into the interior. The committee turned to engineers and specialist consultants, and technical staff in the university's planning office, the contractors responsible for construction works, and other professionals to ask their views regarding the penetration of natural light and the general functionality of the design. The committee's solicitation of a second opinion eroded the architects' credibility, leading to technical negotiations between experts on the side of the client and others who represented the architects and supported their design. The two sides quarreled and were unable to agree, causing the debate to escalate. This in turn led to the involvement of even higher authorities at the Technion, who were asked to reach a verdict and propose a solution.

During these disputes of 1966, Neumann was outside Israel on sabbatical leave in Canada, leaving the less experienced Zvi Hecker to negotiate with Technion officials. At that point, the disagreements between the architects and the Technion were centered on the design and implementation of the windows and the coloring of the façades. The Technion officials were concerned that the window design originally proposed would not admit enough light into the building's interior. They therefore halted the production order for the window frames until the matter was resolved. Zvi Hecker, Technion President Dr. Alexander Goldberg, and Al Mansfeld, a leading architect and respected teacher at the Technion, soon met to address the matter. They came to an agreement, which was later referred to as "Dr. Goldberg's Memorandum." In short, this required the architects to present a signed personal declaration, guaranteeing that the design would indeed meet the light penetration specifications after the proposed windows were installed, and confirmed that the color scheme of the building would be maintained. The shape of the windows and the type of window frame were not addressed. Furthermore, Dr. Goldberg insisted that the architects affirm that these requirements could be met within the existing budget. Once signed, the Technion's president would give the order to immediately resume work and to complete the windows and coloring of the building according to Neumann's and Hecker's original design.[11]

Hecker, on behalf of Neumann and himself, signed the agreement, but less than three weeks later, he visited the construction site and discovered that the windows that he and Neumann had designed had not been installed, whereas others had in their place. He also knew that, in order to be properly dimensioned, the kind of windows that had been installed had to have been ordered weeks in advance—prior to the date of his meeting with Dr. Goldberg. He therefore concluded that the Technion had never intended to install the windows that he and Neumann had designed, and that he had simply been misled. "I was cheated in such a simple way," wrote Hecker in a letter to Neumann. "I cannot understand how it didn't occur to me that it was all a trick. At the same time as Goldberg signed our agreement he also gave an order to install the other windows."[12] Hecker's attempts to settle this in an orderly fashion were unsuccessful, as recounted in a newspaper article: "Mr. Hecker complains that he encountered a 'Kafka-like' series of disappointments. Mr. Goldberg was abroad, the stenographer who had written the memorandum was on sick leave, Professor Neumann was in Canada, and Prof. Shklarsky (Academic Affairs) knew nothing of the memorandum." Hecker later explained that he inquired about getting a court injunction to stop the work, "[b]ut they told me that this would take 48 hours, and by then all 32 windows would be in place."[13] Hecker returned to the building site with a copy of the memorandum in hand, and demanded that the contractor stop work on the windows. The contractor refused, claiming that he had received orders to complete the job. Enraged, Hecker decided to take action. On the night of October 31, 1966, he climbed onto the roof of the Danciger Building and with a crowbar bent fifteen of the already installed window frames, damaging them. Explaining his motivation to Neumann, Hecker wrote: "[M]y thought was as follows, until we could receive an injunction from the court to halt all work, the Technion would have already installed all the windows, making the court order irrelevant."[14]

"The saboteur of the building was the architect himself," read the popular headline to the story in the press. This was followed by a series of articles that at first attempted to uncover Hecker's motivation, but that soon began projecting on wider questions and issues of artistic creativity, such as the fight of the individual artist against the institution, the role and place of the public building within Israeli society, the place of artistic expression within the public domain, questions of mediocrity versus the exceptional, and even demands for "beauty versus functionalism."

Within the architectural community, Hecker's act met with criticism, although some colleagues, architects, artists, authors, and musicians jointly signed an op-ed in support of the act, published in the Israeli daily *Ha'aretz*. The way the Technion had handled the situation and fought against the design was a blow to the architects, especially to Neumann, who had not expected such acrimony and ill will from the academic institution he belonged to. A series of letters, some of which were published in the daily papers, reflected Neumann's disappointment and frustration. His main argument was that he had fulfilled his task and responsibilities as the project's architect and that the Technion, as the institution that educates architects in Israel, should be the first to support the professional and creative practice of design, and certainly not undermine it. Reacting to these events, Neumann resigned from the Technion. The telegram that he sent to Dr. Goldberg personally on November 13, 1966 read as follows: "Protest vehemently against vandalism in Danciger Building instigated by you. Disgusted by your equivocal dealings. Resigning from Technion because will have nothing to do with an institute presided over by you." The architects then filed a lawsuit against the Technion, asking the court for an injunction and mandamus to prevent it from making further changes to the building, and to ensure its completion according to the original plan. The statement of claim defined possible alterations such as the inner divisions of the halls, the painting of the building, and the installation of windows. The Technion responded with a counterclaim, and the case passed through several instances, eventually culminating in an appeal to the Supreme Court. Of the court verdicts, the only decision in favor of the architects was an order requiring the Technion to paint the building according to the architects' original design, which was done only years later.

There were several interesting aspects to this controversy that operated on professional, legal, and cultural levels. For the purposes of the broader story, I will focus here on its cultural ramifications, because it reveals something about the role of architecture and the place of creative freedom and artistic expression within 1960s Israeli society, as well as touching on wider questions, such as: What is architecture's place in society and how does it contribute to and express cultural values?

The fact that an ostensibly internal, professional, and technical skirmish over a specific building detail—the kind of argument that is commonplace in architectural projects generally—became a public controversy reveals that the Danciger quarrel was never simply about technical matters; rather, technical matters merely triggered, and eventually exposed, a much larger and more fundamental issue. The rectangular plan and simple organization of the Danciger Building design were not controversial; rather, the main argument concerned the building's envelope, its outer expression. Here, I would argue that what seemed to be the client's dissatisfaction with the functional, utilitarian performance of the building—specifically the natural light levels in the interior—was in fact a pretext intended to mask what was really a rejection of the building's appearance. In other words, the client could not identify with the look of the building. Only later, as the controversy gained purchase in the media, did the true opposition to the design come to light. The engineers and faculty who were to occupy the building claimed it was too modern for their taste, and stated that they refused to be treated as the "guinea pigs of modern architecture."[15]

Beyond the Technion's apparent dissatisfaction with the building's aesthetic, Israeli culture at the time did not support an architect's right to the visual expression of his or her work, nor did it accept the idea that architecture did in fact constitute an artistic contribution. This sentiment impacted the reception of public buildings in particular, as in the case of the Danciger Building. As an architect, Neumann saw it as his task to address the utilitarian demands of the program and also to provide an appropriate architectural expression for a new laboratory building as a symbol of a growing and creative academic institution. He vehemently rejected interventions on the part of engineers in issues of architectural design, believing that they were the responsibility of the architect alone. He believed that as rational and progressive thinkers, scientists and engineers of all people would best understand the importance of progress and creativity in all disciplines, including architecture; but he was let down. Neumann was especially disappointed that this drama had unfolded within an institution responsible for educating architects, and that the institution that sought to undermine his artistic license and authorship would be the very one that had hired him as dean of its architectural department.

The attack on Neumann's "overly modern" designs—by an established, supposedly progressive, research and technology institute such as the Technion—during the Danciger Building controversy can be seen as an early sign of larger shifts within Israeli architecture yet to come. The controversy prompted not only Neumann's resignation from the Technion in 1966, but also sealed his decision to leave Israel for good, having detected the beginnings of a socio-political upheaval that in just a few years' time would render his work irrelevant. He relocated to Quebec City, Canada, with his wife Naomi and their young daughter Eva-Marie, accepted a teaching position at Laval University, and there founded its Master of Architecture program. During his time in Canada, Neumann remained very much involved in the other projects that he had undertaken earlier with Zvi Hecker, and that were either under construction or in an advanced design phase, nearing readiness for construction. Aside from some visits by Zvi Hecker to Canada, the two corresponded mainly by mail, and often sent sketches and design details back and forth. Their correspondence over this period, from 1966 to 1968, has been preserved and served as a valuable resource for this book. Late in 1966, Neumann wrote to Hecker: "The situation in Israel is perfectly irrelevant from an architectural or any cultural point of view. But they reached their goal in cutting our work, which is a typical case of Israeli cultural vandalism. I am unable to fight on that level and feel defense(less) and powerless. That people revolt against creativity could happen anywhere. What is typical for Israel is that there is no voice of any importance in favor of the artist. This shows the true vacuum."[16]

The 1967 shift: Postmodernism in Israeli architecture

The year 1967 marked a dramatic change in Israel's history. The nation's victory in the Six Day War not only increased the area of the state almost threefold, as the ceasefire lines became the new borders, but most importantly, the war led to Israel's conquest of the eastern part of Jerusalem, including the Old City as its heart. The conquest and unification of Jerusalem marked one of the most significant events in the history of Israel and the Jewish people. The city's unification became a symbol of a people's unification with their land, and the return of the Jews to their Biblical origins. The 1967 victory was far more than a political and military achievement; it was a cultural and spiritual triumph, a moment of national euphoria, seen as the historical conclusion of a two-thousand-year-long exile since the time Jerusalem was last under Jewish sovereignty. This event influenced and changed all aspects of Israeli society, including art, folklore, politics, and culture. The idea of unification was also expressed in architecture and urban planning.

After the 1967 war, Israeli urban planners became preoccupied with expressing the unification of Jerusalem under Israeli rule. Their focus on the city was both symbolic, driven by its importance in history, and geopolitical, since Jerusalem had gone from being a city on the border of the state, to its center, and a new cultural-geographical reference within Israeli society. Attention was focused on Jerusalem's historic qualities, and architects were charged with emulating its traditional stone architecture and ancient styles in order to give the city an "oriental character," as the minister of housing advised his planners.[17] The arch, the narrow alley, and the stone-mason walls with narrow openings, all characteristic of the architecture of the Old City, were to replace Israel's infatuation with modern architecture.

The exploration of new modes of architectural expression, which had been a preoccupation of architects in the years before the 1967 war, was replaced by a dramatic turn toward the past, triggered by the historical look of Jerusalem. The national project of building a unified Jerusalem in the image of its past went hand in hand with Israeli architects' interest in exploring the city's vernacular architecture. The State Ministry of Housing adapted the British Mandate's Jerusalem Stone bylaw, under which all

Post-1967 Israeli "postmodernist" Jerusalem stone architecture, Ramat Eschkol, Jerusalem, 1970

new buildings within the greater Jerusalem area were to be clad in stone in order to reference the historical architecture of the Old City.[18] The new neighborhoods, and in time the Israeli settlements that grew up around the city, aspired to echo the traditional architecture of the old Holy City and so to establish a direct connection between present and past. Modernism's aesthetics were replaced by a semblance of local tradition. According to Alona Nitzan-Shiftan, this tradition was most prevalent in Jerusalem, and was rooted in the cultural and professional formation of the generation of architects that was entrusted with the national task of "Israelizing" Jerusalem. Nitzan-Shiftan claims that "post-1967 Israeli architecture clearly drifted away from its predominantly modernist practices, emulating instead the architecture of its Arab Other," and "Israelizing" the architectural forms of another nation.[19] The "Arab Other," in this context, refers to the inhabitants of East Jerusalem and the West Bank prior to the 1967 occupation, who would later be referred to as Palestinians. Yet here I would argue that in the years immediately following the 1967 War, the notion of this "Arab Other"—and a specifically Jerusalemite or Palestinian architectural expression—had not yet been understood as constituting a cultural identity, but was rather regarded more as a naïve, vague notion of a local vernacular. For the Israeli psyche of the late 1960s and the early 1970s, the Palestinians living in Jerusalem and the West Bank did not yet constitute an organized group, let alone a nation. They were not yet politically represented within the international scene, nor did they even exist in the eyes of most Israelis. The Arab vernacular therefore became associated with a non-political locality, with the picturesque quality of the existing landscape. Whether in a conscious or unconscious denial of the Other, architects from all sides of Israel's political map found themselves appropriating the "Arab" vernacular in their designs for Jerusalem's new architecture.

The new architecture of Jerusalem tried hard to look local. It had to look as if it belonged to the Old City, in order to diffuse the visual boundaries between the old and the new and to create one unified image, reflecting how Jerusalem was conceived politically as a reunified city. This Jerusalemite architecture focused on symbolism, memory, and tradition.

It mimicked traditional elements such as arches, narrow window openings, vaults, and domed roofs, and it incorporated materials such as local Jerusalem stone for cladding in a manner similar to the way stone was used in Jerusalem's historical buildings. This Jerusalem stone architecture sought to relate to its historical context through visual similarity and to combine new and old in a single image of a historic city built in stone. Architecturally, most attention was paid to the buildings' façades as the architectural element responsible for establishing this image, while the building plans in almost all cases remained completely modern: Floor plans, for example, were organized and designed along the same lines as the functionalist approach. The façade, however, through the image it projected, was the most immediate political means of expanding the visual and physical territory belonging to Jerusalem, as Eyal Weizman explains: "The extension of the city's 'holiness' to the new suburbs was conceived as part of Israel's attempt to generate widespread public acceptance of the newly annexed territories."[20] The old built environment of Jerusalem described above became the new image of Israeli architecture and replaced the "high modernism" of bare concrete and abstract geometric expression, one of whose strongest protagonists had been Alfred Neumann.

Neumann's space-packing designs differ from this new Jerusalem architecture on several levels: in the use of materials, from the exposed concrete of the former to the stone of the latter; in building form, from abstract geometric shapes to traditional historicism; in construction methods, from the use of industrial building elements and large-scale casts to reliance on traditional masonry work; and in the structural approach, from an exposed structural system to a concealed one. This new architectural expression, while emerging as a coherent image that depended heavily on an "Arab vernacular" rendered accessible through the occupation of the West Bank, did not necessarily repeat traditional Arab building techniques exactly, but rather combined them with modern, at times prefabricated, building technologies. This postmodern condition—postmodern in the sense of the symbolic instrumentality of the façade, and the combination of traditional architectural expressions with modern building technologies—was understood very well by some of the architects working in Jerusalem both at the time and in later years.

Jerusalem's stone architecture was also made possible by the availability of cheap Palestinian labor as a result of the occupation. The local Palestinian population, which was now under Israeli rule, though not as citizens, knew how to build with stone and provided the new construction workforce. In a reversal of the early state's policy of employing advanced technologies that would rely less on skilled manpower and more on factories and prefabrication, in the building industry at least, cheap Palestinian labor obviated the need to use industrialized construction methods. Although industrial technologies such as precast concrete production had by that time become a fully developed industry in Israel,[21] it was cheaper and more profitable for both private developers and the Israeli Housing Ministry to hire Palestinian laborers. The turn to conventional building techniques also constituted a step backward in terms of exploring new architectural expressions.[22]

This new architecture served the nationalist political aim of securing Israel's hold on the Old City of Jerusalem by surrounding it with new

Ma'alot Dafna, residential neighborhood in Jerusalem, 1973

Jewish settlements and neighborhoods. Neighborhood-building constituted a major national building project of the 1970s and onward, and several soon popped up and began covering the hills surrounding the city. The West Bank settlements that were situated further out in the Occupied Territories gained momentum as a national project following the political rise of the right-wing Likud party in the early 1980s. The larger West Bank settlement projects could be described as an extension of the urban planning approaches undertaken in Jerusalem from the early 1970s onward. The borders of Jerusalem as a regional center and source of influence were repeatedly revised and further expanded. Its municipal and visual boundaries continued to grow, and the areas incorporated into the city were eventually termed "Greater Jerusalem" (*yerushalaim rabati*). This change in architecture was also mirrored by a change in architectural leadership and a change in the questions of concern to the profession. In such a politicized environment, the cultural and sociopolitical preoccupation with the nation quickly found its way into architectural discourse as well.

The year 1967 marked the beginning of an internal debate on issues of identity, nationality, and local expression. The questions, "What is Israeli architecture?" or "What should Israeli architecture look like?" were first raised openly in discussions among the circle of Sabra architects, who through their search for a national identity had by this time begun to play a dominant role in Israel's architectural community.[23] Ram Karmi later described the most pressing question of the time: "How could architects establish an architectural language that encouraged personal expression but also defined a vernacular for the national community?"[24] Consequently, post-1967 Israeli postmodernism relied on architectural referents from within Jerusalem's Old City and the Arab vernacular of the territories newly under Israeli rule. The inspiration of this Arab vernacular obviated the need to look outward to the international architectural scene as a resource for styles, trends, ideas, and inspiration. Israeli architects felt at home: They could finally look inward to discover a national style. Post-1967 Israel, unlike the early state, was less interested in understanding its place within the community of Western nations, and no longer looked to define itself in relation to an international context. Israel instead found its identity in adapting and reconstructing a past image associated with the Holy Land, an image which through the occupation could be accessed and reclaimed.[25]

What interests me here is not so much what became of post-1967 architecture in Israel. Rather, I wish to emphasize the impact that the cultural shift of 1967 had in forestalling other architectural lines of inquiry and potential influences, which all came to a sudden, yet predictable halt. Neumann had sought a different architectural expression from that which preoccupied post-1967 Israel. He never saw the need to mimic either the Arab vernacular or the historic stone architecture of Jerusalem, which post-1967 Israeli architecture sought to emulate. The local influences in Neumann's work—those he mentions in the descriptions of his projects—all relate to the larger regional context that extended beyond Israel's national boundaries and were appropriated into his work in an entirely different way. Ottoman architecture, Persian building traditions, Palestinian village building techniques from the Galilee, Islamic ornamentation, traditional solutions to the climatic problems faced by desert cities, and Byzantine colors, among other elements, were all considered valid architectural sources by Neumann, yet as archetypal conditions and principles, awaiting new forms, geometries, and expressions. His architecture of abstract geometric shapes became ever more isolated and out of place within Israel's post-1967 cultural narrative. Alfred Neumann died in 1968, yet it is not hard to imagine his work gaining influence, and his design approach being adopted and perpetuated by a younger generation of followers within the Israeli architecture scene, especially since by the mid-1960s his work was receiving extensive international recognition. But post-1967 Israeli society unfortunately closed the door on his legacy. This book opens a window through which his work can be re-evaluated and appreciated in a broader historical perspective. The following section presents a chronological account of all of Neumann's buildings and designs known to date. Revealed in the drawings, sketches, diagrams, and photos is an artistic development of constant exploration that challenged conventions of architectural thinking and building to produce a most original interpretation of human habitat in the modern age.

1 Rafi Levi quoted by Benno Kalev, *The Ten plus Group—Myth and Reality* (Tel Aviv: Tel Aviv Museum of Art, cat. 1/08, 2008), p. 16. Author's translation from Hebrew.

2 Peter Cook, *Experimental Architecture* (London: Studio Vista, 1970). This book assembles projects from all over the world that were published in *Architectural Design* and other journals.

3 Ibid., p. 61.

4 Ibid., p. 12.

5 Ibid., p. 68.

6 Maria Bottero, editor, *Zodiac*, 16 (1966), p. 237.

7 Ada Louis Huxtable, "Tinker-Toy City Hall in Israel is 'Space-Packed,'" *The New York Times* June 5, 1969, p. 49.

8 This includes Arieh Sharon's reference to Neumann's work as experimental in Arieh Sharon, *Kibbutz + Bauhaus, An Architect's Way in A New Land* (Stuttgart: Karl Krämer Verlag, 1976), p. 186.

9 An international committee that included the British architects O. A. Saunders and Robert Mathews, and the Israeli architect Benjamin Idelson, who designed the Technion's new campus center.

10 Around this time Eldar Sharon left the partnership of Neumann-Hecker-Sharon to join his father's firm, which is why he was not considered an architect involved in the design. This explains the omission of Sharon's name from the list of architects responsible for the design and his non-involvement in the later Danciger Building controversy.

11 Memorandum dated October 11 and October 18, 1966, Alfred Neumann, personal archives.

12 Letter from Hecker to Neumann dated November 2, 1966. Author's translation from Hebrew.

13 Macabee Dean, "Outraged architect strikes at 'mutilated' building," *The Jerusalem Post*, November 3, 1966.

14 Letter from Hecker to Neumann dated November 2, 1966 (see note 12).

15 As reported by *Ha'aretz* correspondent, "Mechanical Engineering Building Inaugurated at the Technion, Haifa," *Ha'aretz*, October 11, 1966. Author's translation from Hebrew.

16 Letter from Neumann to Hecker dated November 12, 1966.

17 Alona Nitzan-Shiftan, "Seizing locality in Jerusalem," Nezar Al-Sayyad (ed.),*The End of Tradition?* (London and New York: Routledge, 2004), pp. 231–56. See also endnote 3 of the same chapter, in which Nitzan-Shiftan references publications dealing with guidelines for building in Jerusalem, among them: "Planning and Building Methods in East Jerusalem," *Ha'aretz*, February 2, 1968 and David Kroyanker, *Jerusalem Architecture-Periods and Styles: Modern Architecture outside the Old City: 1948–1990* (Jerusalem: Keter, 1991).

18 The Jerusalem Stone bylaw, introduced in 1918 by the British military governor of Jerusalem, Sir Roland Storrs, and later adapted by the Israeli state, assured the continuous appearance of stone throughout the greater Jerusalem area. See Eyal Wiezman, "The Subversion of Jerusalem's Sacred Vernaculars," Michael Sorkin (ed.), *The Next Jerusalem* (New York: Monacelli Press, 2002), pp. 120–45.

19 Nitzan-Shiftan (see note 17), p. 232.

20 Eyal Wiezman, "The Subversion of Jerusalem's Sacred Vernaculars" (see note 18), p. 132.

21 Israel's prefabricated building industry developed in the 1950s in answer to the growing demand for housing to accommodate the waves of new immigrants. The objective was to produce large numbers of housing units using minimum skilled labor and to decrease reliance on foreign builders. The Israeli government imported advanced technologies and equipment from France and subsidized the prefab building industry in order to minimize its reliance on manual labor in construction and to maximize the production of building elements at the factory. Since building, particularly housing, as a means of assuring the presence of a permanent population in a given territory, played a crucial political role in the emerging Israeli state, the Israeli government was directly involved in the building industries and had a Ministry of Construction and Housing devoted only to housing. By the 1960s, prefab construction accounted for 20 to 25 percent of all building in Israel. In the early 1970s, 44 percent of all government-supported housing was made using prefab building methods.

22 The shift from prefab building to manual masonry was gradual and continued throughout the early 1970s. During the first years of the occupation, all government-sponsored projects still required the involvement of the prefab industry in new building developments. Several attempts at combining the two building techniques can be seen in those Jerusalem neighborhoods that were built in the early 1970s.

23 "The national and professional sentiment of the Sabra, I argue, underline the Israeli architectural praxis that shaped the urban landscape of post-1967 Israeli Jerusalem. These sentiments were developed as an internal Israeli debate." Nitzan-Shiftan, *Seizing Locality in Jerusalem*, (see note 17), p. 241. Yehuda Safran also supported the notion that the post-1967 sociopolitical situation had sparked an inner-Israeli debate on the character and national identity of Israeli architecture. From the author's discussion with Yehuda Safran in New York, April 14, 2006.

24 Nitzan-Shiftan (see note 17), p. 244.

25 Ada Karmi Melamed, "White Architecture in Palestine: 1917–1948," lecture delivered at the Department of Art and Archeology, Princeton University, April 17, 2006. Further discussed in the author's conversation with Ada Karmi in Princeton, April 17, 2006.

Buildings and Designs

(1922–1968)

1 Student Work
Vienna, Austria
102

2 House for California
104

3 Addition for the Reichstag
Berlin, Germany
106

4 Government Palace of
Agriculture and the
Centenary Hall
Algiers, Algeria
108

5 School
Boulogne-Billancourt,
France
112

6 Moravia Sanitorium
Tatranská Lomnica,
Czechoslovakia
116

7 Villa
Paris, France
118

8 Justice Hall
Competition
San Salvador, Chile
120

9 Renovation and Extension
of Dr. Josef Slezak's House
at 179 Viničiá Street
Brno, Czechoslovakia
122

10 Family Houses
Brno, Czechoslovakia
126

11 Dormitory and
Housing Schemes
128

12 Bat Yam Town Hall
and Civic Center
Bat Yam, Israel
136

13 Club Méditeranée
Holiday Camp
Achziv, Israel
166

14 Michmoret Holiday Camp
Michmoret, Israel
182

15 Kiryat Yam Holiday Camp
Kiryat Yam, Israel
188

16 Housing Complex,
Arab Village
Ein Rafa, Israel
192

17 Dubiner Apartment House
Ramat Gan, Israel
204

18 Netanya City Hall
Competition
Netanya, Israel
230

19 Danciger Building
Mechanical Engineering
Faculty Laboratory
Building: Technion–Israel
Institute of Technology
Haifa, Israel
240

20 Ashdod City Center
Ashod, Israel
270

21 El-Al Terminal Pavilion
Tel Aviv, Israel
278

22 Synagogue
Competition
286

23 Beit Zeit Youth Camp
and Restaurant
Beit Zeit, Israel
292

24 Amsterdam Town Hall
Competition
The Netherlands
302

25 *Studies* in Polyhedral
Geometries
304

26 Synagogue at the Officers'
School Training Base I
Mitzpeh Ramon, Israel
308

1 Student Work Completed at the Meisterschule für Architektur under Peter Behrens Vienna, Austria 1922–23

RAUM DER SINNE
LANGSCHNITT

2 House for California 1923

The House for California was a project Neumann designed during his third year of studies under Peter Behrens at the Vienna Academy of Fine Arts. The proposal was for an open-plan, single-family home in California. Neumann revisited this project in the early 1930s, and revised his earlier Expressionistic concept by outfitting the building with a large glazed steel skeleton.

VILLAS MODERNES

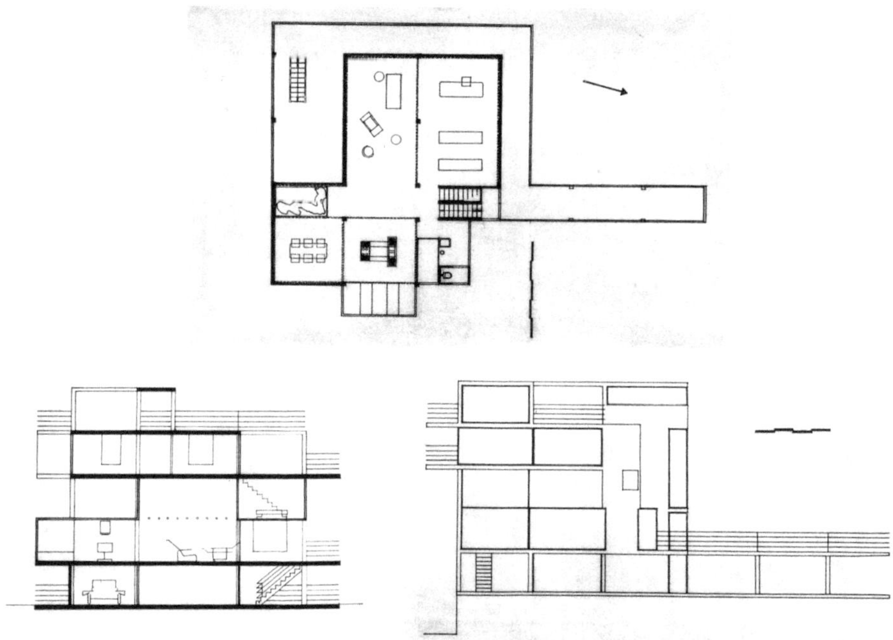

NEUMANN, architecte à Paris
Villa pour la Californie (1923)

2.1 Plan, section, and elevation
2.2 Perspective view

3 Addition for the Reichstag 1927
Berlin, Germany

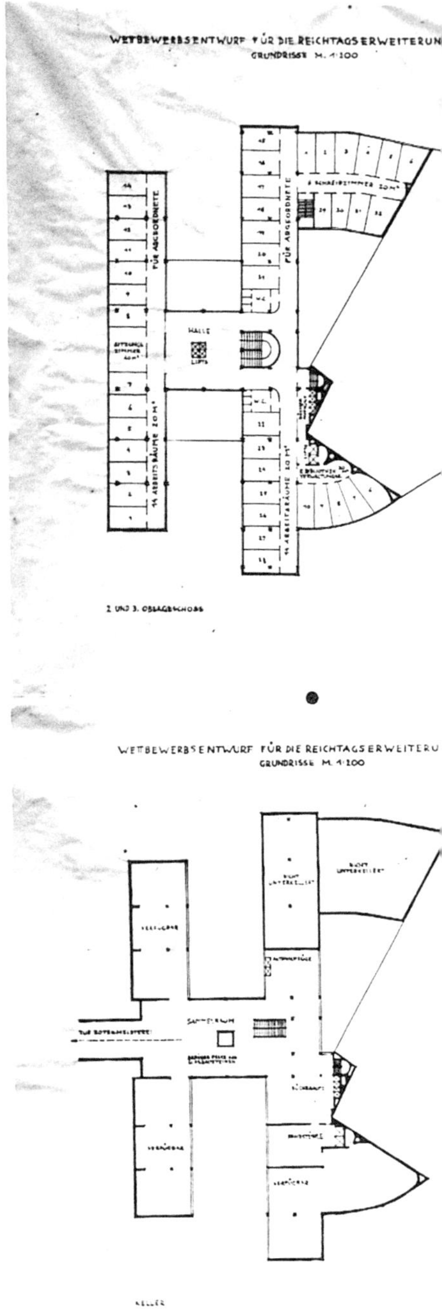

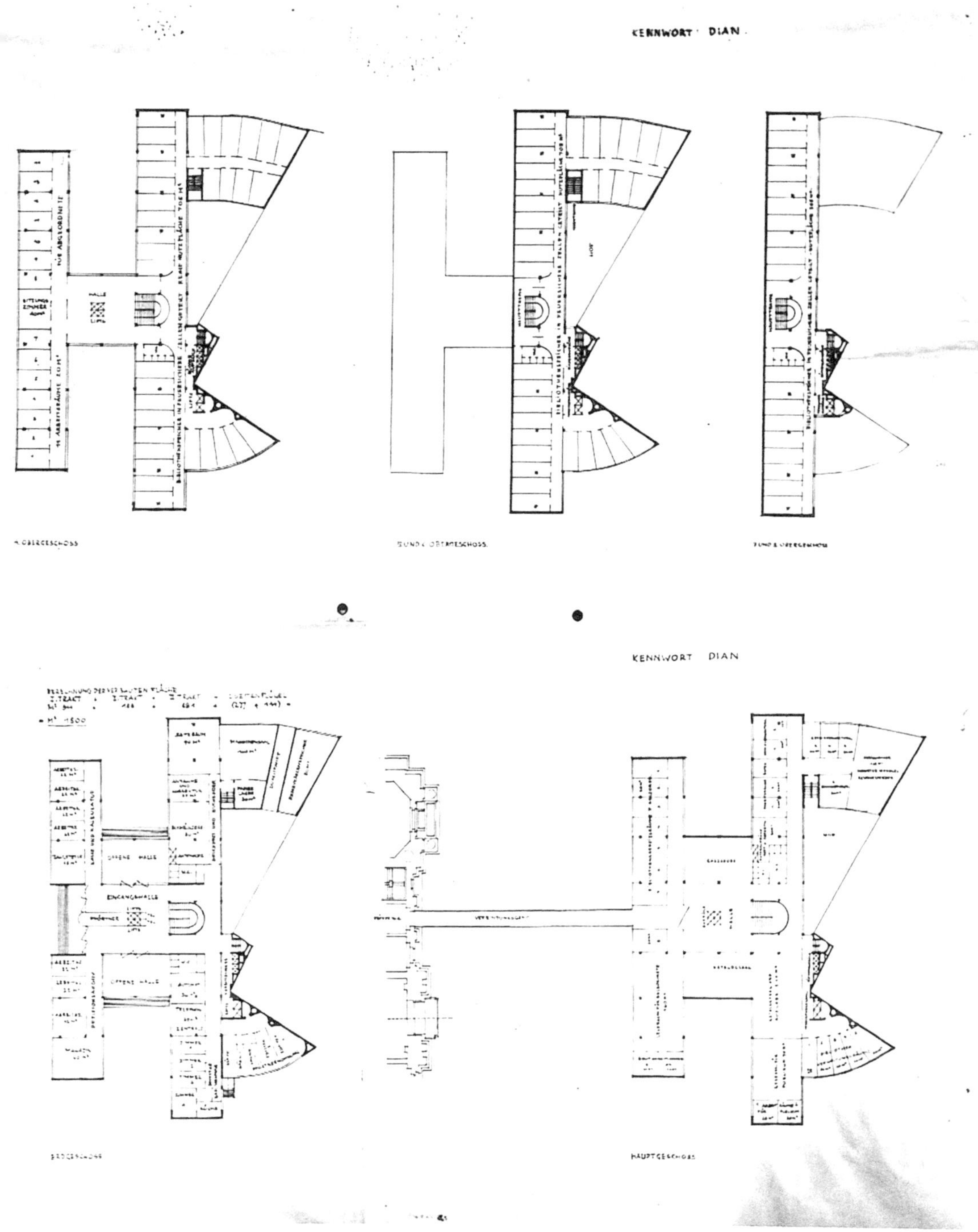

3.1 Competition entry for an addition to the Reichstag, which Neumann submitted while working for Peter Behrens

4 # Government Palace of Agriculture and the Centenary Hall Algiers, Algeria

1928

Project architect for Jacques Guiuchain

Neumann worked on the designs for the Government Palace of Agriculture and Centenary Hall, both important, high-profile buildings in Algiers, for the architect Jacques Guiuchain in 1928–1929. These buildings were informed by Auguste Perret's classic structural principles and marked the arrival of a new kind of modernism in North Africa.

4.1 View of Algiers
4.2 Government Palace of Agriculture

4.4 Centenary Hall

5 # School
Boulogne-Billancourt, France

1929

With Pierre Forestier, Lucien Beugnet

Upon returning to Paris from Algiers, Neumann designed a school in collaboration with Forestier and Beugnet. The structure was terraced and contained large promenade spaces.

ÉCOLES

1

2

NEUMANN, FORESTIER, BEUGNET, architectes à Paris
Groupe scolaire, à Boulogne-sur-Seine
1. Façade sur la rue des Moulineaux. — 2. Façade sur la cour.

5.1 View from the rue des Moulineaux
5.2 View from the yard

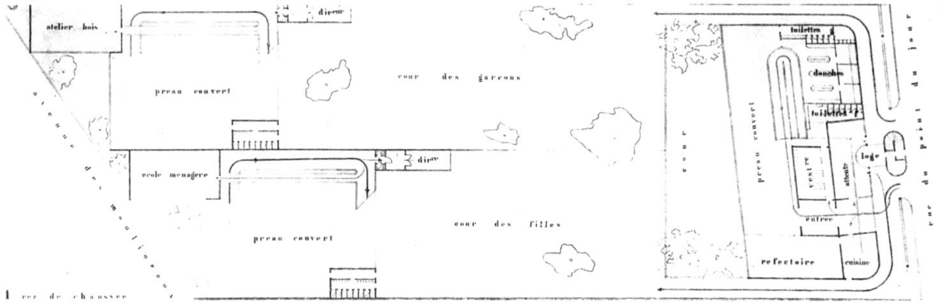

1 rez de chaussée

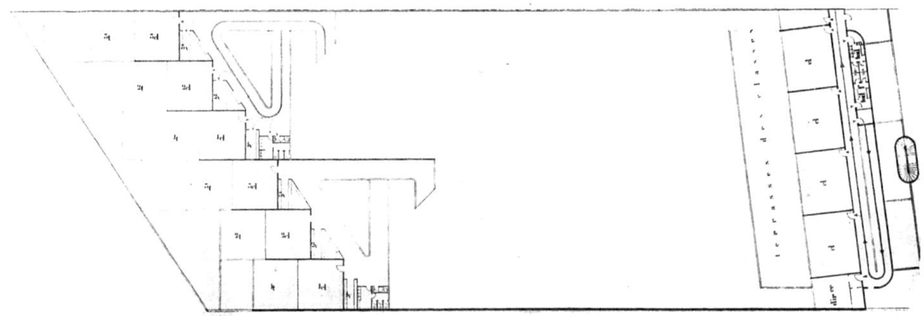

2

NEUMANN, FORESTIER, BEUGNET, architectes à Paris
Groupe scolaire, à Boulogne-sur-Seine
1. Plan du rez-de-chaussée. — 2. Plan au niveau de la première rampe

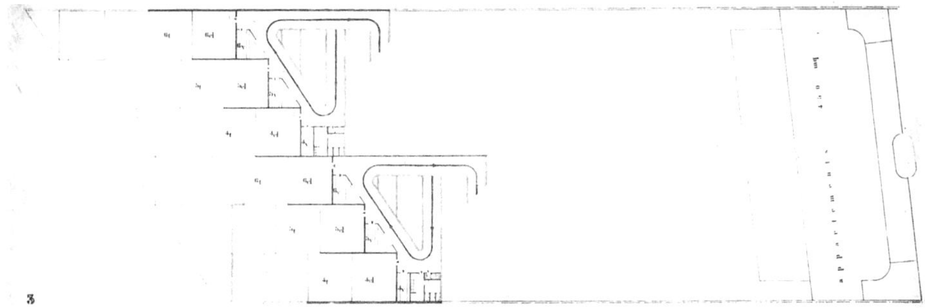

3

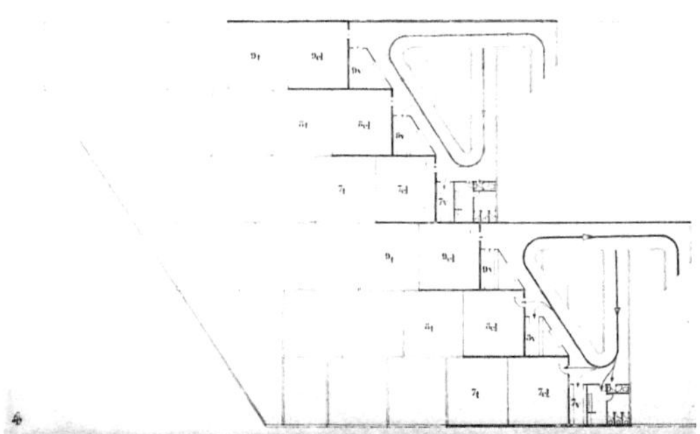

4

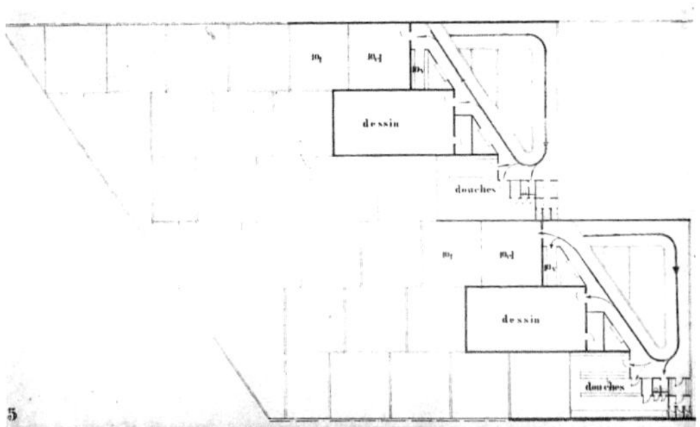

5

NEUMANN, FORESTIER, BEUGNET, architectes à Paris
Groupe Scolaire, à Boulogne-sur-Seine
3. Plan au niveau de la deuxième rampe — 4. Plan au niveau de la troisième rampe. — 5. Plan au niveau de la quatrième rampe

5.3 [1] Ground floor plan, [2] Plan at level of first ramp
5.4 [3] Plan at level of second ramp, [4] Plan at level of third ramp, [5] Plan at level of fourth ramp

19

ÉCOLES
coupe longitudinale

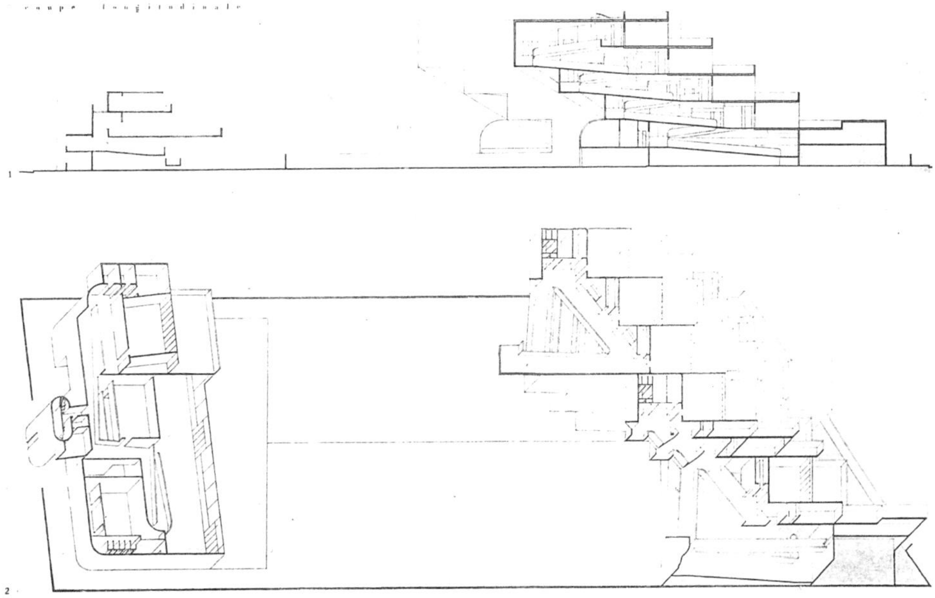

NEUMANN, FORESTIER, BEUGNET, architectes à Paris
Groupe scolaire, à Boulogne-sur-Seine. — 1. Coupe longitudinale — 2. Perspective axonométrique

5.5 View of interior ramps
5.6 [1] Longitudinal section, [2] Axonometric view

6 Moravia Sanitorium 1930
Tatranská Lomnica, Czechoslovakia

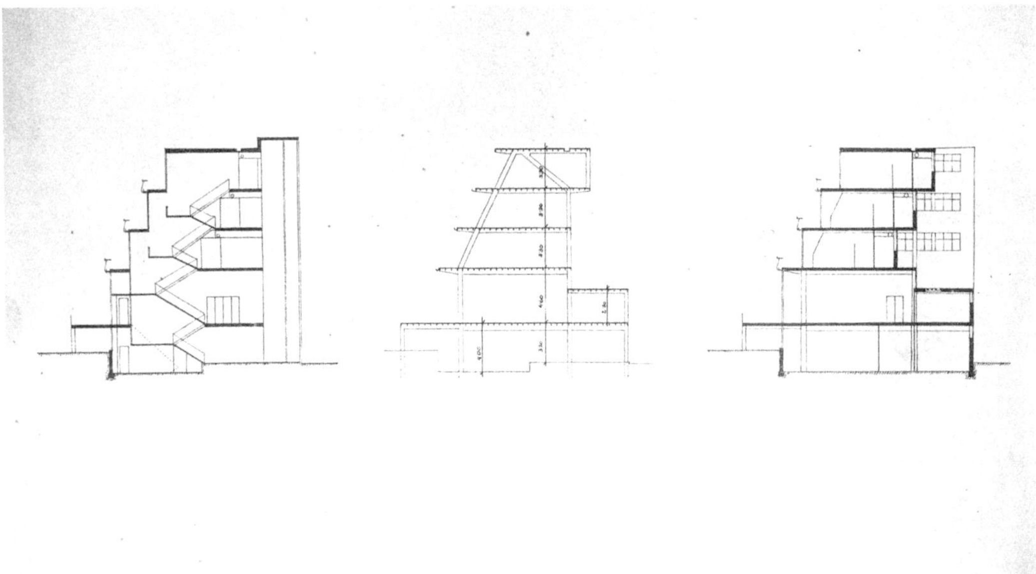

6.1 Perspective view

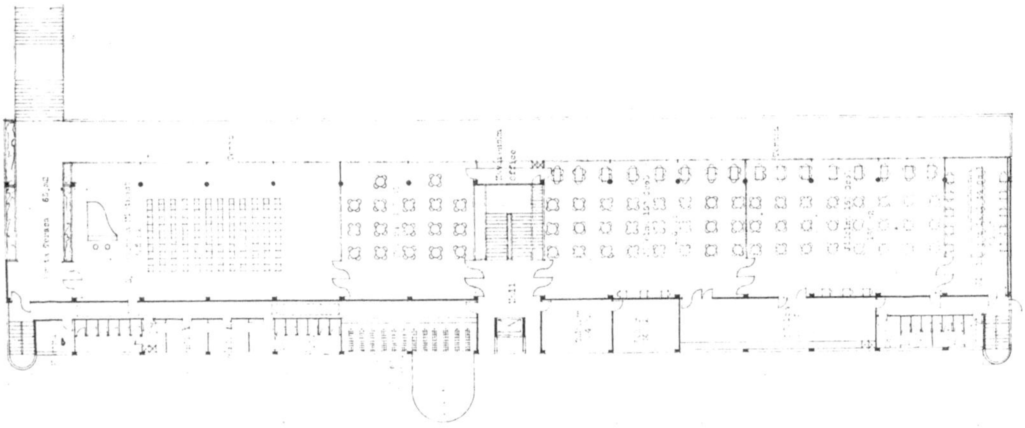

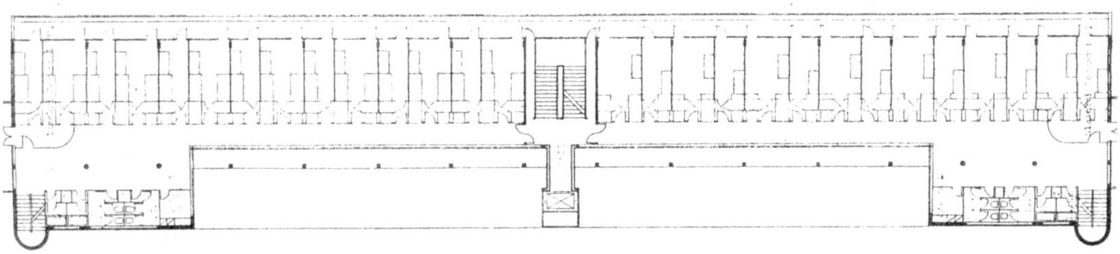

6.2 Sections

7 Villa
Paris, France

1931

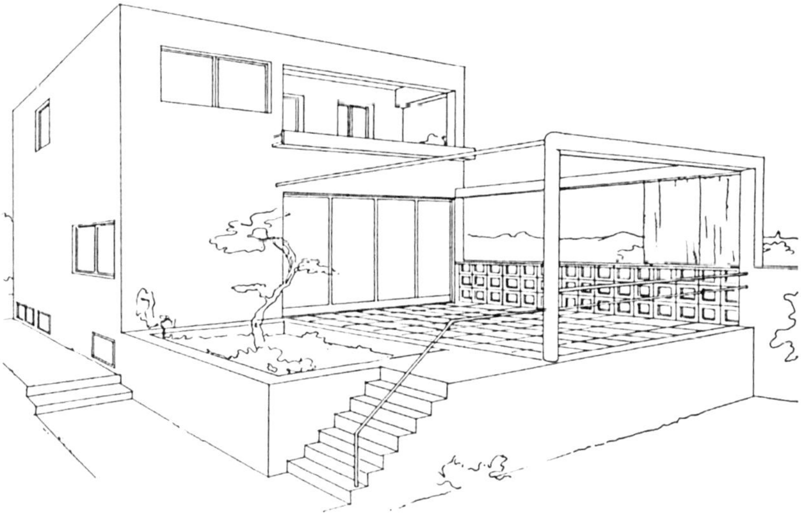

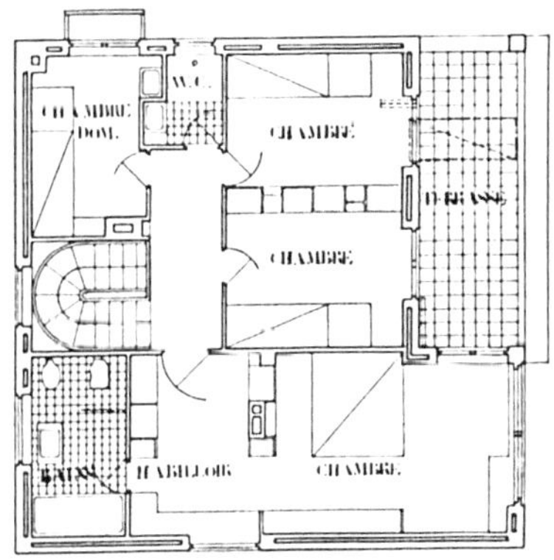

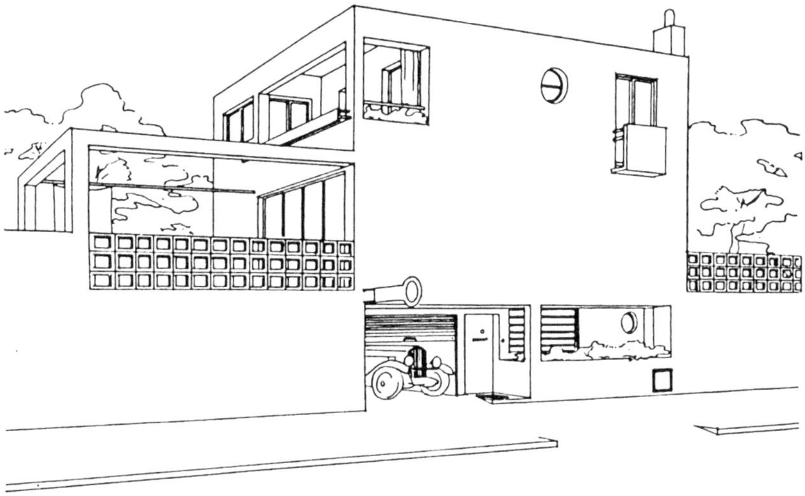

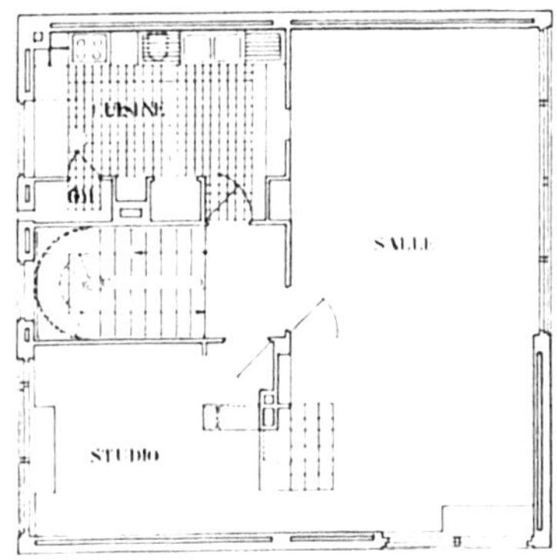

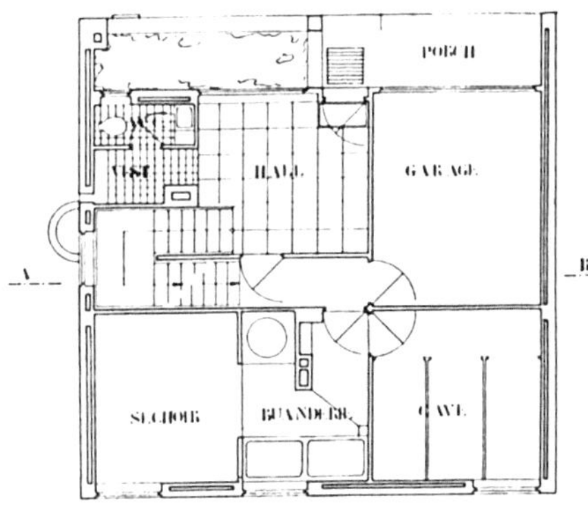

7.1 Designed in collaboration with Jean Ginsberg

8 Justice Hall, *Competition* 1932
San Salvador, Chile

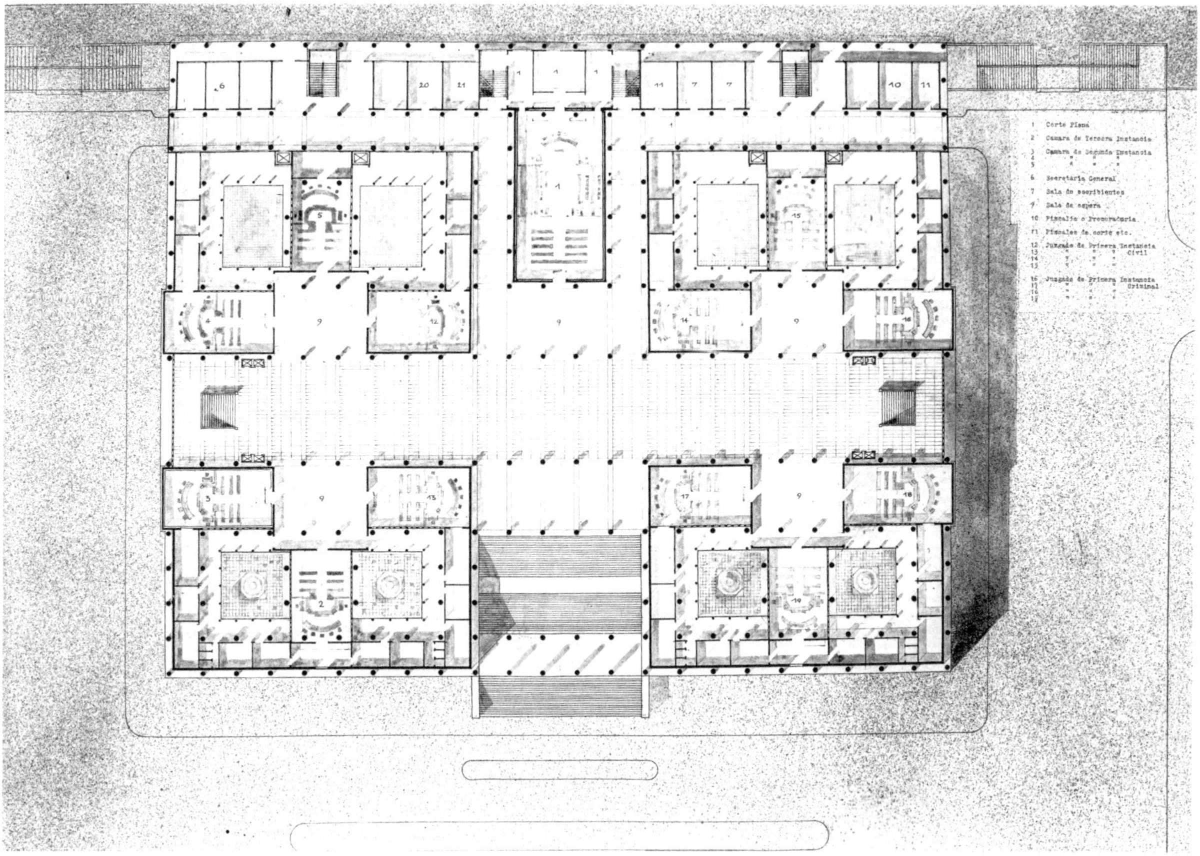

8.1 Ground floor plan
8.2 Perspective view, section, elevation

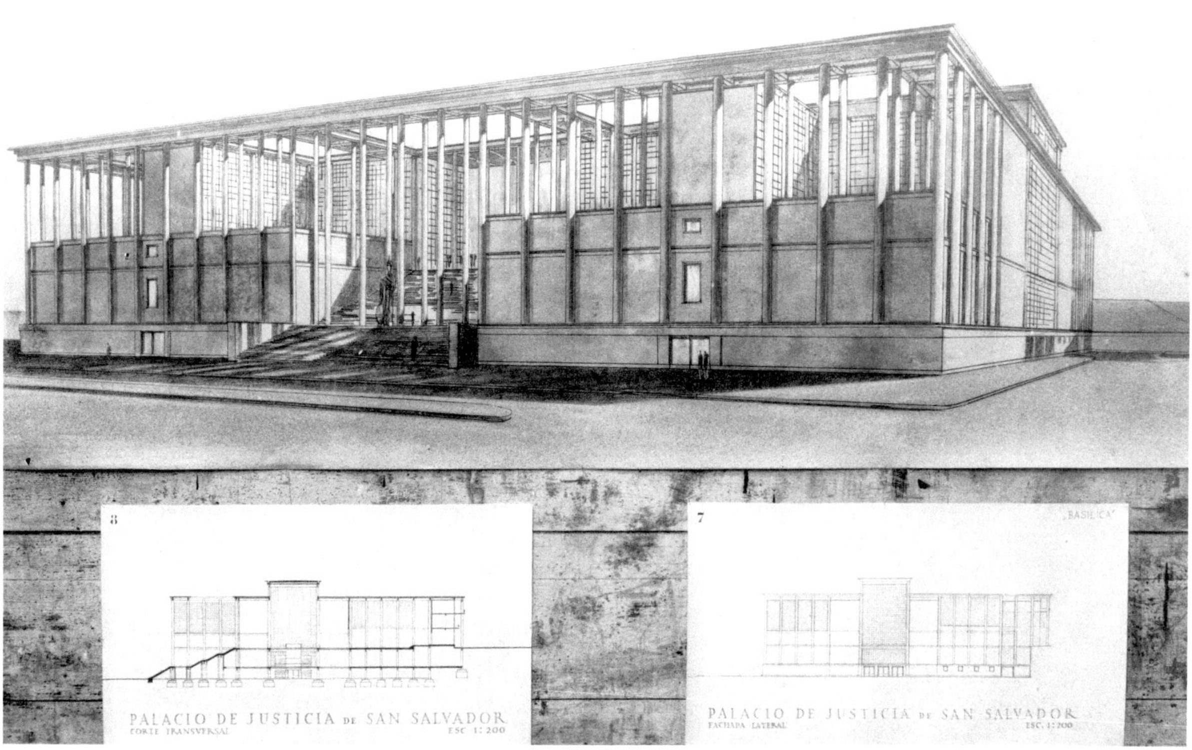

9 Renovation and Extension of Dr. Josef Slezak's House at 179 Viničiá Street Brno, Czechoslovakia

1932–36

Neumann's design for the renovation and extension of Dr. Joseph Slezak's house was influenced by Adolf Loos's "Raumplan" concept, and was to contain built-in and standalone furnishings.

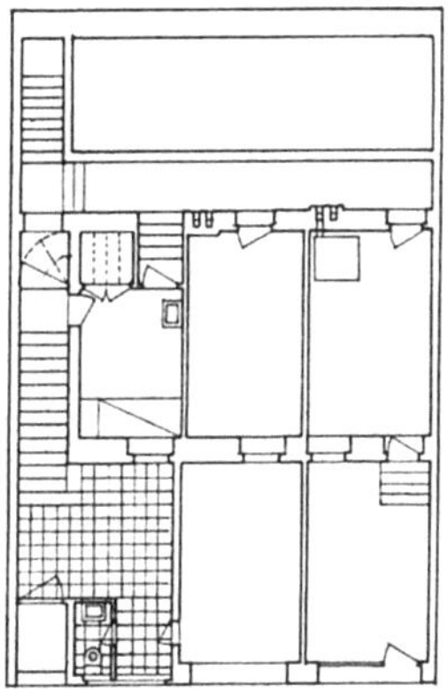

1

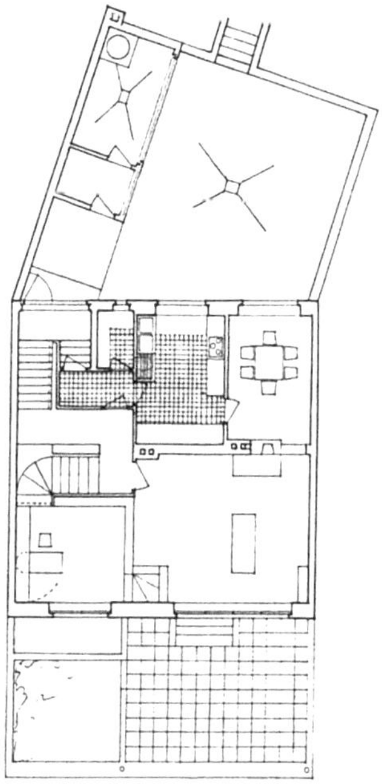

2

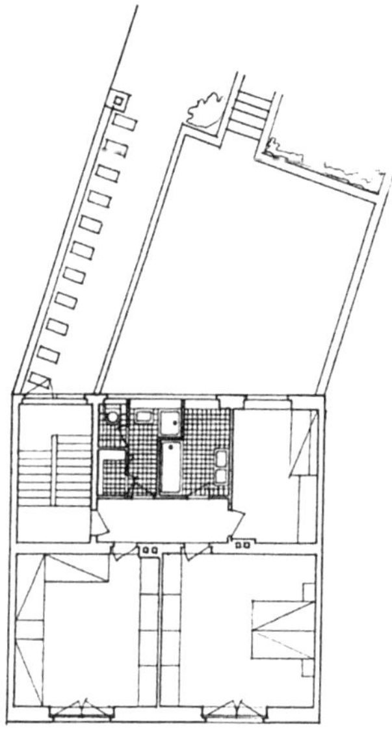

3

9.1 Plan views: 1 Ground floor, 2 First floor, 3 Second floor
9.2 View from the street

9.3 View of the living space; the leather and tubular steel armchair was designed by Neumann

9.4 Built-in sofa and book cabin

10 Family Houses Brno, Czechoslovakia 1937–47

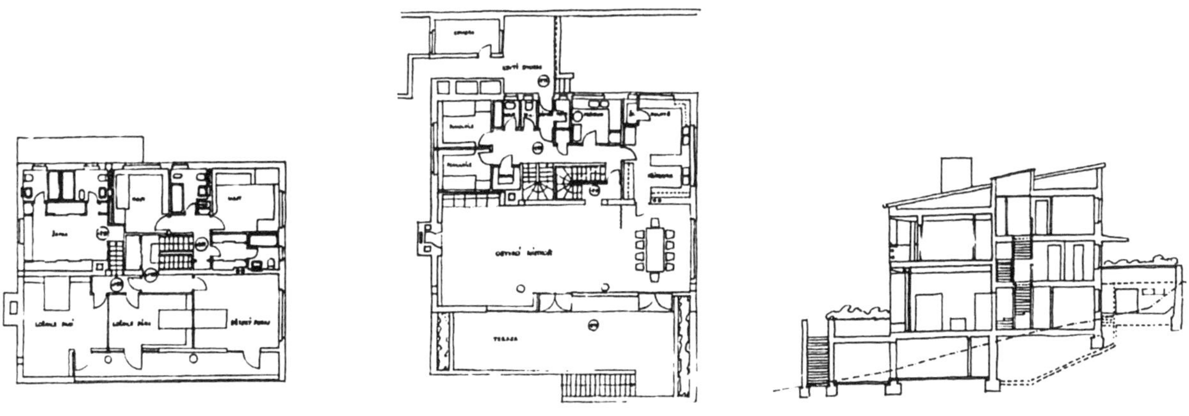

1 2 3

10.1 Perspective drawing, 1937
10.2 Perspective drawing and plan views: [1] Second floor, [2] First floor, [3] Section, 1947

11 Dormitory and Housing Schemes 1950s

The Dormitory and Housing Schemes served Neumann as an architectural experiment in optimizing the use of space in both plan and section. Neumann was of the view that about a third of the floor areas and vertical spaces in buildings are wasted. Furniture and appliances render the spaces above and below them unusable, and Neumann sought to eliminate these gaps. He proposed stacking upright, I-beam-shaped wall dividers to create a building of partitioned units. Each successive row of I-beam-shaped dividers was offset from the one it rested upon, forming a pattern of cruciform spatial units that, from the section cut, resemble the running bond pattern common in brickwork. This arrangement resulted in elevated floors and lower ceilings at the sides of each unit, into which furniture was to be integrated. Neumann's dormitory design permitted more units to be integrated into a given space than was possible in a building formed from rows of cubical units, and was also more cost-effective, he claimed.

A site plan that Neumann made for the project showed rectangular slab-like buildings hemming a hexagonal courtyard, but since this project was never intended for a specific site, the arrangement was arbitrary: The project could take any of a number of forms in plan, since the design was defined in section. Unlike Neumann's later work, the overall form of the dormitory building and the nature of its individual parts were not tightly related. The spatial pattern could be extended infinitely in breadth and height. After Neumann's death in 1968, Zvi Hecker and Naomi Neumann proposed this project to the Canadian housing authorities.

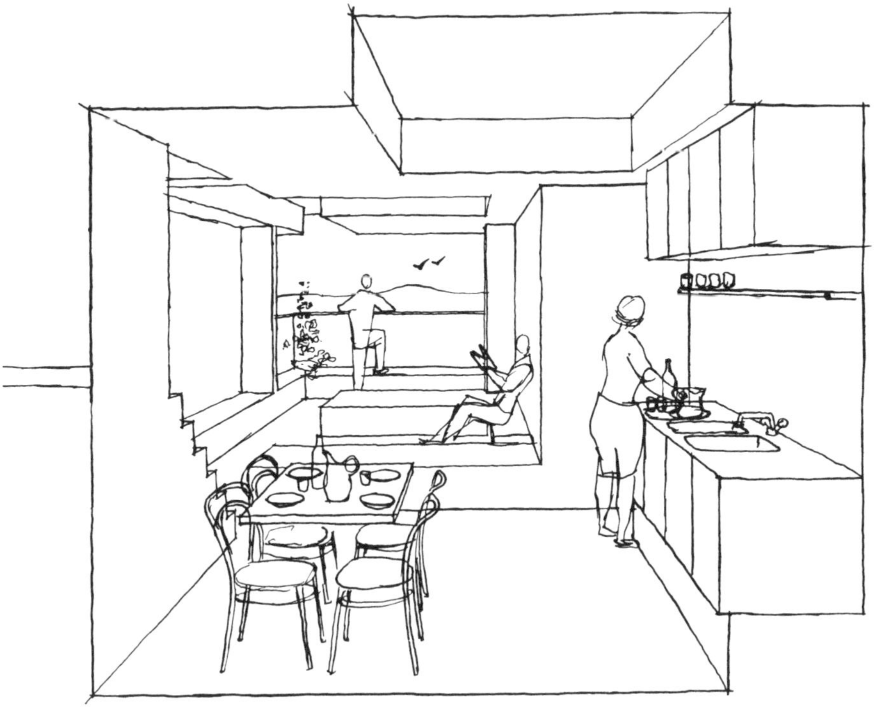

11.1 Interior view of typical unit
11.2 Pattern created by stacking I-beam-shaped units

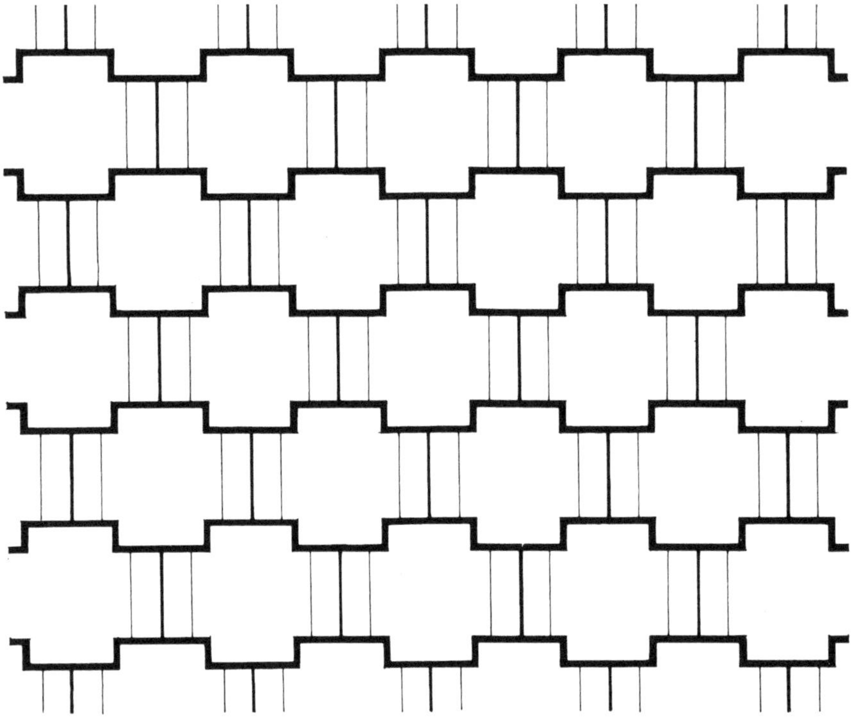

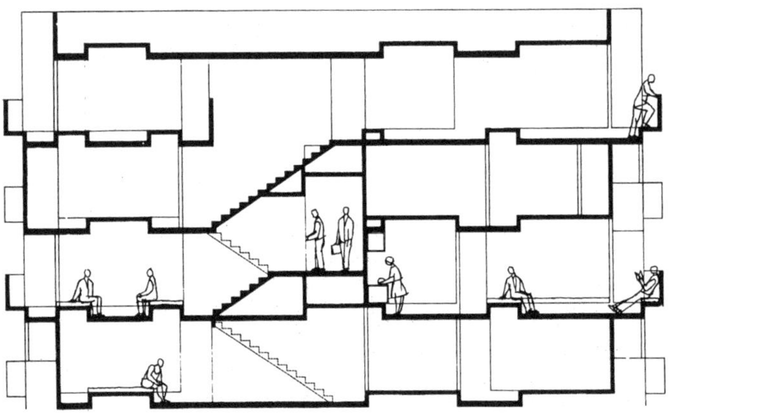

11.3 Pattern and section

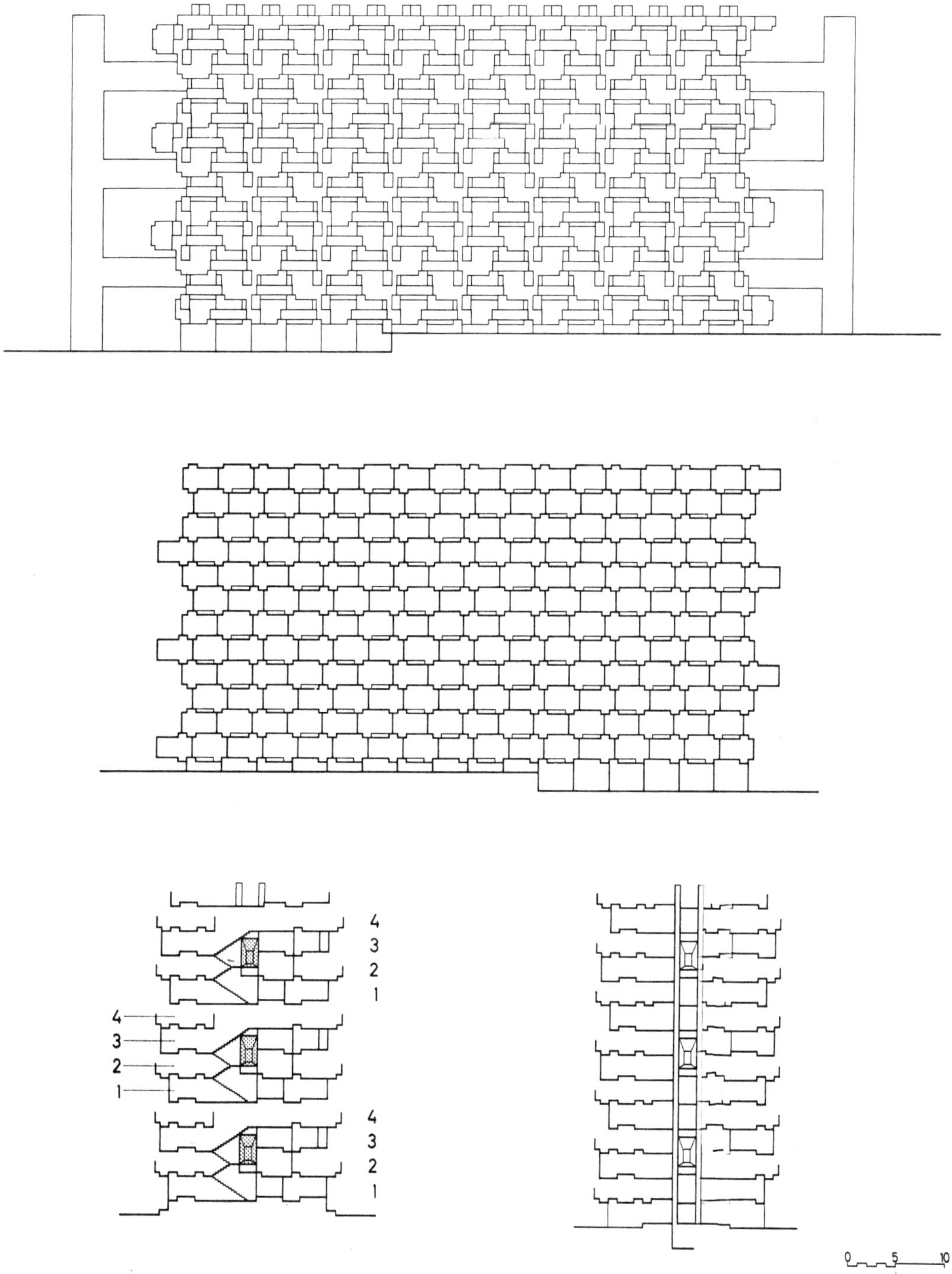

11.4 Elevations and sections

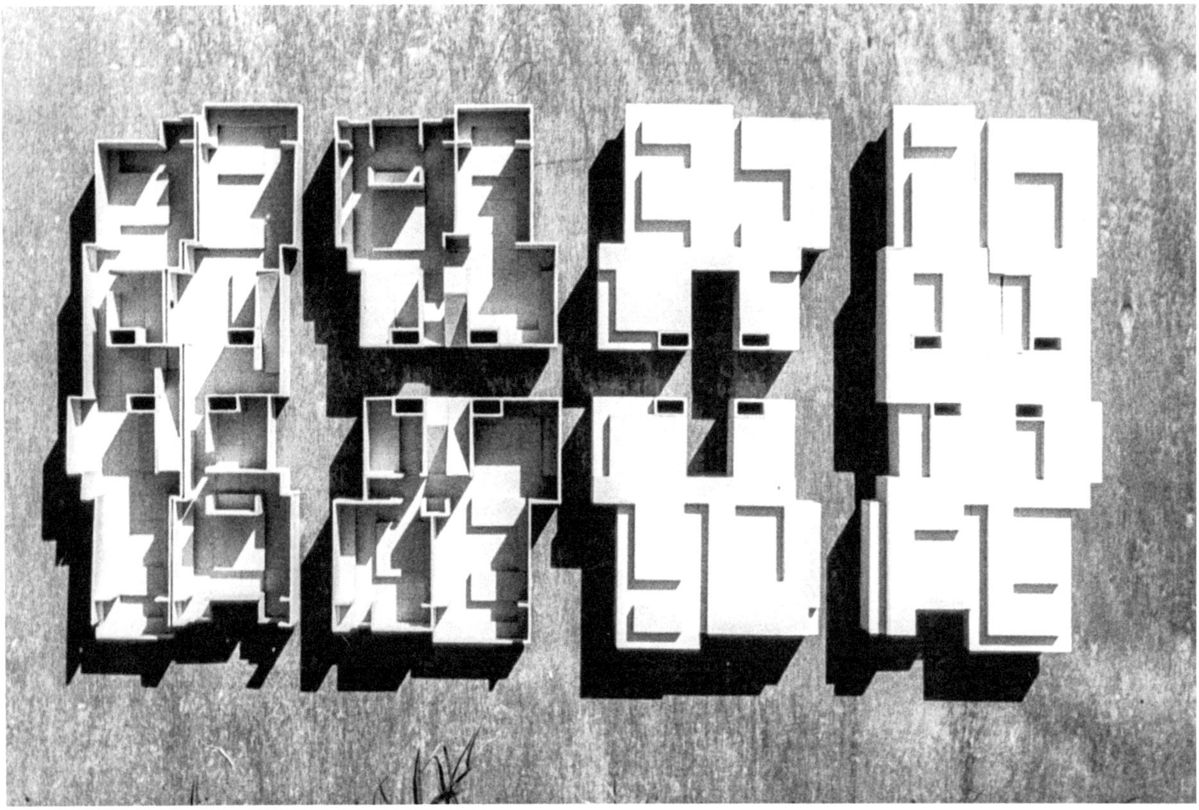

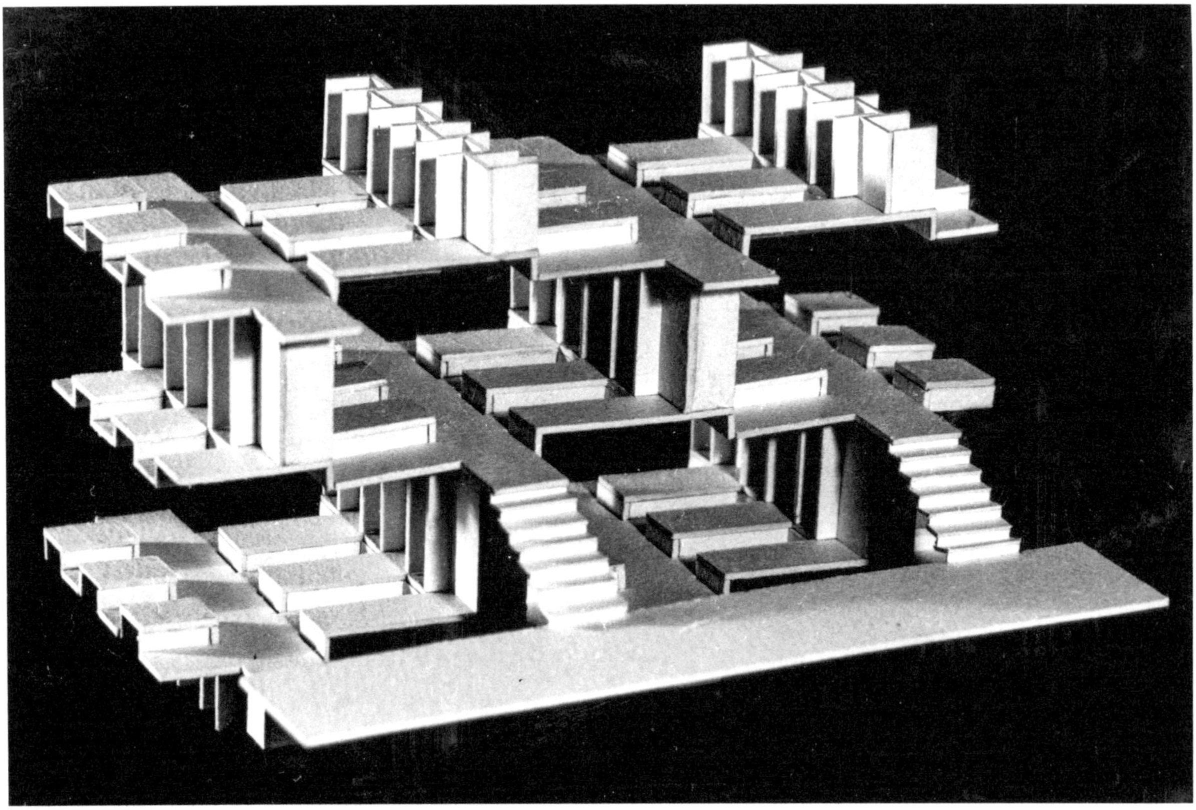

11.5 Models of housing units
11.6 Model showing circulation and floor iterations

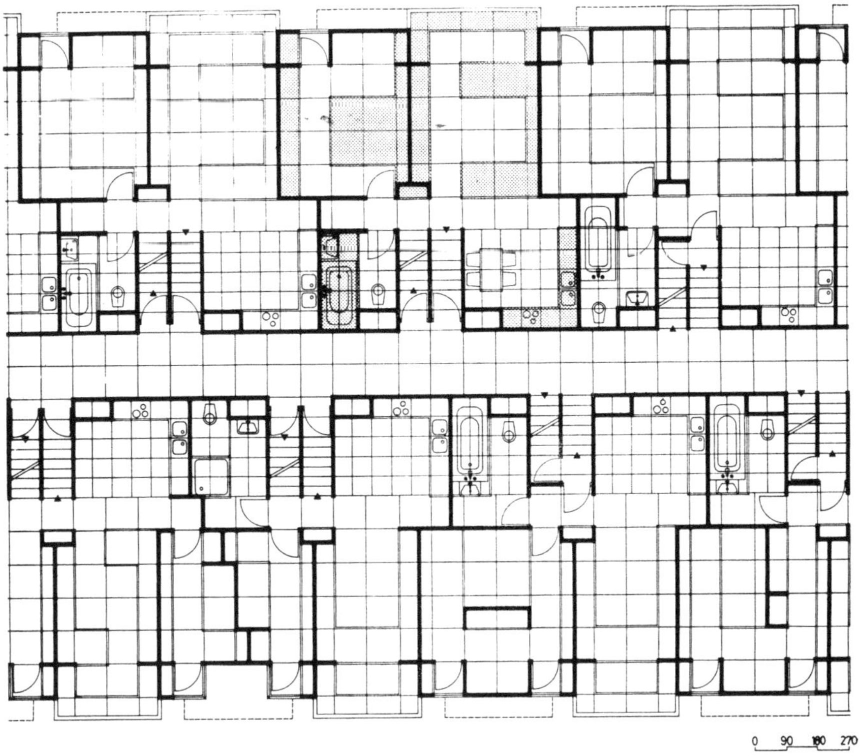

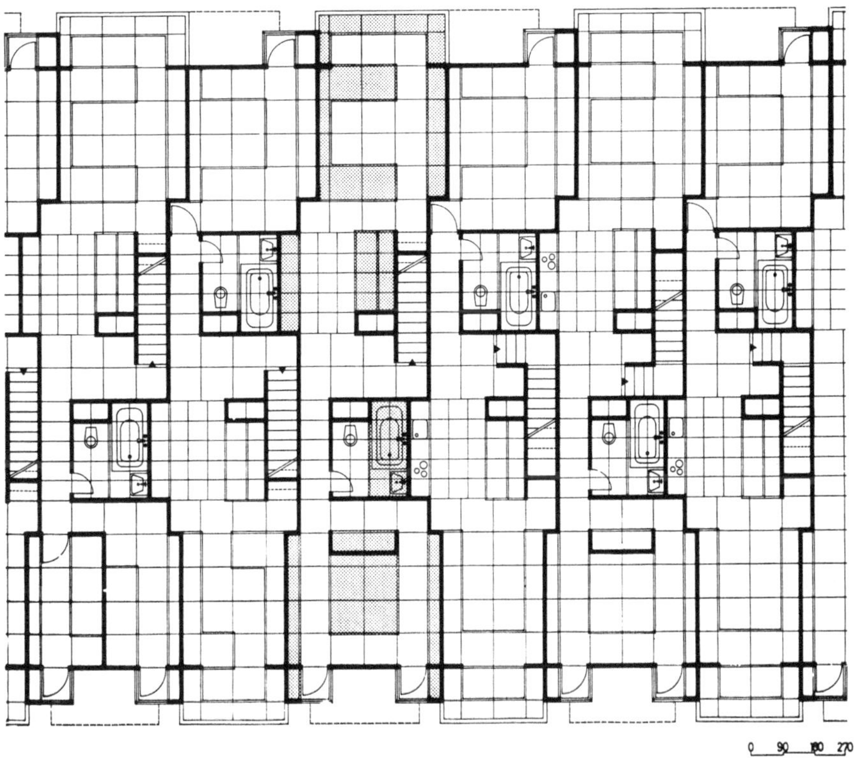

11.7 Variations of the plan arrangement

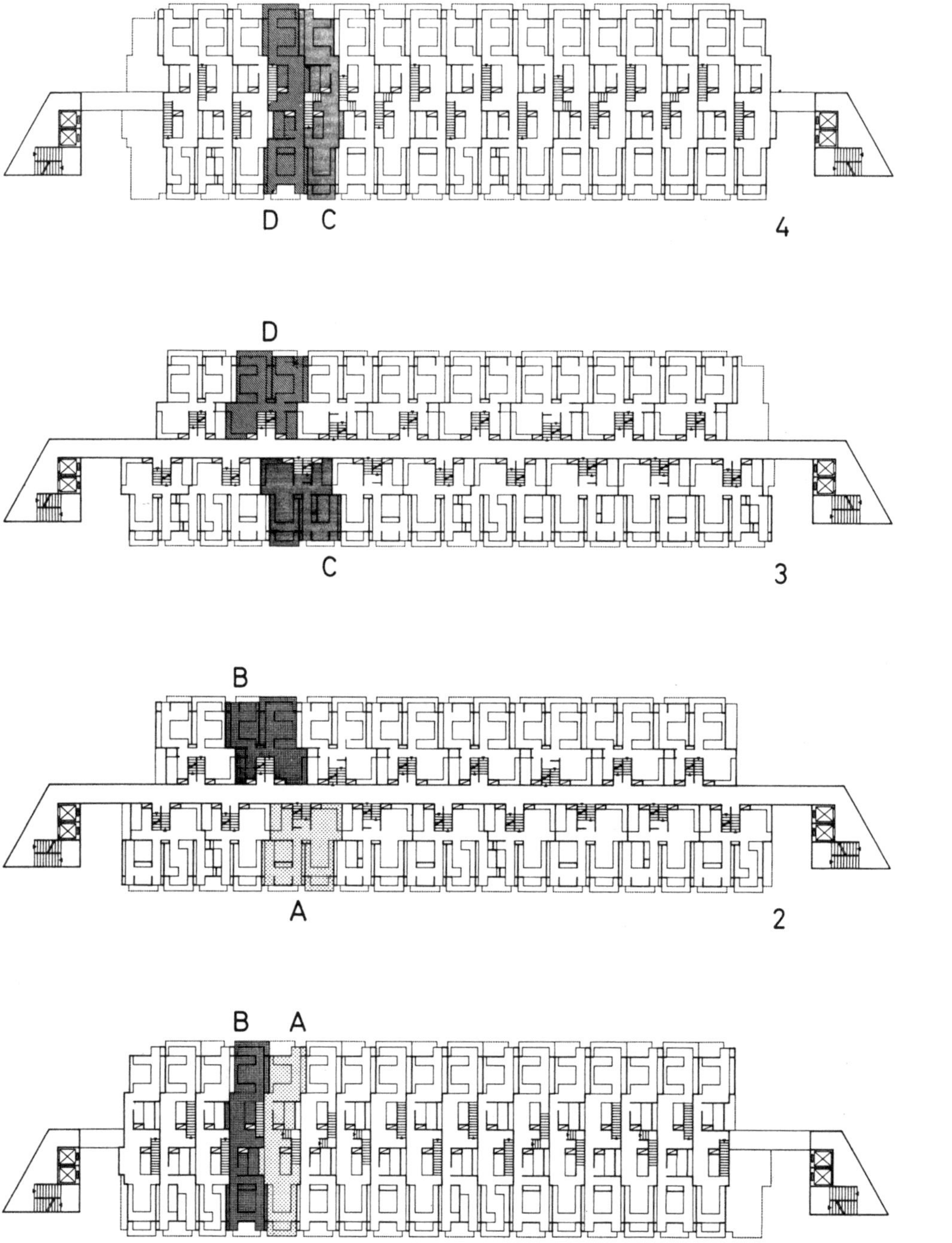

11.8 Floor plans

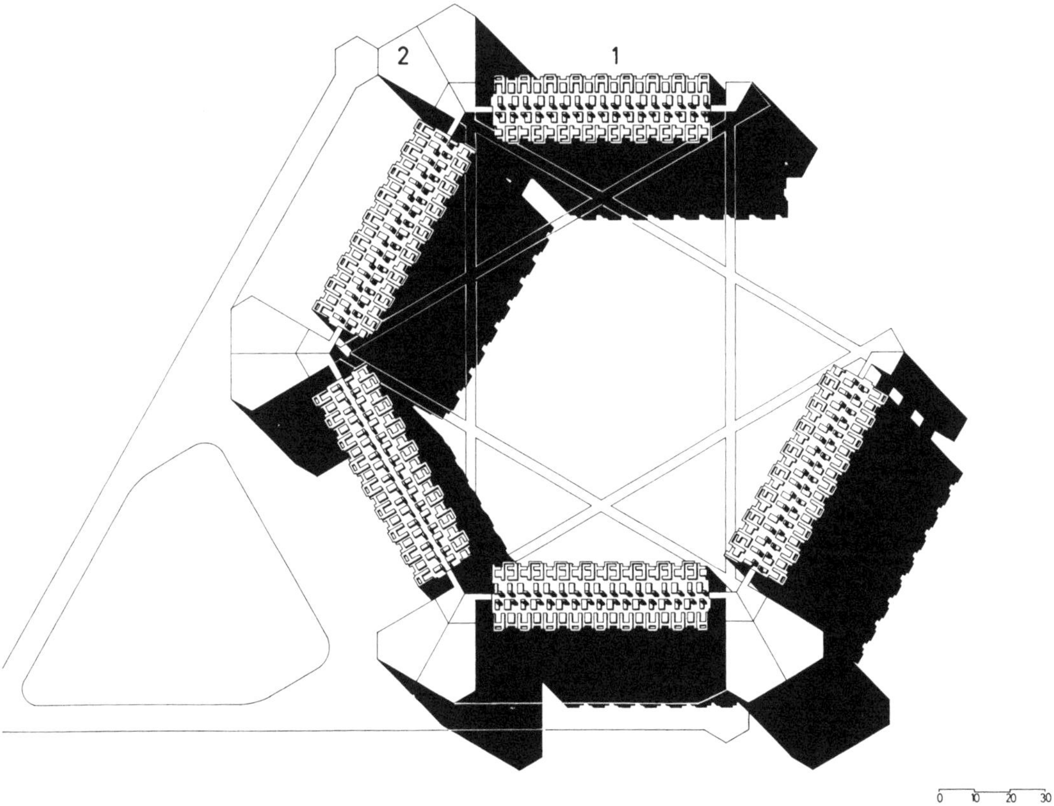

11.9 Layout of dormitory buildings [1] with common shared spaces between them [2]

12 Bat Yam Town Hall and Civic Center 1959–63
Bat Yam, Israel

With Zvi Hecker, Eldar Sharon

The Bat Yam Town Hall and Civic Center began as an architectural proposal, submitted by Zvi Hecker and Eldar Sharon, two of Alfred Neumann's former students, to a national competition for the design of a town hall in the new city of Bat Yam in 1959. The two young architects won the competition, and invited Neumann to collaborate with them on working through the design and realizing the project.

First, Neumann proposed to relocate the town hall from its proposed site in a newly developed part of Bat Yam to a larger, rectilinear lot on the city periphery, a short walk away from the Mediterranean Sea. The greater size and openness of this new site impelled the architects to expand the design into a larger urban civic space. Neumann proposed a large rectangular public square enclosed by a continuous, three- to four-story building with retail space on the ground floor and offices stacked above. The town hall, oriented at 45 degrees to the axis of the public square, is a freestanding, built object inside its southern end.

Neumann also reworked Hecker and Sharon's design of the town hall building itself. In their competition submission, they had proposed a three-story building with each floor extended beyond the one below it, yielding an inverted ziggurat form, with an open, public, atrium-like space in the center of the plan. Neumann retained this initial massing, but reworked the spatial logic of the building by implementing his proportion system and early space-packing ideas. He conceived of the structure as a composition of several small, repeated office-space modules along the exterior periphery of each floor, scaled optimally to human use according to the EM-PHI system. These units formed a pattern on the building's façade, uniting the building's spaces, structure, and façade into one complete system. This pattern was created by Neumann's imposition of a 45-degree structural grid over the rectilinear building to define the forms of the volumetric units and ultimately govern the building's overall visual and spatial pattern.

In the Bat Yam Town Hall and Civic Center design, Neumann realized for the first time the use of his space-packing approach and EM-PHI system—methods that would inform all his subsequent architectural projects. Although Neumann wrestled with new architectural ideas and applied them to the building design often, as in this case, while the building was being constructed, in the Bat Yam Town Hall and Civic Center project, they produced an icon of 1960s Israeli architecture.

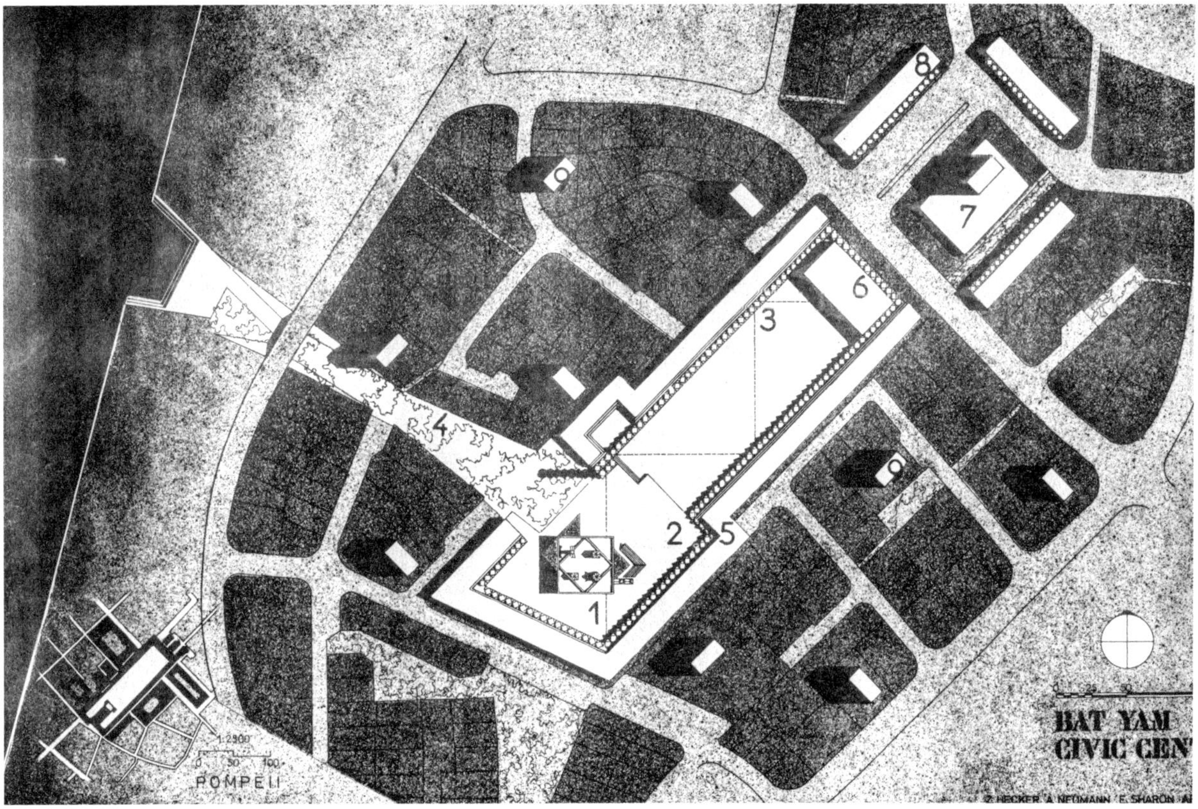

12.1 Site plan: [1] Town hall, [2–3] Public square, [4] Pedestrian boulevard leading to the sea, [5] Three-story retail and office building

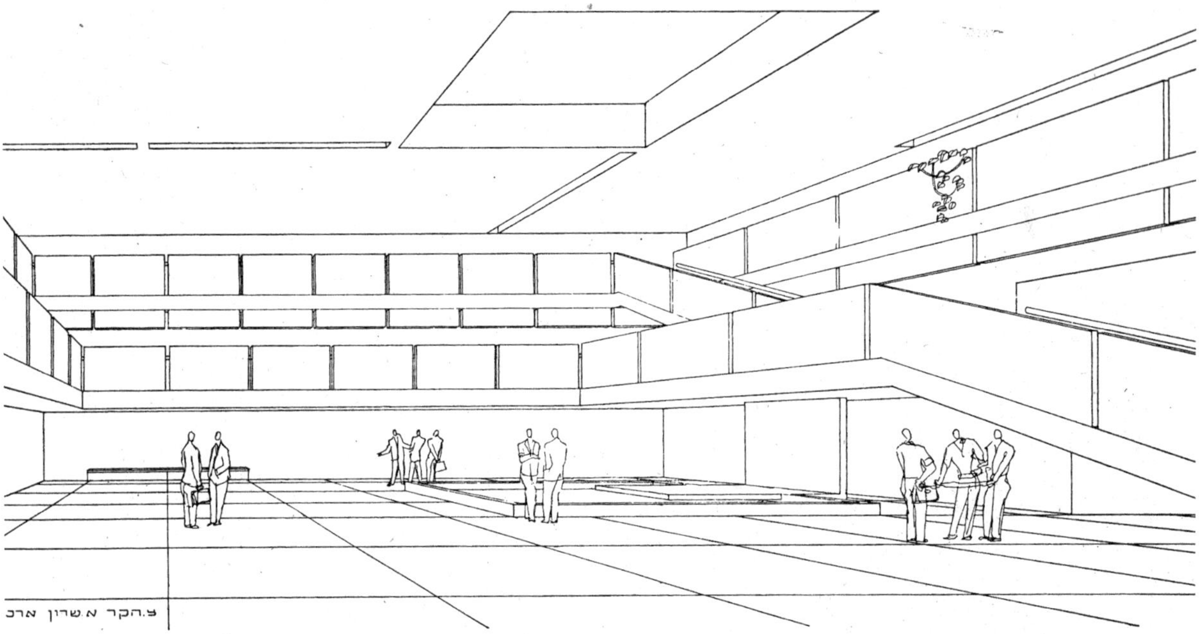

תכנית (אולם הכניסה) בנין בית עירית בת־ים

12.2 View of interior, competition entry for Bat Yam Town Hall, by Zvi Hecker and Eldar Sharon

12.3 Early model for town hall
12.4 Early version of model right after the competition stage

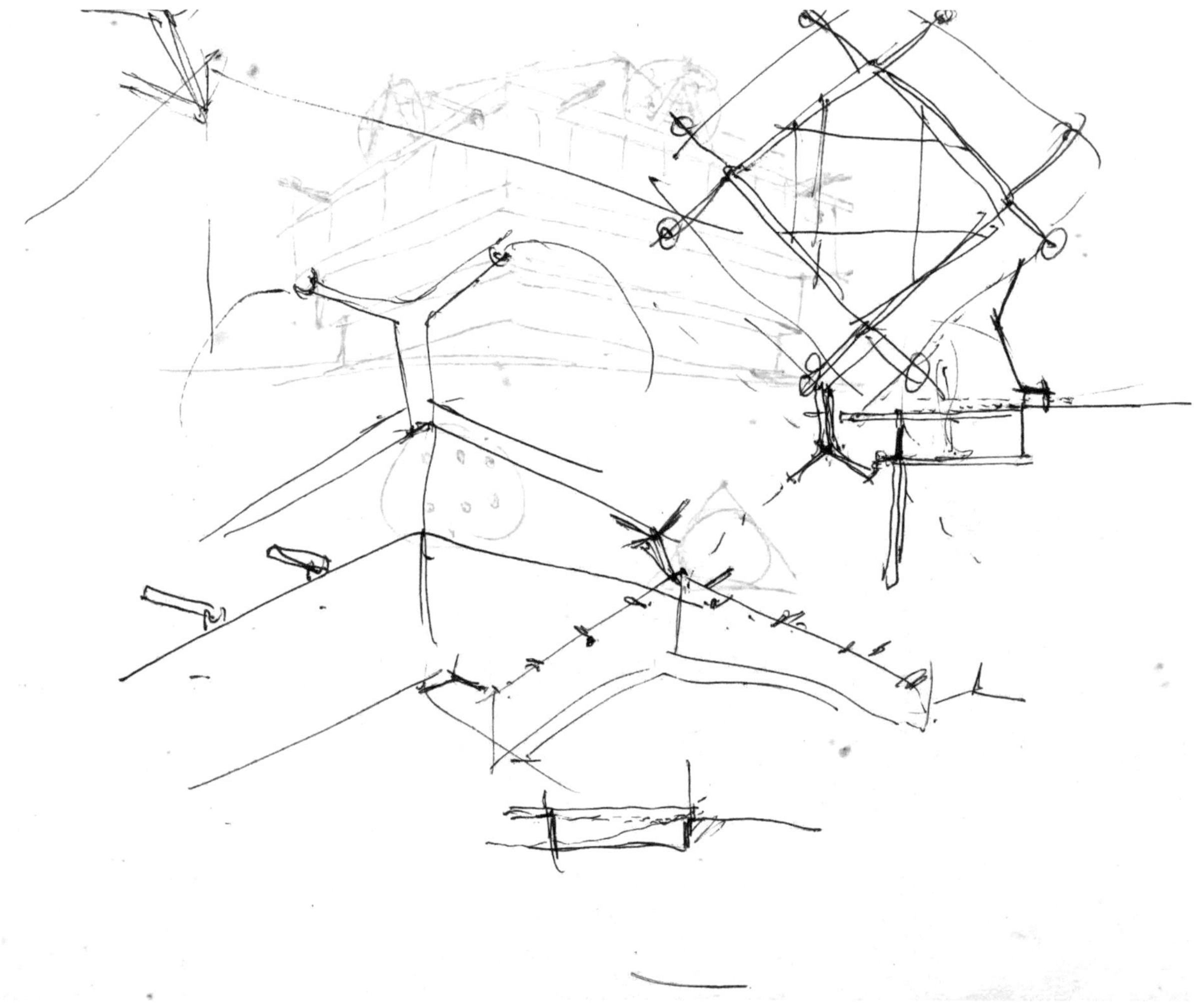

12.5 Early sketches by Neumann exploring the 45° geometry imposed onto the orthogonal structure

12.6 View of the town hall at completion, southern fringe of Bat Yam

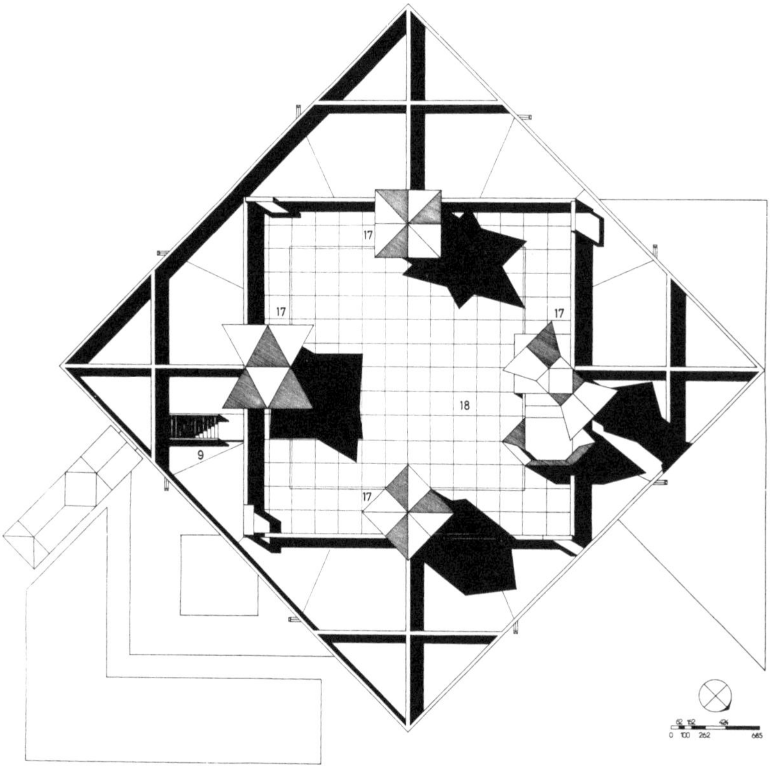

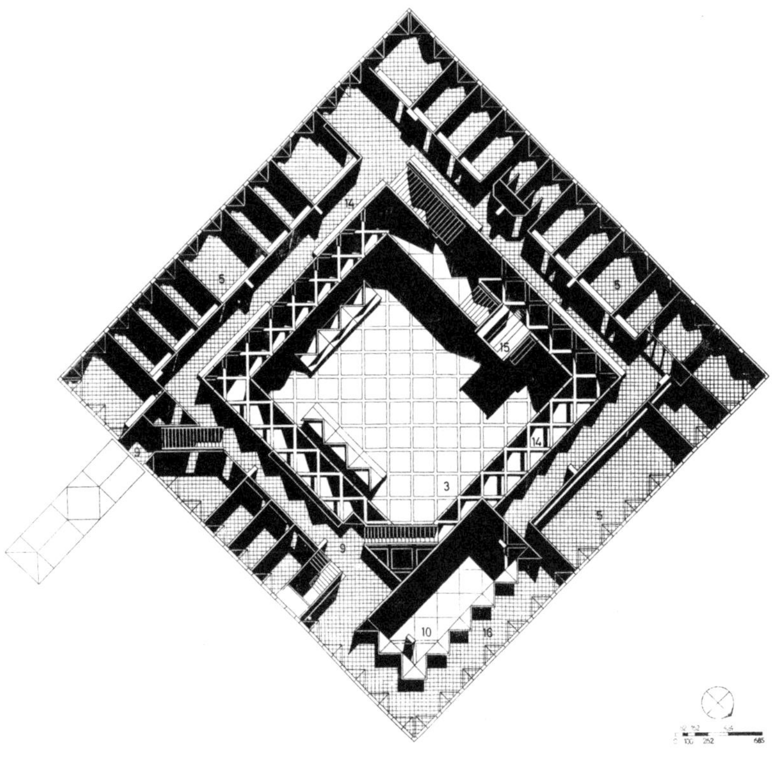

12.7 Roof plan
12.8 Shaded plan showing central space open to the public

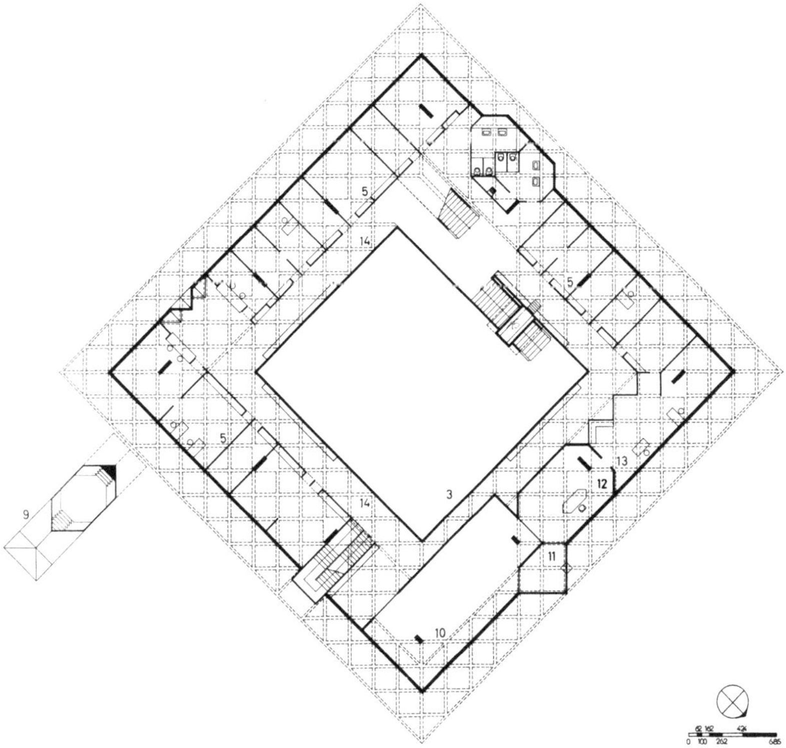

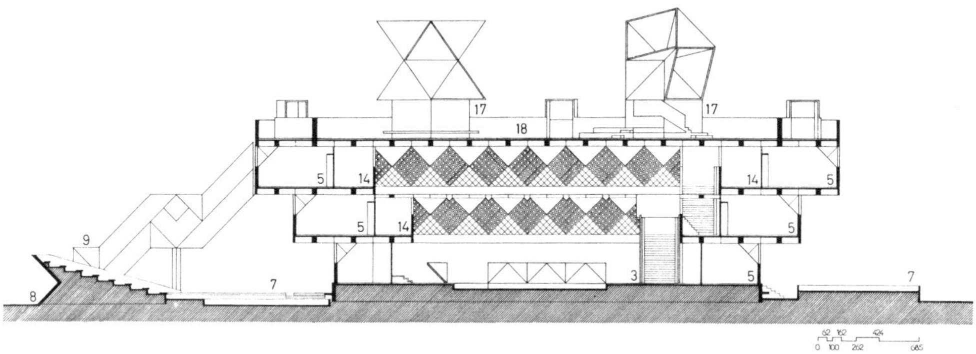

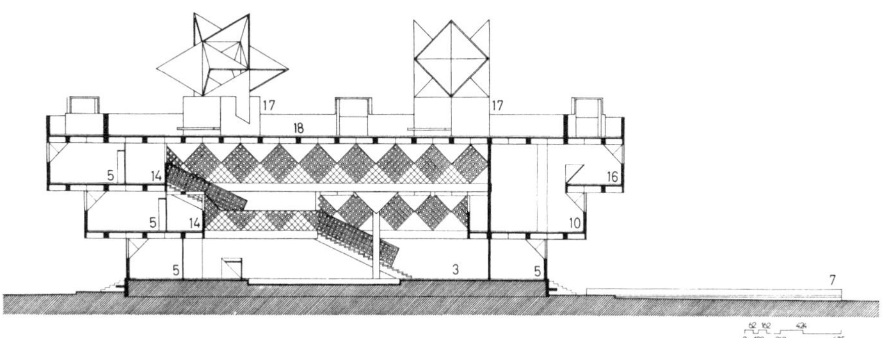

12.9 Third floor plan
12.10 Sections

12.11 Model view without roof exposing interior space

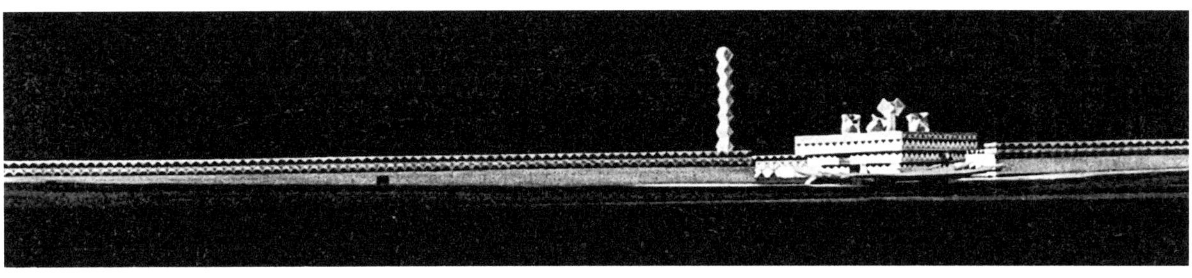

12.12 Model views of proposed Bat Yam Civic Center complex

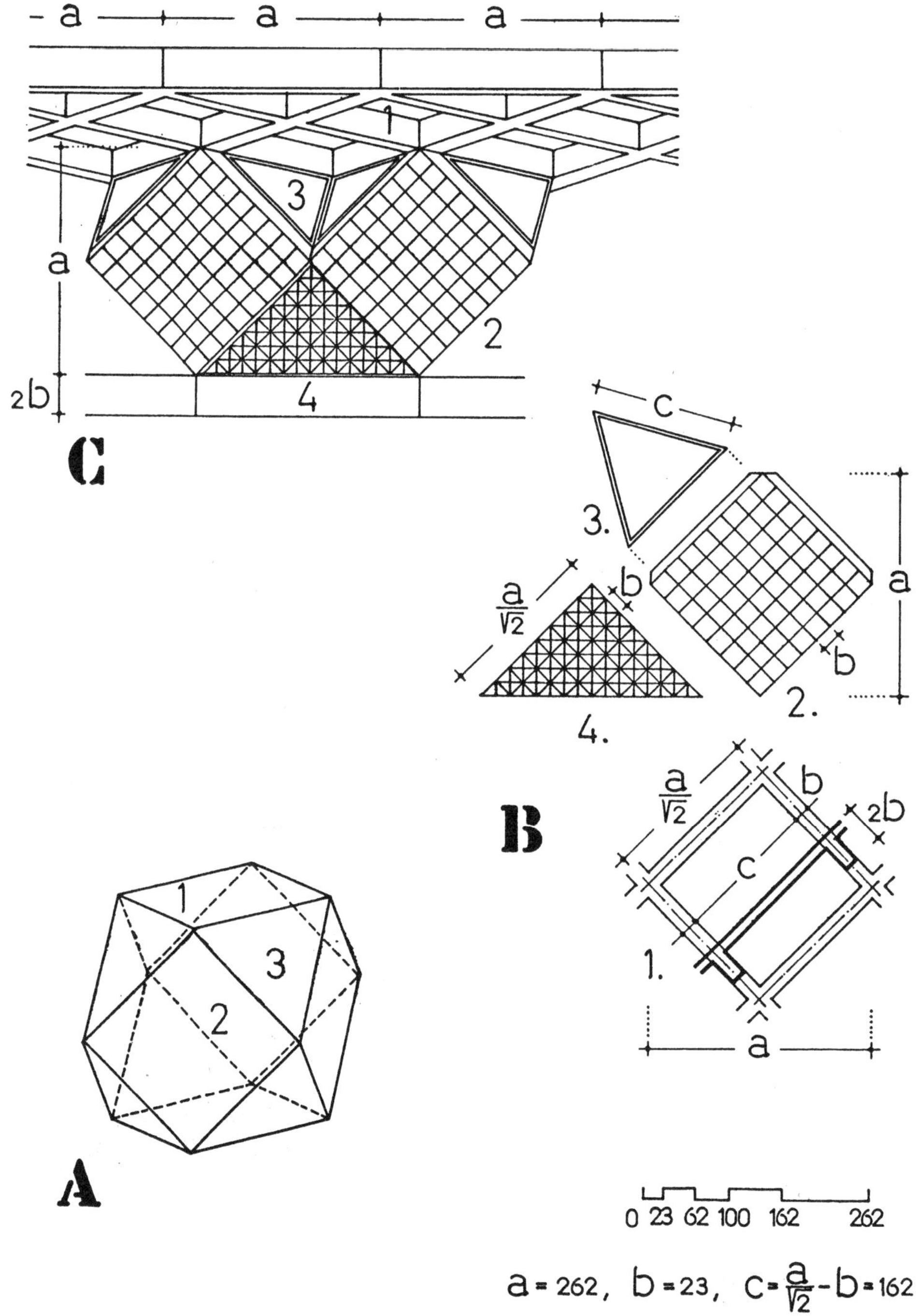

12.13 Basic geometric unit, cuboctahedron; fit to the dimensions of Alfred Neumann's MΦ system

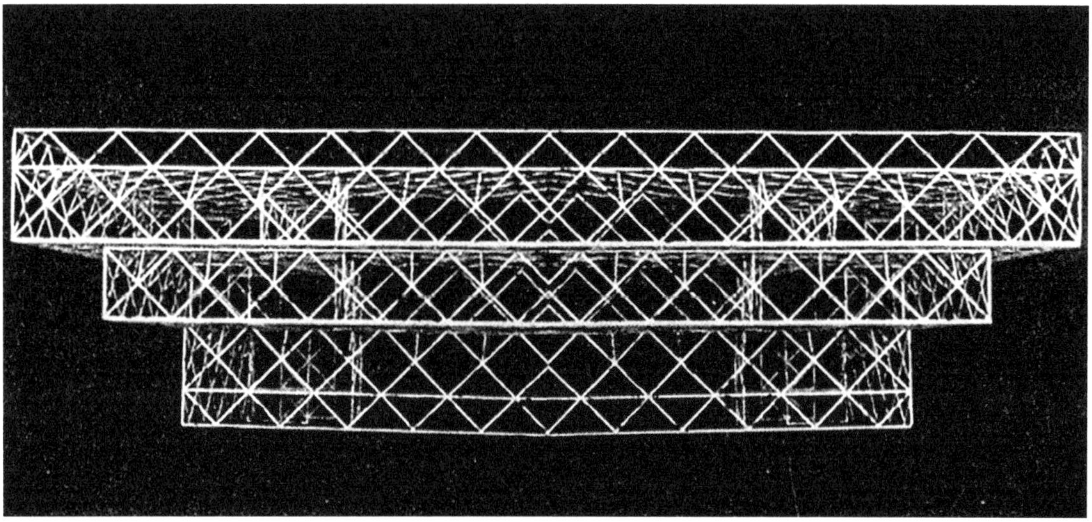

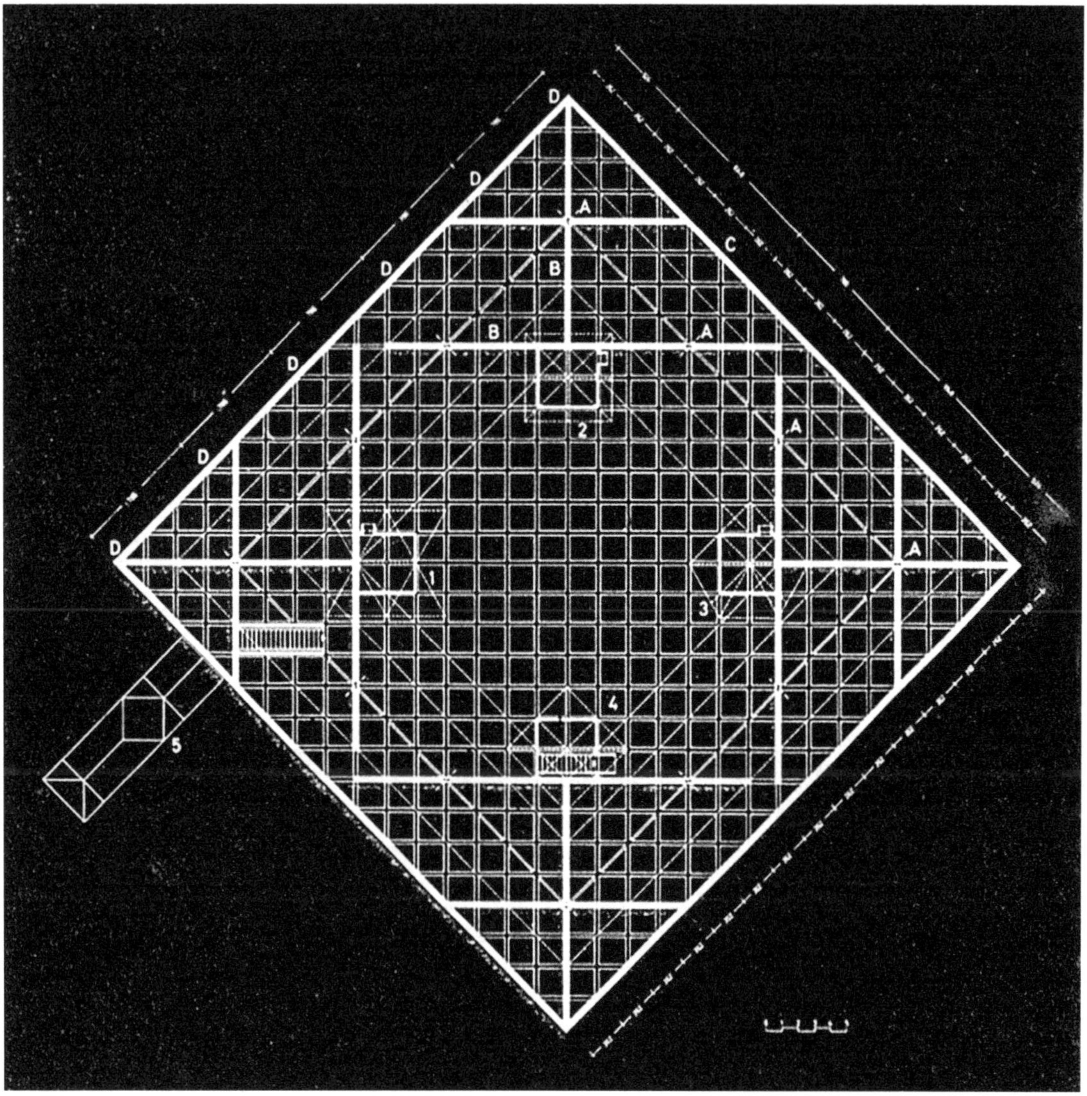

12.14 Model of structural system
12.15 Structural ceiling plan

12.16 Model of units
12.17 Model view with light chimneys

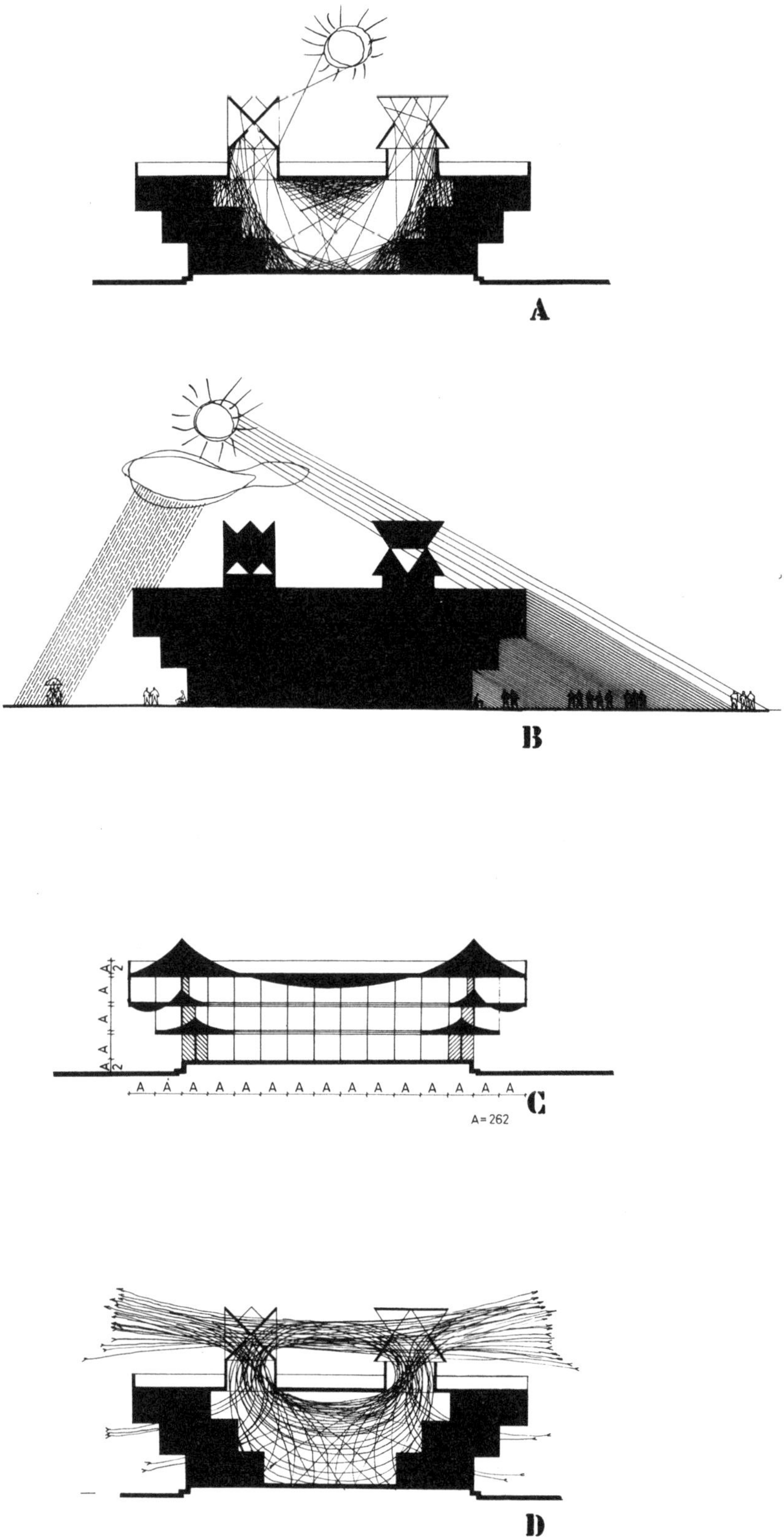

12.18 Diagram showing reaction of building to environmental conditions: (A) Sunlight, (B) Rain and shade, (C) Structural behavior, (D) Natural ventilation.

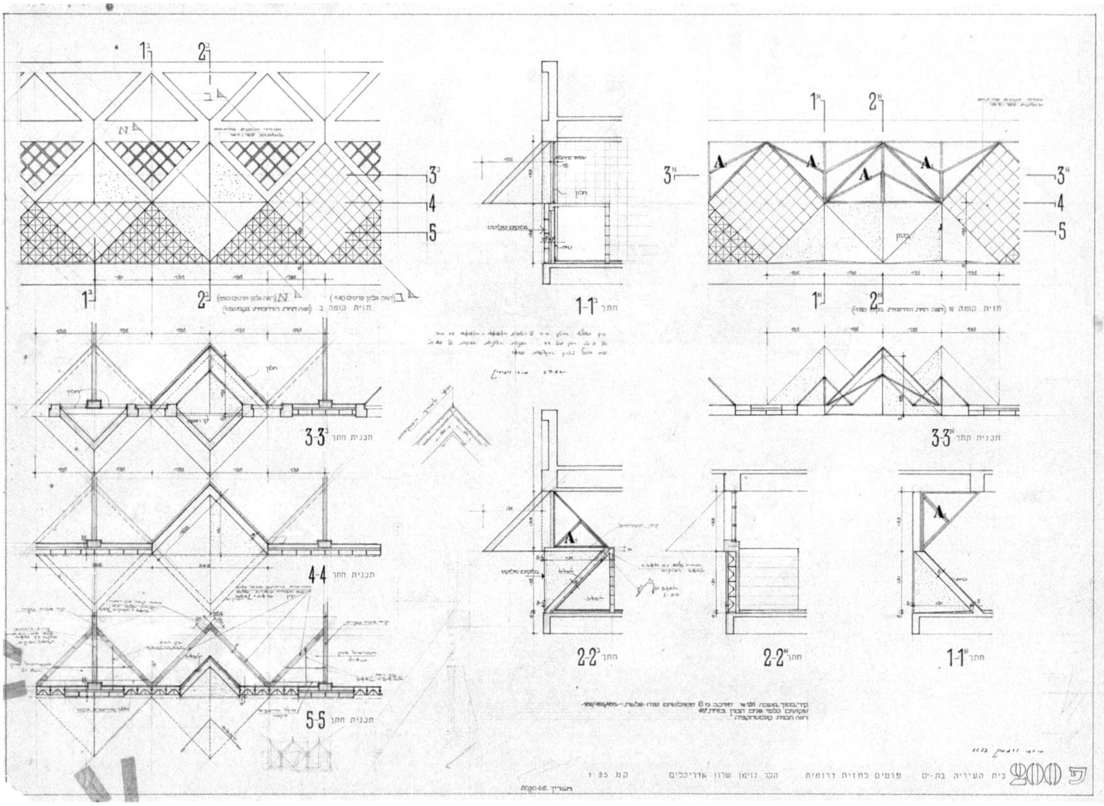

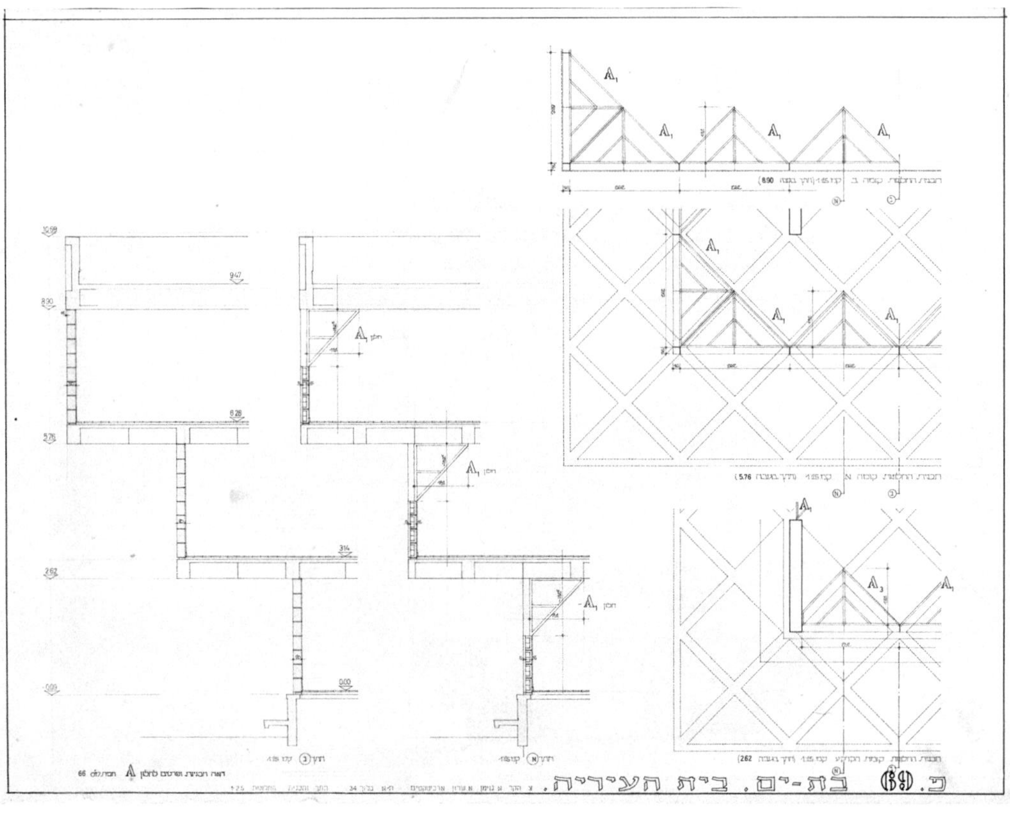

12.19 Original construction drawings

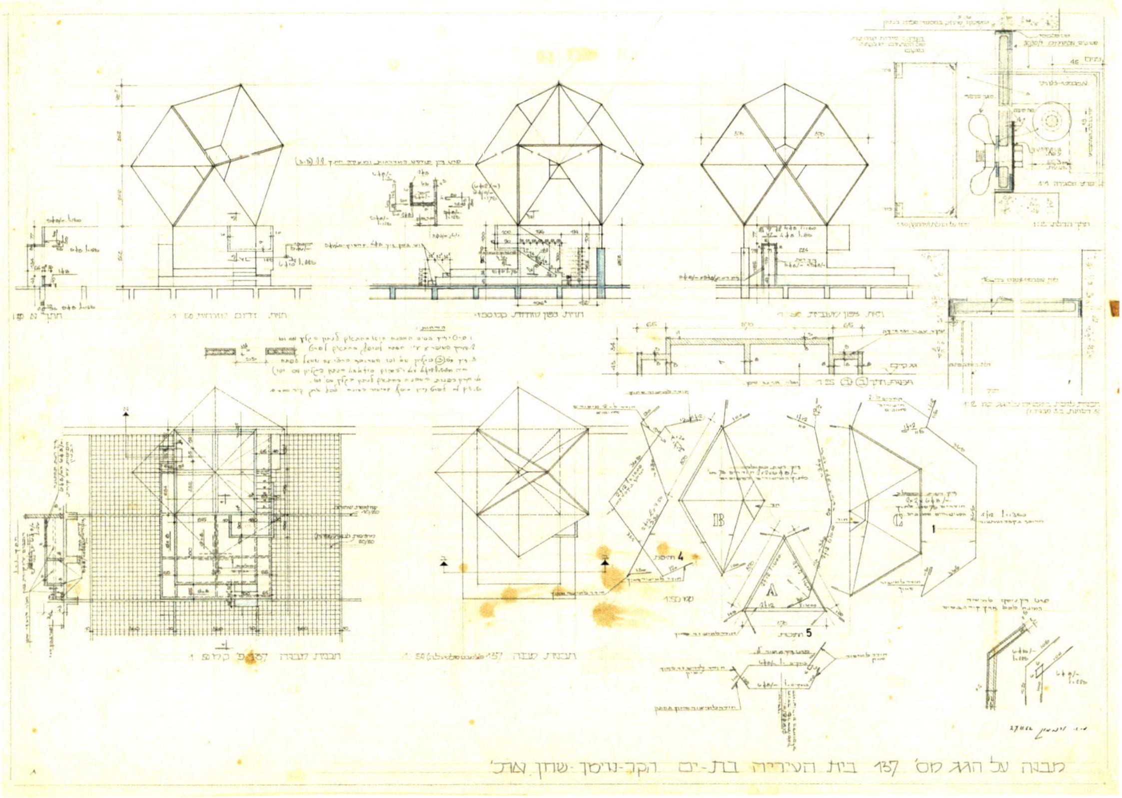
מבנה על הגג מס' 137 בית העיריה בת-ים הקר-נוימן-שרון ארכ'

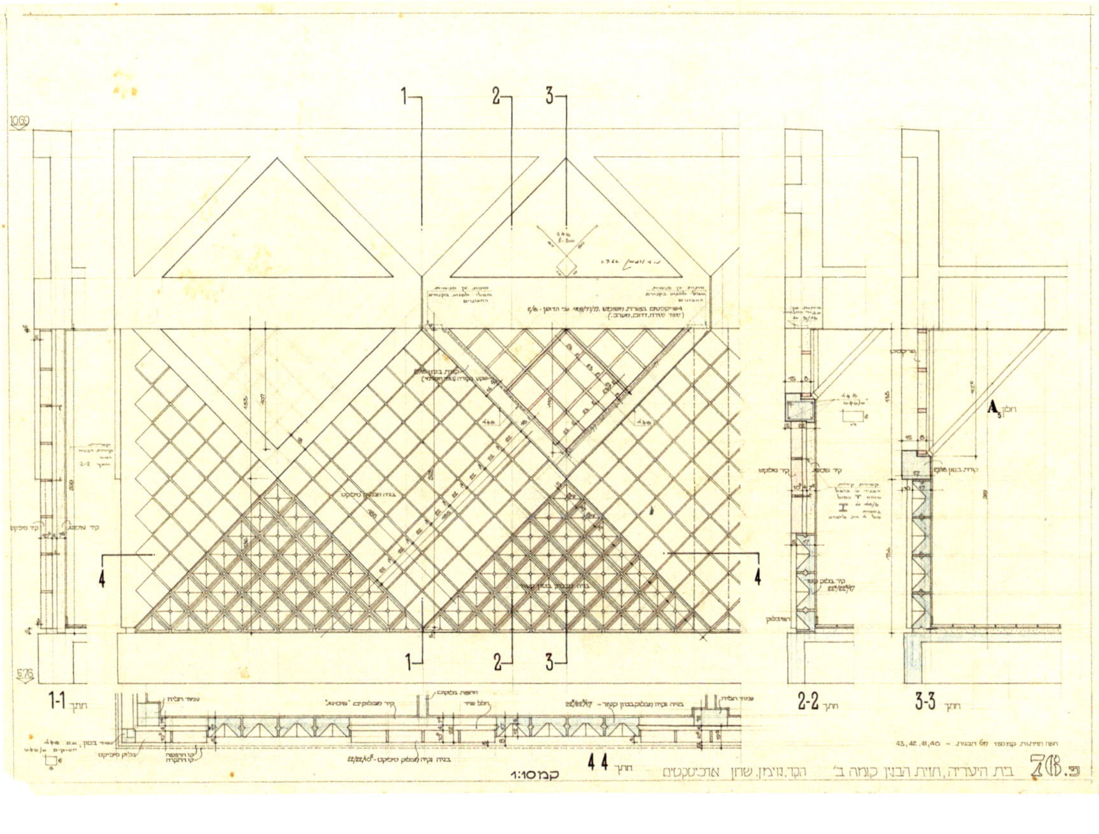
בית העיריה, חזית הבנין קומה ב' הקר, נוימן, שרון ארכיטקטים
קנ"מ 1:10

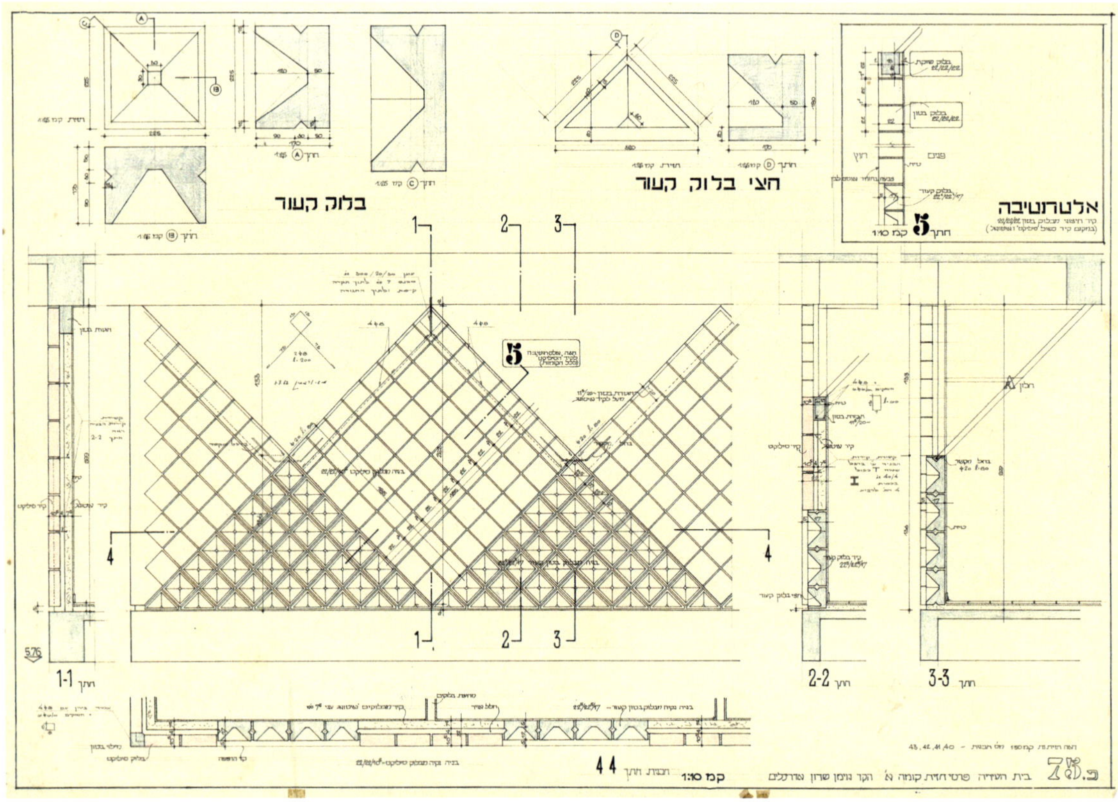

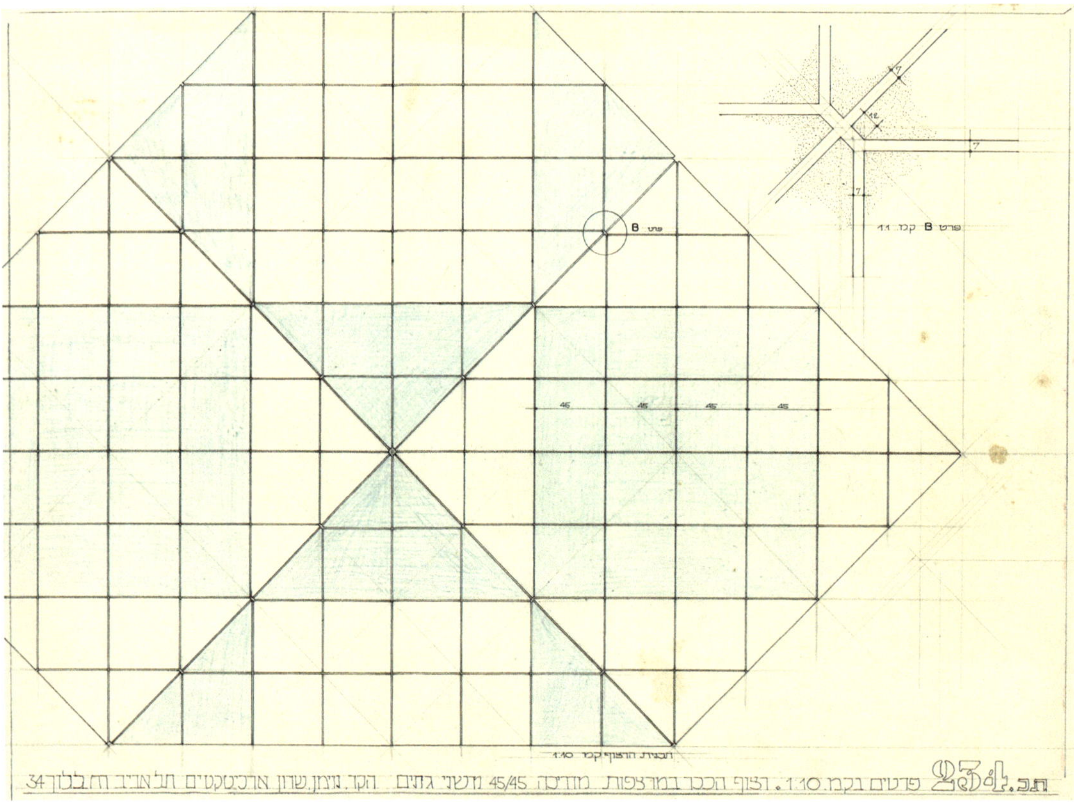

 12.20 Original construction drawings

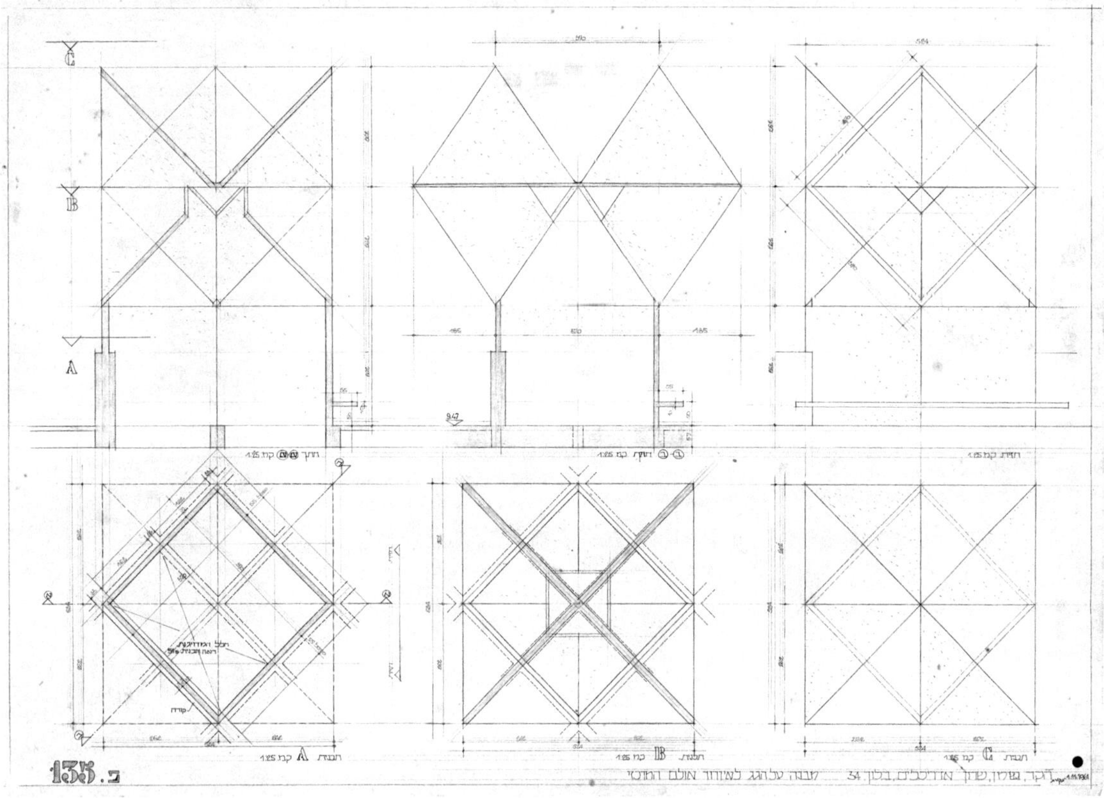
ב. 135

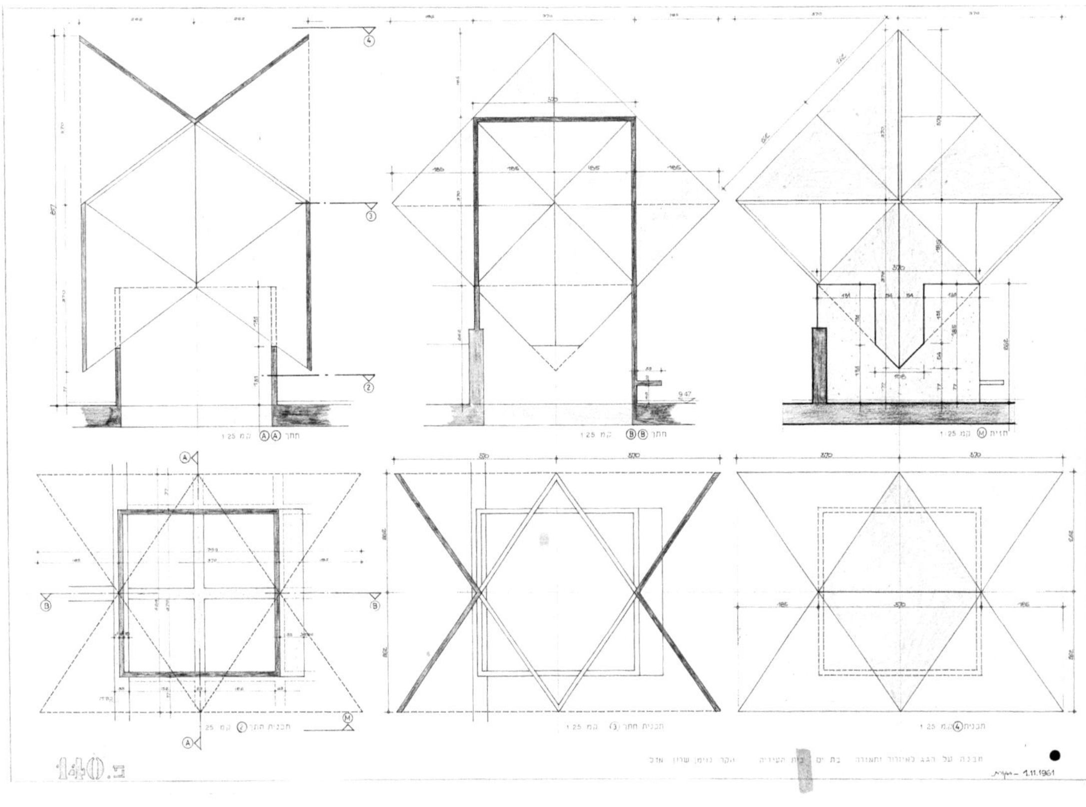
ב. 140

12.22

12.23

12.24 Views of building during final stages of construction

12.25
12.26

12.27
12.28

12.29 Interior views of offices

12.30
12.31

12.32
12.33

12.34

13 Club Méditeranée Holiday Camp 1960–61
Achziv, Israel

With Zvi Hecker, Eldar Sharon

In the late 1950s, the French resort company Club Méditerranée (Club Med) began to expand into the Middle East. They chose to build in Achziv, a white sandy beach beside the ruins of a Palestinian village in northern Israel. Club Med first asked Eldar Sharon's father's firm to design a holiday camp for the Achziv site. As A. Sharon-Idelson Architects—by that time one of the largest and most established architectural firms in Israel—was preoccupied with a number of other significant commissions, however, in 1960 Sharon senior passed the project along to his son's new architectural partnership, Neumann-Hecker-Sharon.

Club Med's early resort villages were essentially clusters of straw huts on beach sites, and this concept was part of the brief the company presented for the new Achziv location. Once Neumann-Hecker-Sharon received the commission, however, Neumann decided to revise the conventional hut design, and instead proposed a truncated-tetrahedron form for each accommodation unit. Initially Club Med was skeptical of Neumann's design, and the French representative in charge of the commission requested to see a full-scale mock-up before approving his plan. As a result of the hut's multifaceted, tetrahedral geometry, its entrance openings were rather small and triangular, and would force users to bend down in order to pass through them. The Club Med representative who came to inspect Neumann-Hecker-Sharon's plywood mock-up was exceptionally tall, and the architects momentarily feared that their design would be rejected. To their great relief it was approved, however, and soon thereafter construction commenced in earnest.

Neumann's tetrahedral hut design was visually complex, but exceedingly simple. First, six triangular wooden frames were arranged radially and joined together with metal cleats to form a hexagonal panel. These protruded slightly toward the center to yield a mildly convex form that enhanced their structural rigidity. Next, the panels were were filled in with dried and pressed straw and bound together with wire. Finally, three of the hexagonal panels were joined together to form a floorless truncated tetrahedron. Ample shelter, along with openings for sunlight, air, and entryways, were affordances intrinsic to the planar geometry of the design. Neumann's use of dried, pressed straw was not

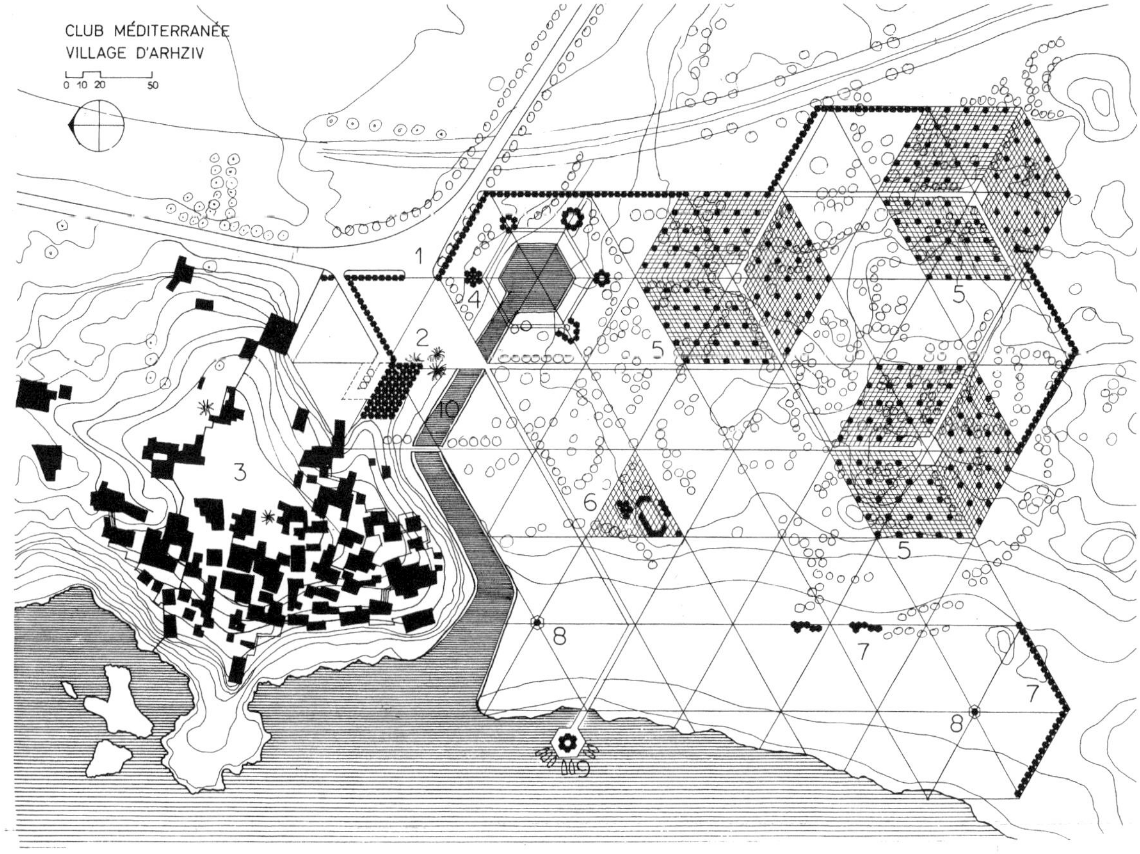

only in keeping with Club Med's conventional resort village designs, but this construction method also reflected the region's local building traditions. Palestinians in the villages of northern Galilee crafted straw and reed mats which they often used as cladding for their round agricultural huts. Further, straw construction was simple and inexpensive, and the structures could be disassembled for winter storage and re-erected in the summer season.

The site plan at Achziv comprised 300 tetrahedral accommodation units spaced evenly across a hexagonal grid plan. Some of these huts accommodated two vacationers, but most were built to house three people, in support of Club Med's policy of bringing strangers together and encouraging singles to meet. The architects' proposal also included several similar structures, such as offices, a restaurant, kitchen, and bar, which were also fashioned from hexagonal, pressed-straw panels. The site also had a dance floor and areas shaded by parasols.

The holiday camp project at Achziv was Neumann-Hecker-Sharon's first completed and published project. Their innovative design was praised in Israel and also gained extensive international exposure, which was likely also due to Club Med's expanding presence and the growing popularity of its resorts. Neumann-Hecker-Sharon's inventive solution for a new kind of beach village led them to receive commissions from local Israeli companies for other holiday camp projects.

13.1 Site plan: [1] Entrance, [2] Dining hall, [3] Ruins of a Palestinian village, [4] Offices, [5] Cabins, [6] Bar, [7] Beach shade, [8] Showers, [9] Dock, [10] Canal

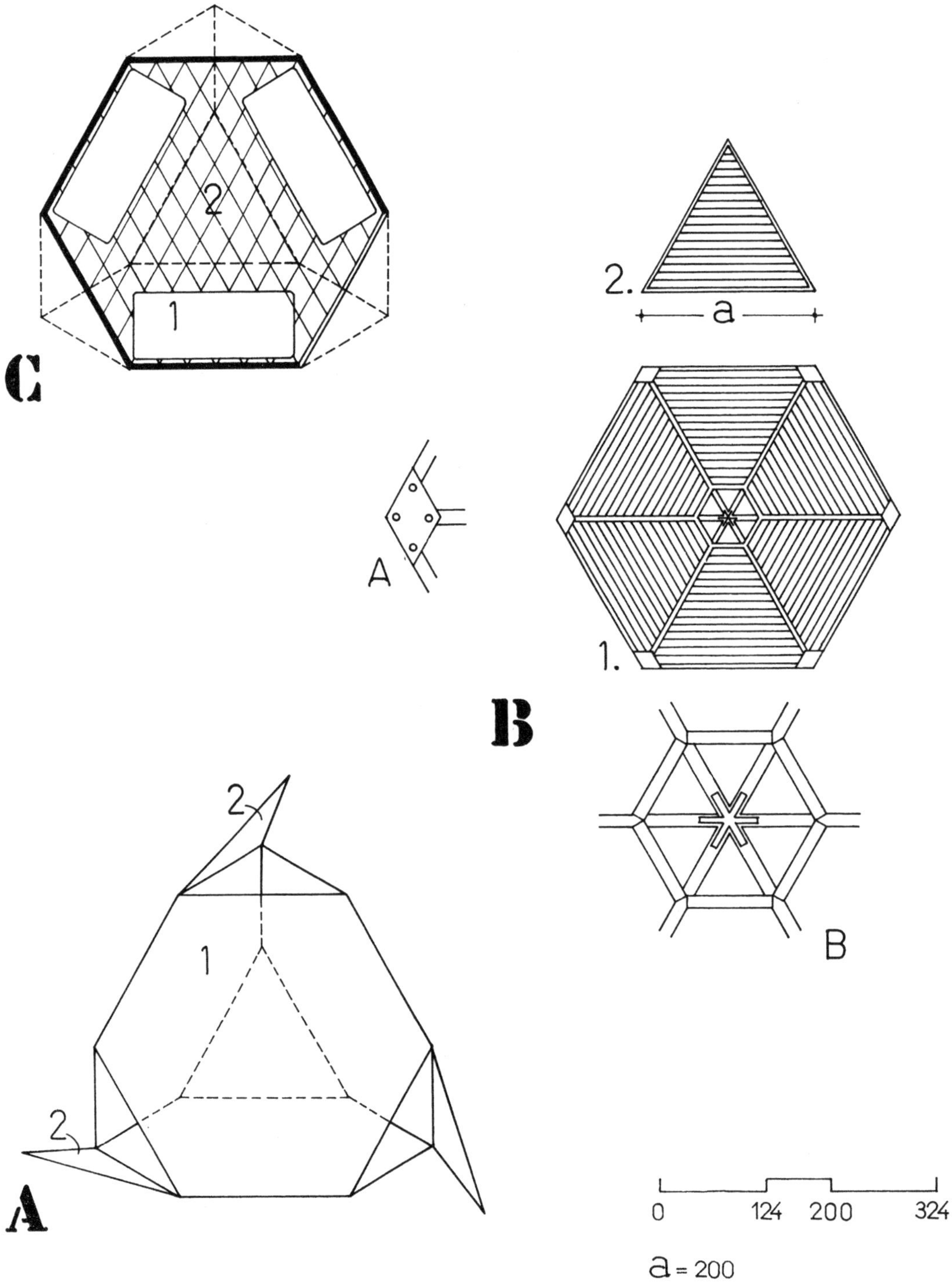

13.2 Unit comprising the three-bed cabin; dimensions follow Alfred Neumann's MΦ system

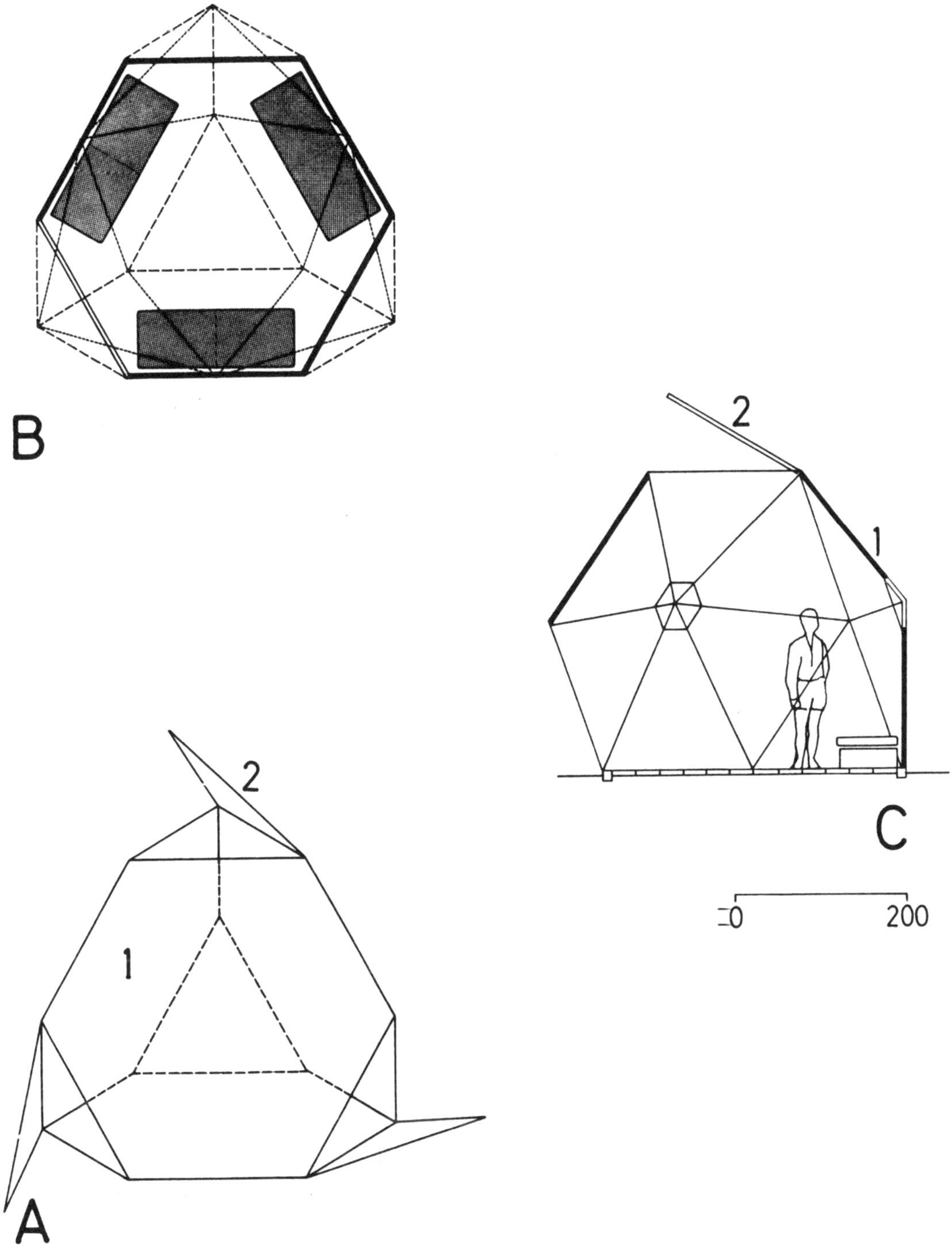

13.3 Drawings of cabin unit

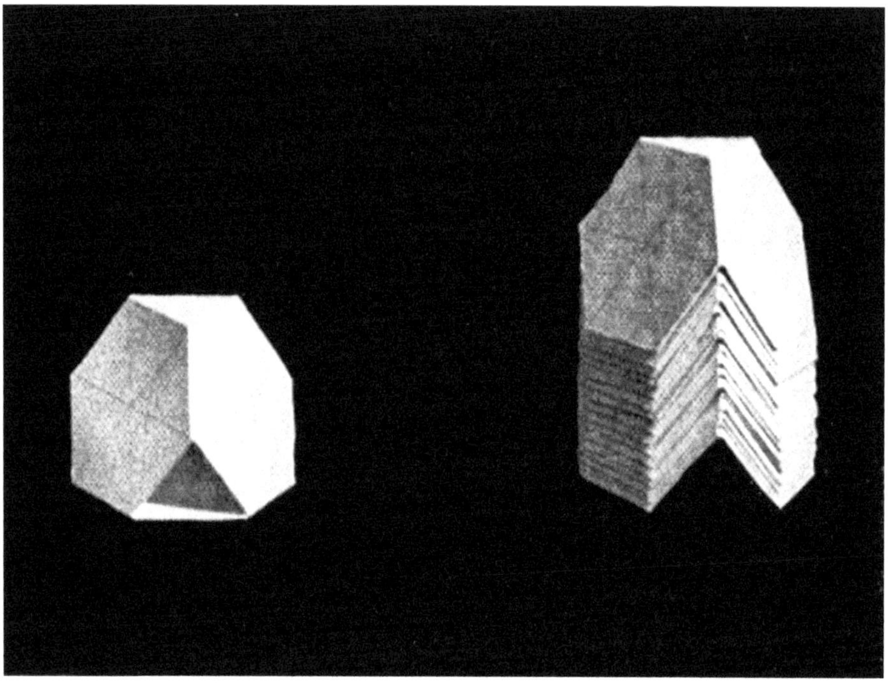

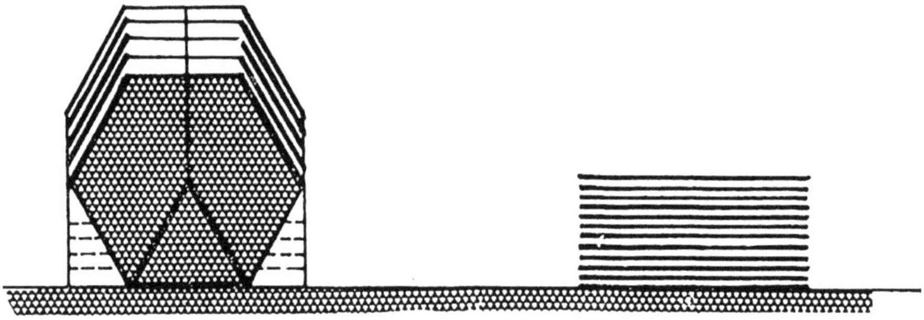

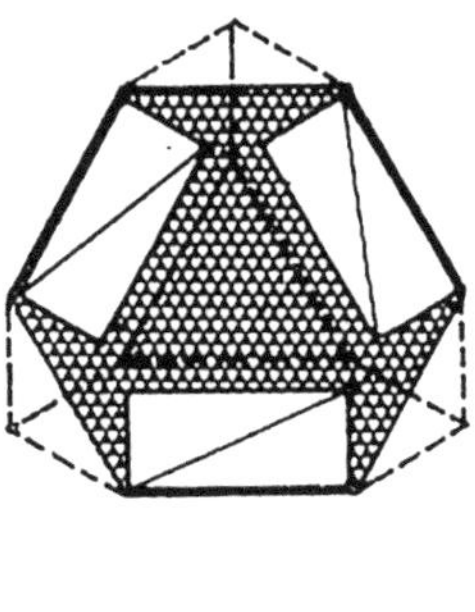

13.4 Model of unit and stacking system
13.5 Diagram of unit, stacking system for storage

13.6 Sun and wind diagrams

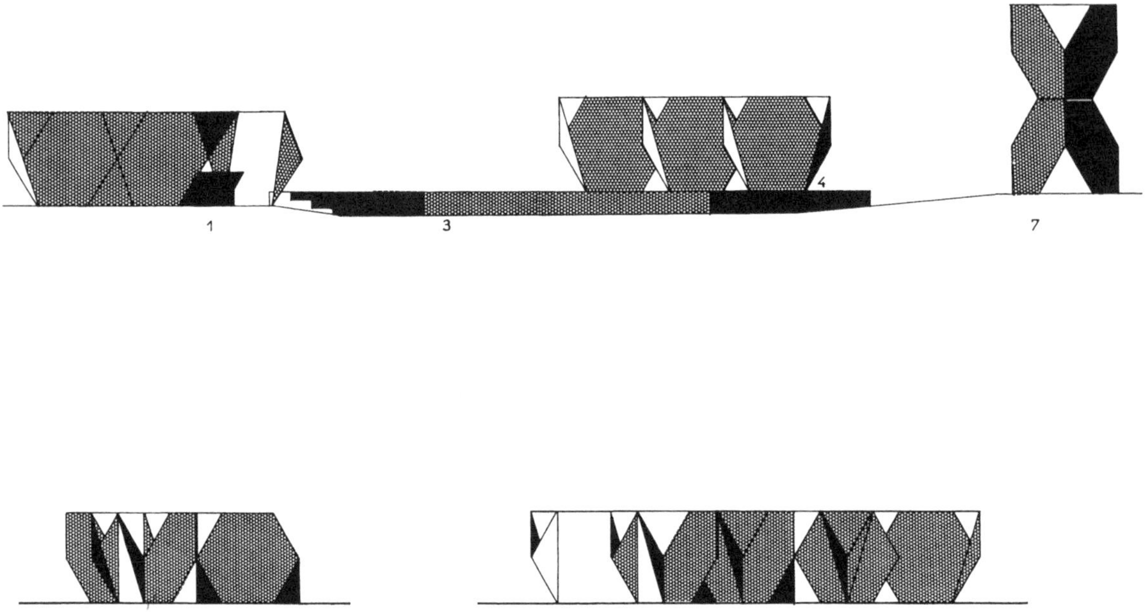

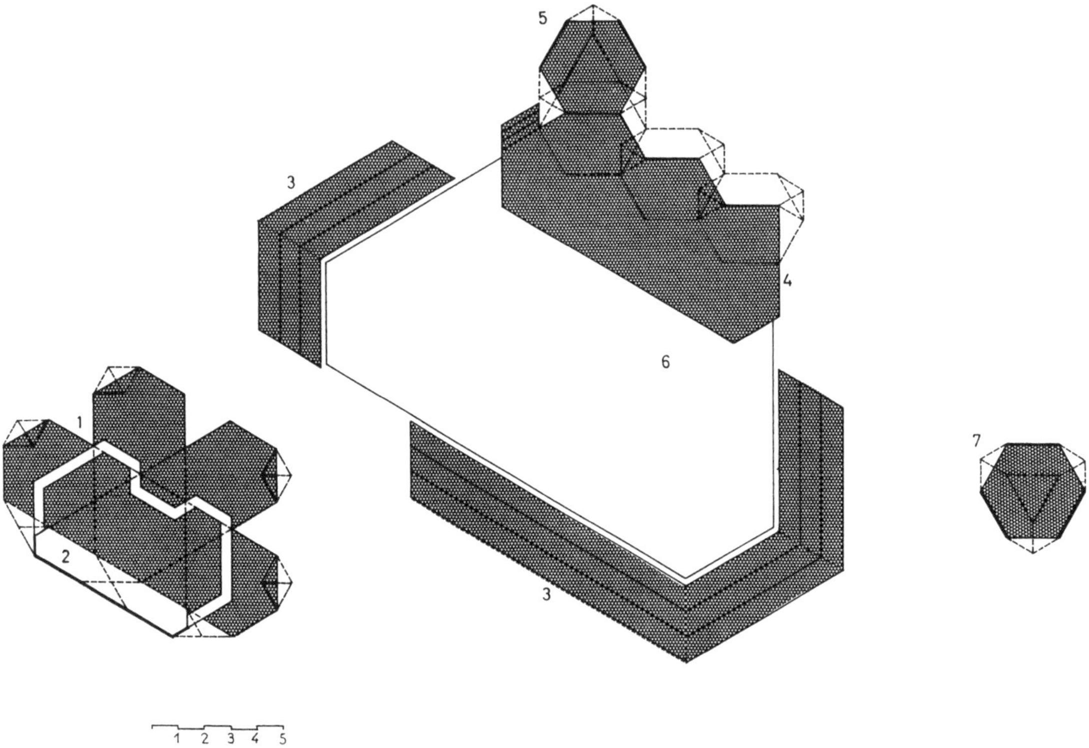

13.7 Outdoor bar and stacked lifeguard booth unit; section
13.8 Outdoor bar and lifeguard booth; plan

13.9 View of outdoor bar from the beach

13.10 View during construction of small water canal
13.11 View of dining area from the sea
13.12 View from the beach toward cabin area within the trees

13.13 View of dining area
13.14 Lifeguard booth composed of two units

13.15

13.16 Cabin units under construction in the office area
13.17 Detail of cabin units, a few units were constructed of plywood and some painted

13.18 View of offices structure
13.19 Beach shades

13.20 Beach shades

13.21 Inside view of beach shades
13.22 Cabin made of wooden frame and pressed straw

14 Michmoret Holiday Camp Michmoret, Israel 1963

With Zvi Hecker, Eldar Sharon

Thirty kilometers north of Tel Aviv near Netanya lies the Michmoret Holiday Camp designed as a resort village consisting of seventy small huts arranged along a gently sloping site around an artificial canal which pumps water in from the sea.

The huts were designed in the form of a truncated tetrahedron, like the units at Neumann-Hecker-Sharon's earlier holiday camp at Achziv. They were formed by four hexagonal panels made from timber frames filled in with dried and pressed straw, materials chosen for their light weight, shading and ventilation capabilities, and low cost. Each panel was bent to form three small hyperbolic paraboloids, which caused it to be slightly convex and pointed at its center. The creases in the panel served as openings for light and air ventilation.

Most of the cabins were constructed on the ground, using three panels joined together to form side walls, and sand as their base floor. Some of the units were elevated by being propped up atop a fourth panel, which served as the hut floor and was reinforced by an interior column 1 meter in height. Small triangular panels covered the apertures in the truncated tetrahedron, and could flip downward to form an entrance ramp from the ground up to the hut interior.

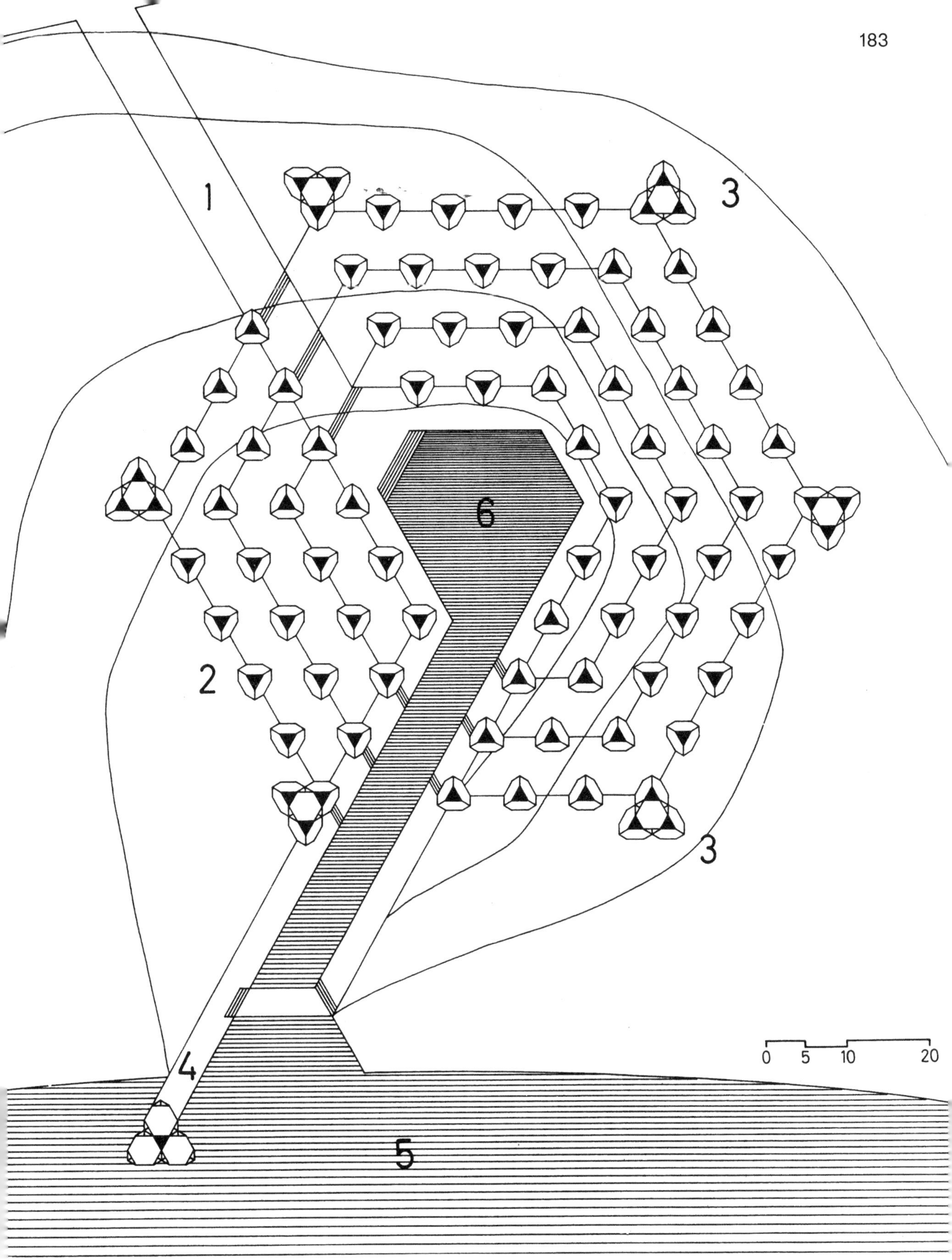

14.1 Site plan: [1] Entrance, [2] Cabins, [3] Combined larger units, [4] Dock, [5] Sea, [6] Pool

14.2 View of cabin area

14.3 View of cabins
14.4 Interior view of wall panel

14.5 Elevated cabin

15 Kiryat Yam Holiday Camp 1961
Kiryat Yam, Israel

With Zvi Hecker, Eldar Sharon

The Kiryat Yam Holiday Camp was built as a recreational site for schoolchildren in Haifa. At its center was a rectangular multi-use hall, which was surrounded on three sides by a line of octahedral hut units. Together, the units accommodated groups of 150 children often visiting for two weeks at a time.

Since the project brief stipulated that each hut was to house between seven and ten children, Neumann-Hecker-Sharon designed the units in the form of a truncated half-octahedron to yield a greater floor area than other polyhedral structures would have allowed. Each hut was 28 square meters in area, and was formed from four slightly convex panels with fixed apertures for light and ventilation. Neumann-Hecker-Sharon opted for timber and Canadex frames and straw thatching as building materials, as at the Achziv and Michmoret Holiday Camps.

The Kiryat Yam Holiday Camp was located in an area with strong winds and blowing sand, so the low hut units were designed on a continuous concrete bench profile 40 centimeters thick.

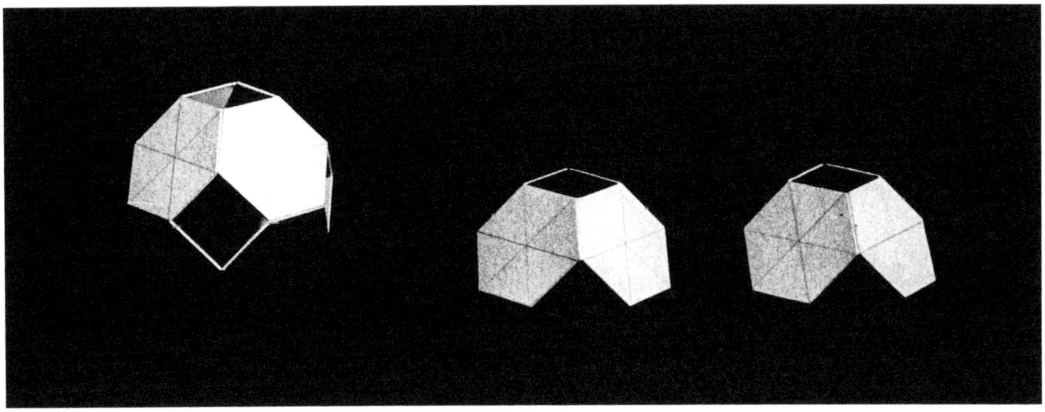

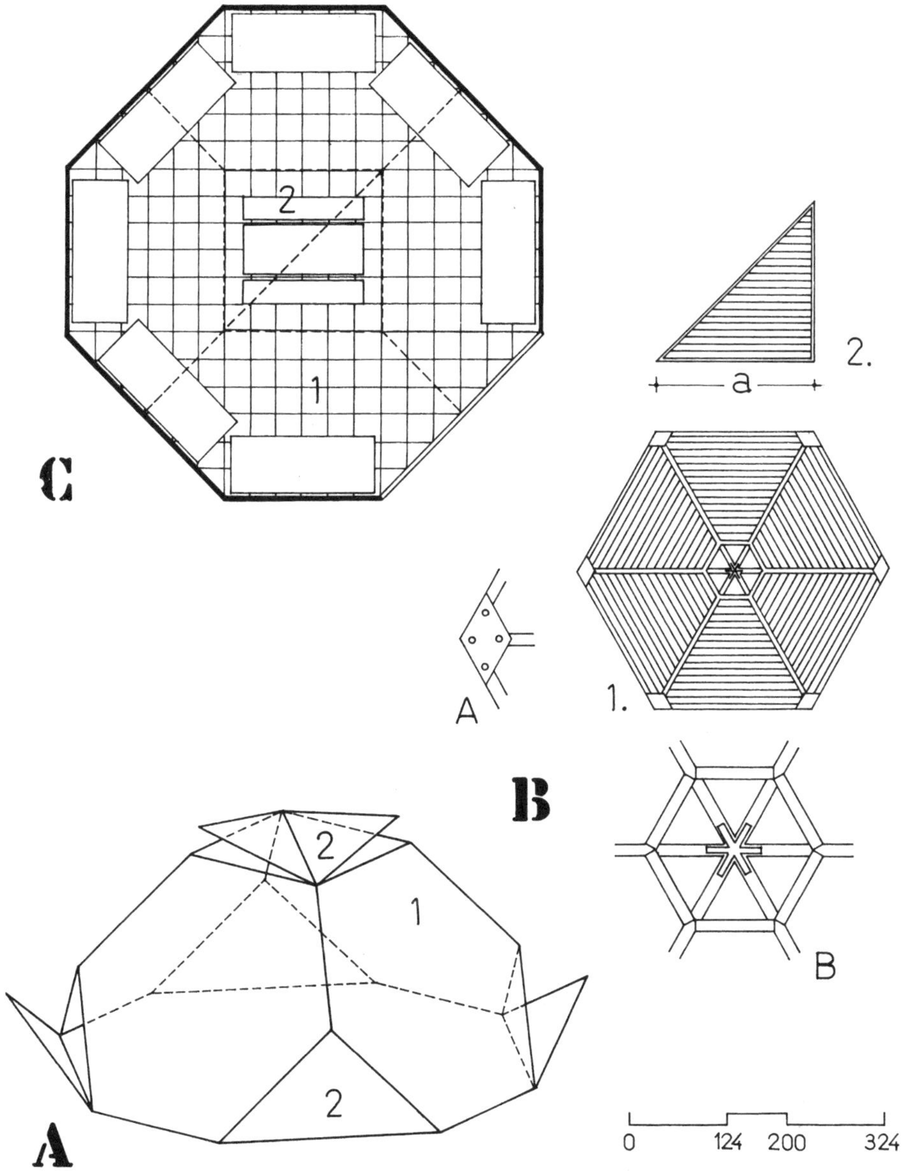

15.1 Models of unit
15.2 Larger cabin unit with seven beds and table (2) in the center

15.3 Views of shared dining area

15.4 View of seven-bed cabin
15.5 Cabin entrance

16 # Housing Complex, Arab Village Ein Rafa, Israel 1961–62

With Zvi Hecker, Eldar Sharon

The Ein Rafa project is a village complex for farmers and livestock breeders in the countryside near Jerusalem. The settlement comprises twenty housing units grouped around a central open area. The distinguishing feature of the housing units are their vaulted asbestos-cement roofs, positioned over bearing walls constructed using traditional methods by local laborers.

The project's design was funded by the Israeli Ministry of Housing as part of a nationwide initiative to provide permanent and modernized housing (with electricity and plumbing) for the Palestinian minority in the state, many of whom were beset by poor living conditions, occupying mud housing in some cases. This housing initiative affected some forty villages around the country. In many cases the construction of the homes was undertaken together with the tenants to reduce the building costs and the amount of the government mortgage provided to pay for it. Most of the housing units in this initiative ranged between 45 and 60 square meters, and typically each was allocated a small outdoor space.

The Ein Rafa project features two housing types. One is a long, rectangular-plan residential unit, topped by a single-vaulted roof, and the other is a square-plan unit, formed by two bays and topped by two roof vaults. Both of these variations cover about 50 square meters in total, and contain a living room, bedroom, kitchen, bathroom, and covered terrace. The housing designs also include traditional vernacular elements, such as a living-area niche, small fireplace, and terrace bench. Each housing unit is positioned within an irregularly shaped enclosure of approximately 280 square meters, where animals can roam and graze.

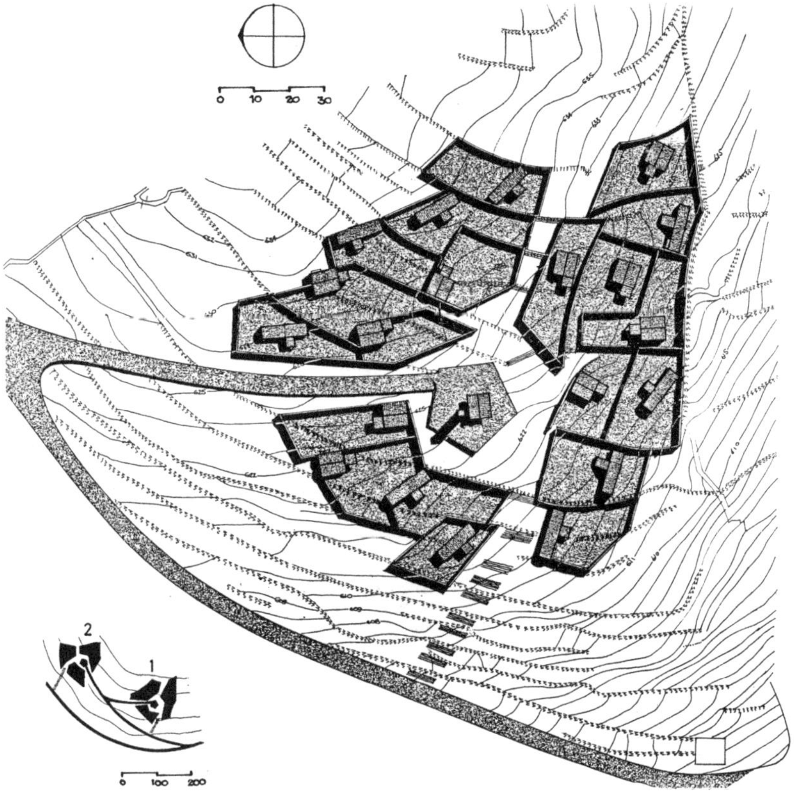

16.1 Site Plan
16.2 Drawing of village with retaining walls and fences

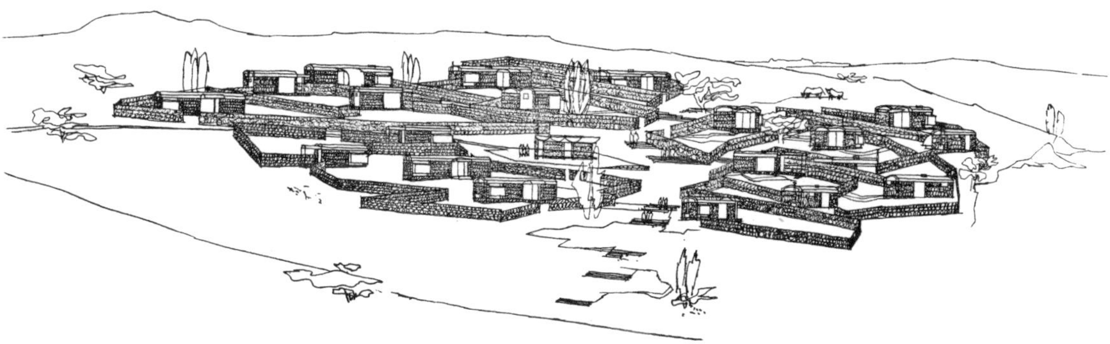

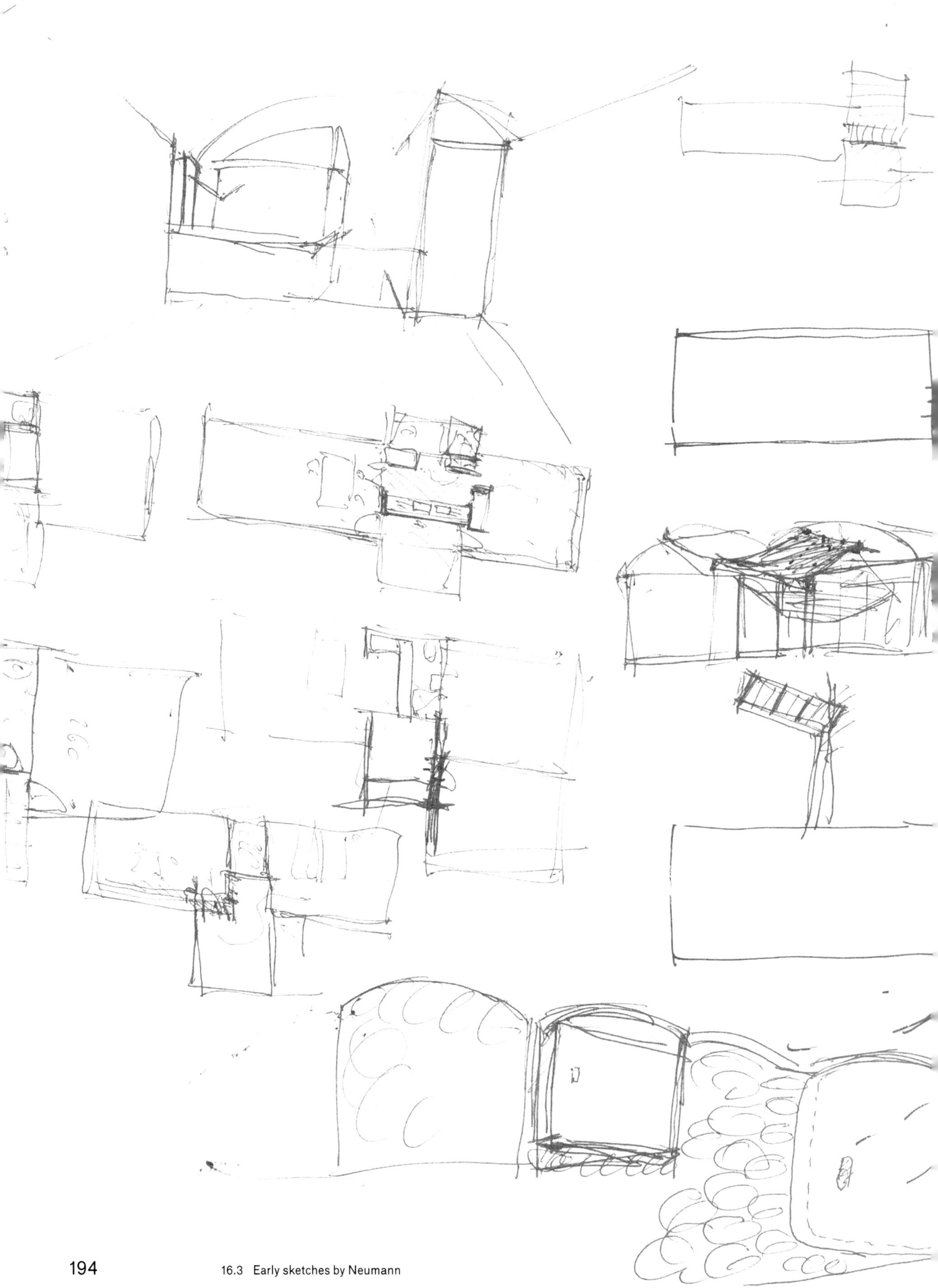

16.3 Early sketches by Neumann

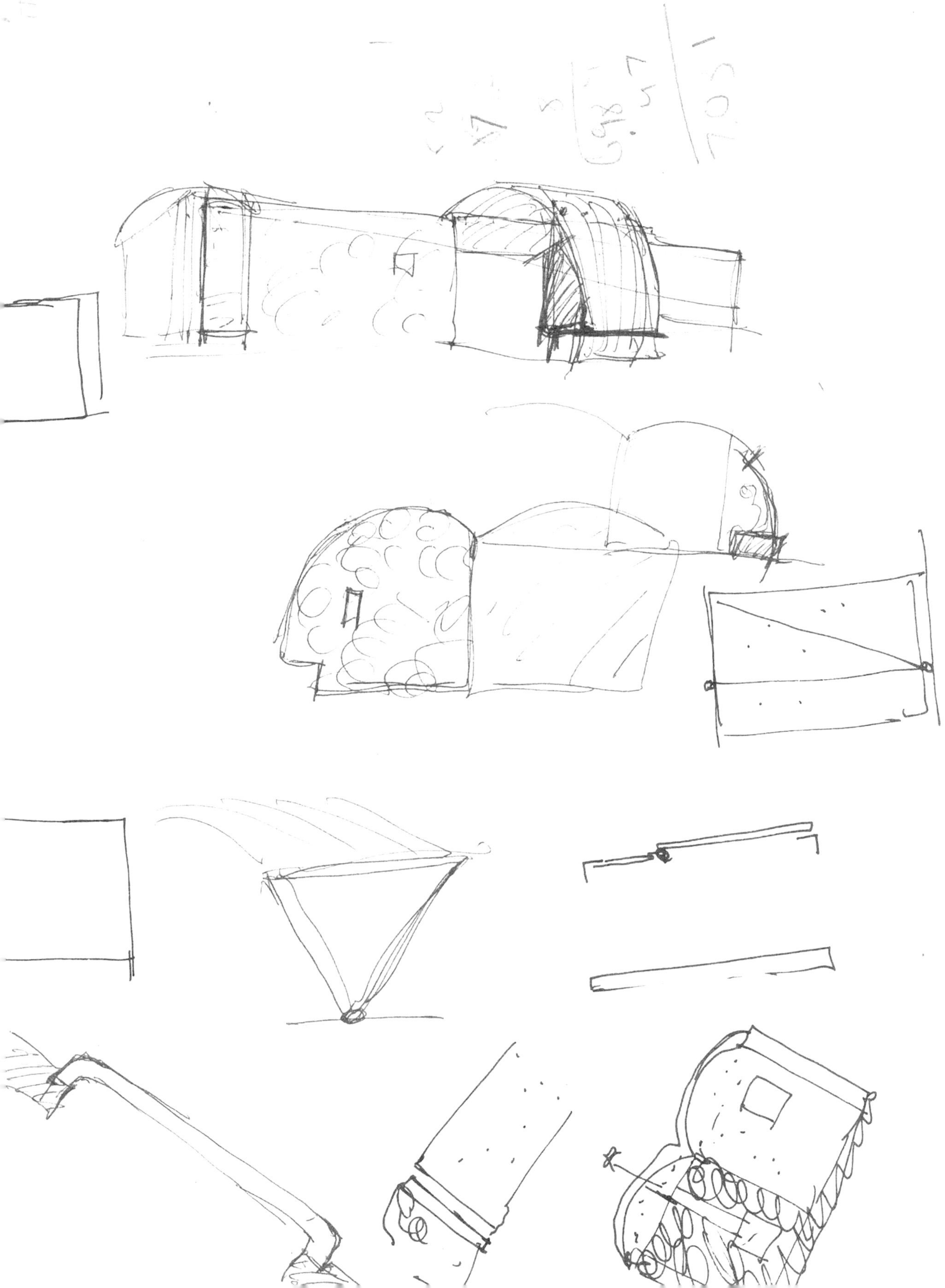

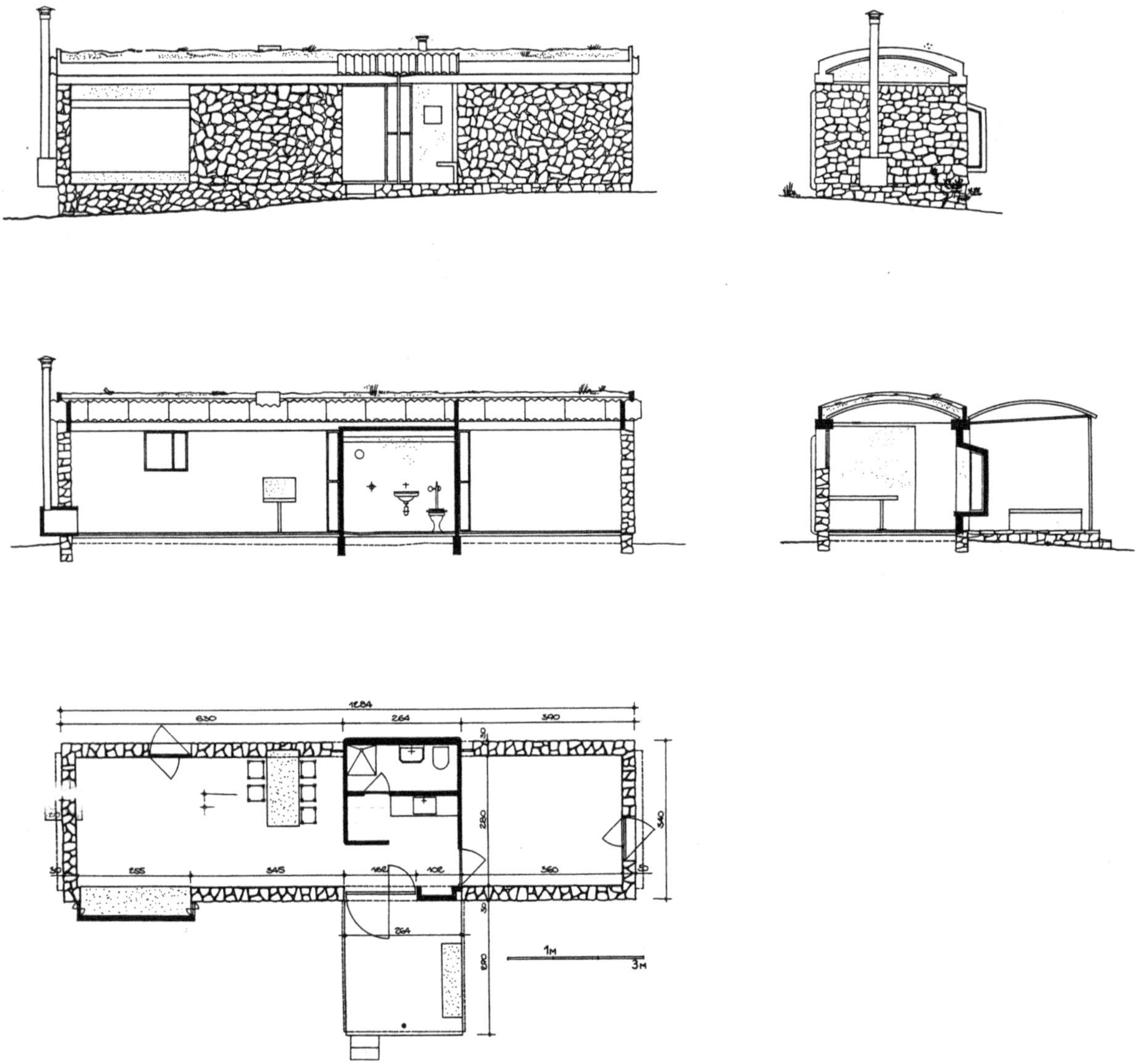

16.4 One-vault unit: elevations, sections, and plan

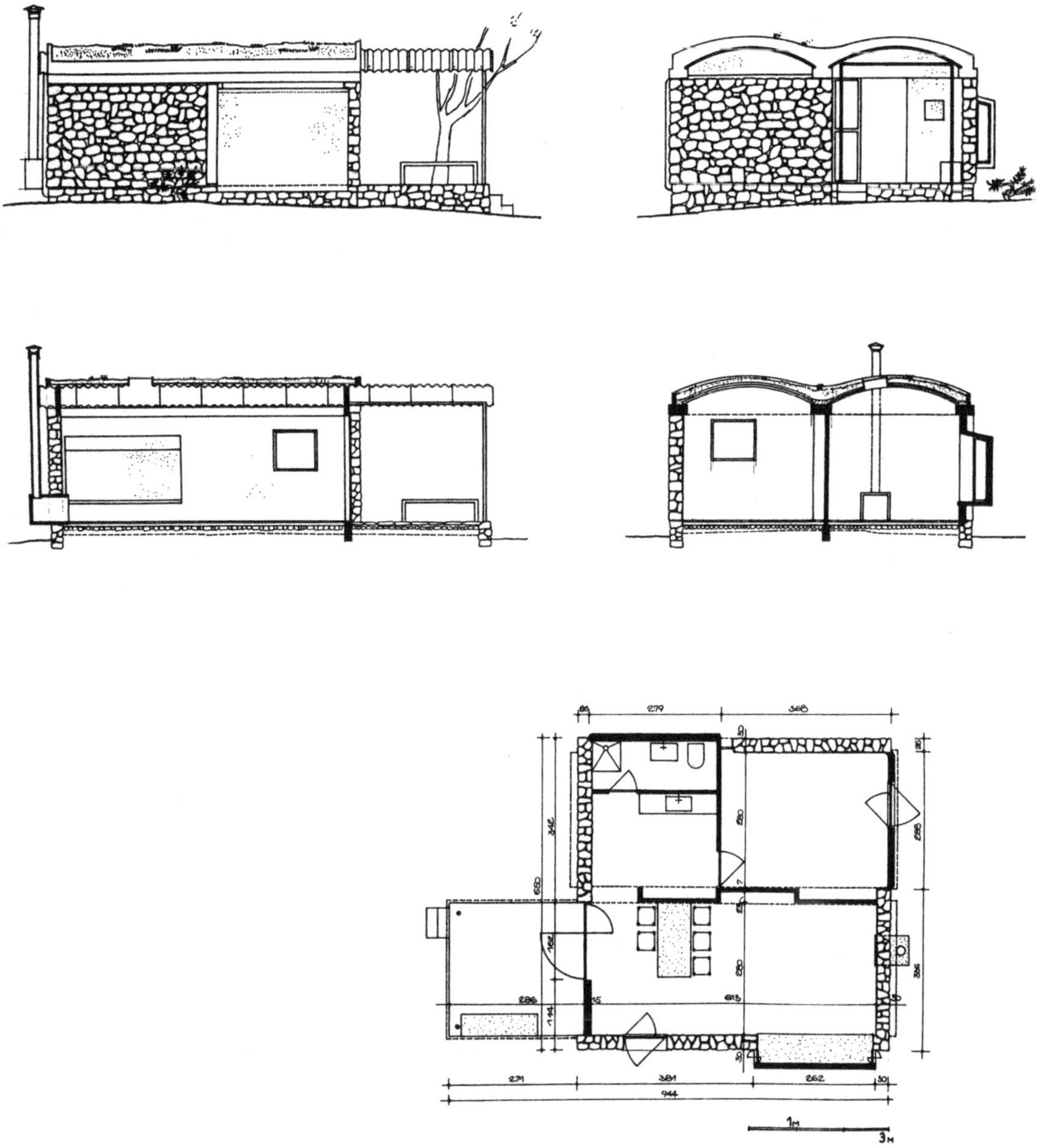

16.5 Square (two-vault) unit: elevations, sections, and plan

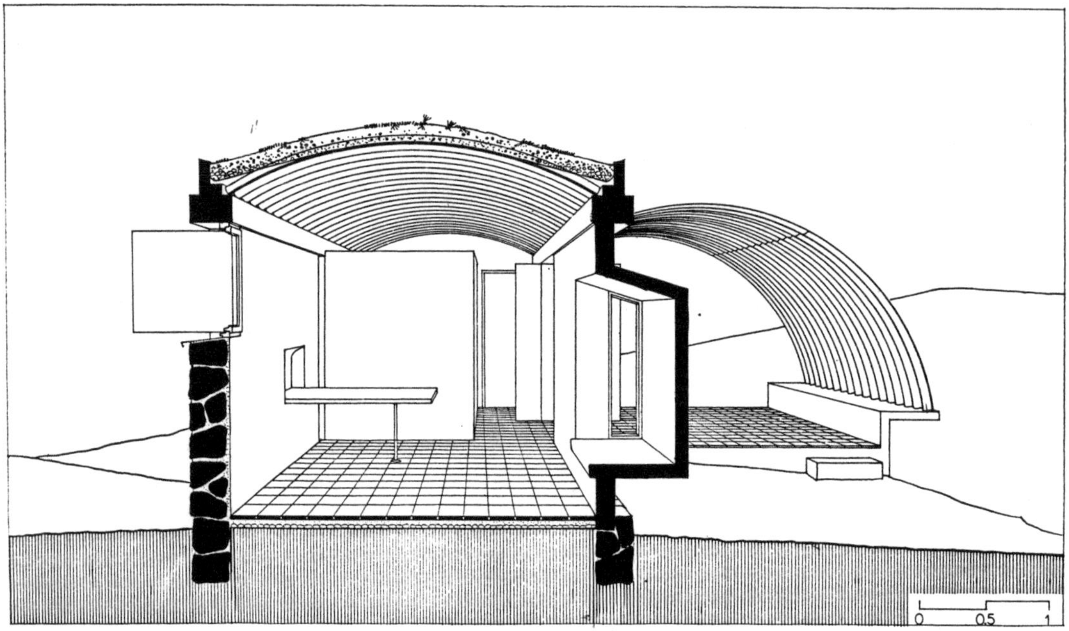

16.6 Perspective section of one-vault unit
16.7 Perspective section of two-vault unit

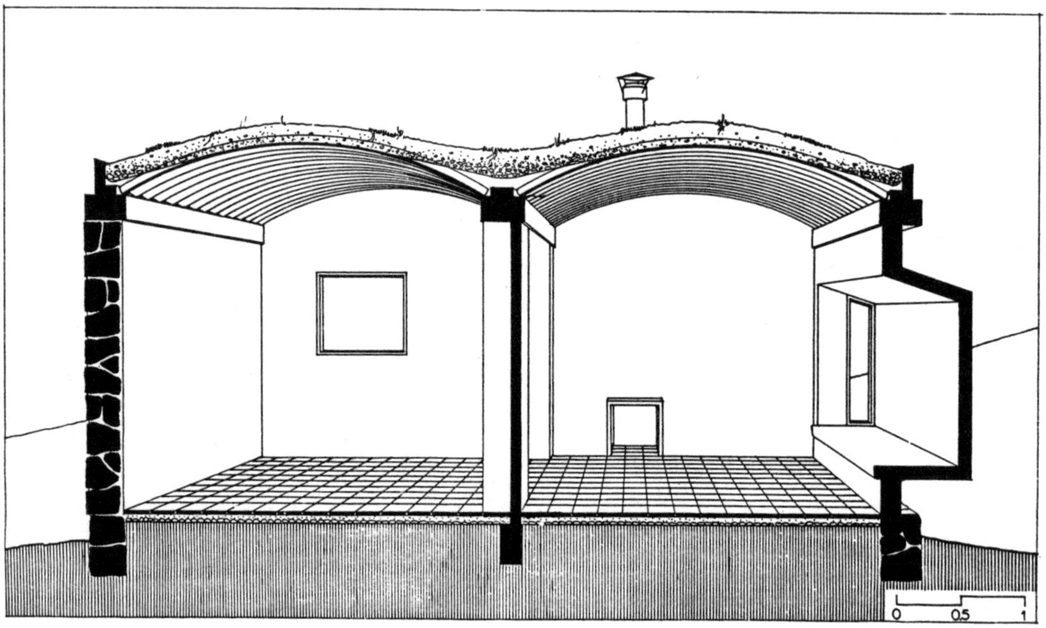

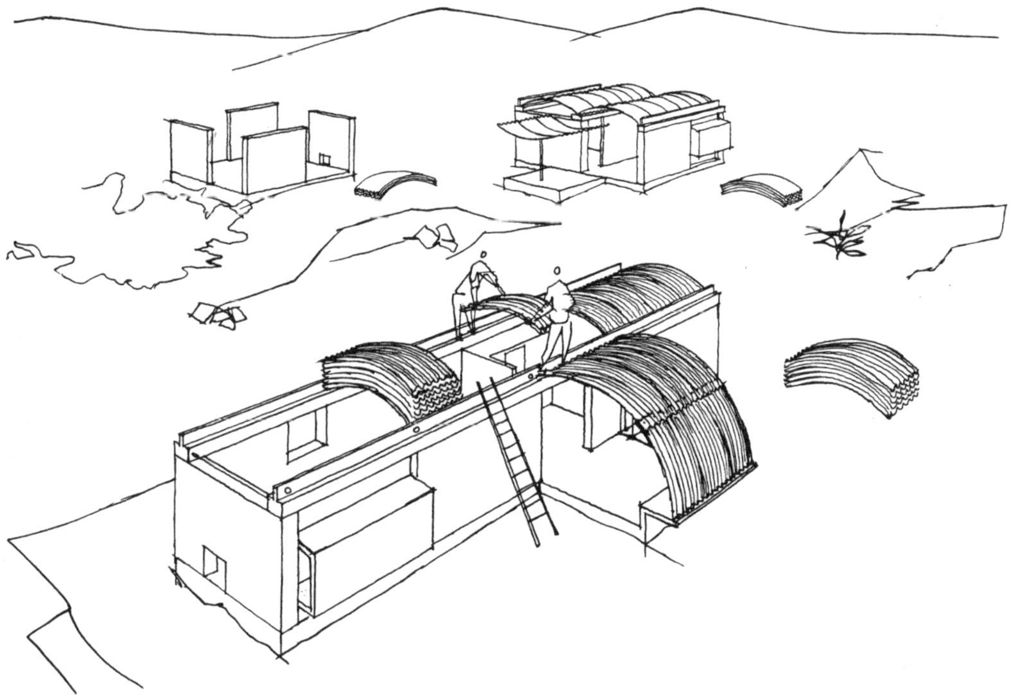

16.8 Roof construction with asbestos sheets
16.9 Perspective view of unit

16.10 View of one-vault and two-vault units
16.11 Units freely arranged along the sloping site

16.12 Side view of two-vaulted unit
16.13 View of shaded entrance with the terraced Judean-Samarian landscape

16.14 View of unit showing living-area niche and fireplace as elements puncturing the stone walls
16.15 Variation on shaded entrance area

16.16 Local stone used for wall construction
16.17 Detail of asbsestos shade

17 Dubiner Apartment House Ramat Gan, Israel

1961–64

With Zvi Hecker, Eldar Sharon

In 1961, Sam Dubiner, a wealthy Canadian entrepreneur, approached Neumann-Hecker-Sharon to design a house for him and his family on a southwest-facing, steep sloped plot of land in Ramat Gan, a town on the outskirts of Tel Aviv. Dubiner wanted to build a large detached home on the site, but Neumann proposed an apartment building instead, as it would better integrate into the urban fabric of Ramat Gan, a small town of apartment blocks and attached houses. Dubiner agreed to the suggestion, but the site's zoning regulations did not permit the construction of an apartment building there. However, the mayor of Ramat Gan, hoping to ingratiate himself with the affluent Dubiner, fought to have the zoning regulations changed to grant Neumann's and Dubiner's wishes.

Neumann's initial design concept was for a stepped building with entrances at both the top and bottom of the hill, linked to one another via an interior pathway. Neumann wanted each apartment to be directly accessible from this central pathway as well, although he and his partners found it a challenge to conceive of a design that satisfied both of these conditions. Their solution was to design apartments larger than was typical in Israel at the time, and to connect them to the central artery by short bridges. This solution worked because increasing the size of the apartments meant that fewer of them would need to be built to fit within the building footprint, and thus fewer bridges needed as well. Furthermore, the more generous wall space around a larger apartment allowed for flexibility and variability in the placement of entrances.

The building was divided into seven stories that each contained two to three apartments. The three lower stories were stepped following the slope of the hill and took the form of a bent line with the point of the bend facing away from the foot of the hill. The upper three stories rested on the fourth, and took the same form but with an orientation that mirrored the lower floors, with the point facing the peak of the hill. The massing of these bent floor bands opened a void in the centre of the apartment block for an outdoor courtyard. The central courtyard opened onto the access bridges to each apartment. However, this area was not only a waypoint: It also channeled airflows, provided shade from direct sunlight in

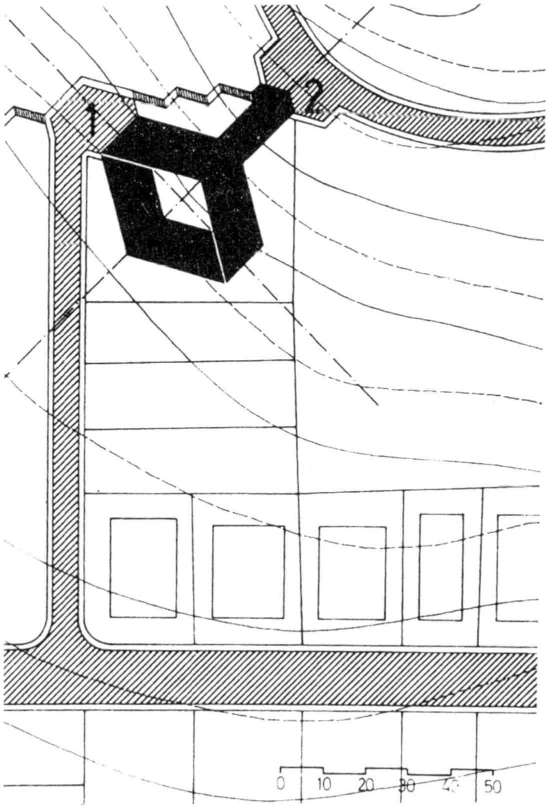

the summer, and absorbed direct sunlight in the winter, creating its own microclimate that furnished a pleasant, semiprivate outdoor space.

After the building's general massing strategy had been determined, Neumann subdivided the rooms on each floor into a honeycomb pattern of hexagonal spaces whose dimensions were derived from his EM-PHI system. Each hexagonal space served as a single unit or module; larger rooms were formed from a few of these modules, while smaller rooms occupied only a single module. Because the floors were stepped, each apartment had a balcony formed by the roof of the level below it.

Concrete was used for the structural frame and concrete blocks for the walls of the building, and the entire structure was covered with stucco to cover construction joints and emphasize its planar geometry. It articulated the jagged outer face of the building, giving the impression of an open, accreting form, yet it also unified the building's many surfaces and distinguished it from its surroundings as a single patterned object.

17.1 Site plan: [1] Lower street; [2] Upper street

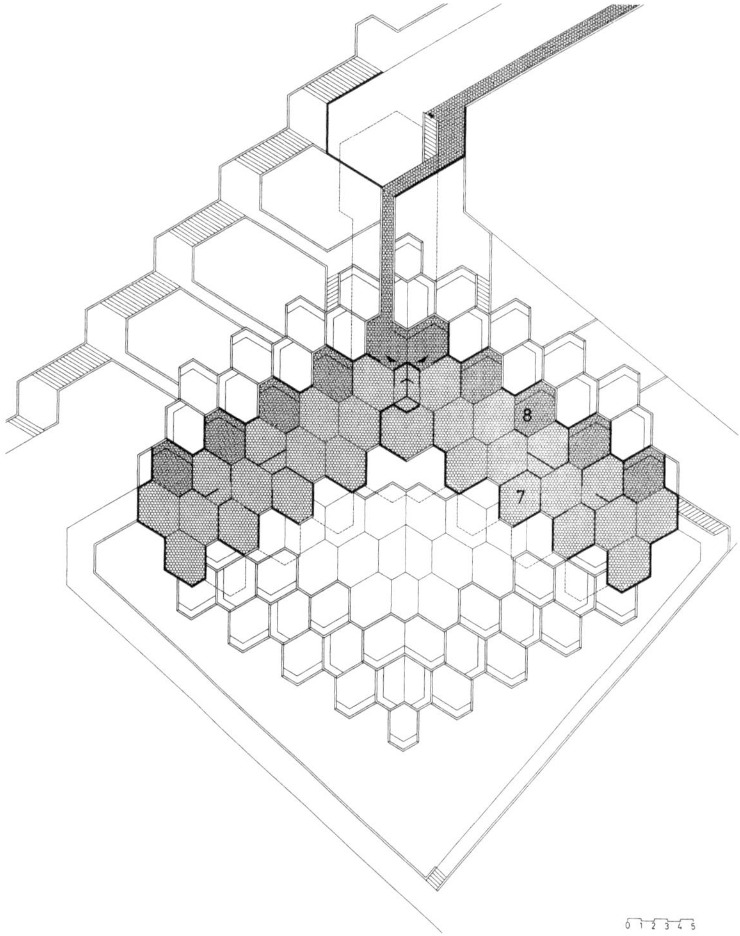

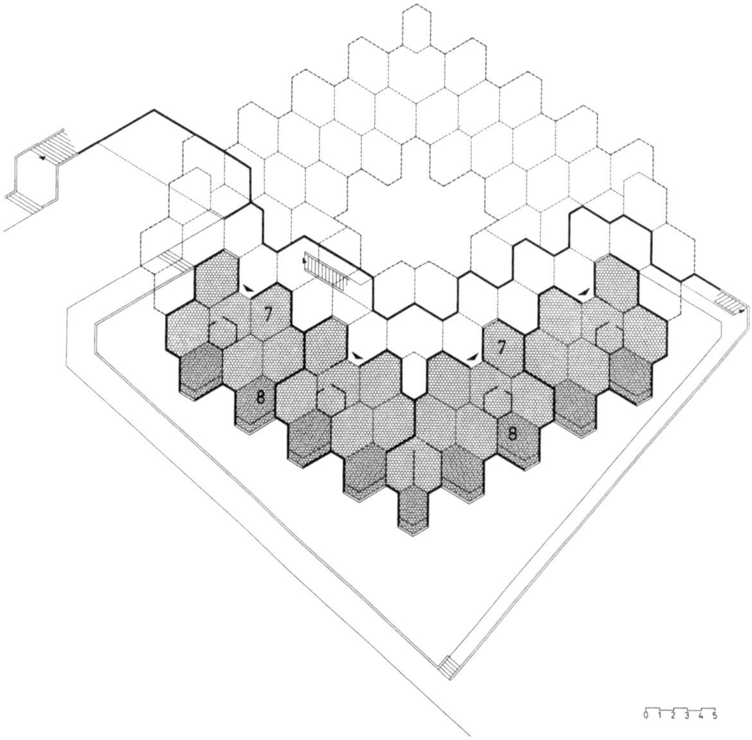

17.2 Fourth-floor plan (first upper level)
17.3 First-floor plan (first lower level)

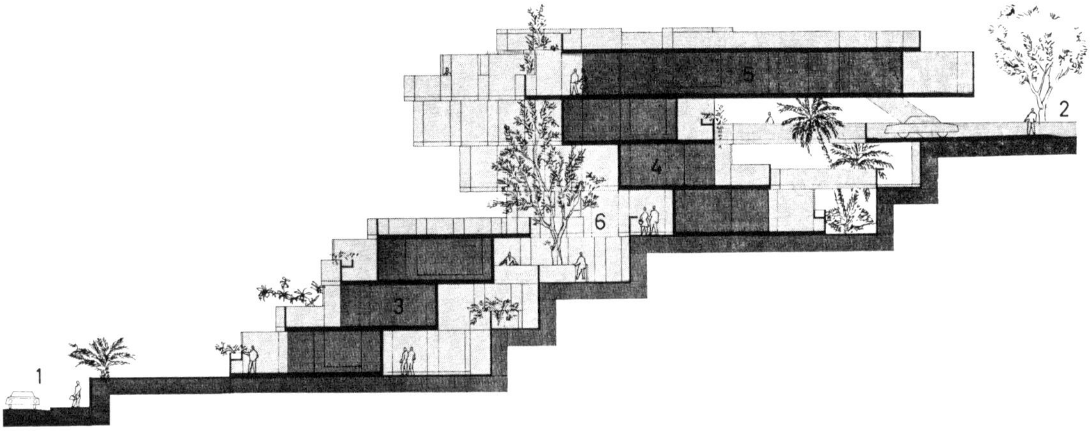

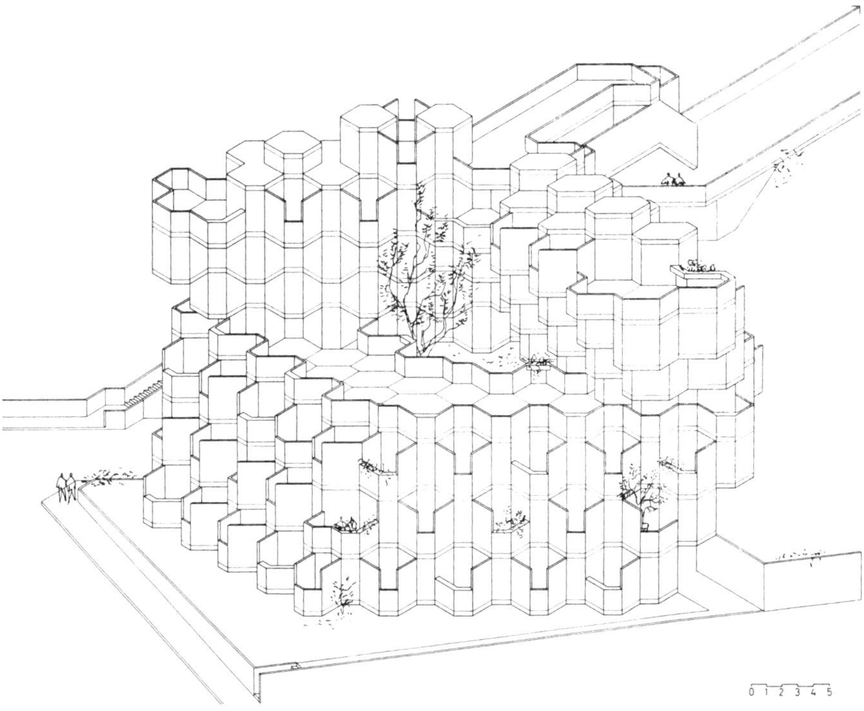

17.4 Section through inner (stepped) courtyard
17.5 Axonometric view

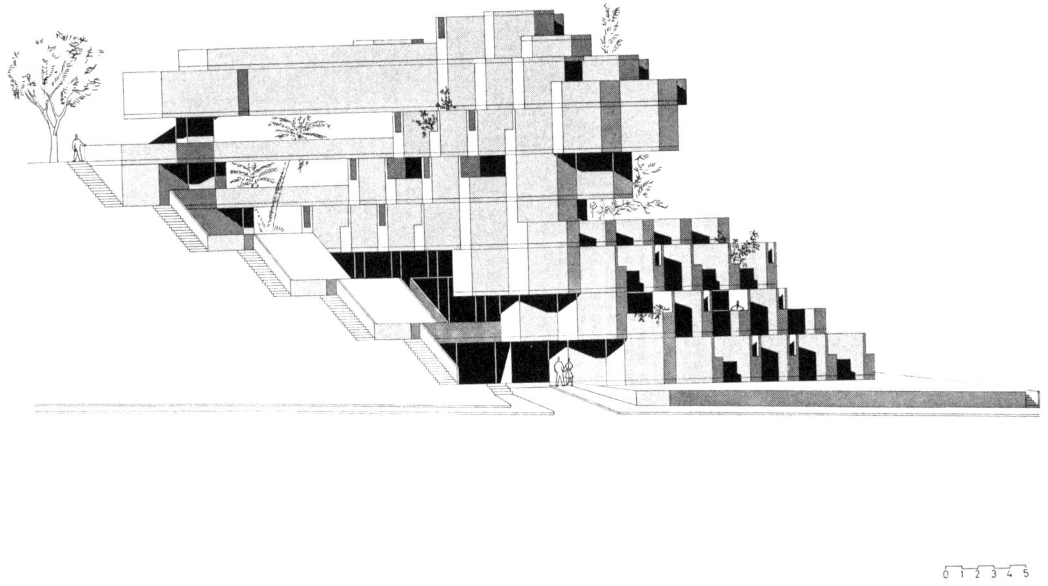

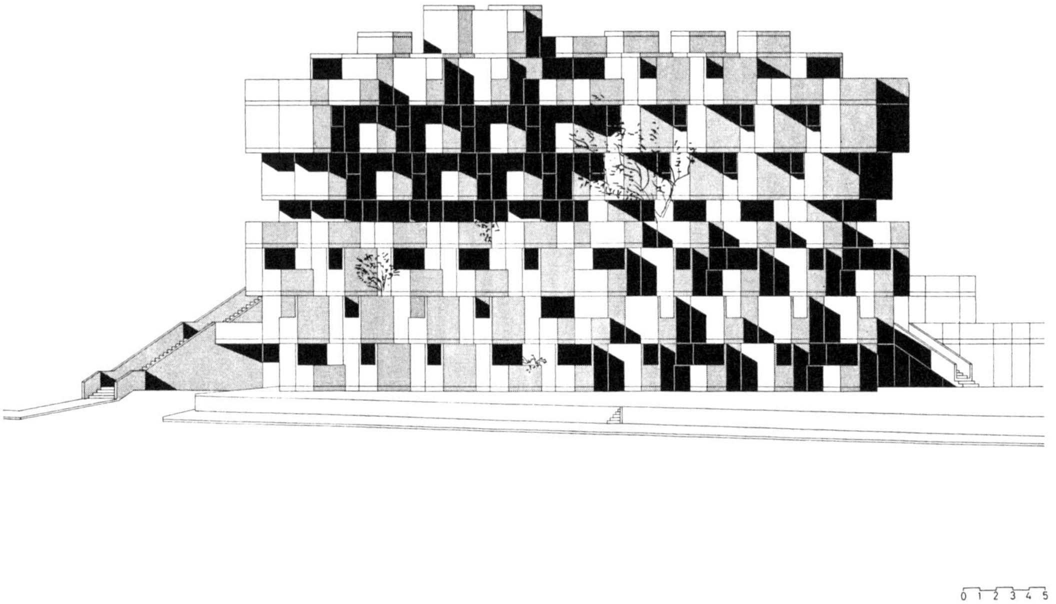

17.6 Side elevation
17.7 Front elevation

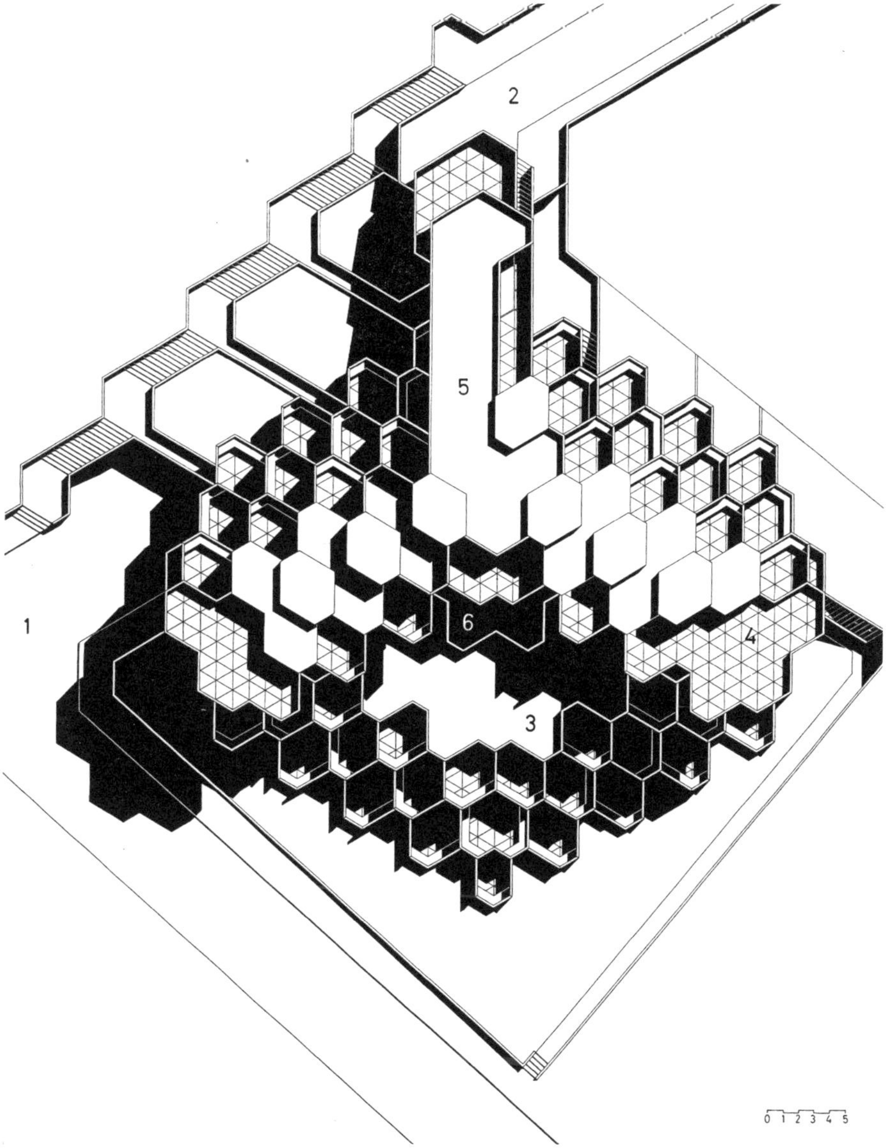

17.8 Roof plan: [1] Access from street below, [2] Access from street above, [3] Top level of lower section, [4] Larger edge balconies, [5] Dubiner's own apartment, [6] Inner courtyard

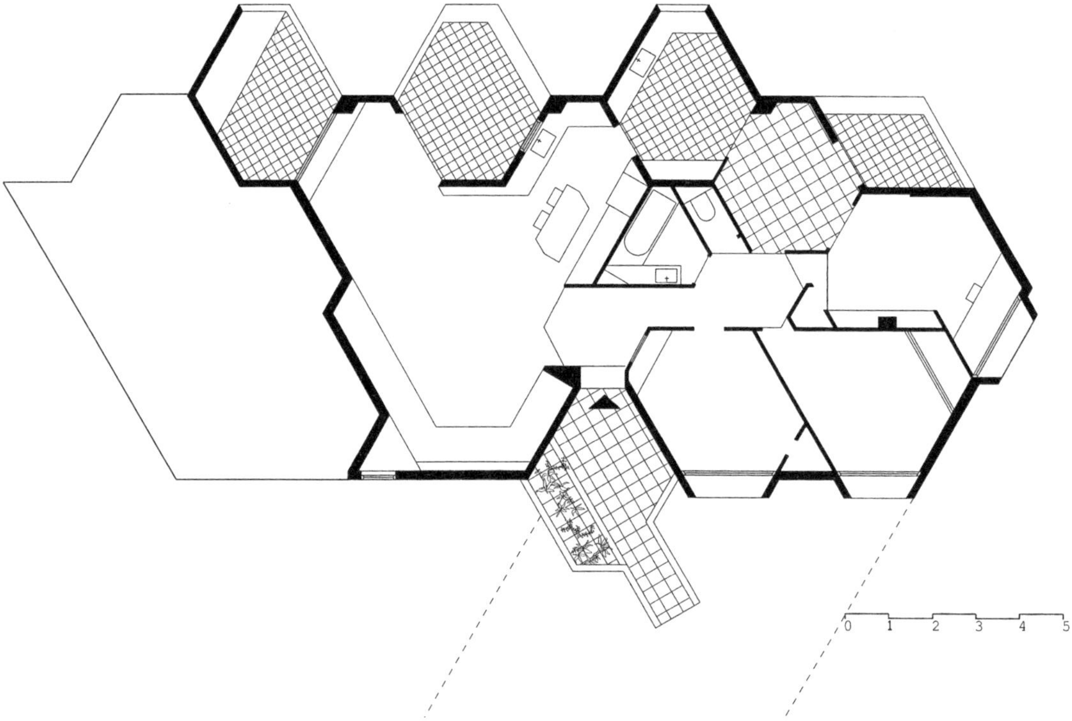

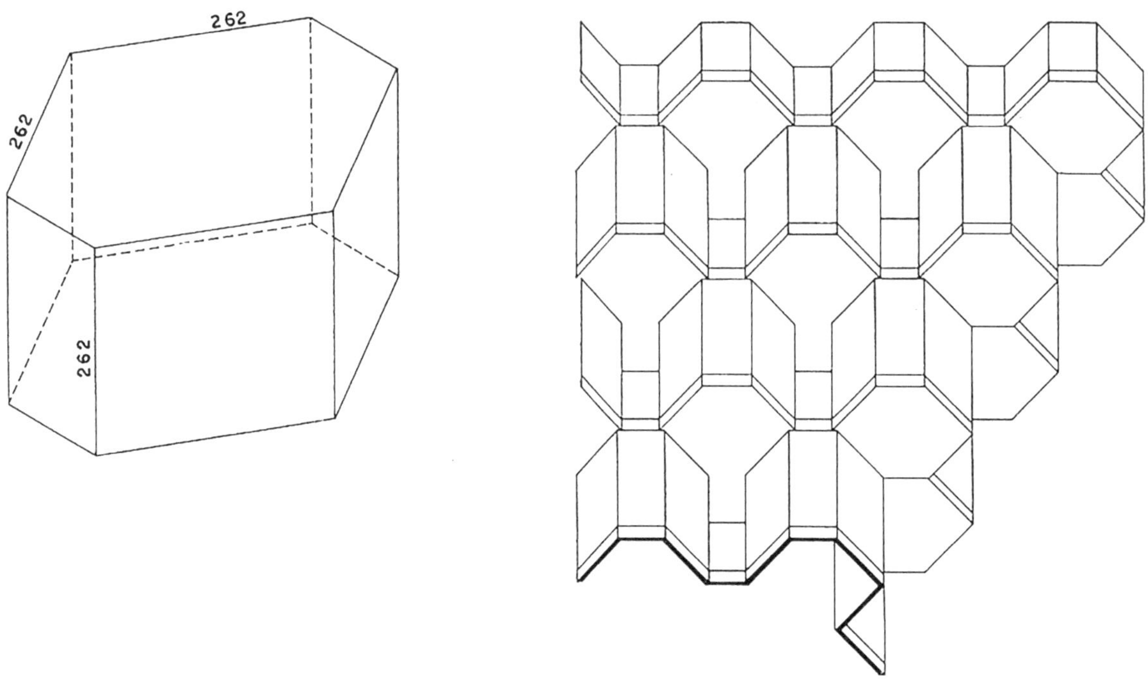

17.9 Second-floor apartment plan; redrawn by Rafi Segal
17.10 Elongated hexagon unit; dimensions according to Alfred Neumann's MΦ system, and hexagonal unit pattern

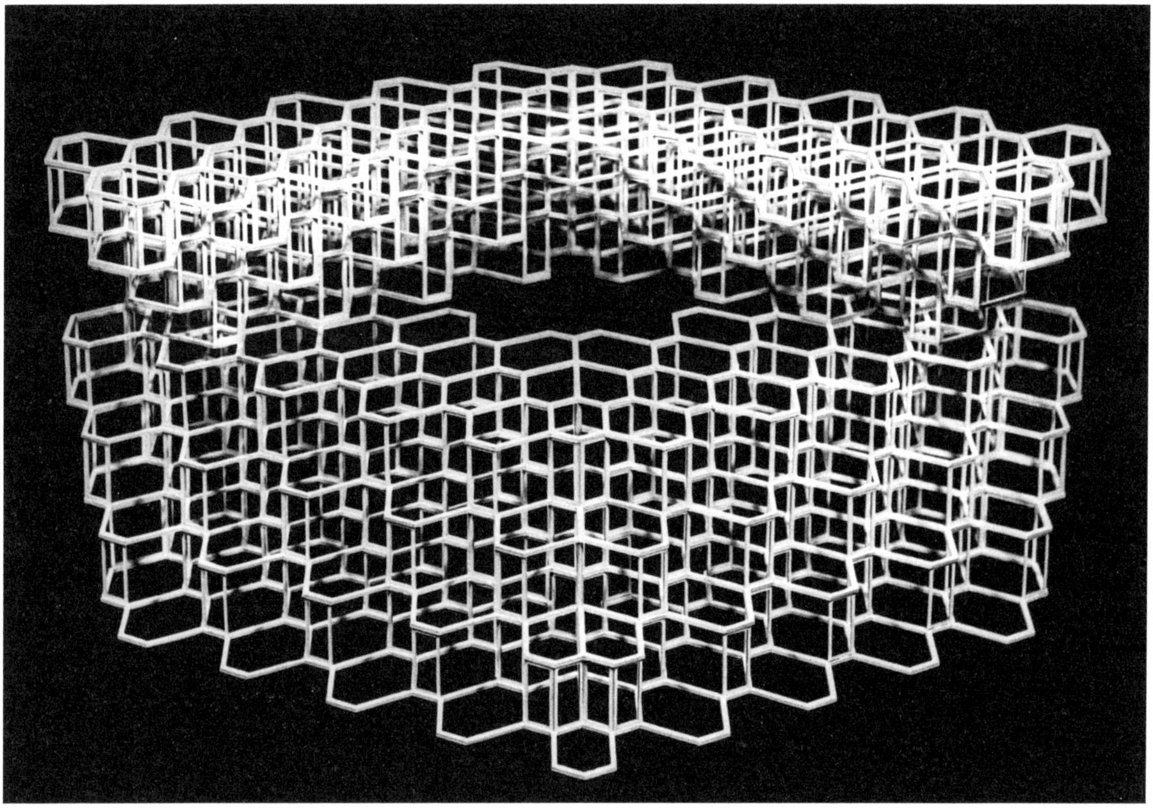

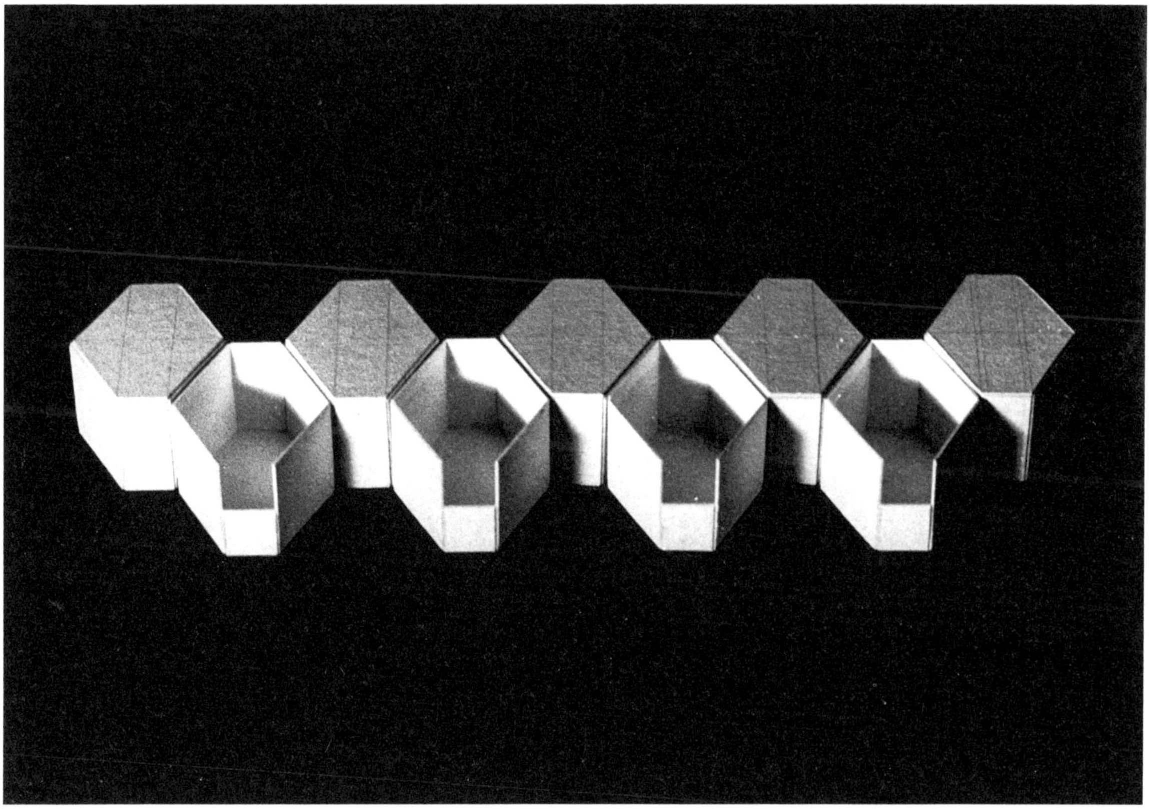

17.11 Wire frame model of structural system
17.12 Model of unit organization

17.13 Preliminary model of early scheme

17.14 Study model showing bridges leading to different floors and circulation of stairs traversing the building and connecting lower and upper streets
17.15 Working model with topography

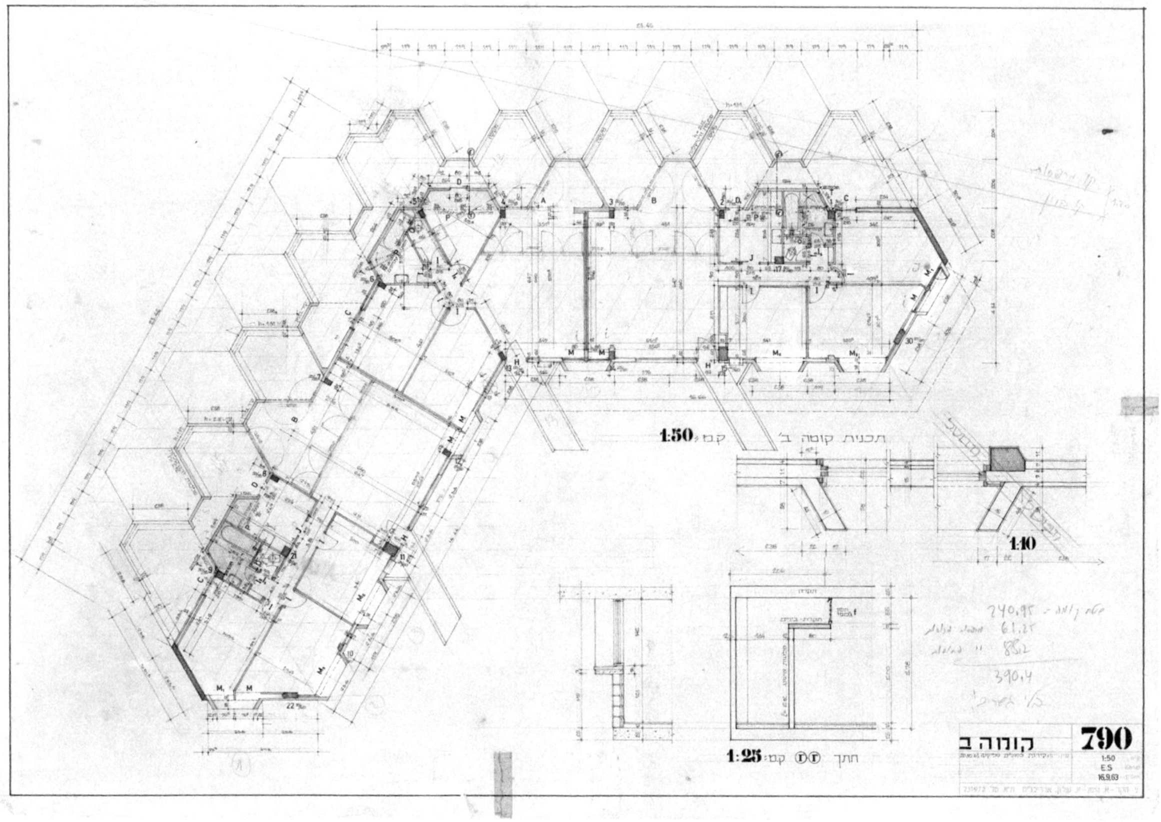

17.16 Original construction drawing of second floor
17.17 Original construction drawing of sixth floor

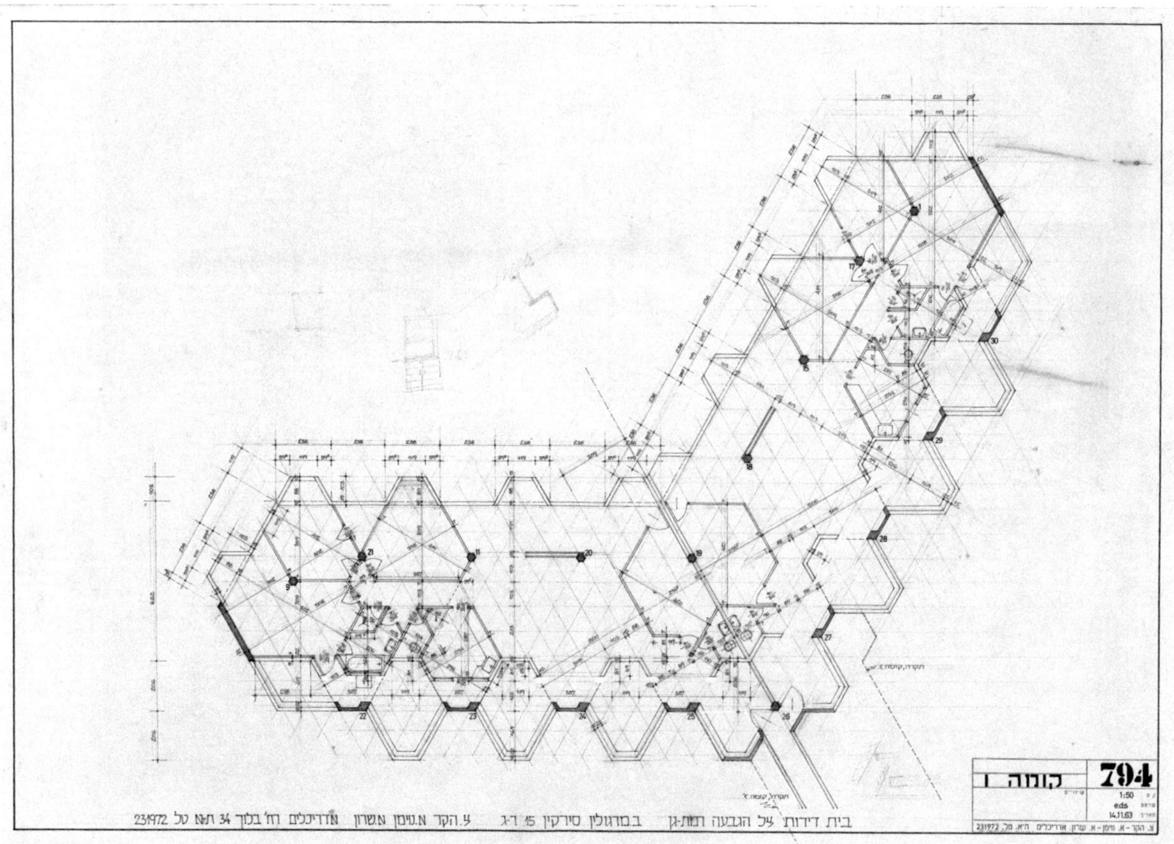

17.18 Neumann (left) on site during construction
17.19 Dubiner Apartment House under construction

17.20

17.21 View of main elevation
17.22 View from above

17.23 View of side elevation
17.24 Stepped balconies

17.25 During construction

17.26 View at third-floor height
17.27 Open and semi-enclosed balconies which align and create the building envelope

17.28 Unit roofs become terraces for units above

17.29 Side elevation showing the shift in floors

D 19

18x24 x 2

27.

33

35

39.

45

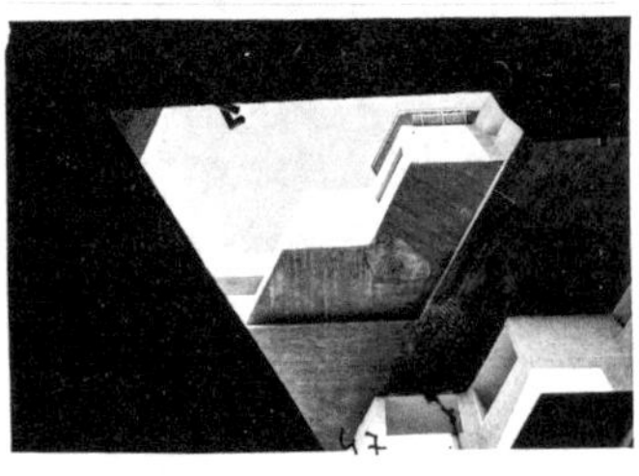

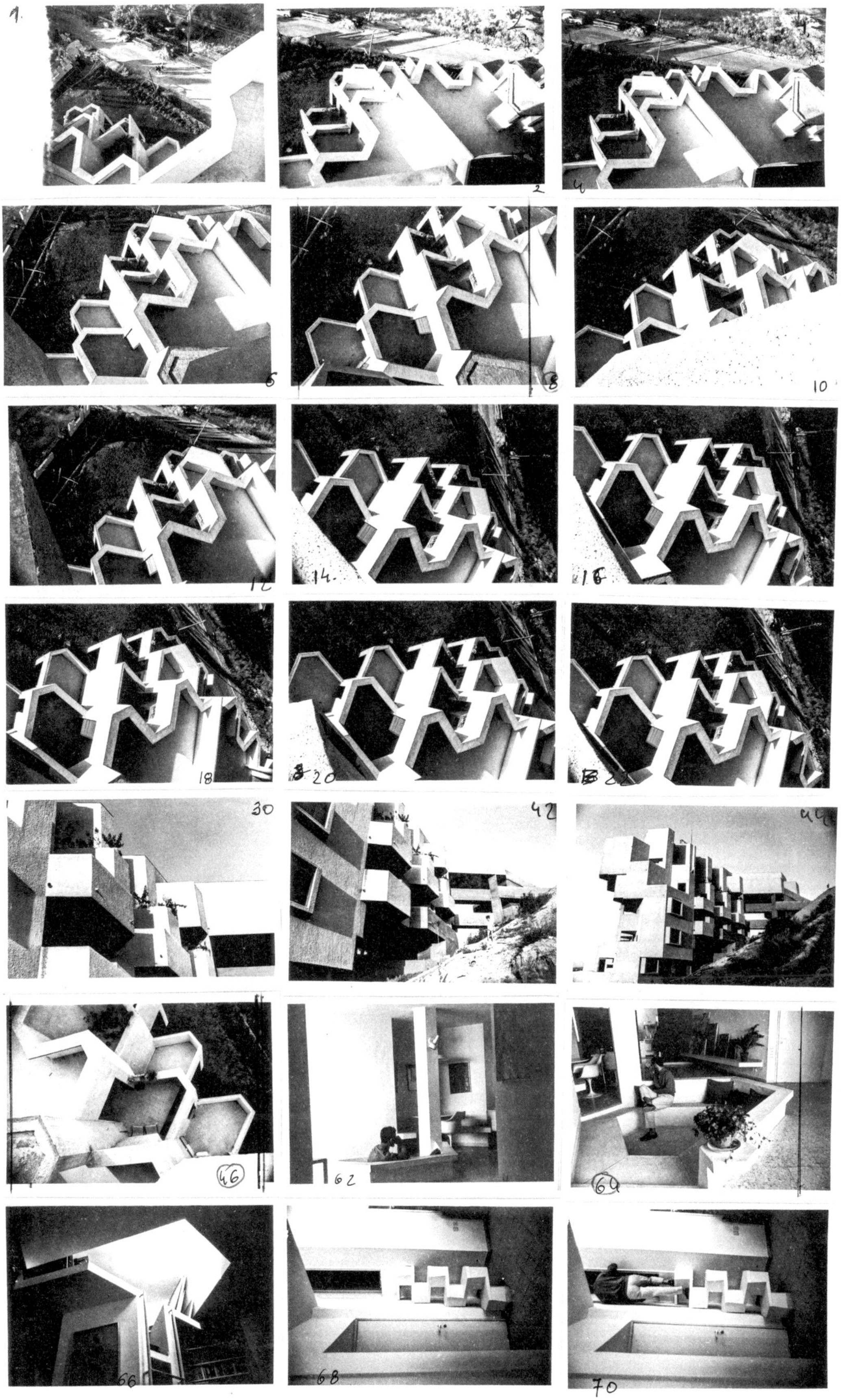

17.30 Semi-covered courtyard allows shade during hot summer months and sun during the winter
17.31 Views from inner courtyard toward entrance from lower street

17.32 View of inner courtyard
17.33 View of open staircase traversing the courtyard and connecting lower and upper street

17.34 View after the building was inhabited

17.35 The building featured on the cover of Italian publication *L'Industria Italiana del Cemento*, 1971

18 # Netanya City Hall, *Competition* Netanya, Israel

1964

With Zvi Hecker

In the 1960s Netanya was a town of 60,000 inhabitants about 25 kilometers north of Tel Aviv on the Mediterranean coast. Known as a recreation site and diamond industry center, it had just experienced rapid growth and therefore needed a new civic center. The civic center was to be located in a pedestrian plaza right by the shoreline, and was to be accessible via three streets.

Neumann and Hecker's proposal for a new city hall and civic plaza for Netanya won first prize in a national architecture competition. The project envisioned the civic plaza as a triangular site at the intersection of three axes: two of them pre-existing city streets and one that Neumann and Hecker proposed as a terraced path leading to the seashore. The city hall was to be located in the center of the civic plaza, and was also conceived as triangular in plan to echo the urban condition of its site. This city hall was to have three overhanging stories to resemble an inverted triangular pyramid in elevation.

The walls of each floor are formed by space-packed, hollow, truncated tetrahedrons, built from hexagonal concrete panels which, when joined, create triangular window openings. Inside, the building contains a three-story central atrium, around which offices are grouped. Positioned over this atrium is a pyramidal element that houses the council chamber. Three wind towers, also conceived of as rooftop pyramidal elements, stand at each point of the triangular upper floor. Light penetrates the central court through the openings in the roof structure.

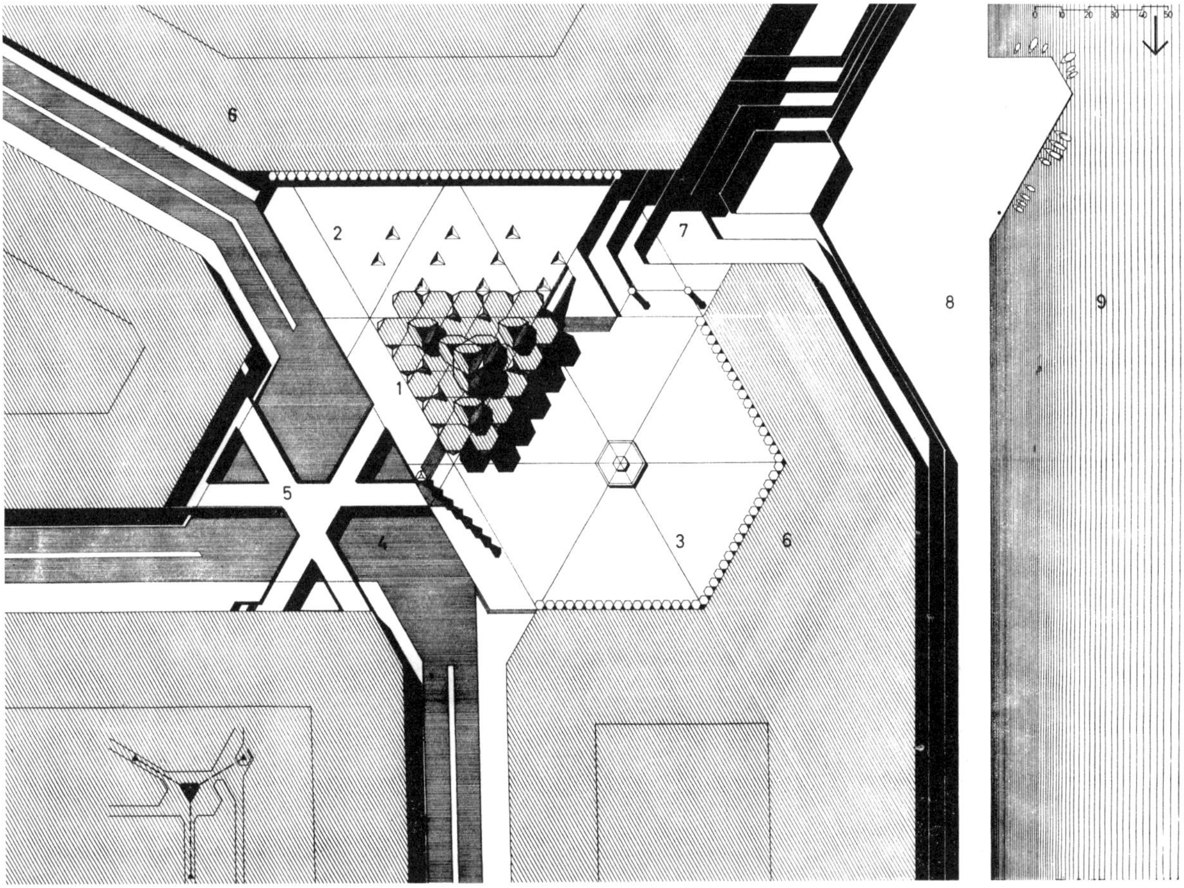

18.1 Site plan: ¹ City hall; ² Upper plaza; ³ Lower plaza; ⁴ Traffic square; ⁵ Bridge over the road; ⁶ Shops, offices, and community buildings; ⁷ Terraces to beach; ⁸ Seashore

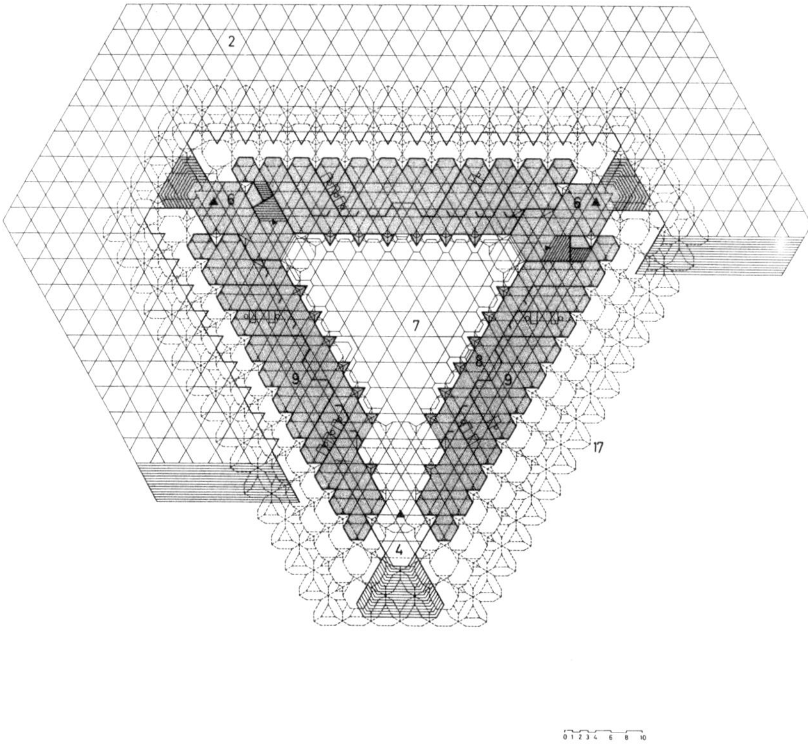

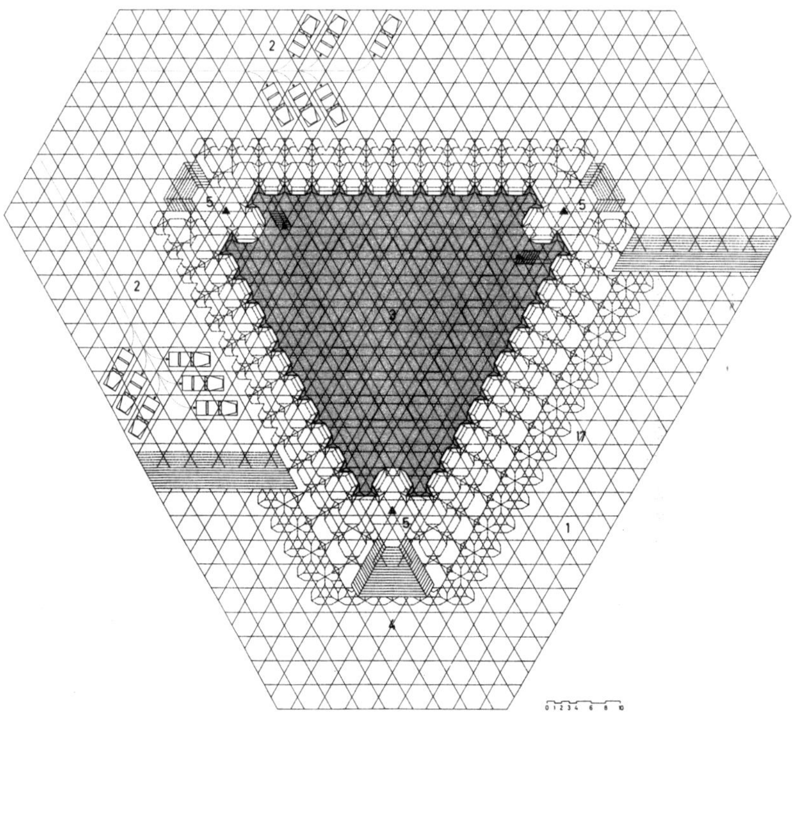

18.2 Third-floor plan
18.3 Ground-level plan; darker area showing interior space

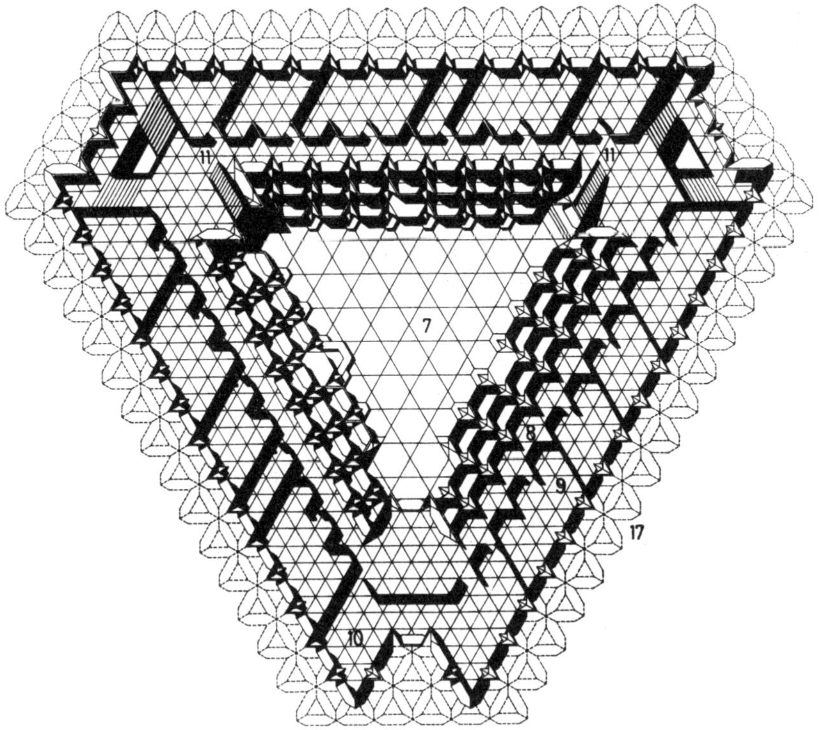

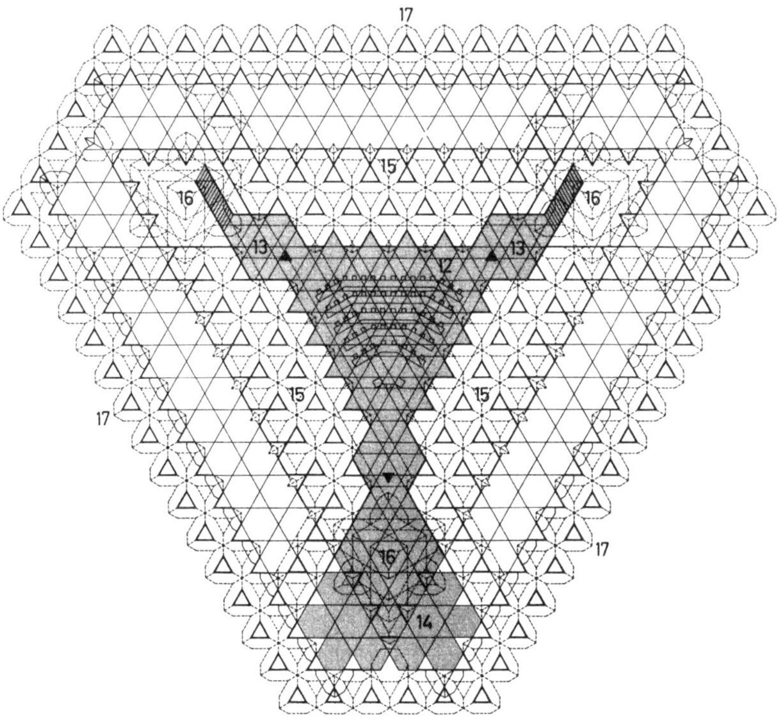

18.4 Shaded plan showing stepped inner public space and perimeter offices
18.5 Fourth-floor plan; assembly hall

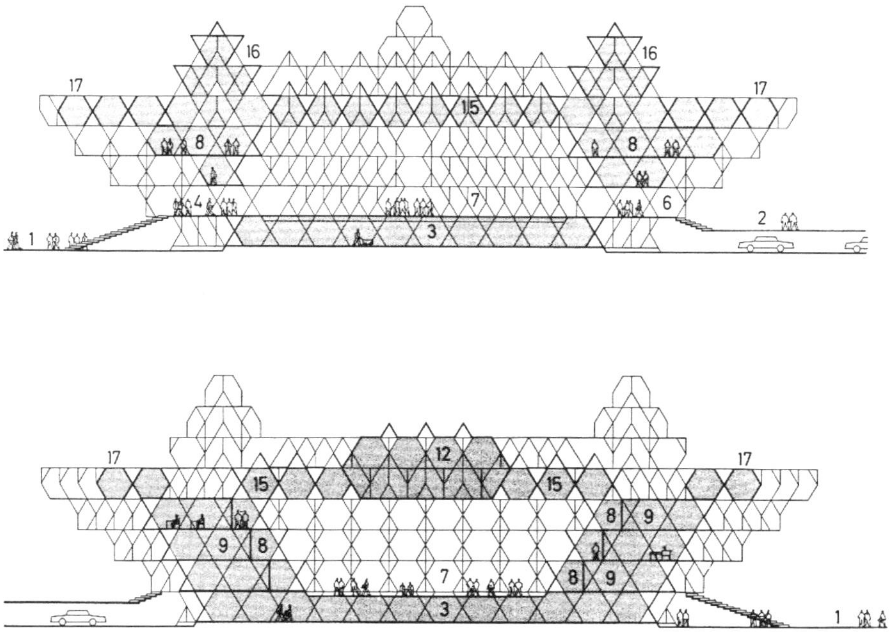

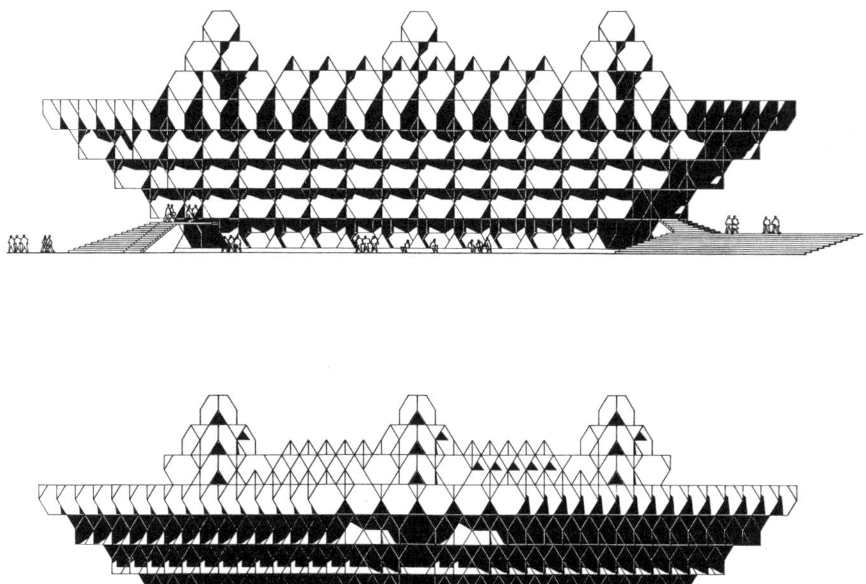

18.6 Section through the main and side entrance
18.7 Section through the council chamber and offices. Key to 18.6 and 18.7: 1 Lower plaza, 2 Upper plaza, 3 General service equipment area, 4 Main entrance from the lower plaza, 6 Side entrance from upper plaza, 7 Triangular central court, 8 Interior galleries, 9 Offices, 12 Triangular council chamber, 15 Triangular tetrahedron bearing structure introducing diffused light to interior court, 16 Pyramidal wind towers, 17 Truncated tetrahedron hollow roof structure
18.8 Elevations

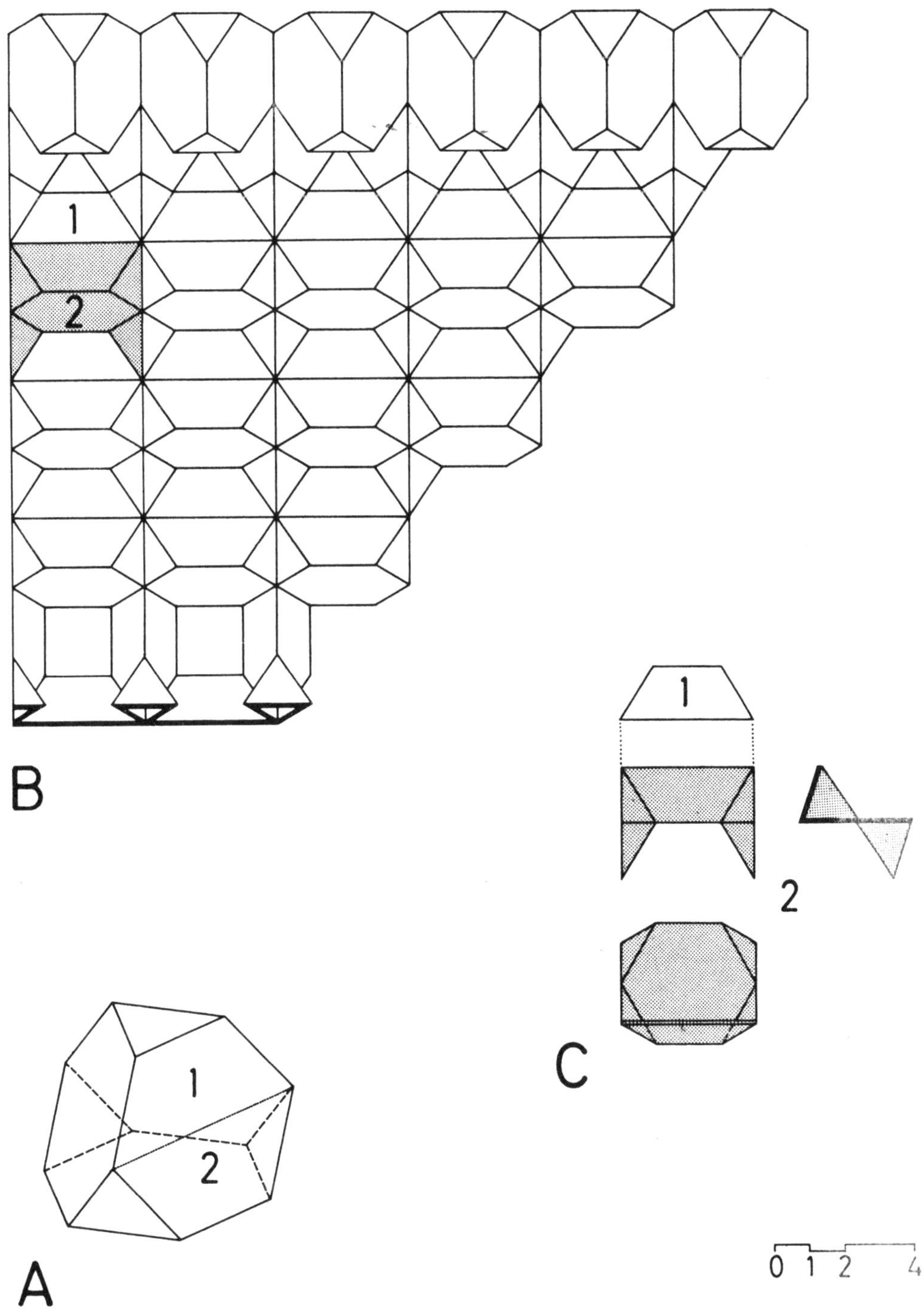

18.9 Unit and space-packing pattern

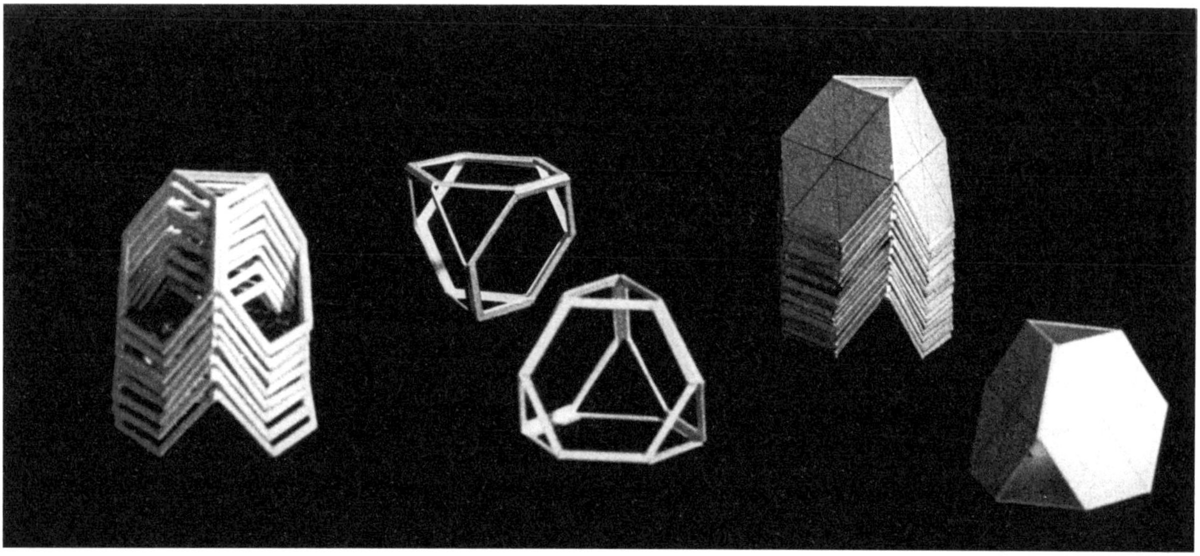

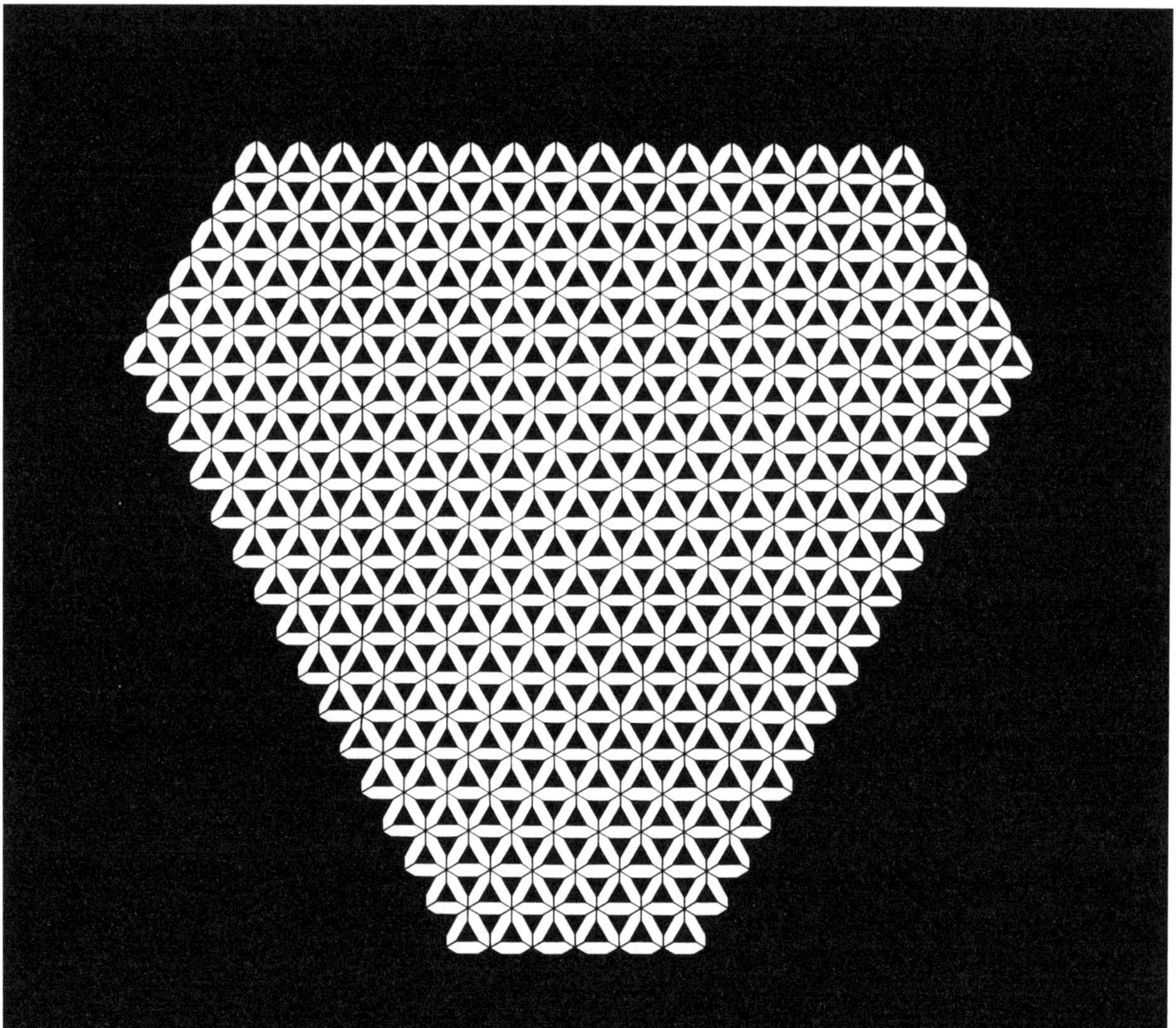

18.10 Models of unit
18.11 Drawing of pattern in plan

18.12 Model views

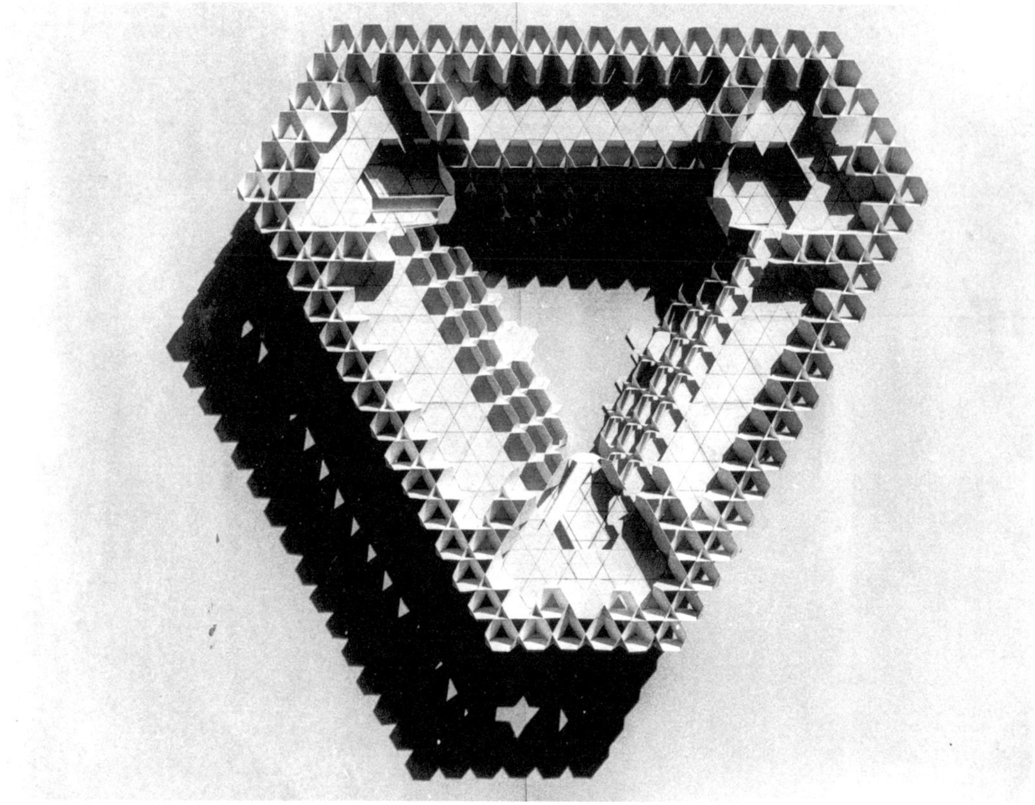

18.13 Model view
18.14 Model showing view of interior public space

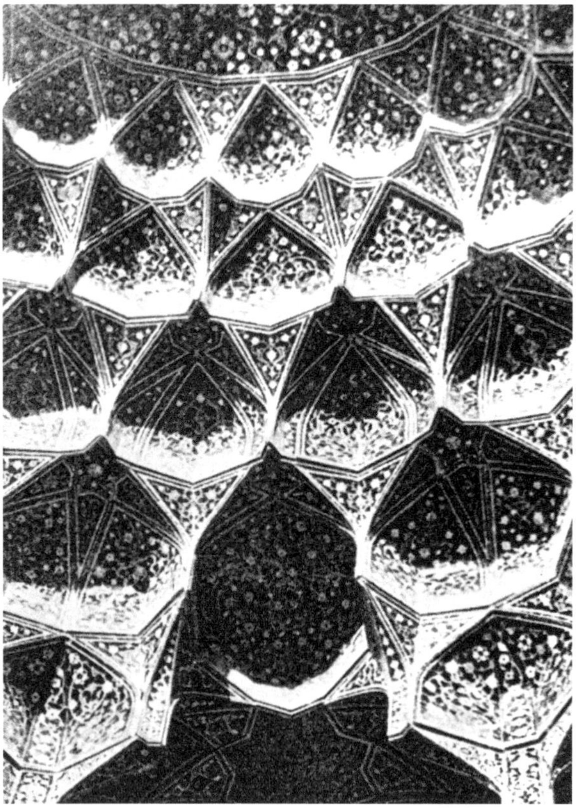

18.15 Model view of building elevation (left) compared by the architects, Alfred Neumann and Zvi Hecker, with an Islamic motif; a detail from Sheikh Luftullah Mosque, Isfahan (right)

18.16 Study model: light and shade

19 Danciger Building Mechanical Engineering Faculty Laboratory Building Technion-Israel Institute of Technology Haifa, Israel 1963–66

With Zvi Hecker

During the 1950s, enrolment at the Technion–Israel Institute of Technology increased rapidly, and the university decided to establish a new campus at Mount Carmel to accommodate the growing student population. The university undertook a massive building campaign to construct the new campus, and in 1956 Technion's president, Yaakov Dori, recruited Neumann to design the new buildings for the Faculty of Mechanical Engineering.

Neumann first worked with a committee assembled by the Technion to determine the programmatic requirements for the new engineering buildings. This slow process was put on hold after a few years and resumed again in 1963, the year Neumann collaborated with Hecker and the Technion came to some conclusions, deciding to first construct one of the laboratory buildings as a pilot project before proceeding with the others. This first laboratory was to be named the Danciger Building, in honor of the family that funded its realization.

Among the functional requirements mandated by the Technion committee for the Danciger Building were certain specified dimensions for its central halls, and an open plan that could permit large pieces of machinery to be moved throughout the building. To accommodate these measures, Neumann proposed a long, rectangular-bar building to be aligned axially across the mountain's gentle slope, and in order to keep the interior spaces open, he decided to locate all load-bearing functions in the building's outer envelope. Neumann and Hecker proposed a radical new vision for the building's structural envelope. It was to be built from triangular slabs of concrete, standing upright and oriented in plan at alternating 45-degree angles, lined end-to-end to create a jagged perimeter wall. Narrow spaces between the triangular planes would allow light to enter the building's interior. On the second level, the angles of the triangular planes were inverted so that the upper façade protruded outwards where the lower façade receded inwards, creating shade over parts of the wall and mitigating solar heat intake. A lattice of ceiling beams oriented at 45 degrees to the right angle formed by the building's plan, much like the system implemented at the Bat Yam project, and resting on the upper edges of the first-floor triangular planes, completed the structural system.

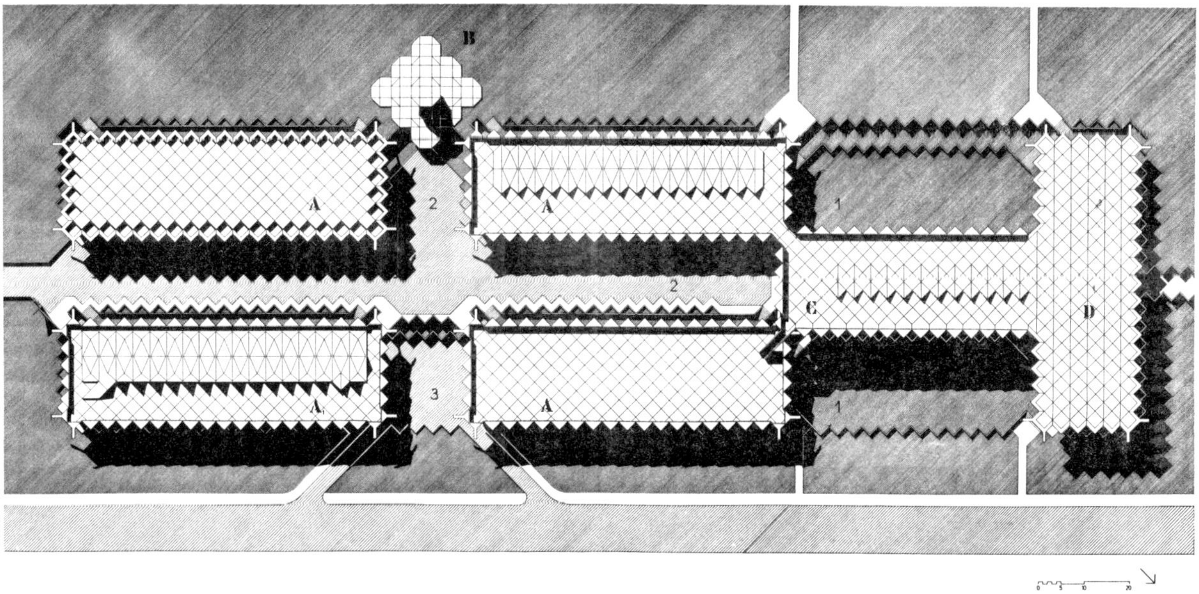

The Technion officials were not satisfied with Neumann and Hecker's inventive geometric design for the Danciger Building envelope, and quarreled with the architects about it well into the building's construction phase. The Technion officials' primary concern was that the linear slits between the triangular planes in the façade design would not allow enough light into the building, and they made Neumann and Hecker sign a memorandum promising that their design would meet the desired daylighting requirements while adhering to the existing budget.

Weeks later, Hecker visited the construction site to discover that the wrong windows were being installed. Despite their approval of the memorandum that Hecker and Neumann had signed, the Technion had had doubts about the architects' proposal and had ordered their own windows instead of those originally designed. The architects were furious. On the night of October 31, 1966, Hecker climbed onto the roof of the Danciger Building and bent fifteen of the installed window frames with a crowbar in hopes of slowing construction to allow time for him and Neumann to request a court injunction to halt work. Neumann, appalled by the Technion's furtive dealings, resigned from his professorial position at the university. The architects filed a lawsuit against the Technion, which responded with a counterclaim. After several hearings and an appeal to the Supreme Court, the only verdict in the architects' favor was an order that the Technion paint the building according to their initial design. This was not done until several years later.

Although the Technion complained about the façade's ability to create proper interior light levels, this grievance likely concealed what was in fact an aversion to the appearance of Neumann's radical modern design. This controversy suggests that the architects may not have been understood or well-respected in Israel, or at least not by the Technion, at the time of the Danciger Building project. Neumann's steadfast defense of his design shows that he refused to be a servile implement: He believed that architecture was a discipline fuelled by artistic expression, creativity, and innovation.

19.1 Plan of the Mechanical Engineering Faculty complex, of which only one laboratory buidling (bottom left) was built

19.2 Site of the new Technion Campus on Mt. Carmel, Haifa

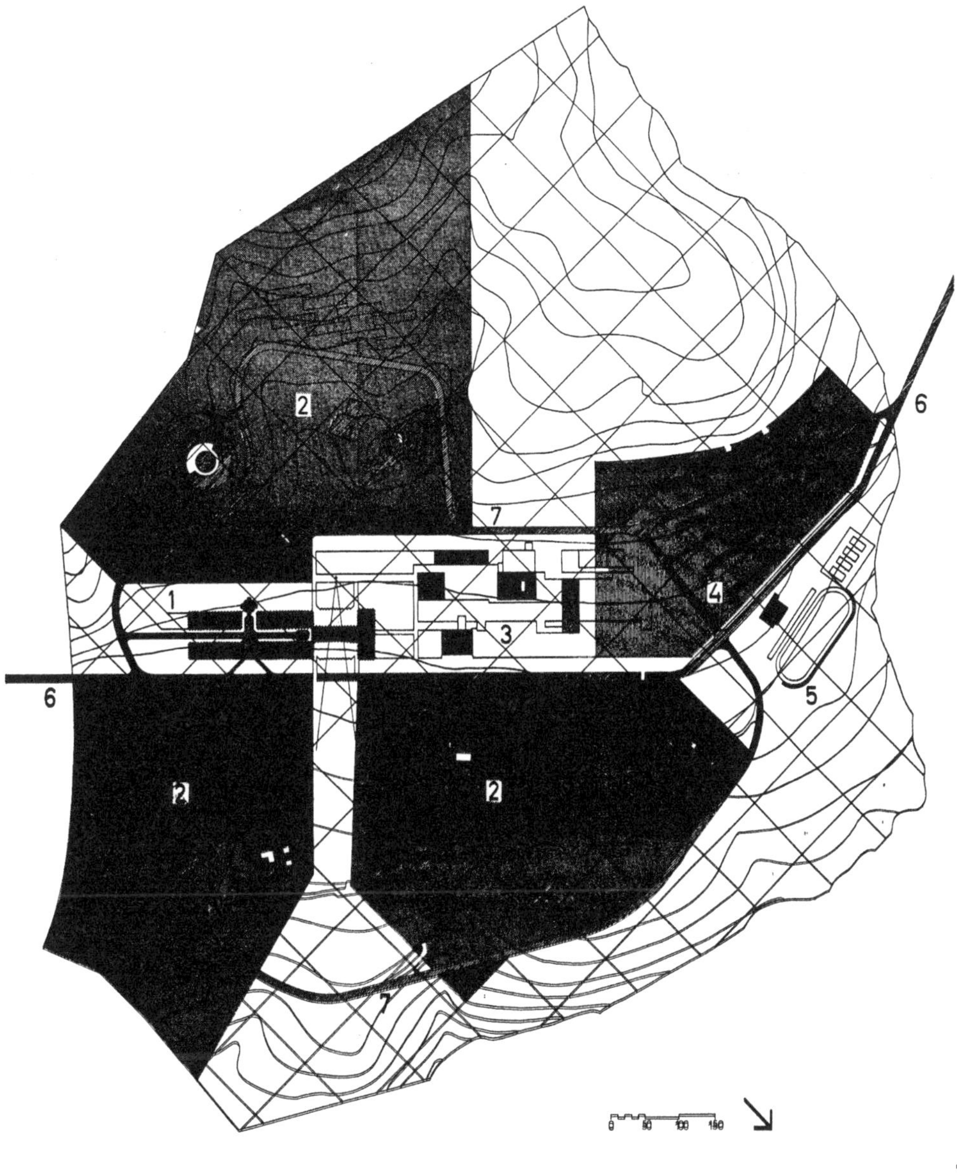

19.3 Site plan of east Technion campus area; [1] Mechanical Engineering Faculty complex at center left

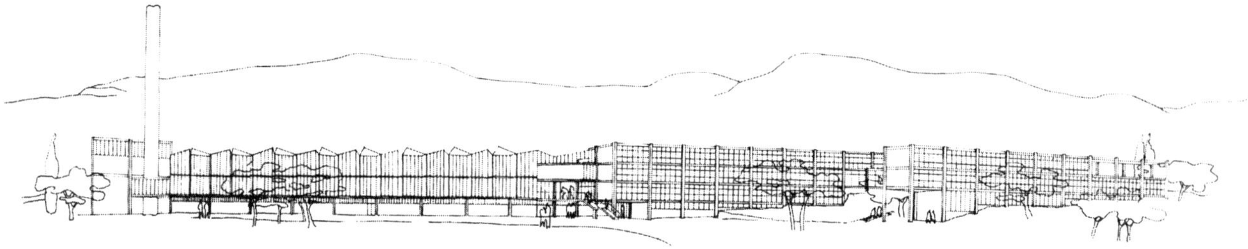

19.4 Early drawing of the Danciger Building before the triangular unit system was conceived

19.5 Early sketch of the triangular unit system
19.6 Detail of the building envelope

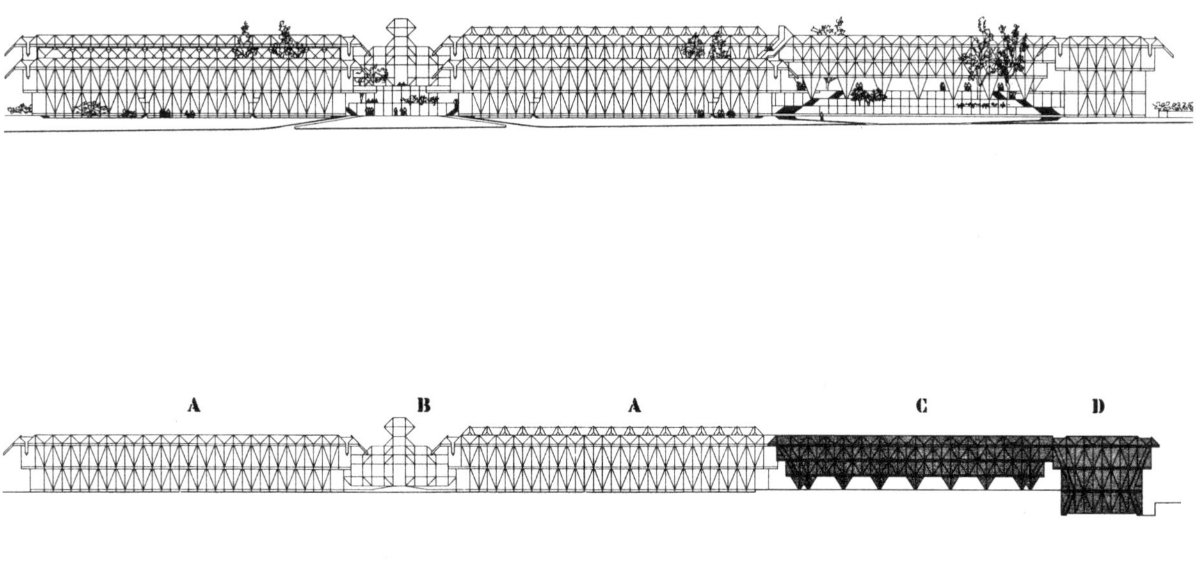

19.7 *Above*: Model of the proposed complex of five buidlings
19.8 Elevations of the complex

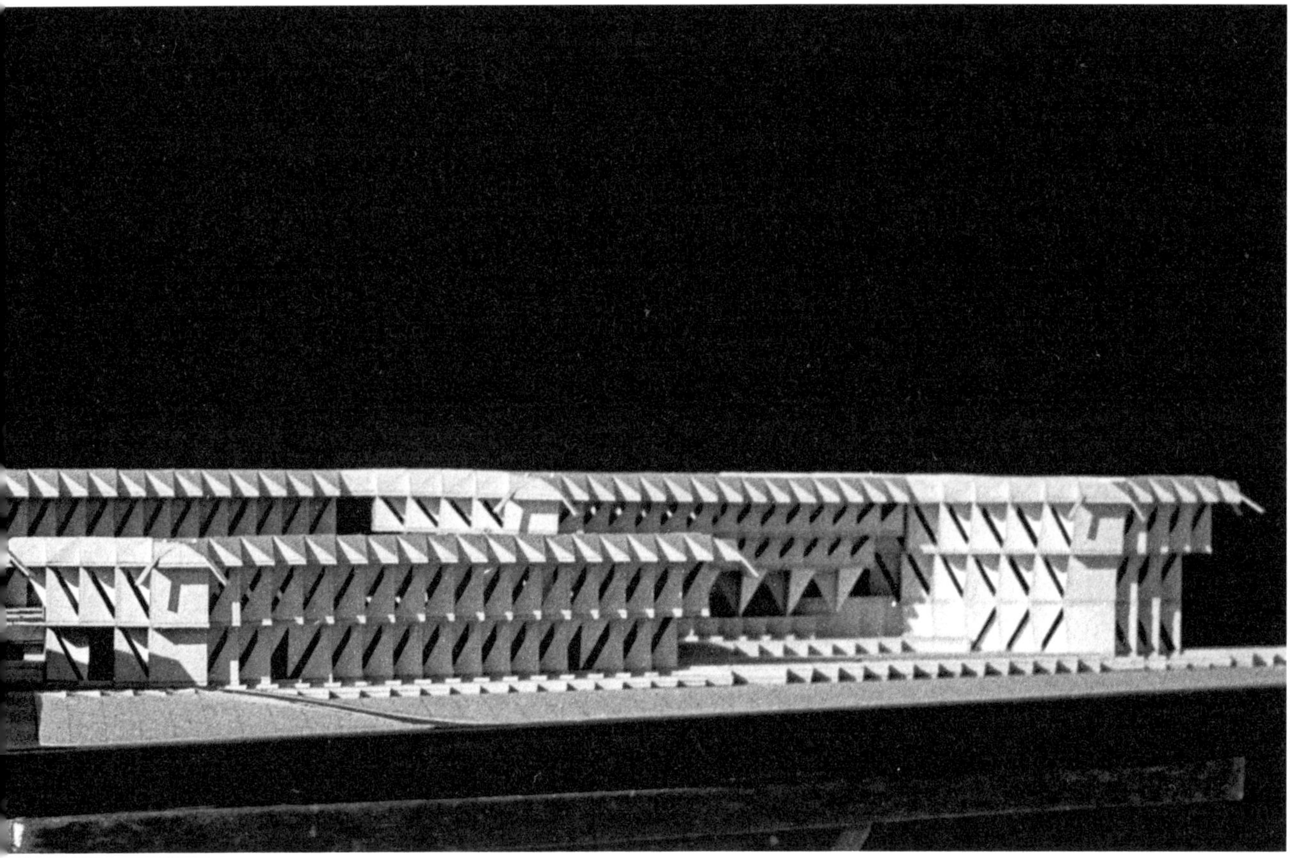

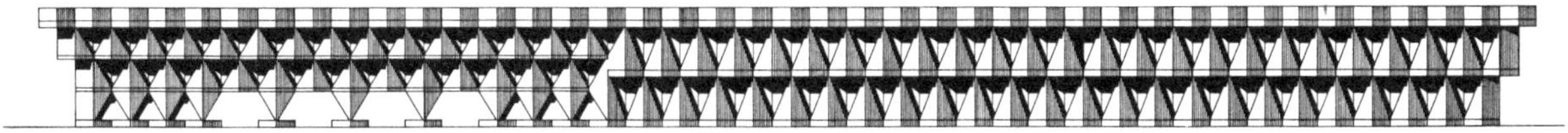

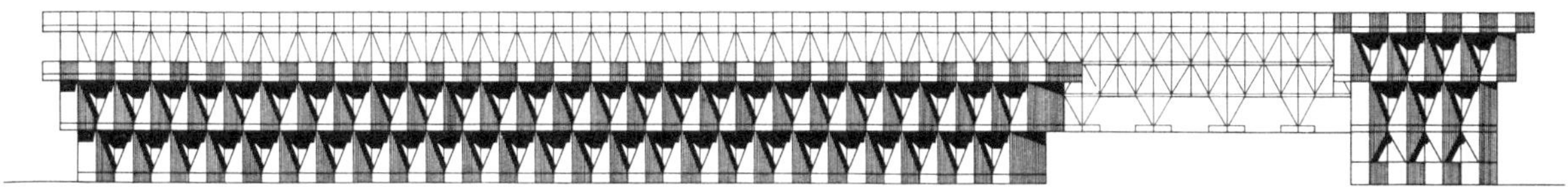

19.9 Elevation and section of the complex

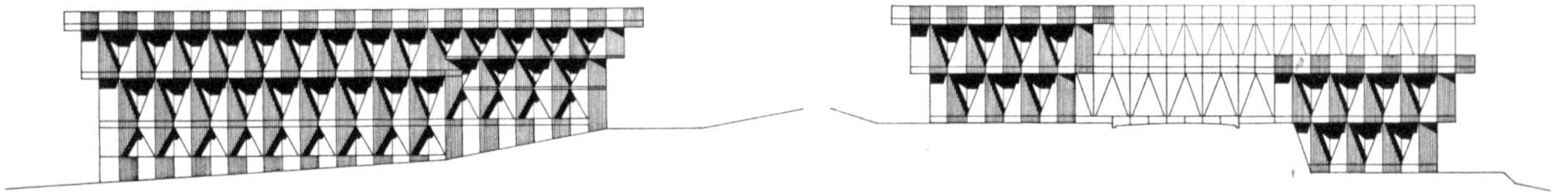

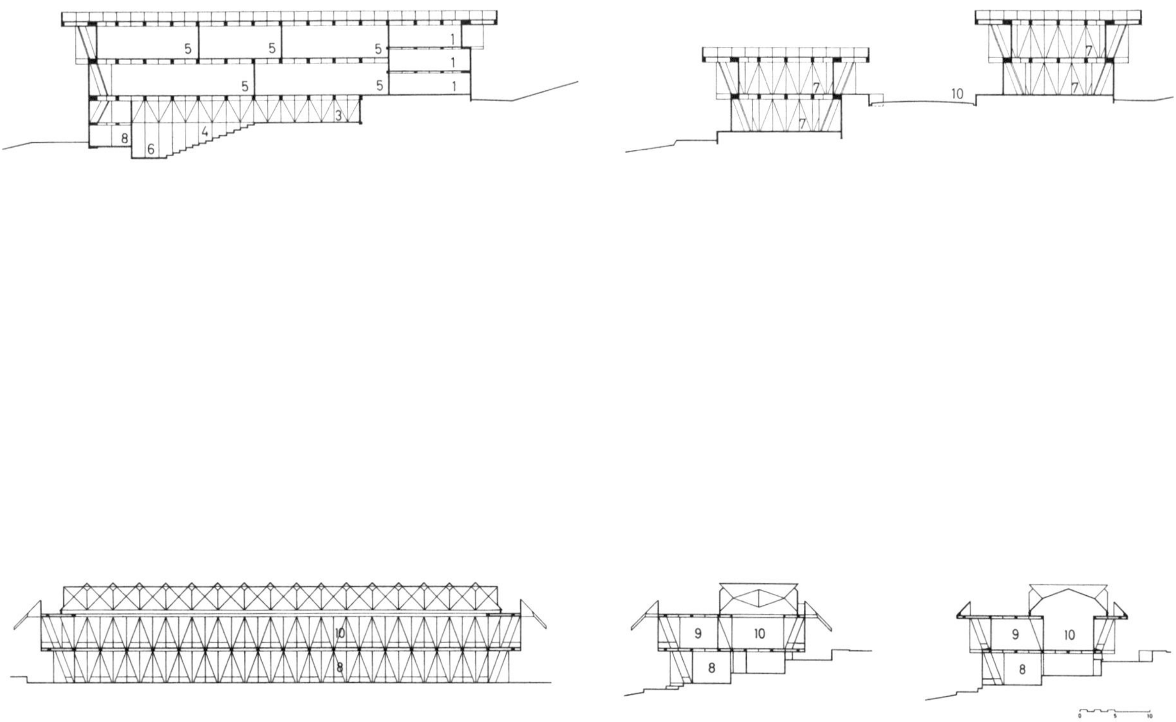

19.10 Side elevations of the complex
19.11 Sections of the complex

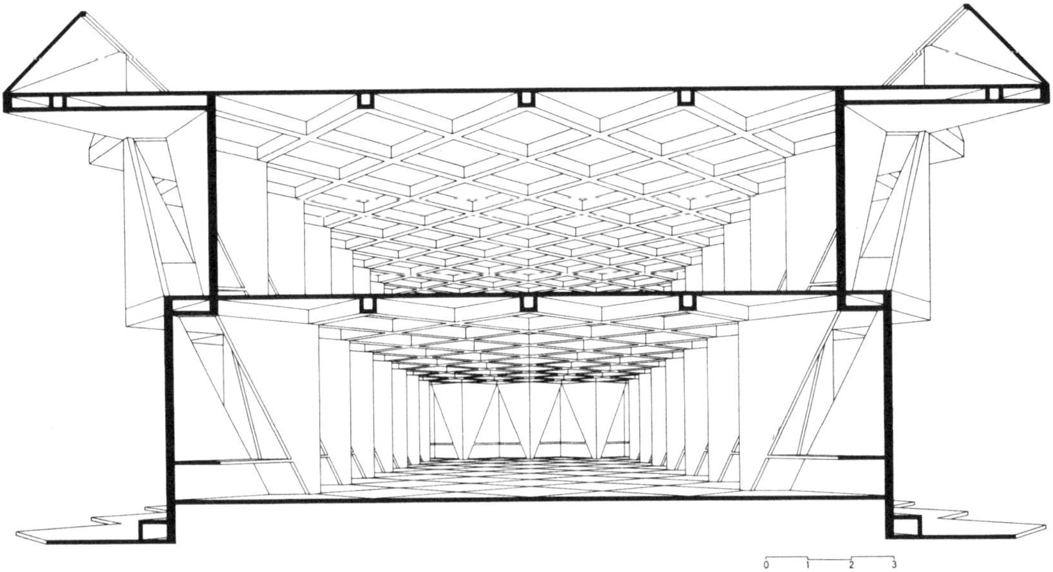

1 2

19.12 Perspectival section of a single building
19.13 [1] Diagram of a single building reacting to sun and ventilation, [2] Structural diagram

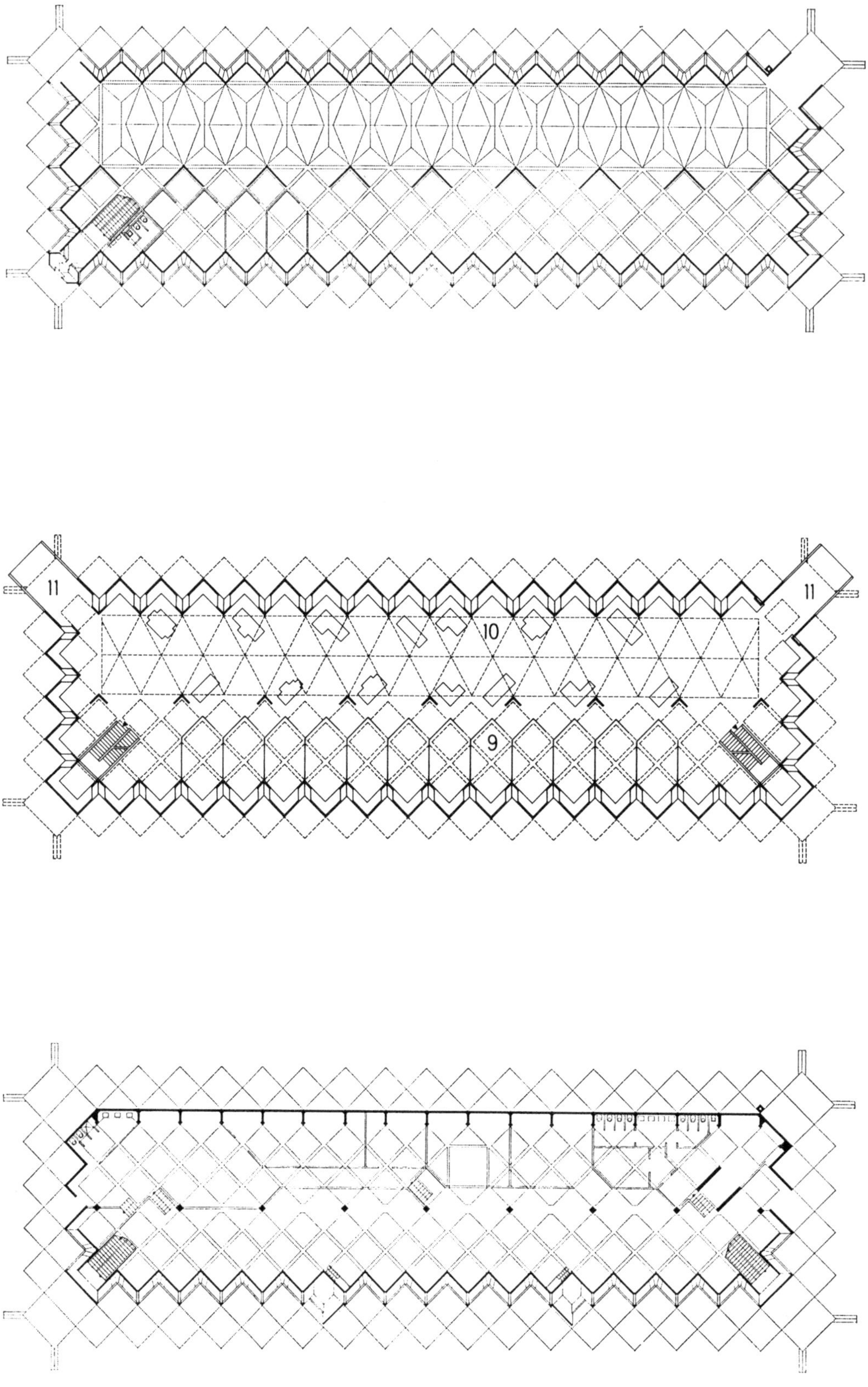

19.14 Plans of the single laboratory building that was constructed, top floor (top, center), ground floor (bottom)

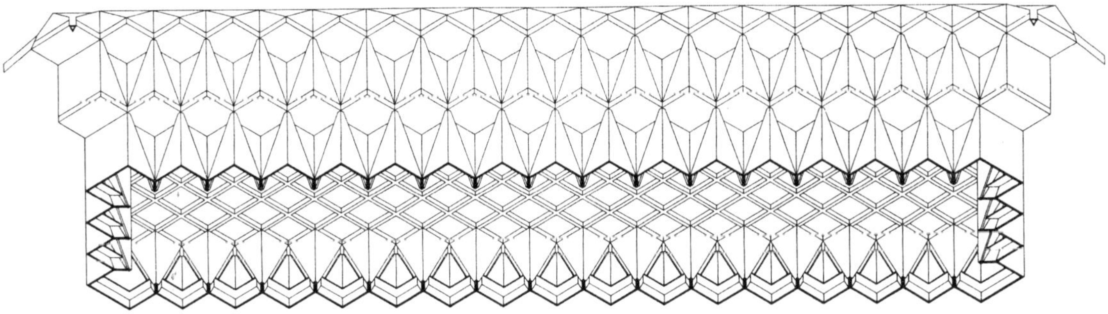

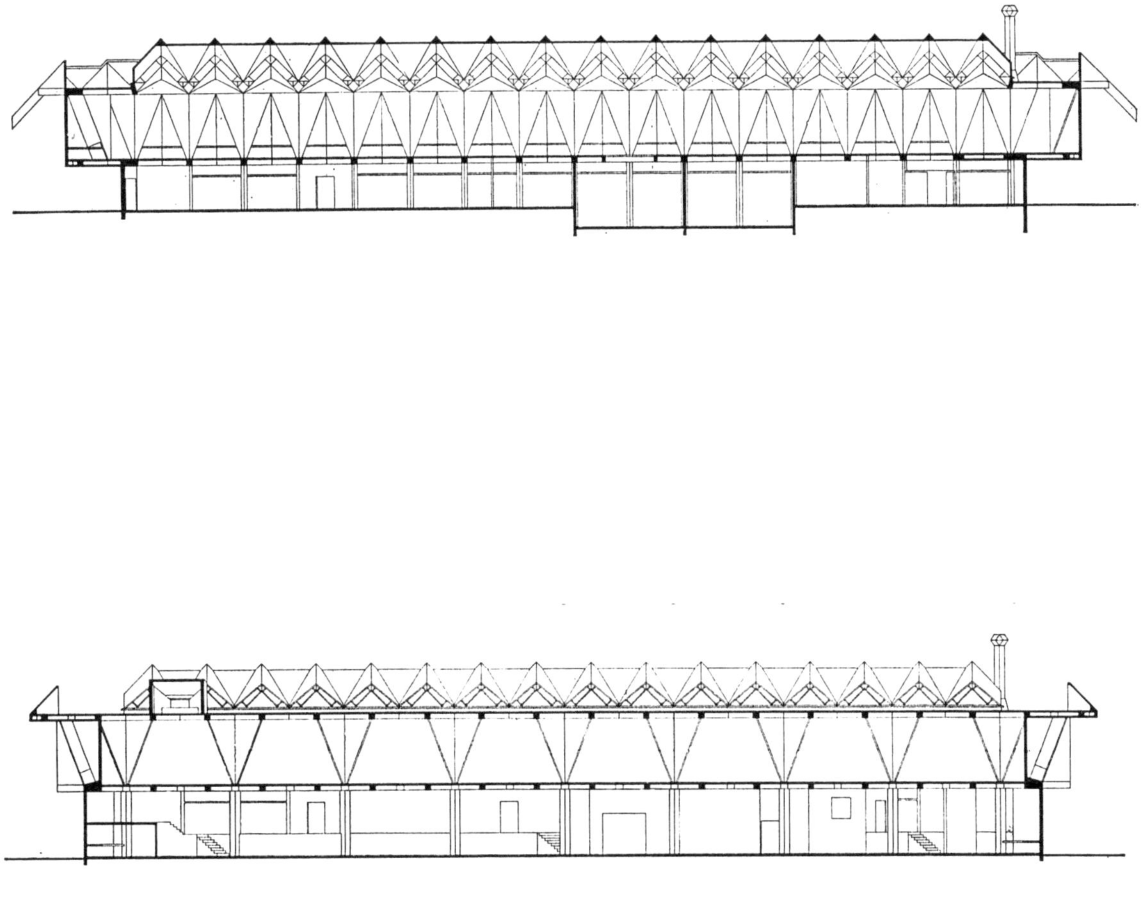

19.15 Axonometric view from below
19.16 Longitudinal sections

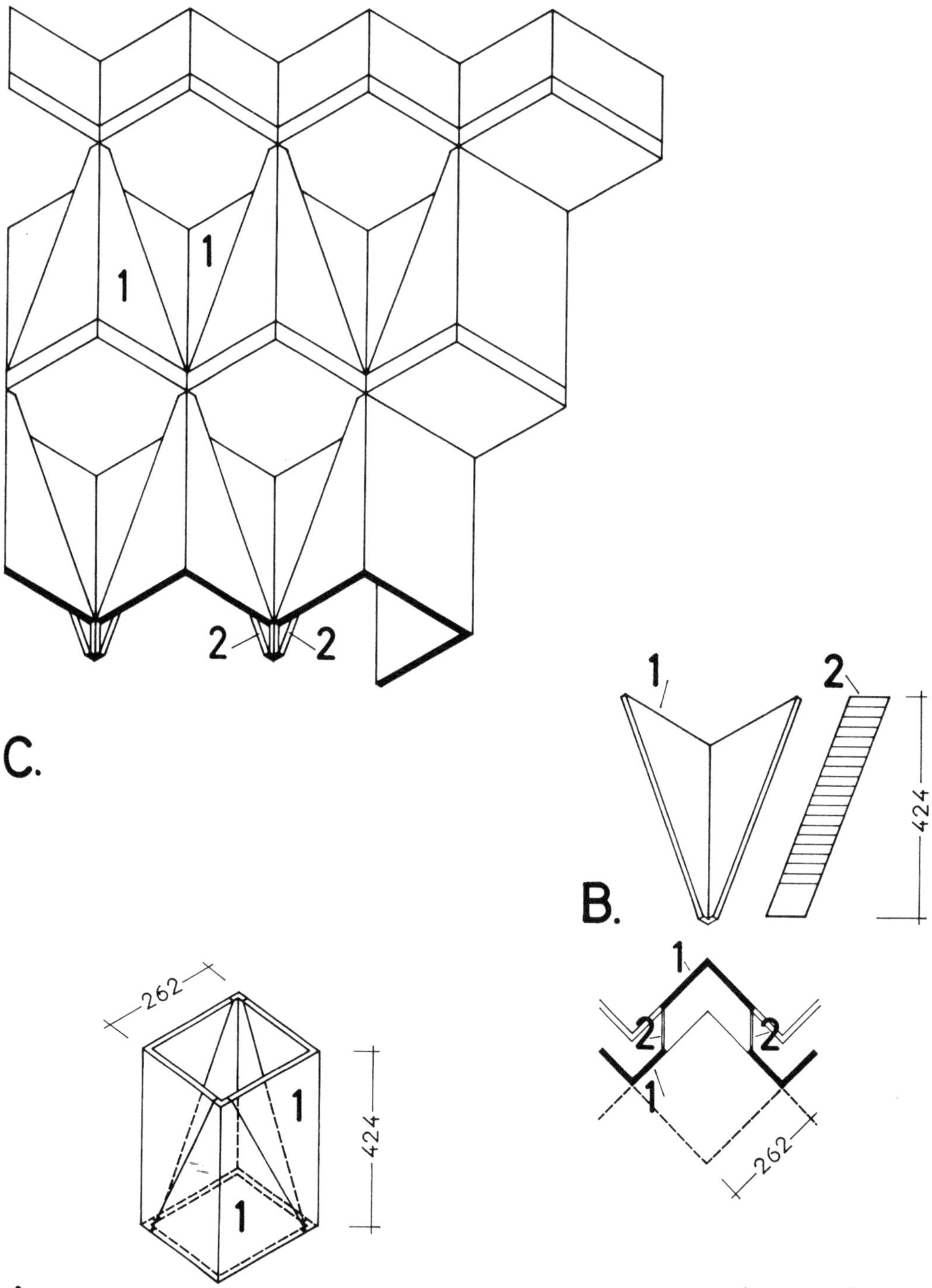

19.17 Basic unit; dimensions following Alfred Neumann's MΦ system

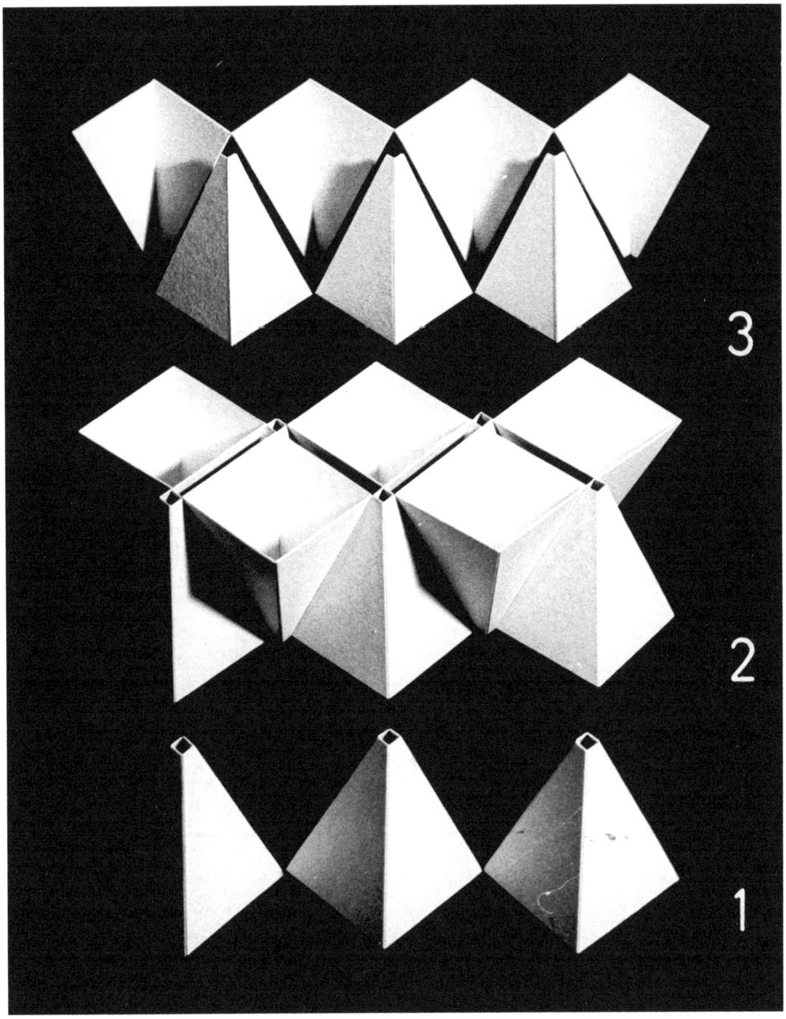

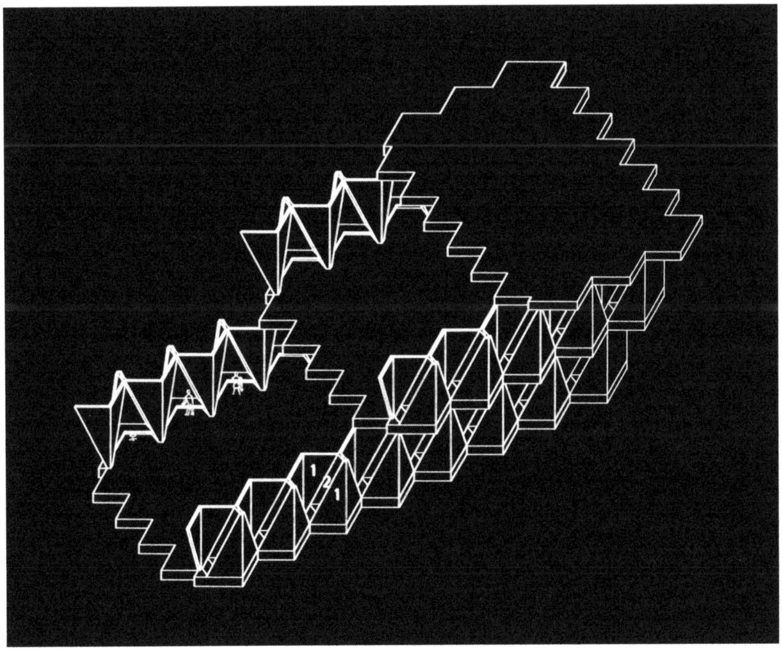

19.18 Model of the triangular units in combination
19.19 Organization of the triangular units to form a structure and building envelope

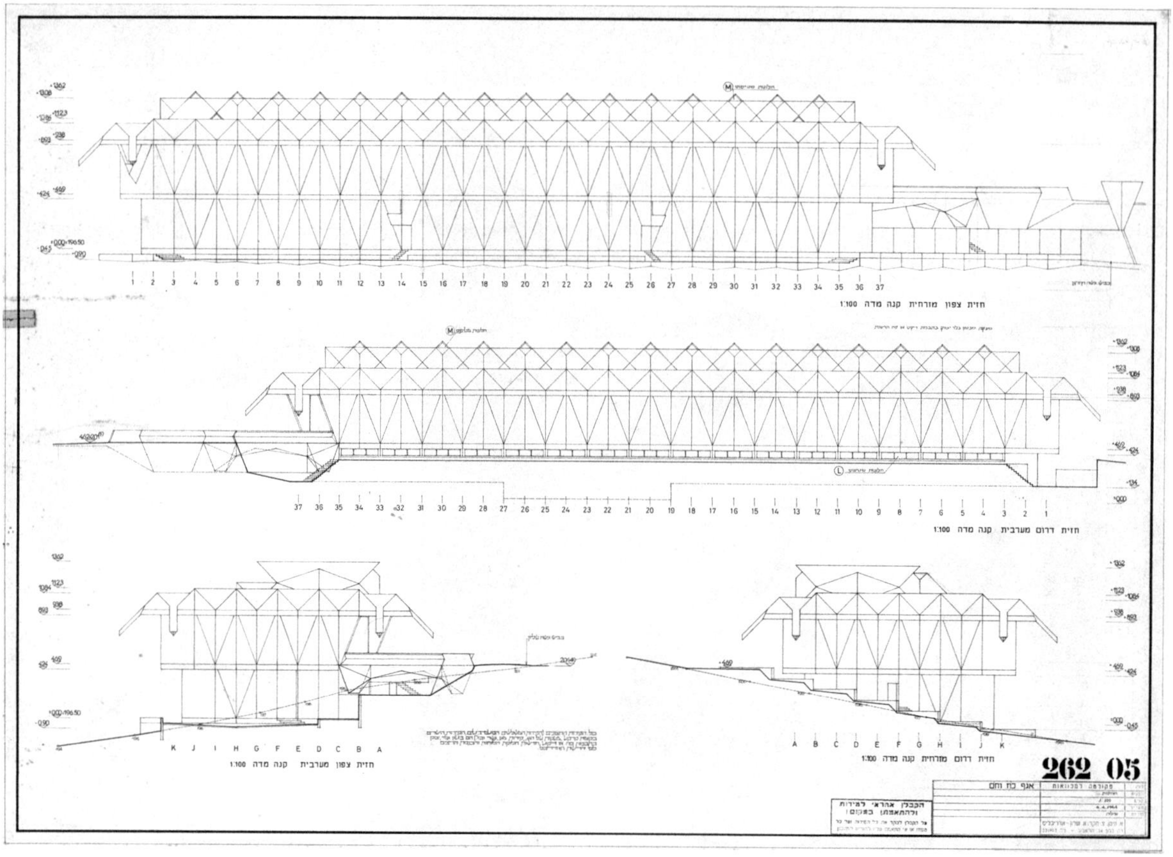

19.20 Original construction drawings: elevations
19.21 Original construction drawings: roof plan

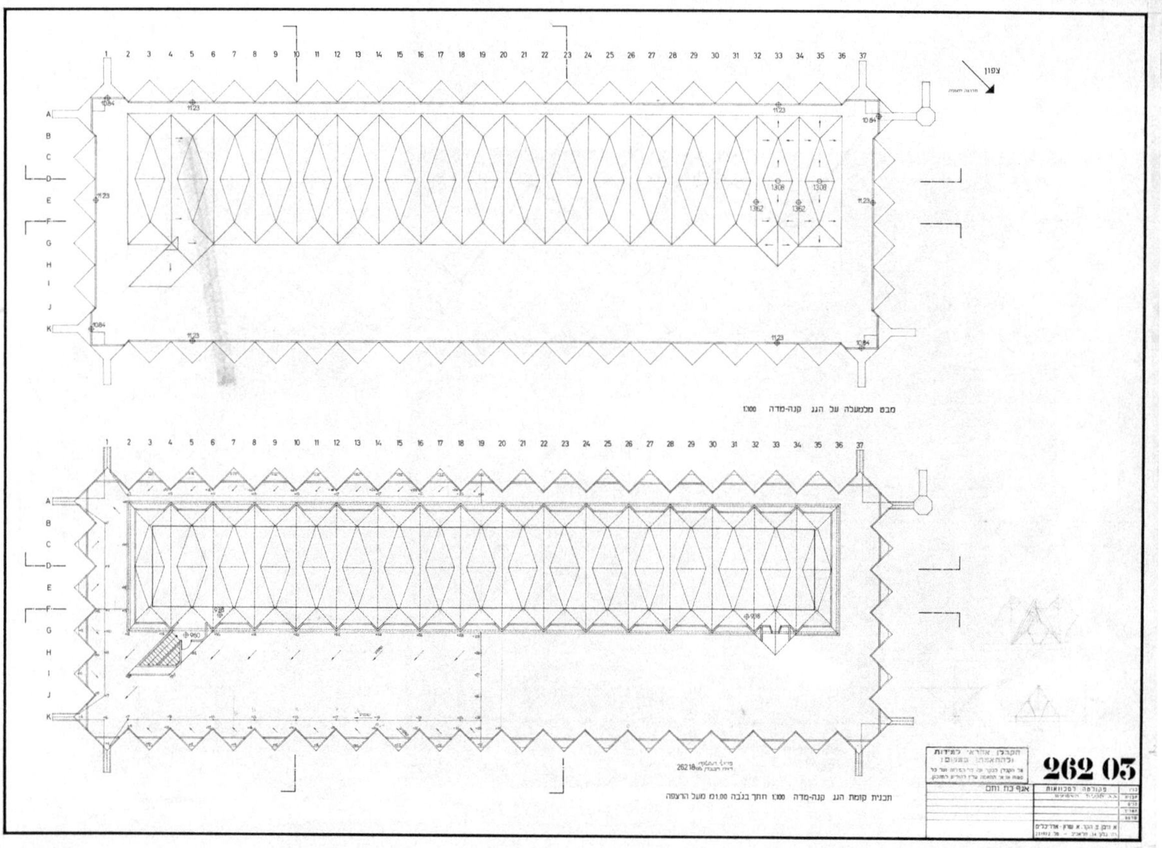

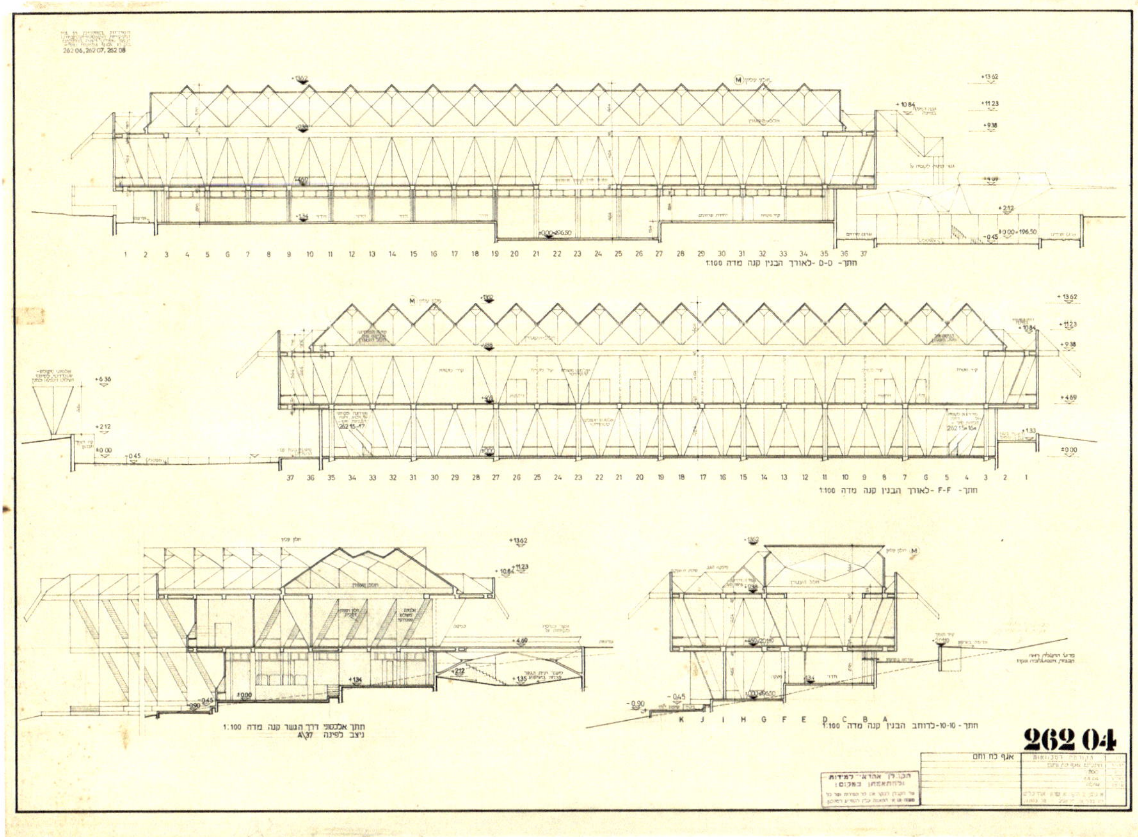

19.22 Original construction drawings: sections
19.23 Original construction drawings: plans

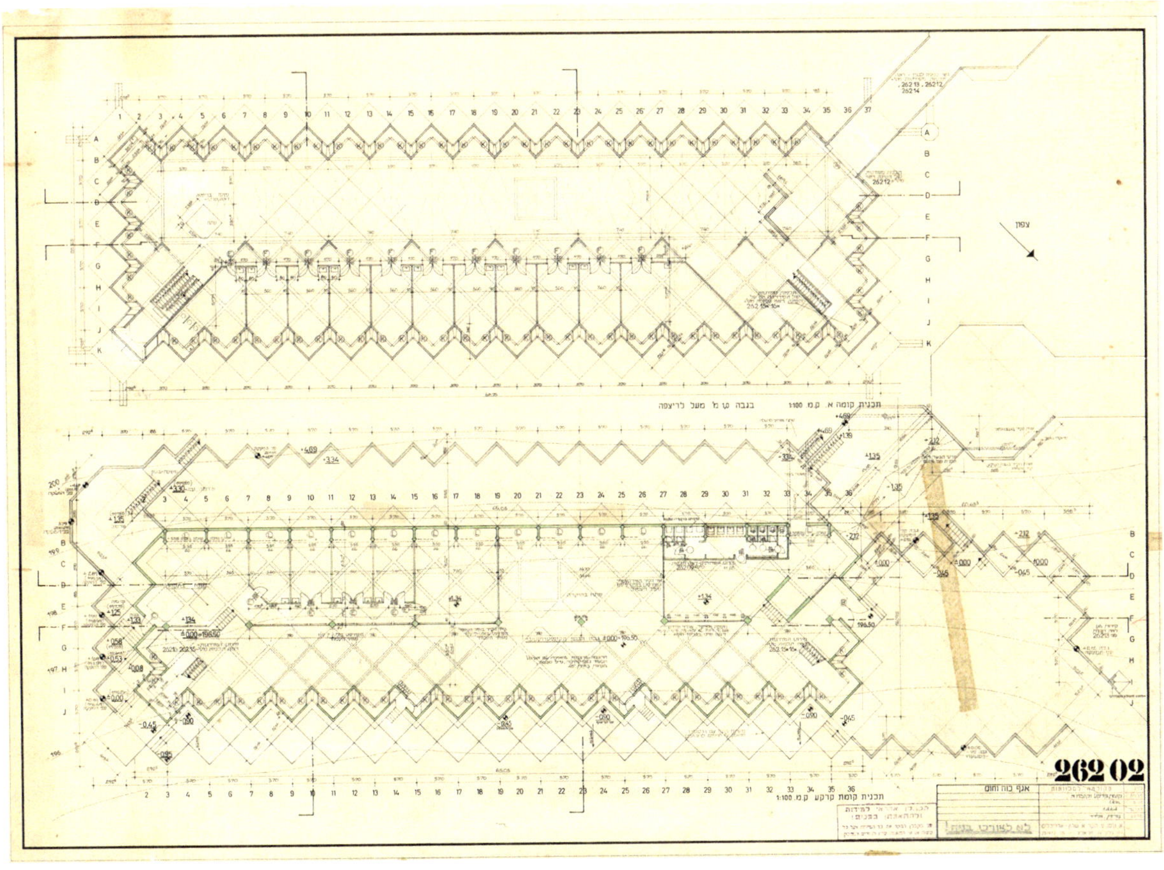

19.24 Construction of lower triangular units
19.25 Construction of jagged building envelope and structural system

19.26 Triangular unit; reinforced concrete, 14cm thick

19.27 The Danciger Building under construction during Neumann's site visit

17

18

19.28 Interior view of the upper hall during construction
19.29 Interior view of the lower hall during construction

19.30 Interior view of the lower hall during construction

19.31 Sketches showing color scheme of exterior
19.32 Sketches showing interior color scheme of the upper hall; alternating yellow and blue

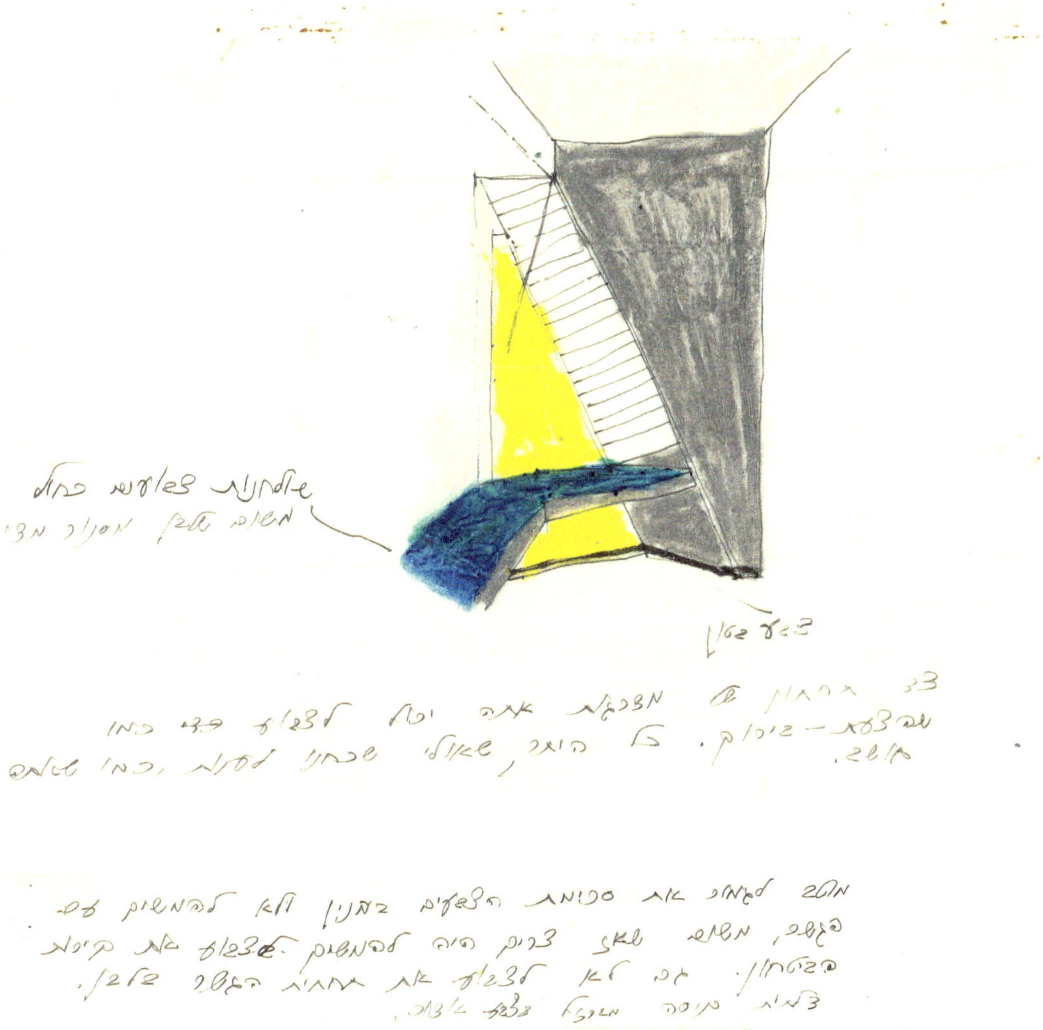

19.33 Sketch detailing the color of a single interior workstation unit created between every two alternating units
19.34 Sketches showing exterior color scheme for the side elevation indicating where to leave the concrete exposed. The four sketches were among several others sent from Neumann, residing in Canada at the time, to Zvi Hecker in Israel. The handwritten notes in Hebrew are by Naomi Neumann, recording Neumann's comments

19.35 View of the constructed laboratory building from downhill showing Mt. Carmel in the background

19.36 Side entrance detail

19.37 Side elevation and main entrance bridge

19.38

20 Ashdod City Center 1965
Ashdod, Israel

With Zvi Hecker

Sited on the shore of the Mediterranean, the Ashdod City Center was designed to form the heart of the new city of Ashdod. The project, which was undertaken for a competition, comprises three elements arranged axially that form a pathway linking sea and land: an artificial basin, a tiered plaza, and a residential quarter.

The basin is octagonal in plan, and is formed by two arms built out over the sea. At the outermost point of the basin is an opening through which boats may enter, over which an administrative building is raised up, anchored on each side to the two enclosing arms of the basin. The basin serves as a marina and fishing port, augmenting the functionality of the existing commercial port of Ashdod. Furthermore, various hotels are situated around the basin, and are connected to the arms of the port. In the project submission for the competition, the architects referenced the port of Ostia as a historical precedent for a hexagonal water basin in the Mediterranean.

Across the basin, opposite the port entrance and administrative building is a plaza, which serves as a central connection point between the basin and the residential quarter. The plaza has three stepped levels ascending the shore, and contains restaurants, cafes, nightclubs, and travel agencies, along with various cultural amenities such as a theater, museum, concert hall, and cinema. The north and south sides of the plaza are each flanked by three high-rise office buildings. Behind each row of office buildings are recreational areas with parks and pools, leading onto the beach.

Further inland, adjacent to the plaza, is the residential quarter. It contains four nearly identical neighborhoods in the form of large octagons, each containing from 1,400 to 1,800 residential units. These units are distributed among several three- to five-story bar buildings, bent in plan to form the shape of an octagon. The spaces between the buildings are interconnected by a circulatory network of pedestrian and vehicular paths, and in the central area between the four neighborhood quarters is an open area with nurseries, kindergartens, schools, playgrounds, and synagogues, accessible to all residents on foot.

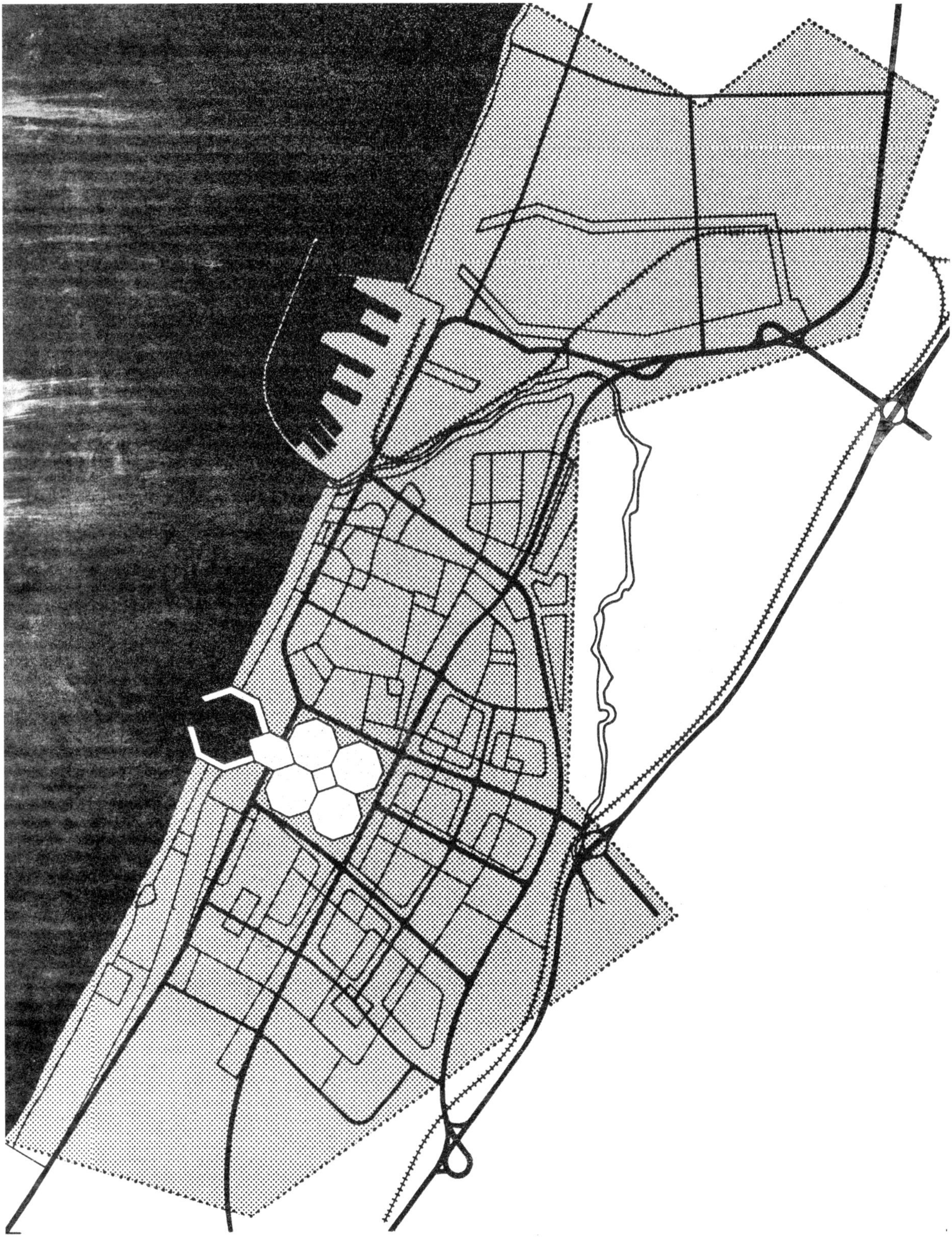

20.1 City of Ashdod; group of octagons marking the proposed civic center and new marina

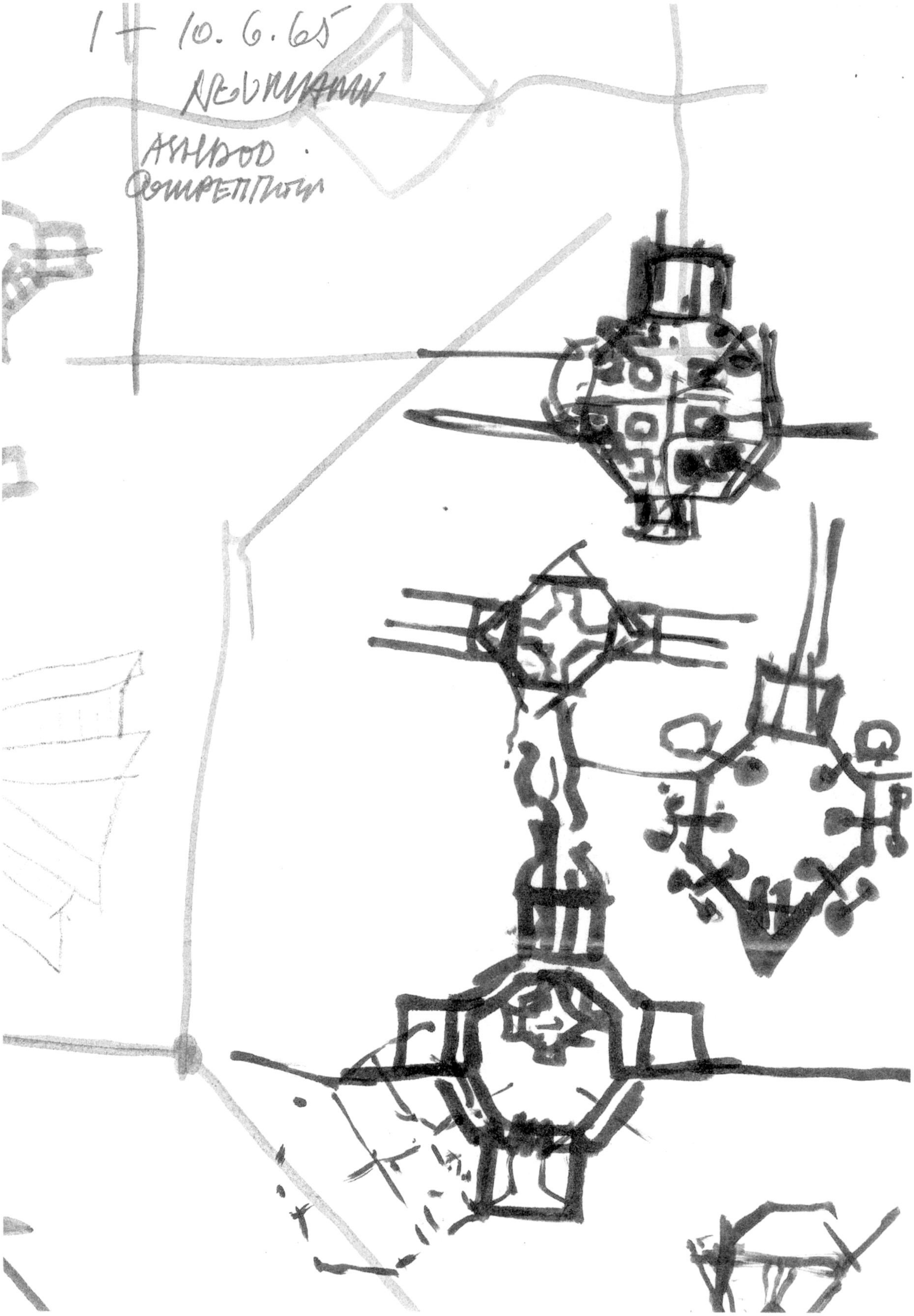

20.2 Early sketches by Neumann

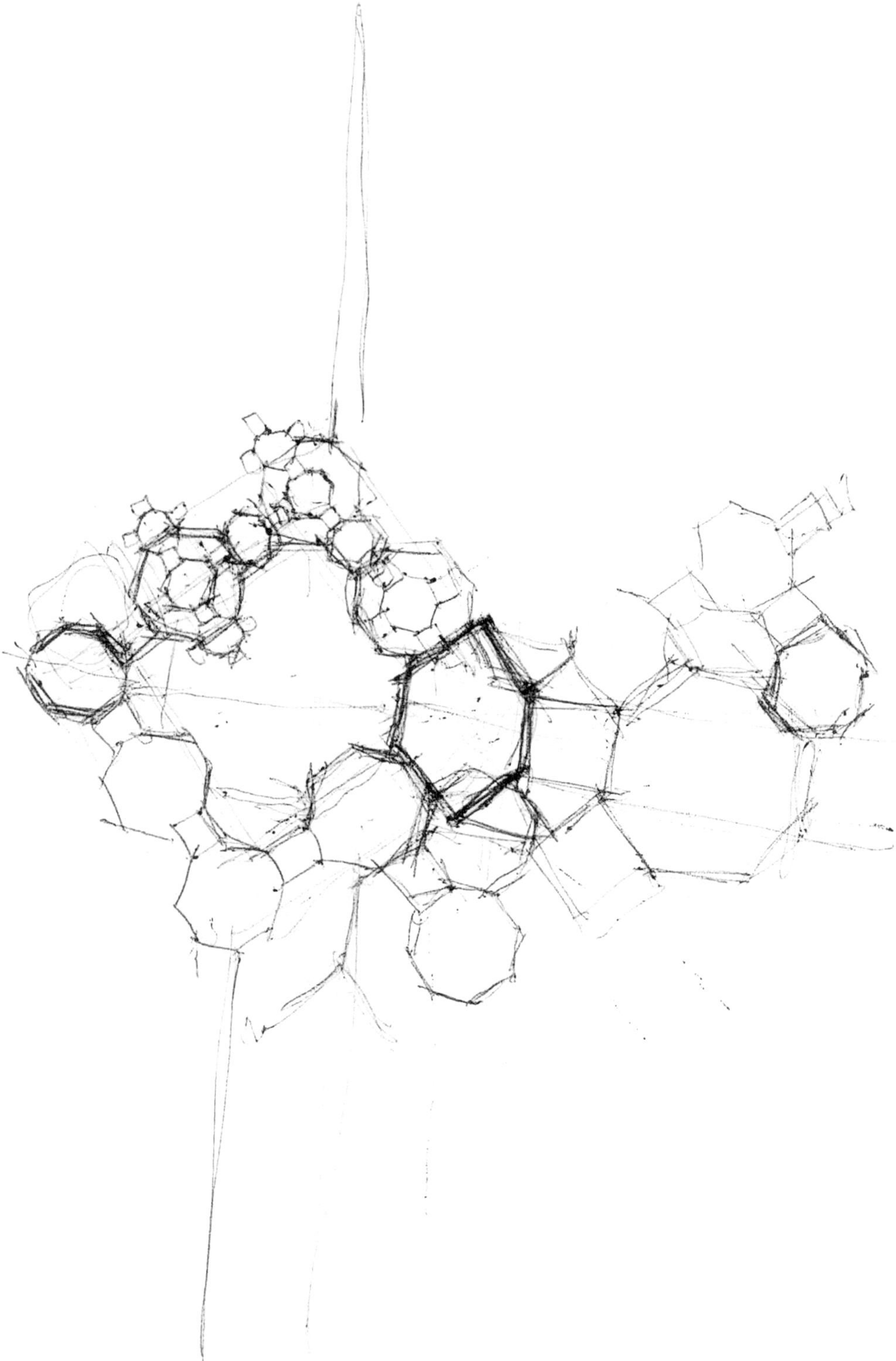

20.3 Sketch showing the octagon and square geometries at their various scales

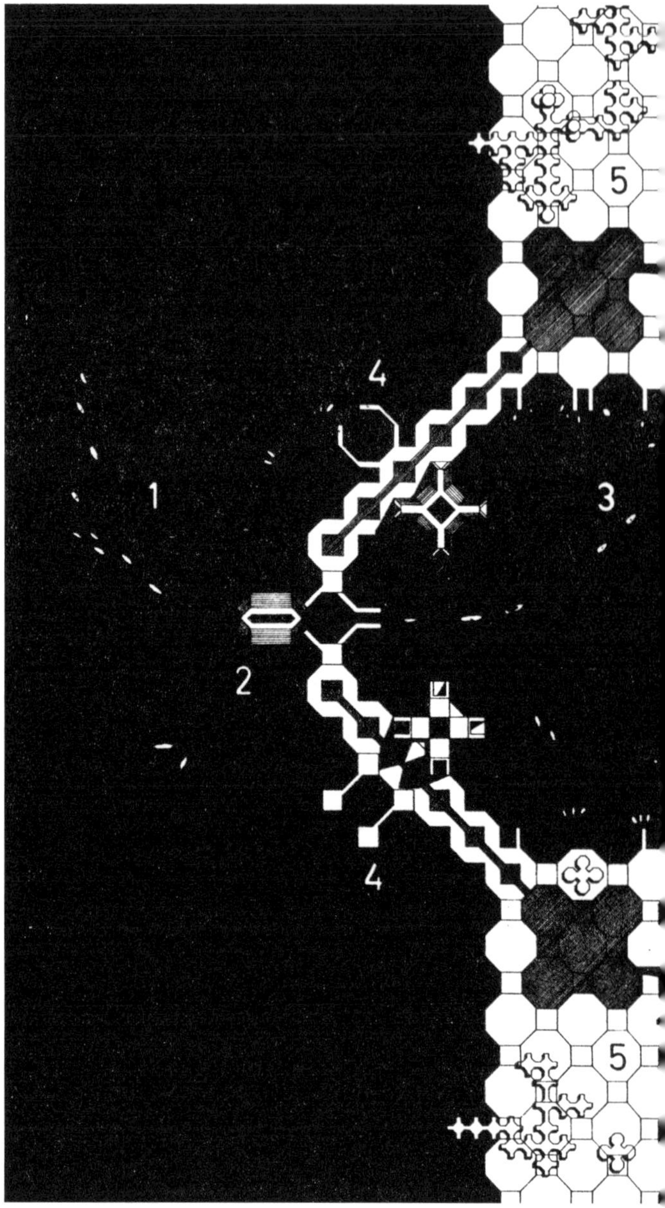
5
4
1
3
2
4
5

20.4 Urban plan and section

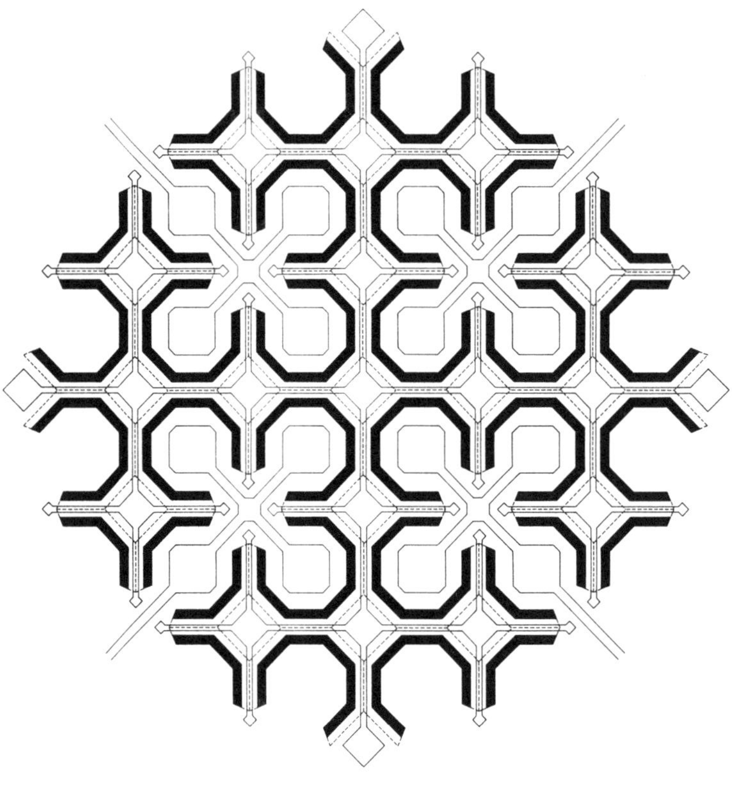

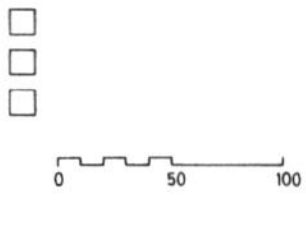

20.5 Urban unit
20.6 Pattern

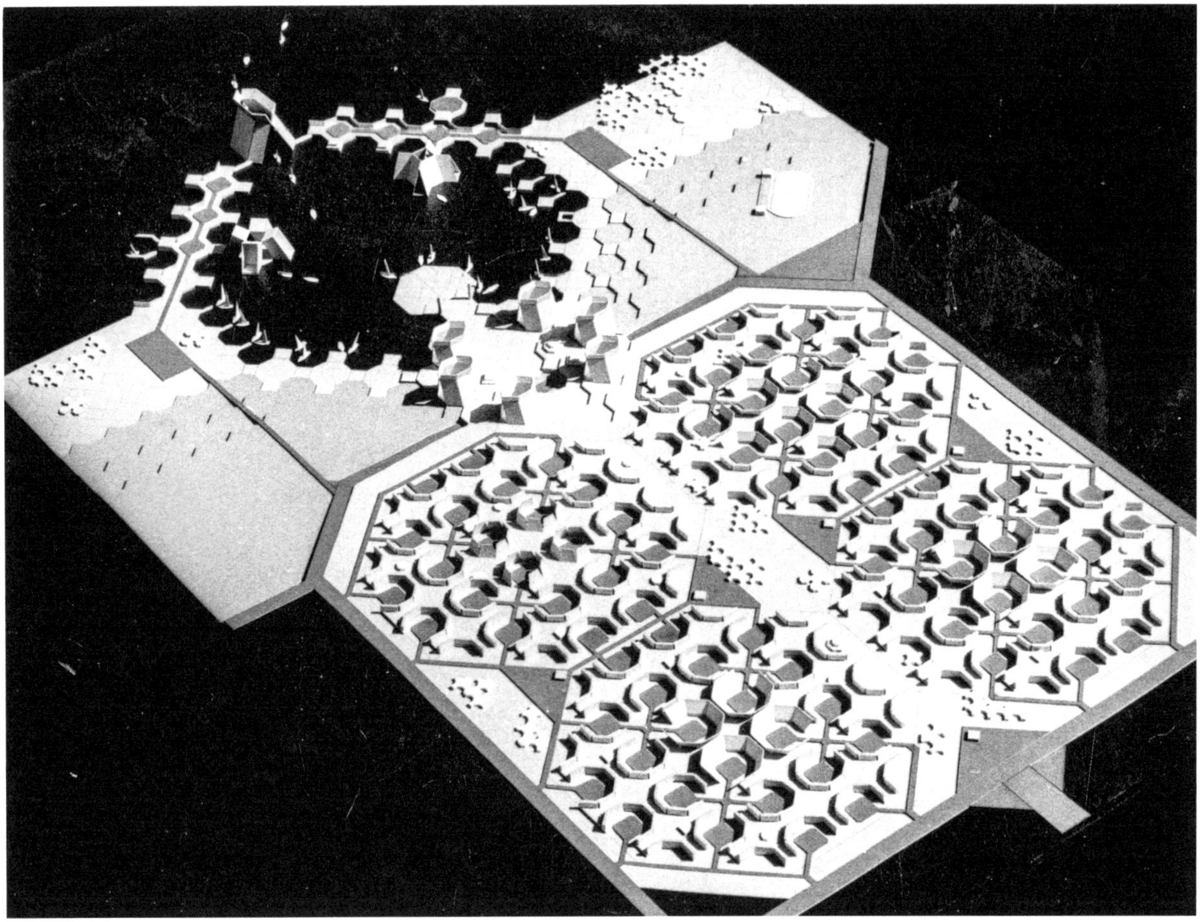

20.7 Model views

21 El-Al Terminal Pavilion
Tel Aviv, Israel

1966

With Zvi Hecker

The El-Al Terminal was conceived as a gathering space for passengers departing from the city by bus for the airport. The terminal was designed in the form of a triangular pyramid with three points of access: a passenger entrance on one side, and taxi and bus loading areas located along the others. The main space inside the terminal is a large triangular room with a waiting area and ticket counters. Offices occupy a small gallery that projects over the pedestrian entrance.

The walls of the terminal are formed from stacked, hollow truncated tetrahedral units. These units are built from hexagonal panels, which yield triangular apertures when joined together. The interior of the building is essentially open to the exterior, therefore, and light freely penetrates the numerous openings, flooding the central space with light. In this building, structure, closure, and lighting are resolved with a single wall element.

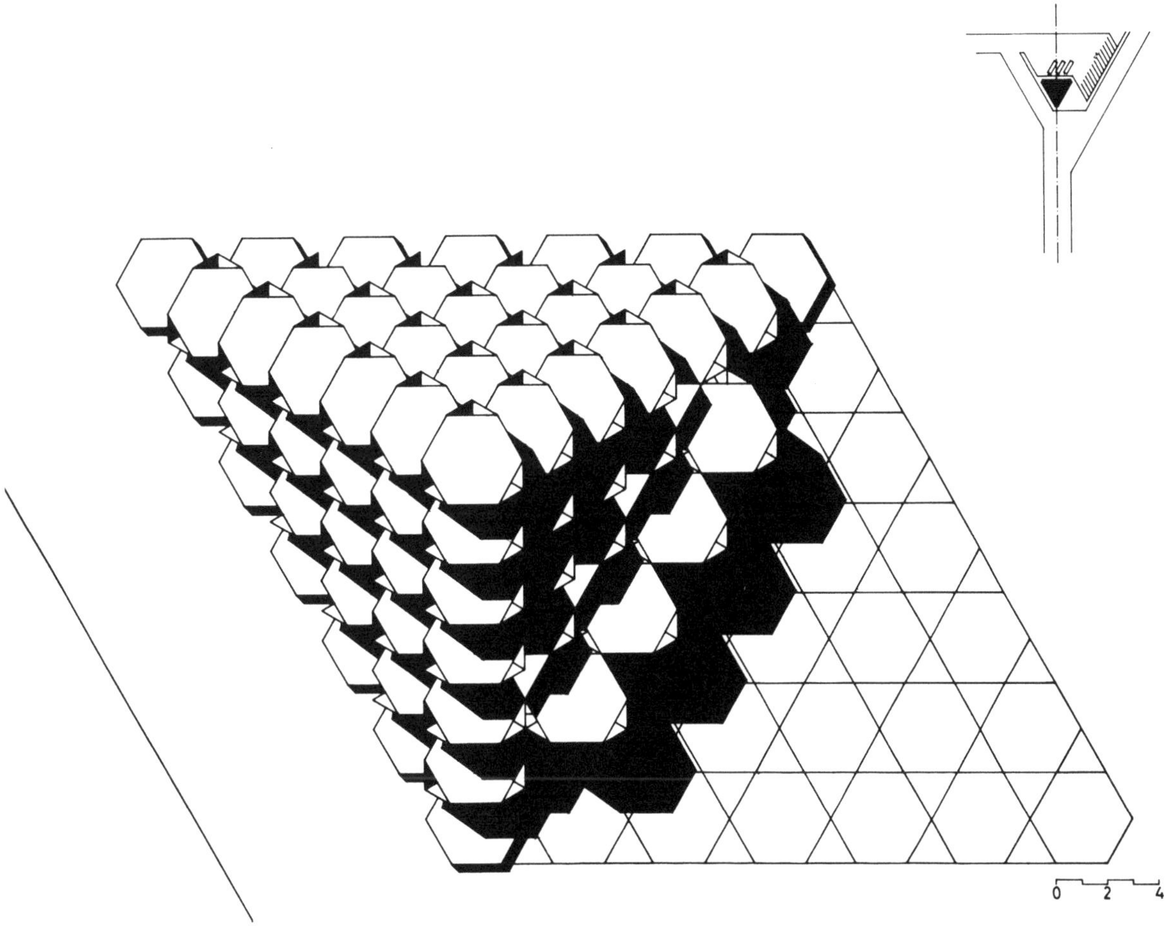

21.1

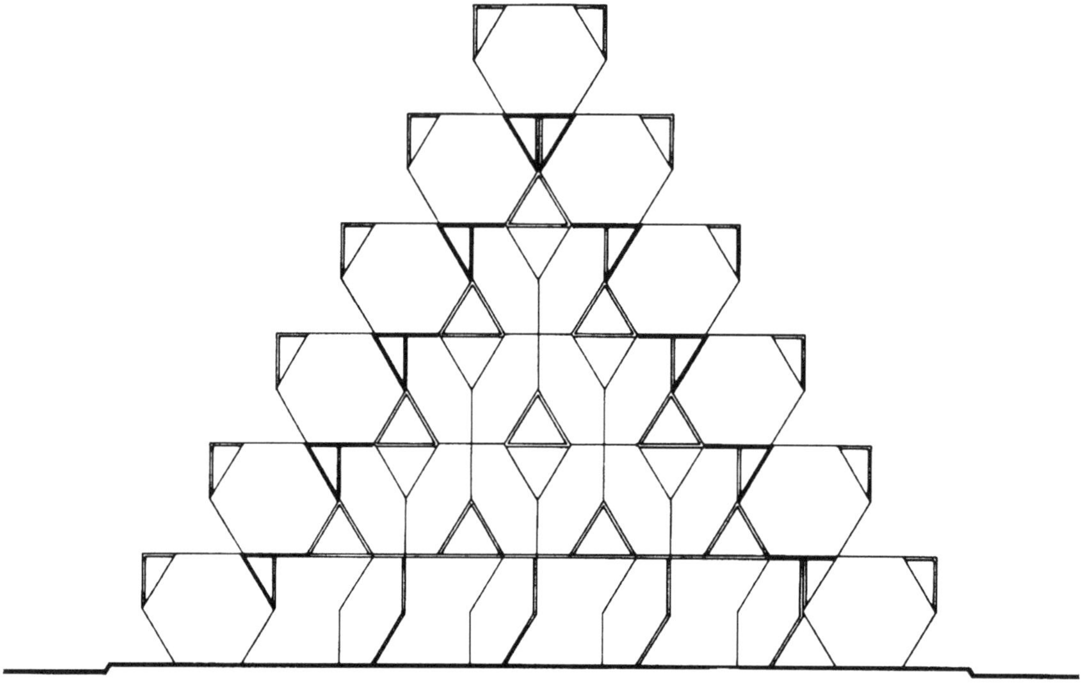

29
COPPER
0 2 4

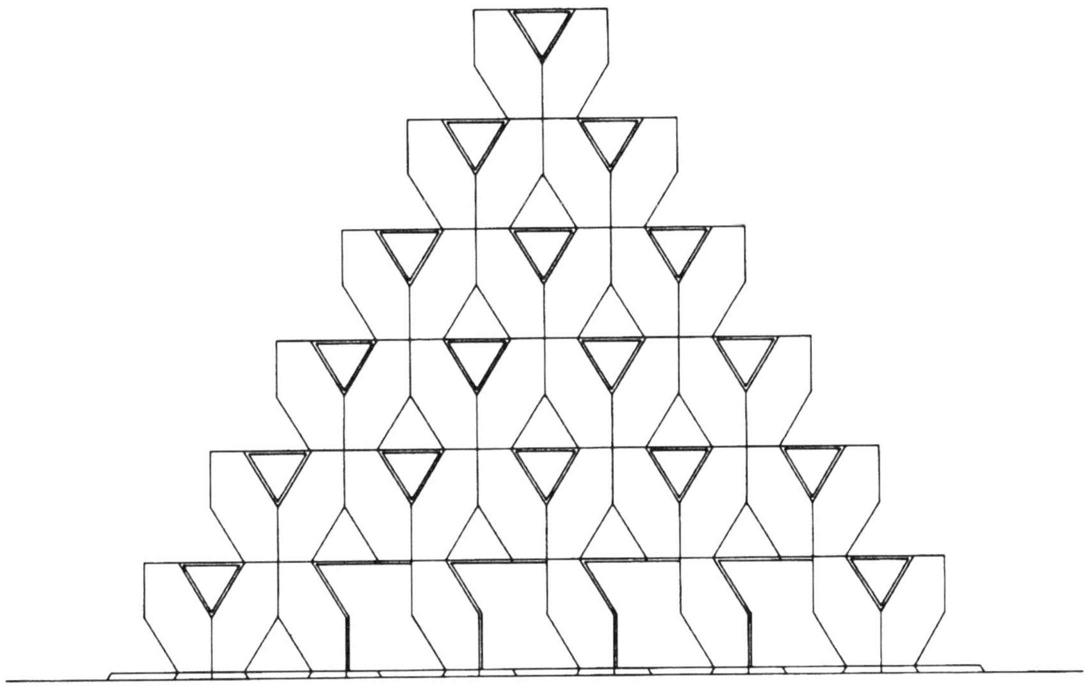

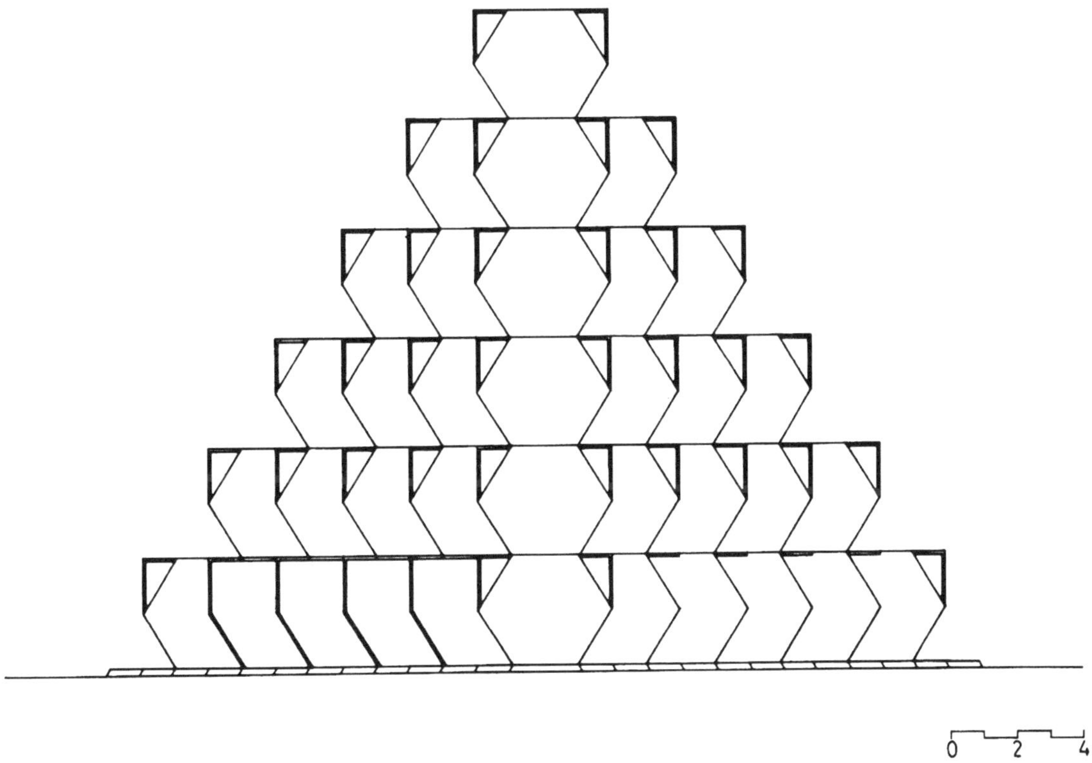

21.3 Elevation view parallel to tetahedron side
21.4 Elevation view facing tetahedron edge

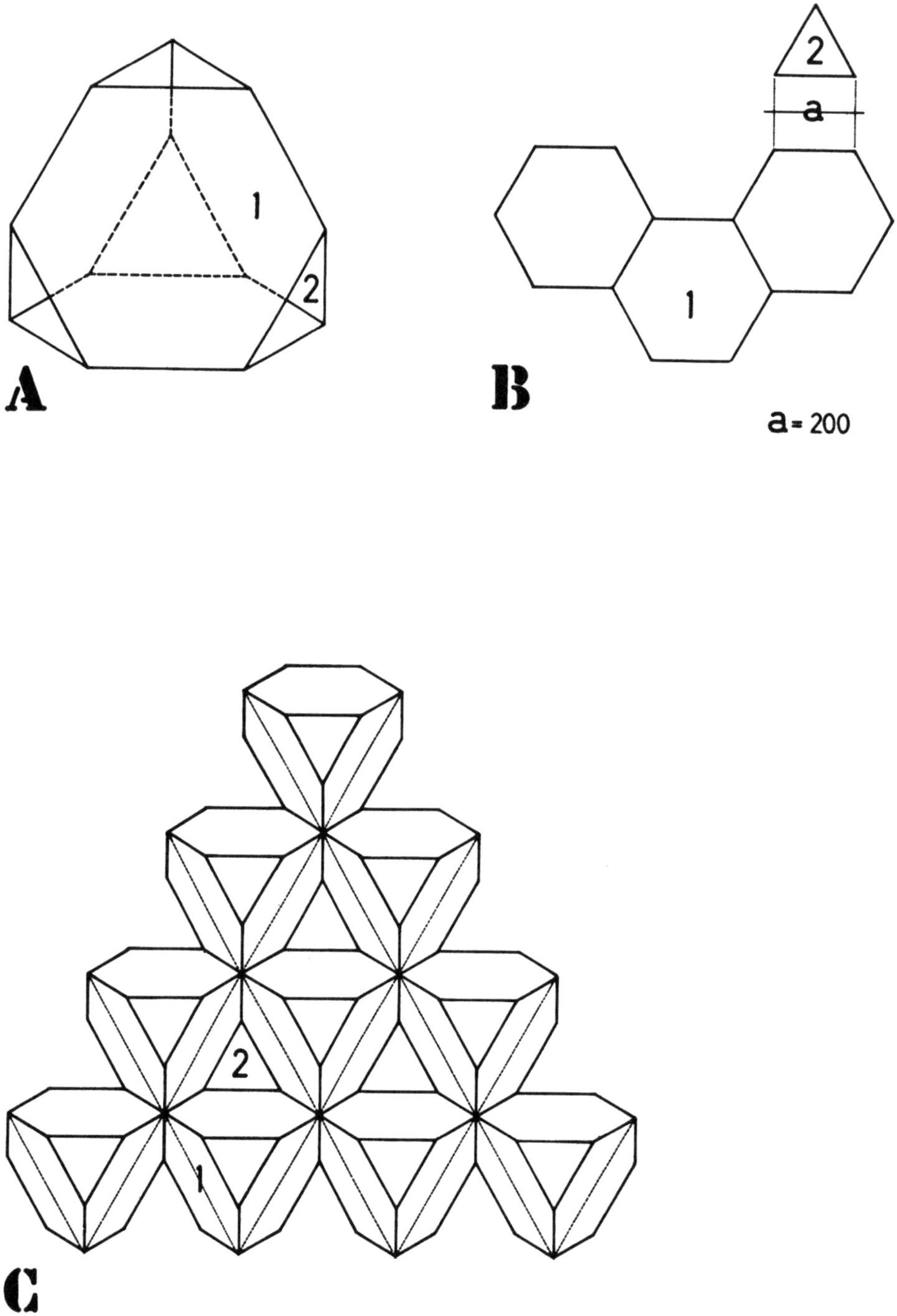

21.5 (A) Unit, (C) Pattern

21.6 Model view

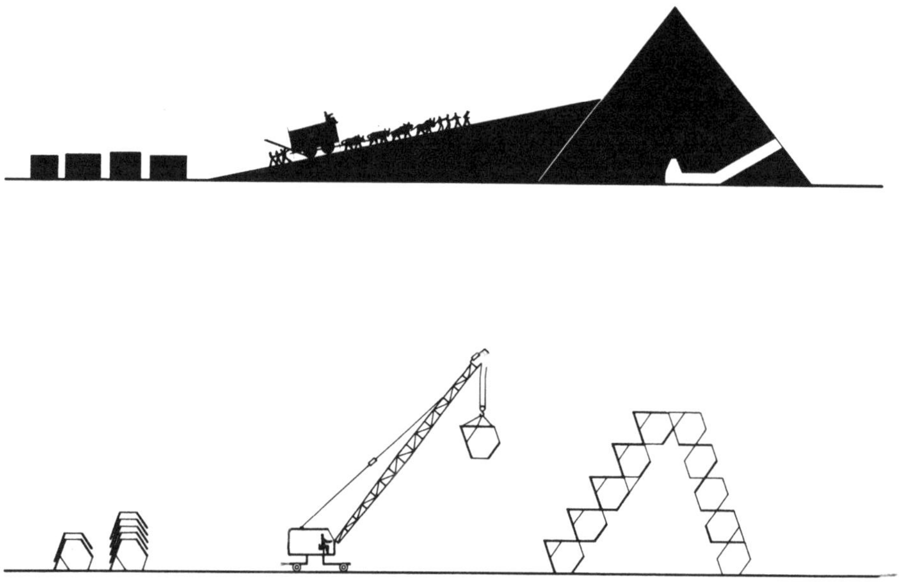

21.7 Model view

21.8 Diagram showing the process of dematerialization of architecture in its historical development; the building mass reduced to constituent, hollowed-out, volumetric elements

21.9 Model showing the lit structure at night

22 Synagogue, *Competition* 1966

With Zvi Hecker

Neumann and Hecker conceived the synagogue building as a large, truncated tetrahedral shell, built up from smaller, space-packed, hollow, truncated tetrahedral units. Each of these units was to be prefabricated from thin hexagonal concrete panels, forming a volumetric wall of about 3 meters deep. The triangular openings that are formed by the joined hexagonal panels serve as windows that allow direct light into the interior. The project aims to create an architectural unit where structure, space, and light are fully integrated to form a single whole. This project represents a clear example of what I term a patterned object.

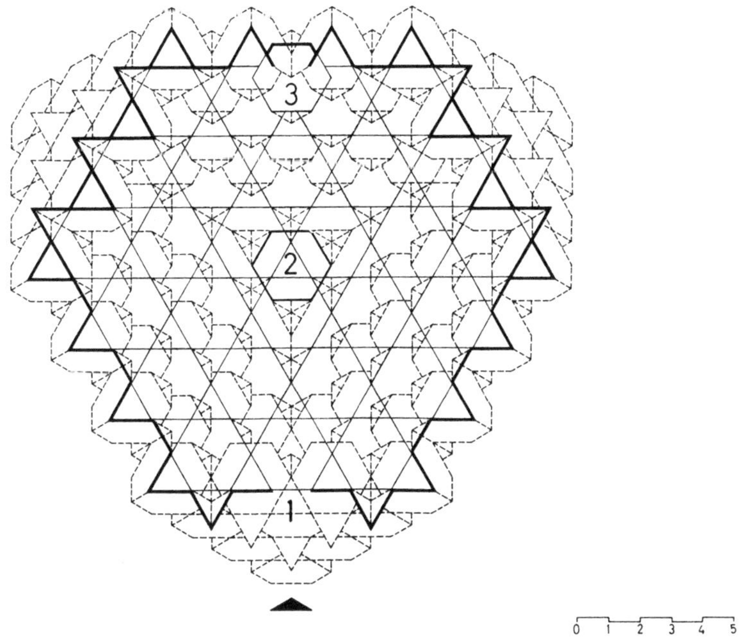

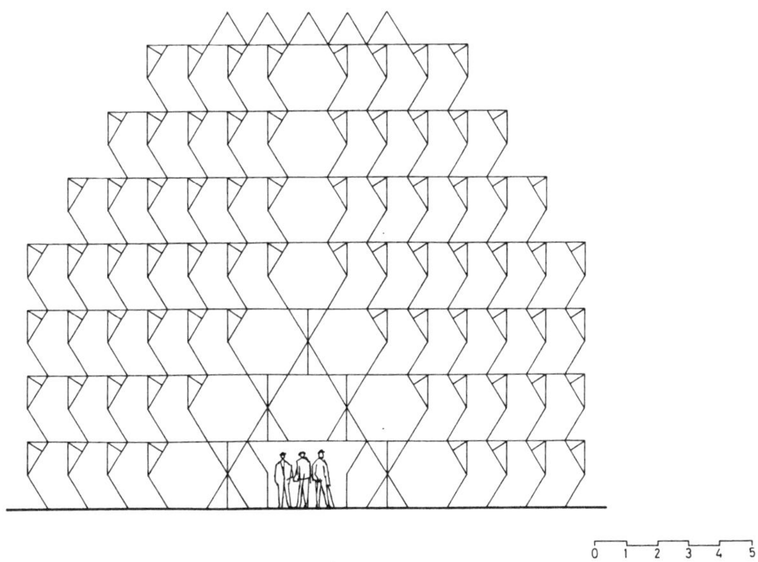

22.1 Synagogue plan: [1] Entrance; [2] Bamah; [3] Aron hakodesh
22.2 Entrance elevation

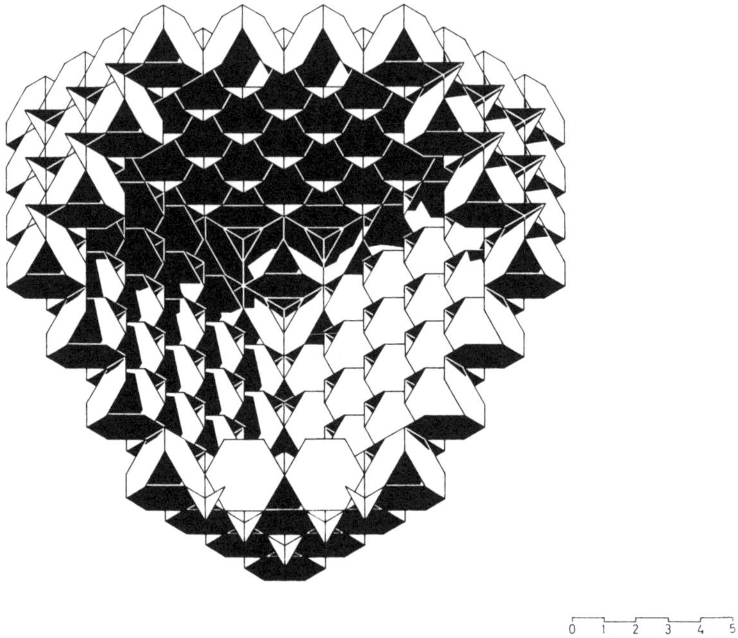

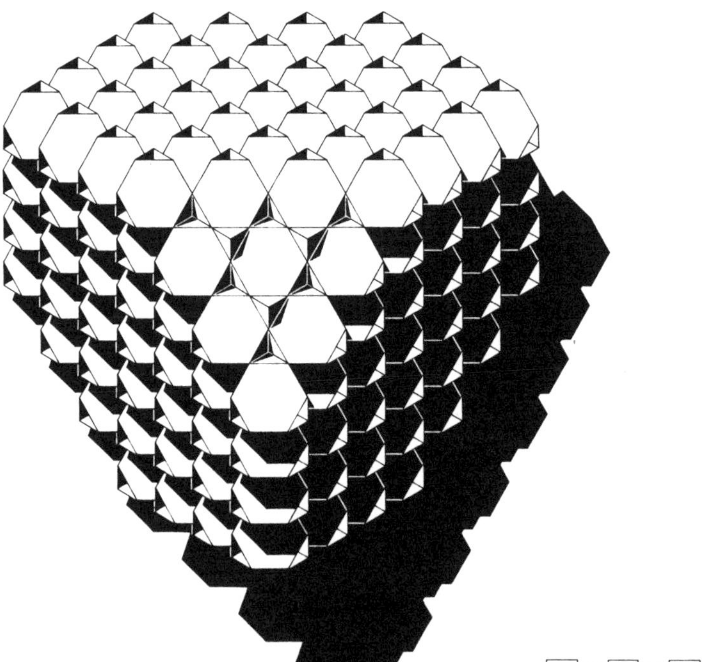

22.3 View of the interior from below looking upward
22.4 Shaded roof plan

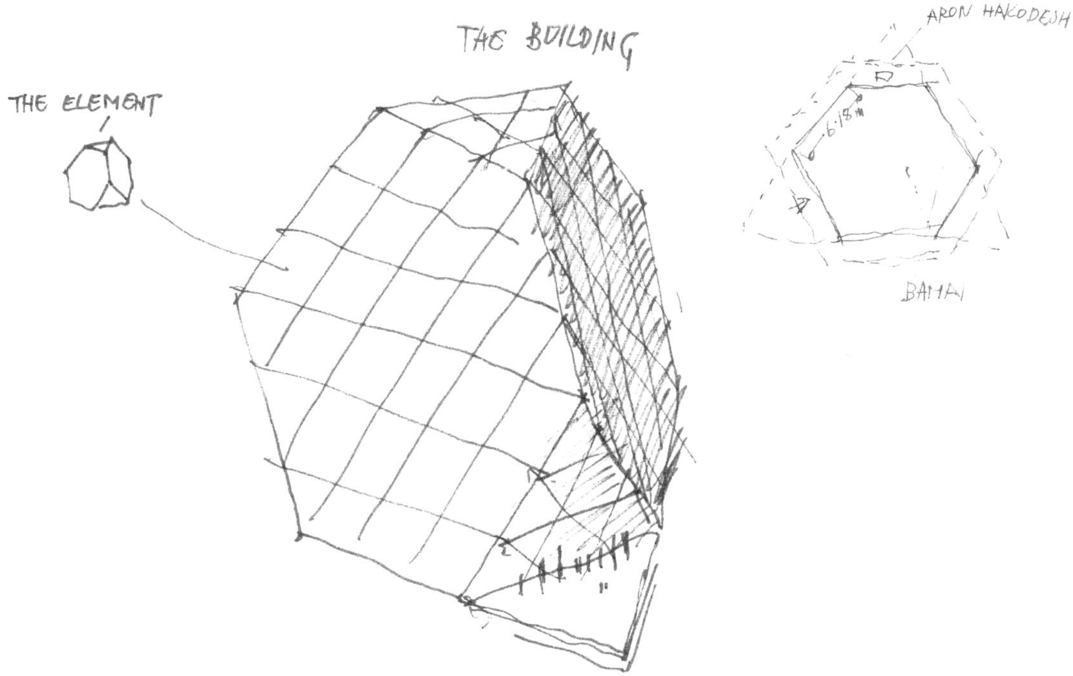

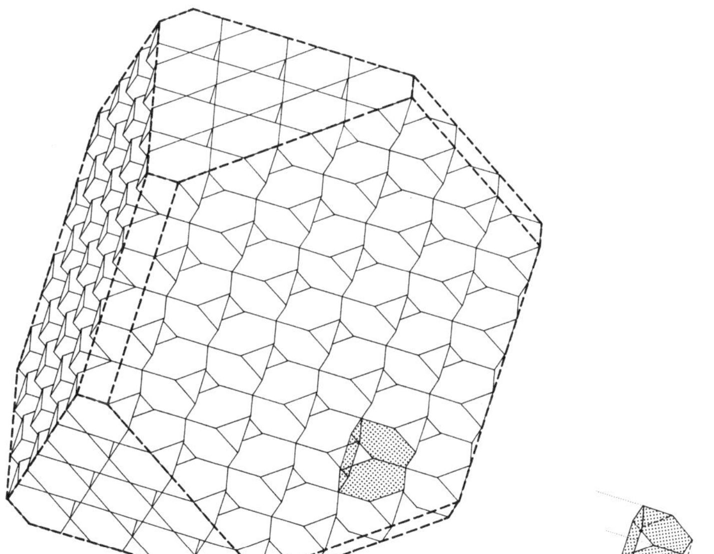

22.5 Sketch by Alfred Neumann explaining the relation between the element (unit) and the building (whole)
22.6 Axonometric view of the design, emphasizing its stereometric characteristics: (A) the form of the synagogue, truncated tetrahedron shell structure created by the packing of truncated tetrahedrons; [1] prefabricated elements

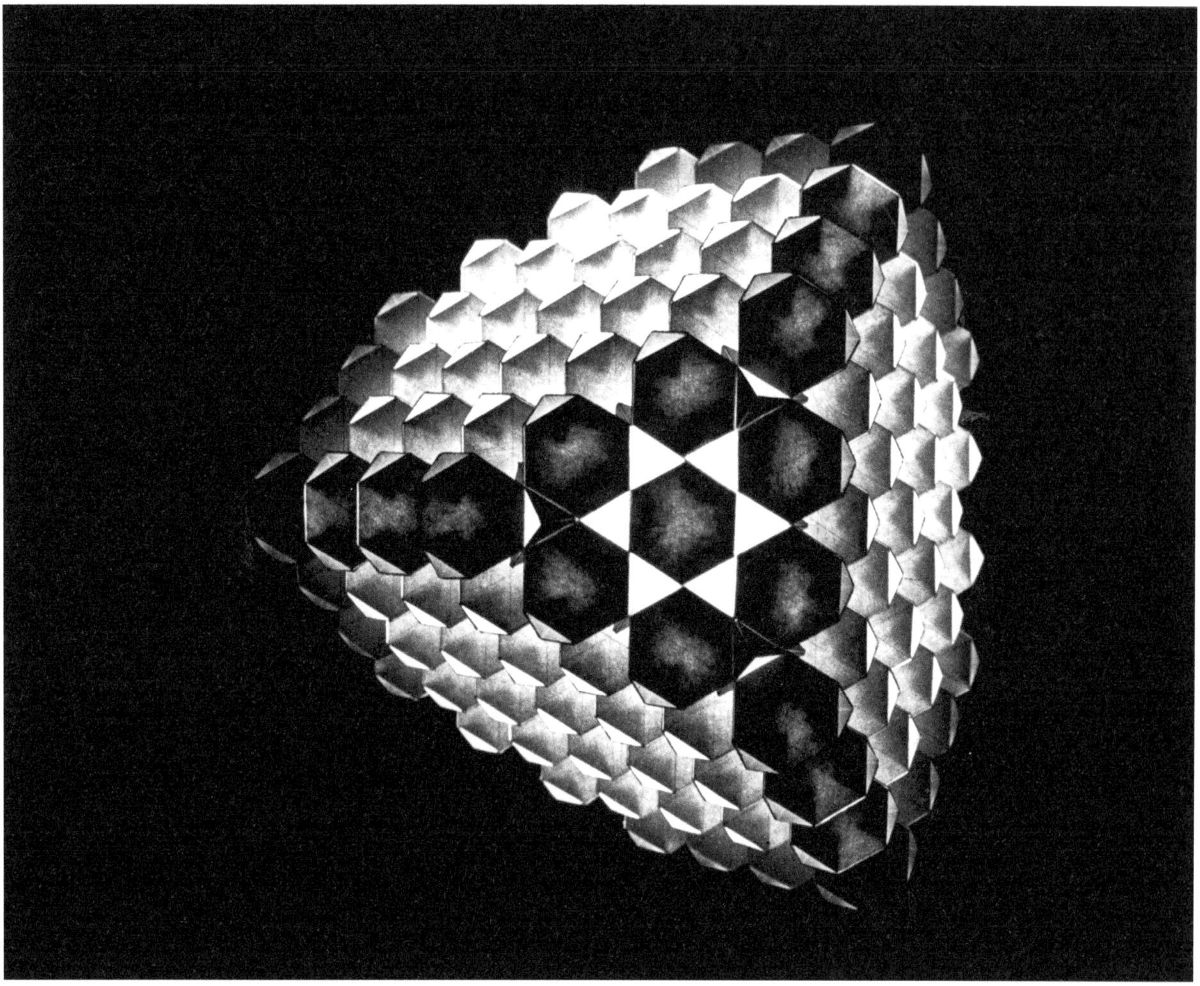

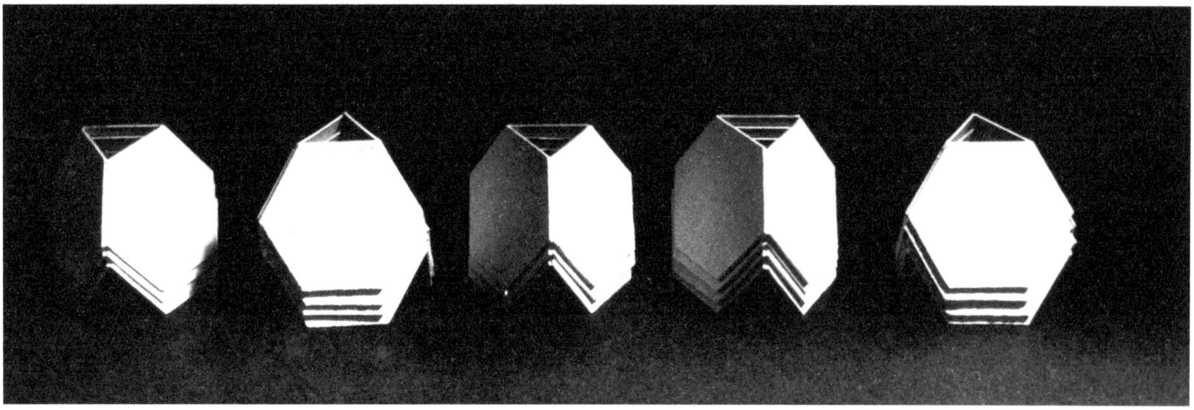

22.7 Model view from above showing the lit structure at night
22.8 Stacked model units

23 Beit Zeit Youth Camp and Restaurant 1961–62
Beit Zeit, near Jerusalem, Israel

With Zvi Hecker, Eldar Sharon

The Beit Zeit Youth Camp and Restaurant was located on a sloping hill in Jerusalem. Its side was hemmed in by trees and accessible via a long ascending road, with a large restaurant on one side, and a dining tent and four clusters of accommodation units on the other. The structures were all made from cloth panels stretched around steel frames and reinforced with wire.

The structure of the dining tent was based on the modular form of truncated cuboctahedrons, and consisted of a canopy formed from four large octagonal panels, abutted by small, diamond-shaped panels, supported on all sides by a zigzagging skirt wall formed from sloping hexagonal panels. The camp's four clustered living units were also formed by adjoining truncated cuboctahedrons, some of them in snaking lines. They were each built atop a terraced cobblestone floor. The restaurant was terraced to follow the slope of the hill, and was formed from four adjoining rows of truncated tetrahedrons.

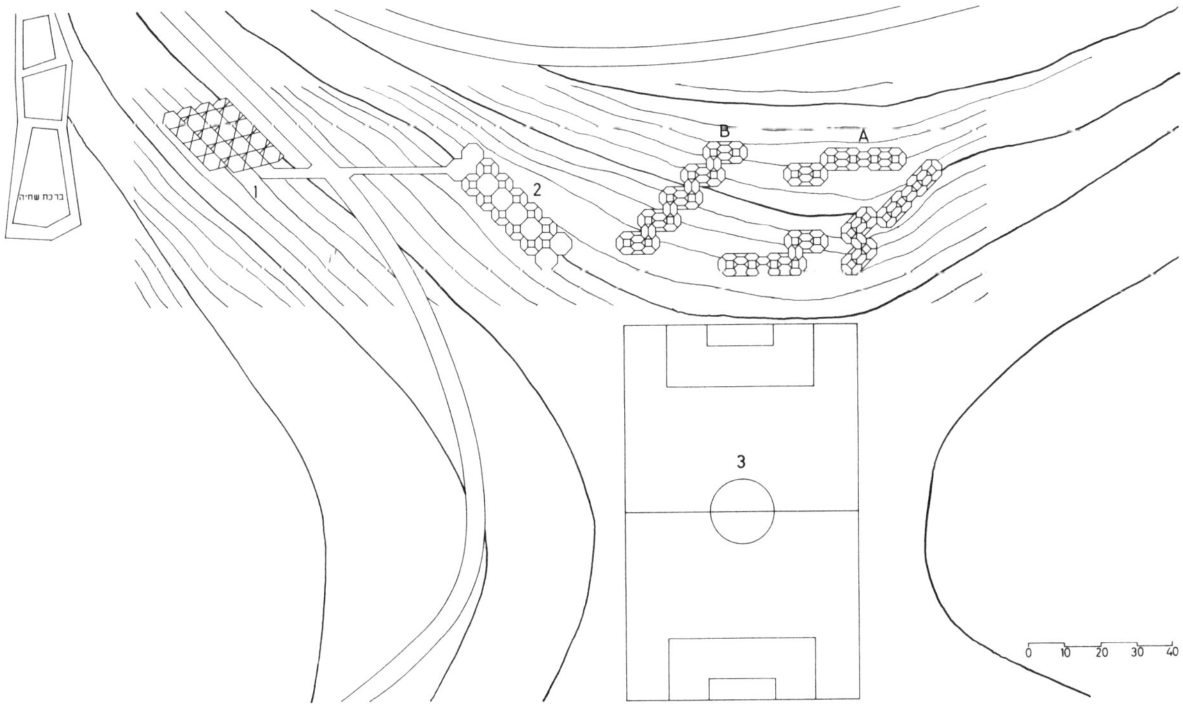

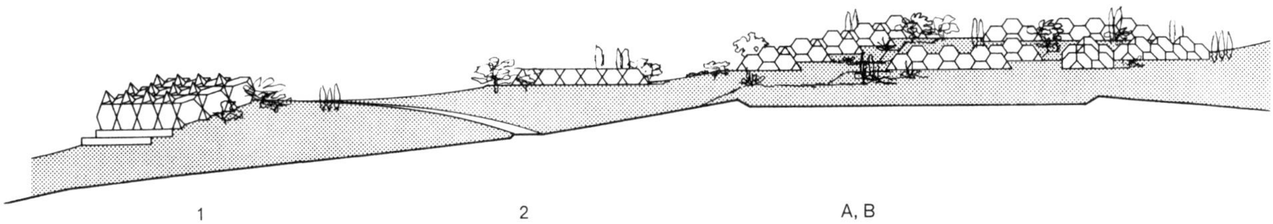

23.1 Beit Zeit Youth Camp site plan: 1 Restaurant, 2 Camp dining tent, 3 Soccer field, (A) Tent type A, (B) Tent type B
23.2 Site elevation

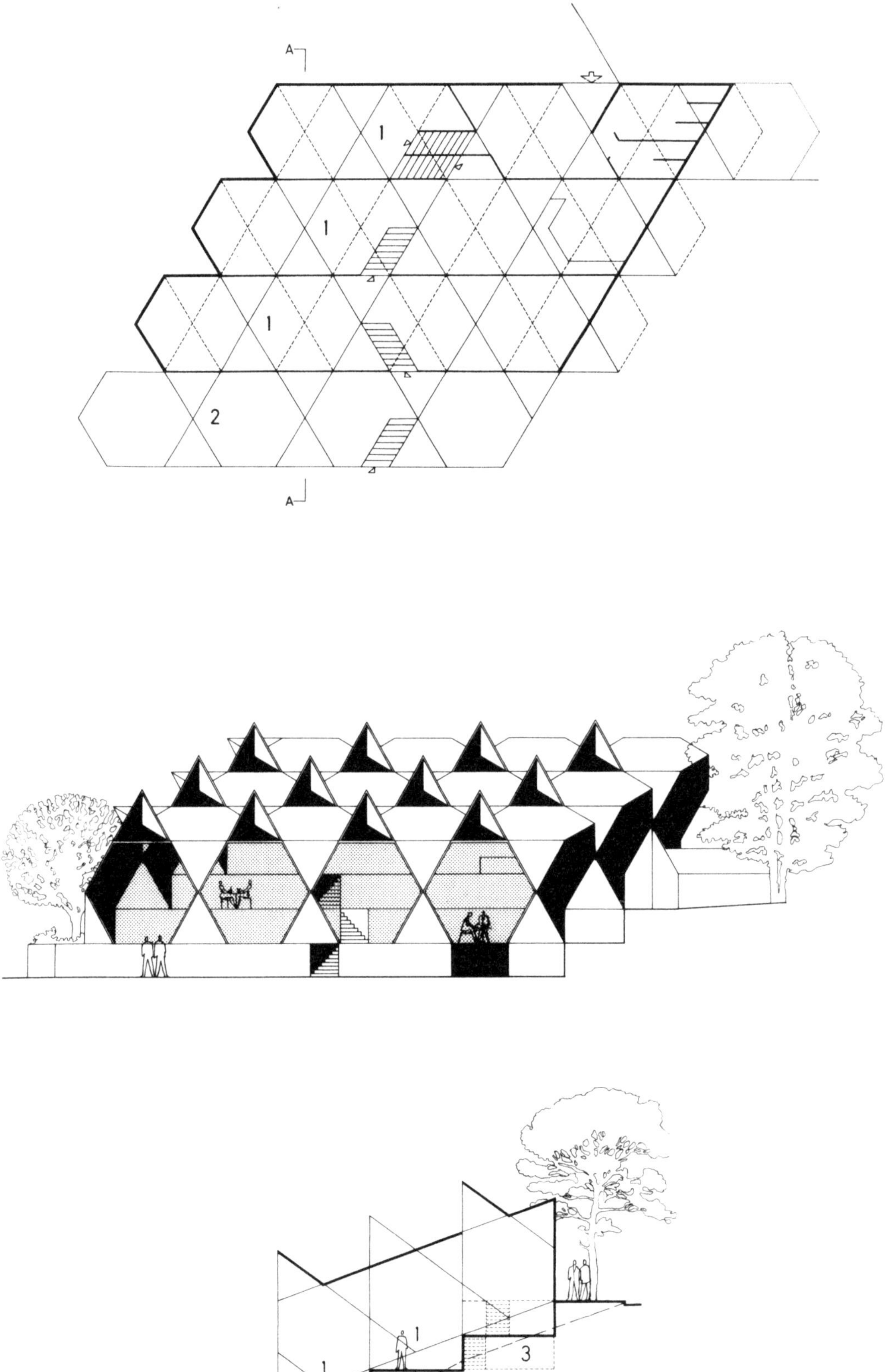

23.3 Restaurant plan, elevation and section: 1 Dining terrace, 2 Open terrace, 3 Kitchen

23.4 Restaurant model views

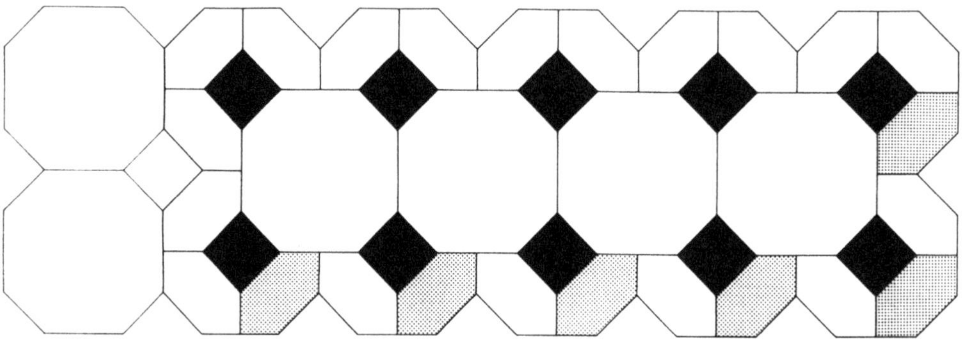

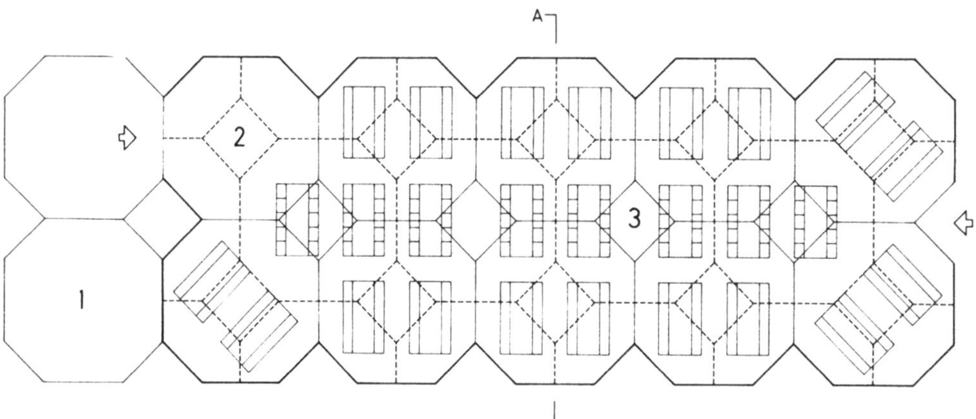

23.5 Dining tent roof plan
23.6 Dining tent plan: [1] Service yard, [2] Food preparation, [3] Dining space

23.7 Dining tent sections and elevations

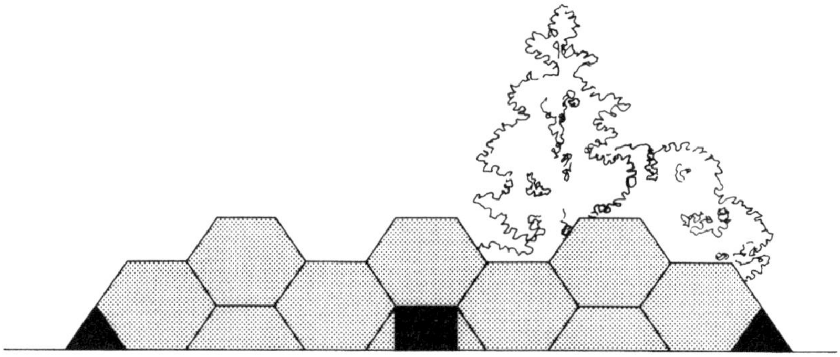

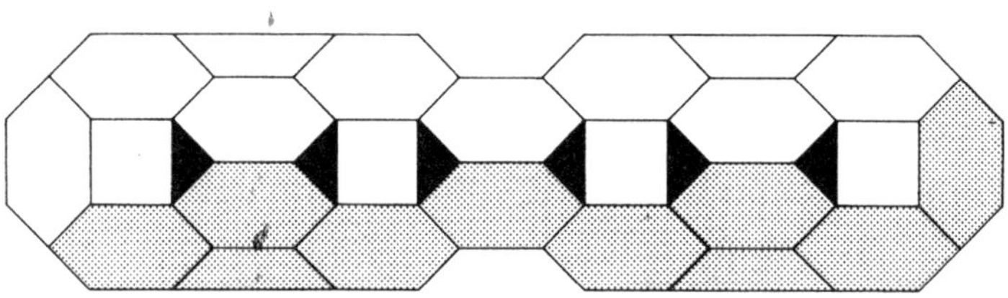

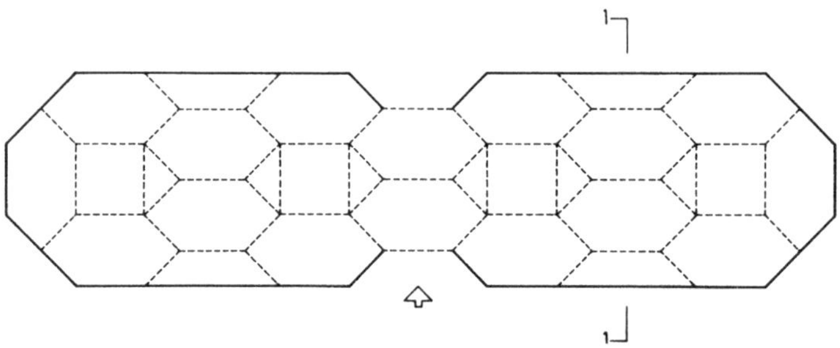

23.8 Cabin unit combinations, plans and elevations

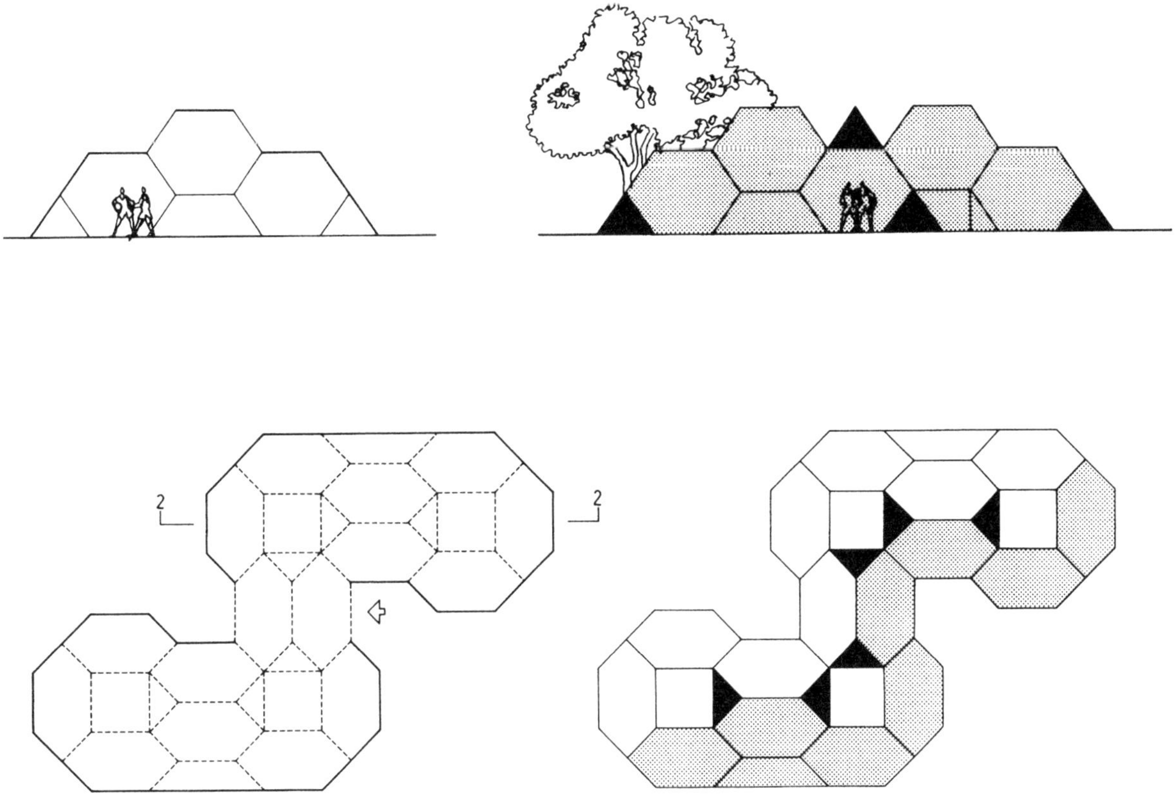

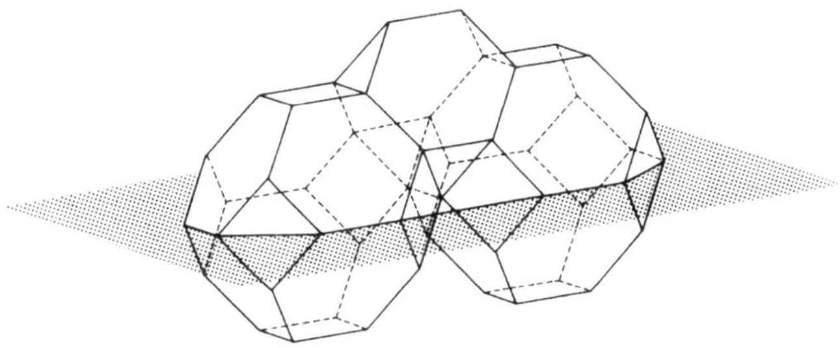

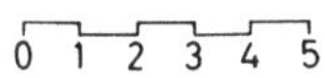

23.9 Plan, section and elevation of cabin units
23.10 Cabin unit geometry in relation to ground plane

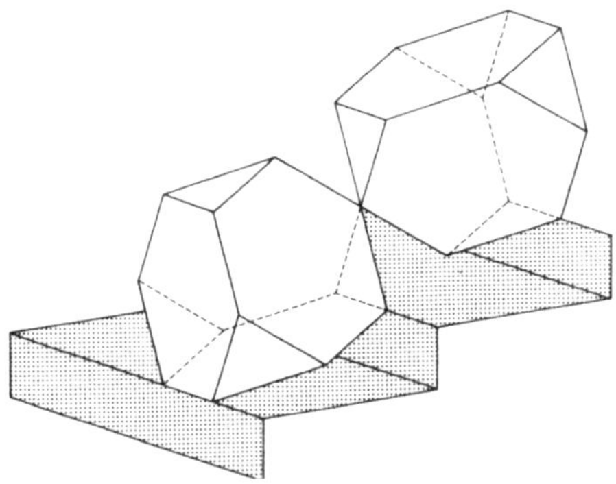

23.11 Perspective drawing
23.12 Modular unit, truncated tetrahedron as arranged along terraces

23.13 Construction of units made of steel frames
23.14 Construction of dining hall, site visit by Zvi Hecker

24 Amsterdam Town Hall, *Competition* 1966
The Netherlands

With Zvi Hecker, Naomi Neumann

In 1964, Amsterdam's city council held an architectural competition for the design of a new town hall. Neumann, Hecker, and Naomi Neumann collaborated on a proposal for the town hall's portside site. They envisioned a building composed of grouped geometric rings arranged symmetrically around a central elongated hexagonal inner court. Each section of the building was to be based on slices of truncated tetrahedrons of varying thicknesses: The central section was to be three stories in height, the section protruding out from it two stories, and the outermost corner sections one story each. The town hall also featured a protruding hub cantilevered out over the shoreline, which likely functioned as an entryway for boat passengers.

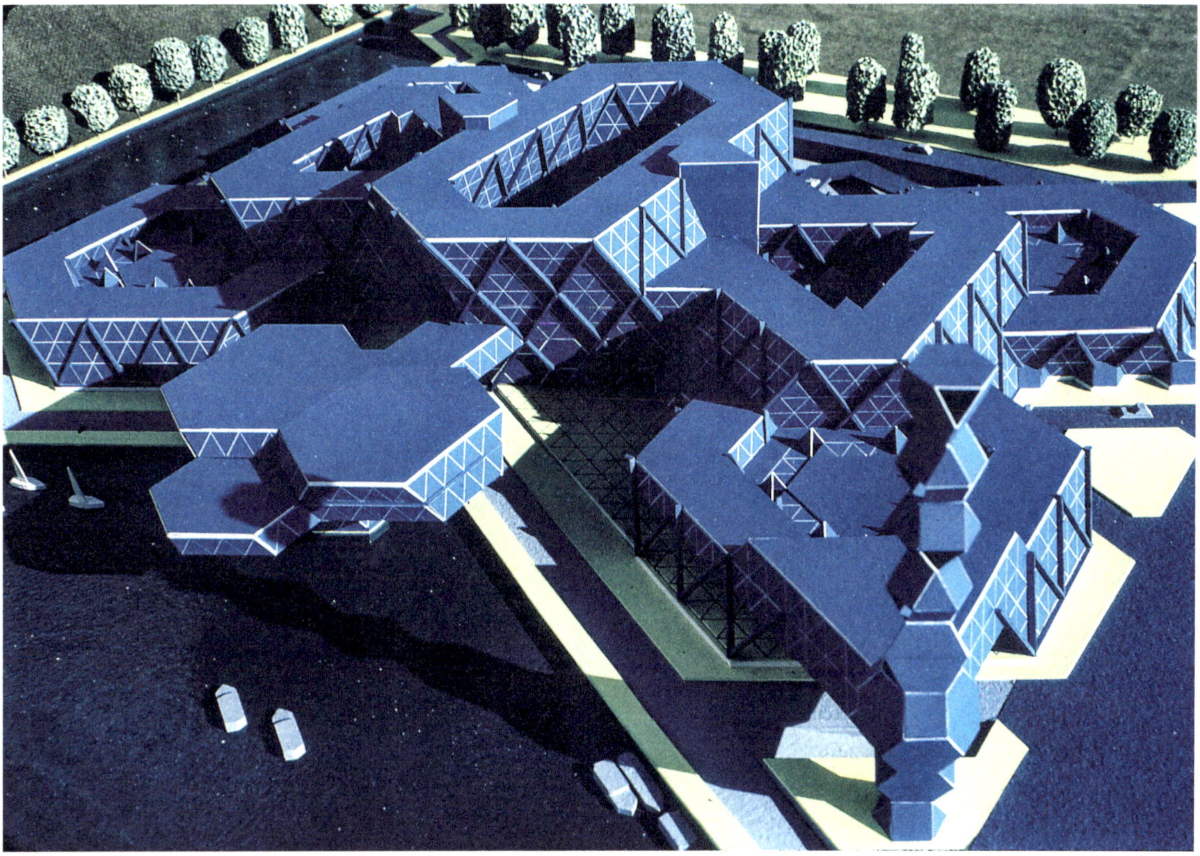

24.1 Model views

25 *Studies* in Polyhedral Geometries 1967

Neumann first experimented with his space-packing approach to architecture in projects of the late 1950s and early 1960s. For these designs, such as the Bat Yam Town Hall and Club Med Holiday Camp at Achziv, he began with one specific polyhedral form, multiplied it, and then combined the multiples together to create buildings. To diversify this approach, in 1967 Neumann undertook a series of design explorations which he titled "Studies in Polyhedral Geometries." Rather than merely accreting together multiples of one particular polyhedral body, in these studies Neumann designed a variety of hypothetical structures from combinations of different kinds of multifaceted polyhedral forms. He and Hecker in fact coined the term "Polyhedric Architecture" to describe this project and others they designed from 1966 onward, which combined different multifaceted geometric shapes.

Neumann's study presented a variety of massing and structural possibilities, all created from three different kinds of polyhedral forms—a truncated tetrahedron, a cuboctahedron, and a truncated octahedron—all with edges of identical length. The purpose of using different varieties of polyhedral elements together in one building was to architecturally distinguish the different parts of a structure that serve different functions, such as apertures for light and ventilation, and elements of spatial enclosure. Neumann colored each of the three kinds of polyhedral forms differently in order to further distinguish them as unique elements. Each of the designs presented in "Studies in Polyhedral Geometries" adhered to one of three basic plans: a square, hexagon, or triangle.

The use of polyhedral geometries in architecture was not unique to the 1950s or 1960s; many architects had experimented with such forms in these and earlier decades. However, while polyhedral forms were often employed at this time as an aesthetic style, Neumann's approach was different in that he used these elements to physically constitute architectural form through his space-packing method. His "Polyhedric Architecture" incorporated Archimedian solids as well as the Platonic solids promoted by the modern movement in architecture.

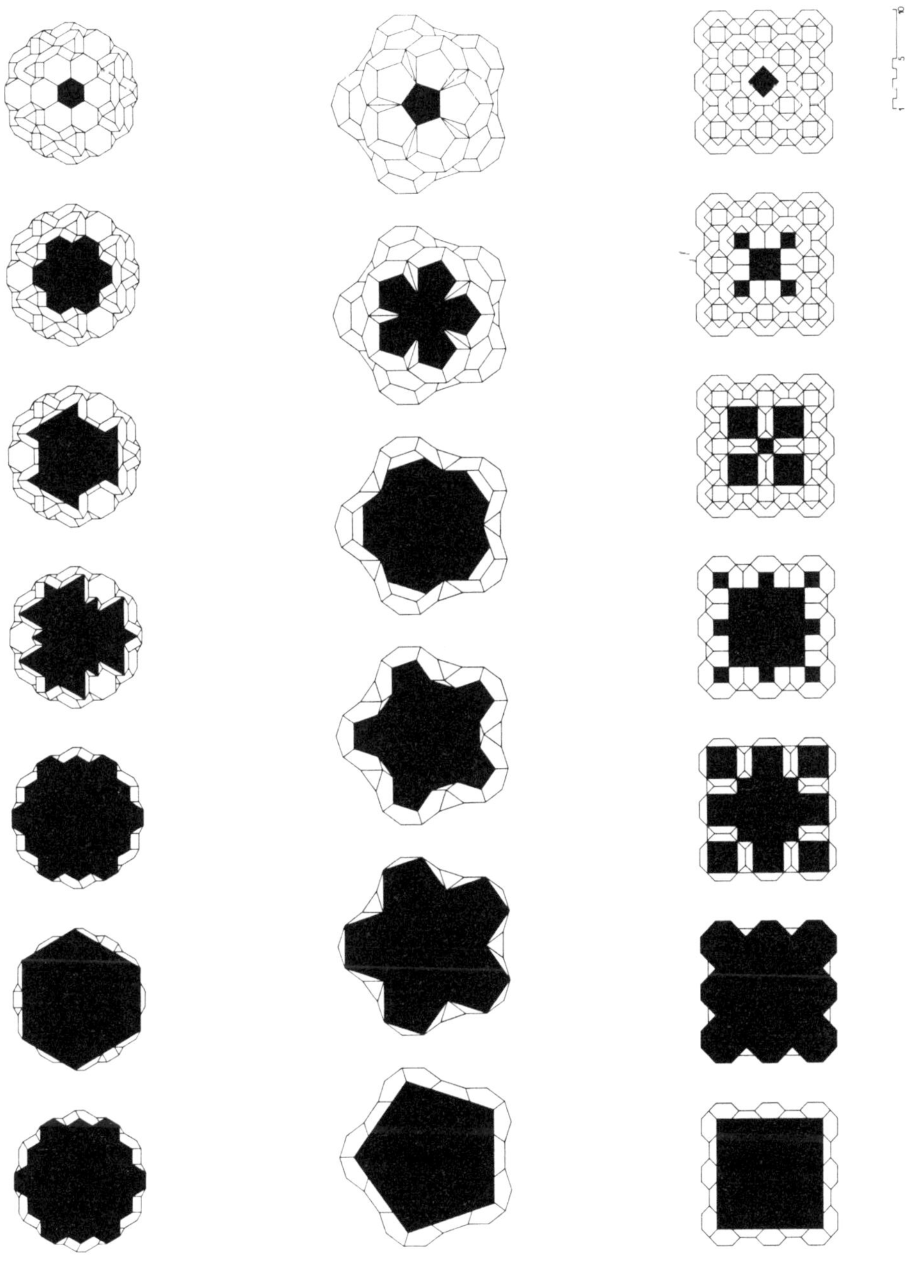

25.1 Studies of polyherdric structures through plan sections, using combined and single repetetive solids (units)

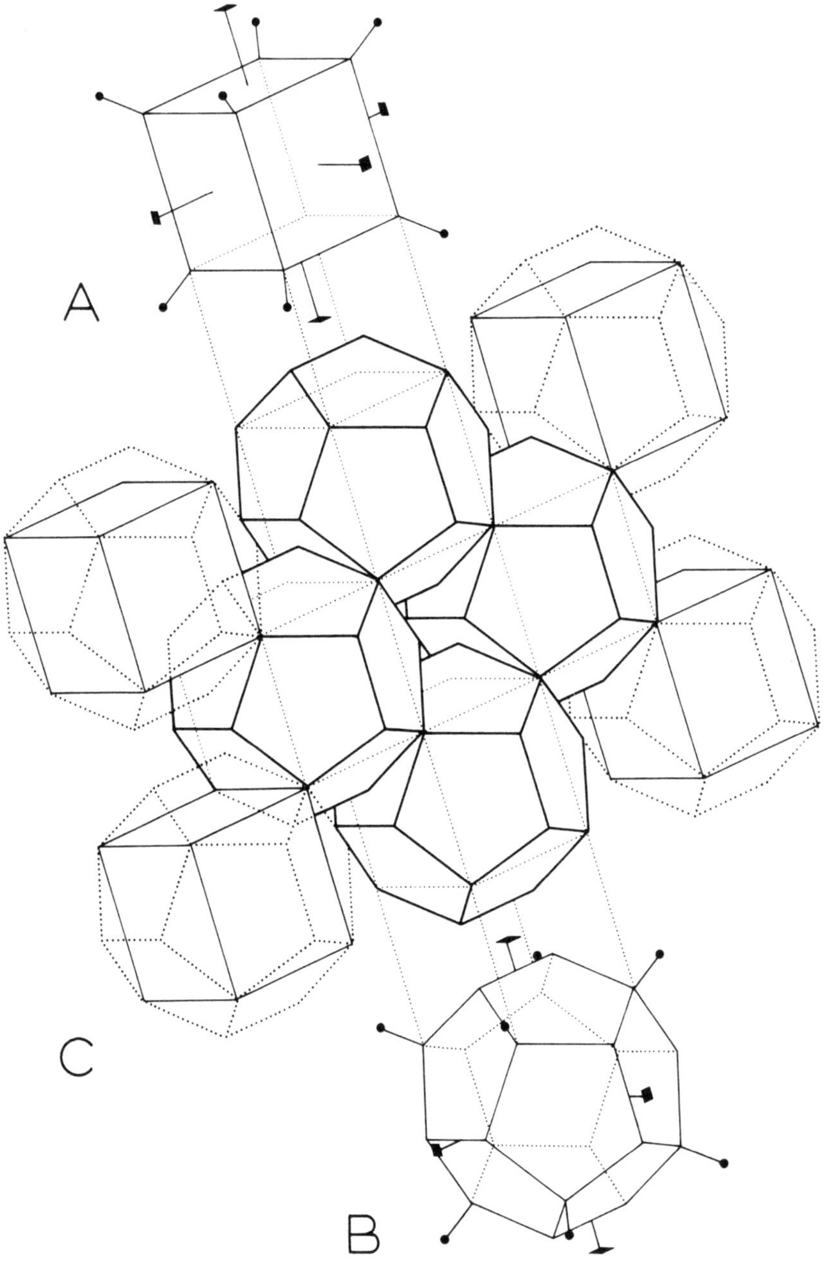

25.2 Axonometric diagram showing relation between cube and dodecahedron in a stacking system

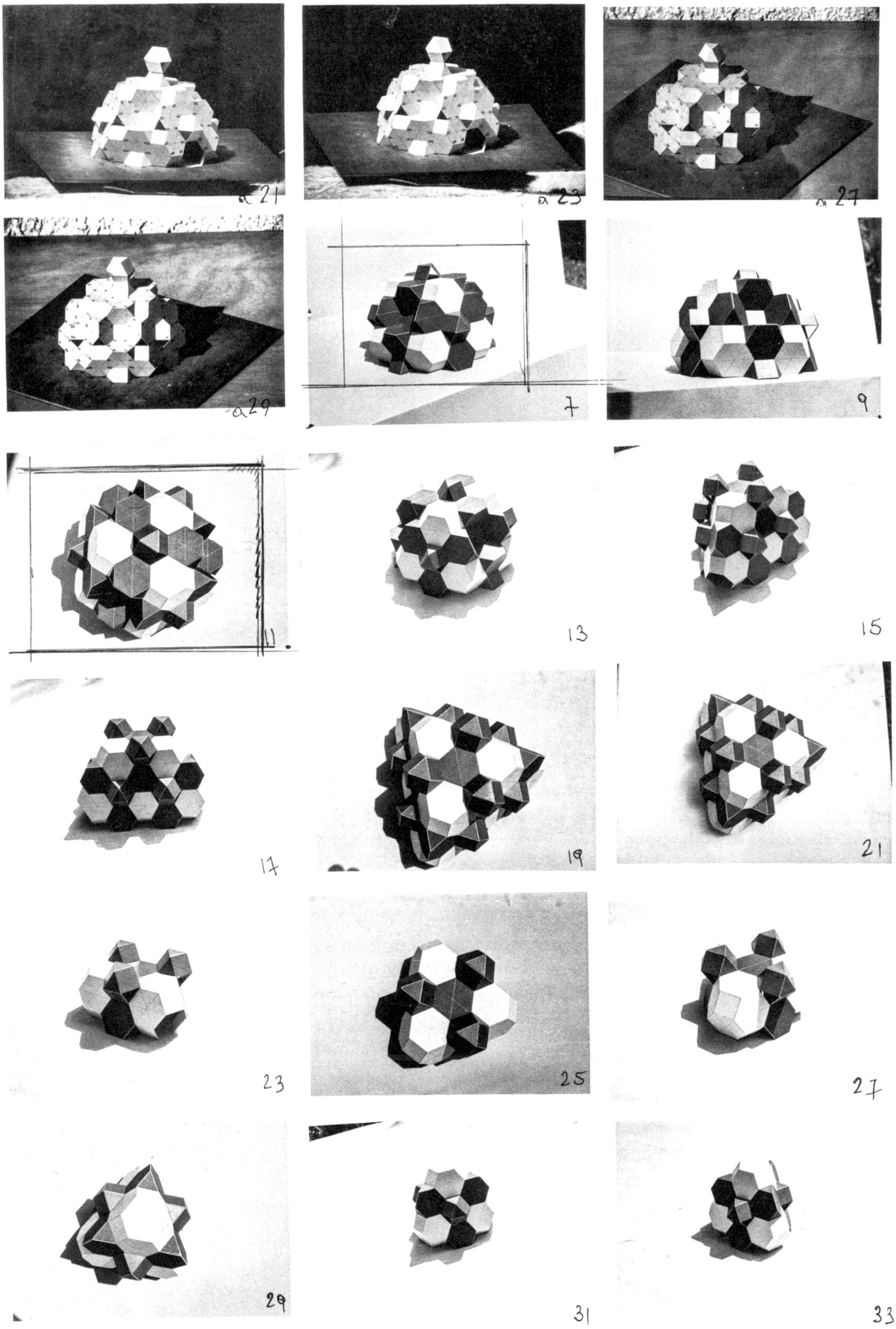

25.3 Model views

26 Synagogue at the Officers' School Training Base I Mitzpeh Ramon, Israel

1967–69

With Zvi Hecker

Work on the Synagogue at the Officers' School began late in 1966, when Neumann was in Canada and Hecker in Israel. Corresponding by mail, Neumann sent Hecker photographs of models, sketches, drawings, and various instructions on the development of the design.

The synagogue is located in the Negev Desert and forms part of the Israeli Army's military camp where officers are trained. It is located at the edge of the compound, on a diagonal axis in relation to the central courtyard of the base. The truncated octahedron shape of the building is composed of three types of polyhedral units. Hexagonal panels are the basic building element of these polyhedral units, while the triangular spaces between them function as ventilation openings that enable air to circulate through the interior, and also as windows that let light in. Painted surfaces on the interior reflect and intensify the color of the light that streams in, creating a radiant effect.

The building is centrally planned and symmetrical. The ark, the receptacle for Torah scrolls, and the Bimah, the centrally positioned, elevated podium from which the Torah is read, are located along the central axis of symmetry which points in the direction of Jerusalem. The synagogue was constructed entirely from concrete cast on site. Its inclined planes meant that large spans could be kept to a minimum, allowing reinforced concrete panels for wall and roof elements to measure a consistent thickness of 14 cm. Its floor area is 40 square meters. The entire officers' training base, which the synagogue is a part of, was designed by Zvi Hecker alone and became the Israeli Army's primary officers' training facility. Of the entire base, only one synagogue was permitted for publication due to army censorship of its facilities. Neumann did not want to take part in the design of the entire military base since he believed the army should not build permanent structures but rather be housed in tents.

26.1 Completed synagogue building, Mitzpeh Ramon, Negev Desert

Letter from Alfred Neumann addressed to Zvi Hecker
December 31, 1966

I understand that you looked for a square plan. It looks a bit like the boiler room house, which would not be bad by itself, but it has the clear shape of a cross, and that should be avoided. Even if they cannot read plans they might object later.

The packing we experimented with consists of three different bodies: 1) truncated octahedron, 2) truncated tetrahedron, 3) cuboctahedron. For convenience's sake they are shown in different colours, but in reality they could be different in colours too. With our play one could arrive at 3 basic shapes: a square, a triangle and a hexagon (there is also a possibility of a rhombic plan shape, which we do not show).

The different structures of the packing as shown in the photographs are as follows:

A A square plan outlay, the elements have the side length of 1.62m, just like in the plans you have sent us. On the roof there is an additional cuboctahedron not shown in the photograph but shown in the accompanying plans. The cuboctahedrons are as shown in the section full and serve for lighting and ventilation, additional lighting could be achieved through the triangles of the truncated tetrahedrons, as shown.

B A triangular outlay consisting of three truncated octahedrons, three truncated tetrahedrons and three cub octahedrons. Here the side length should be bigger than in the previous scheme to fit the programmatic floor area required. There are no plans accompanying this outlay only photos.

C A large triangular outlay, again the side length of the bodies has to be determined according to the area needed.

D A variation of scheme C. with additional truncated tetrahedrons. This creates certain difficult court-yards on the roof which cold be overcome if some of the cub octahedrons would be full like in scheme A.

E A triangular scheme with a vertical buildup. Again the side length has to be determined.

F A high hexagon outlay with side lengths of elements 1.62m. This scheme has accompanying plans and a construction suggestions. The cub octahedrons on three side walls and on the roof are full as shown in sections.

Once Ilan of the Technion told me that according to the Talmudic tradition a synagogue should be square in plan. Anyhow there are many deviations from this rule, not only the famous synagogue of F. L. Wright when deciding the final shape of the synagogue, you have to consider the special desert conditions where little objects stand out very strongly against the monotonous background. The synagogue should be actually higher than any other structure in the surrounding (according to *halacha*), as this cannot be possible the synagogue should at least stand out from the other structures in wealth of form. I have recently seen photos of old Jewish wooden synagogues in Poland, and it struck me that they abound in polygonal configurations.

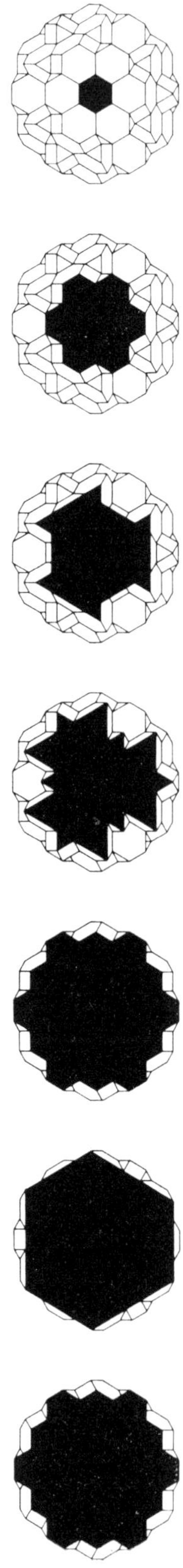

26.2 Different forms of the building envelope as it transforms along the vertical axis of the structure

26.3 Plan view of the synogogue building as its envelope changes along the vertical axis; elevations

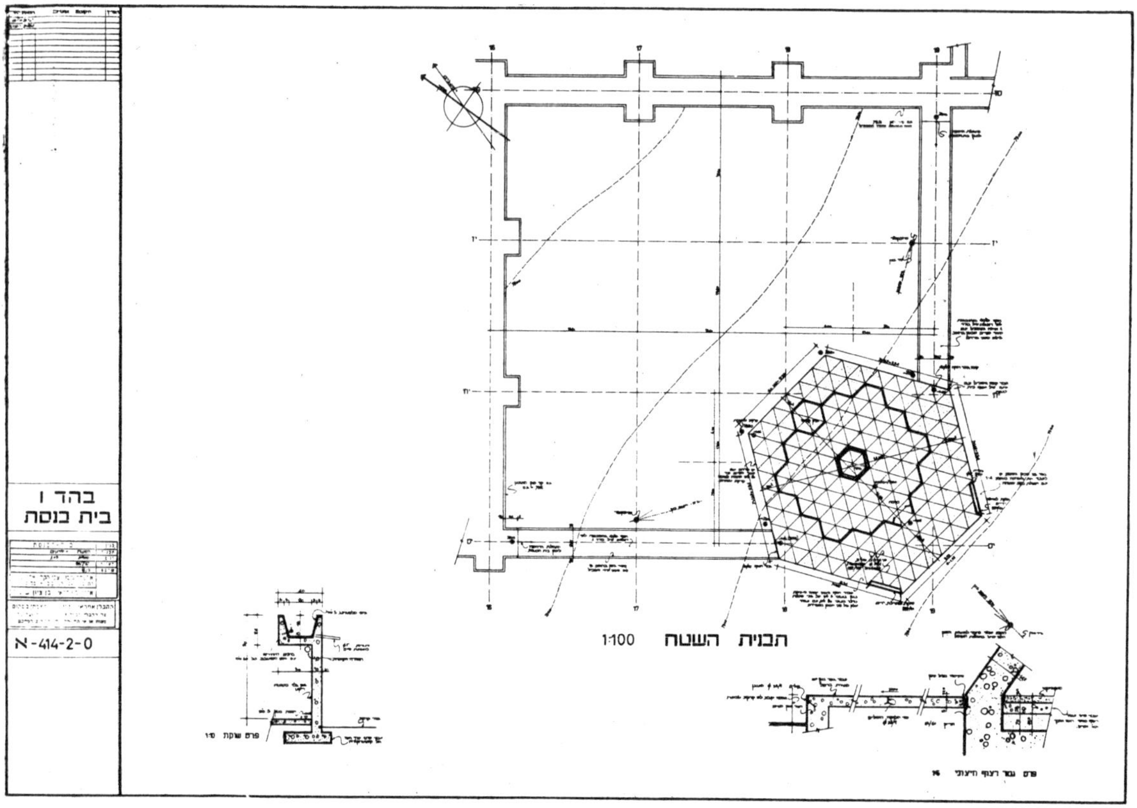

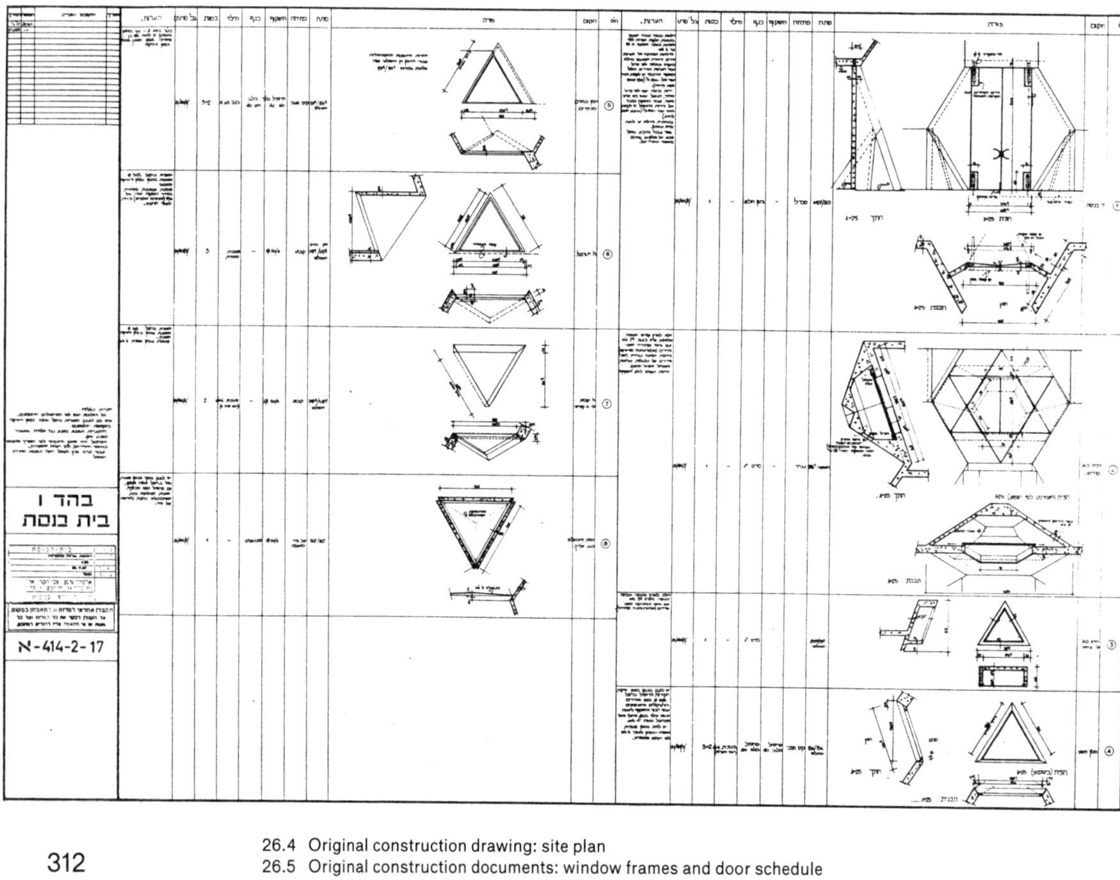

26.4 Original construction drawing: site plan
26.5 Original construction documents: window frames and door schedule

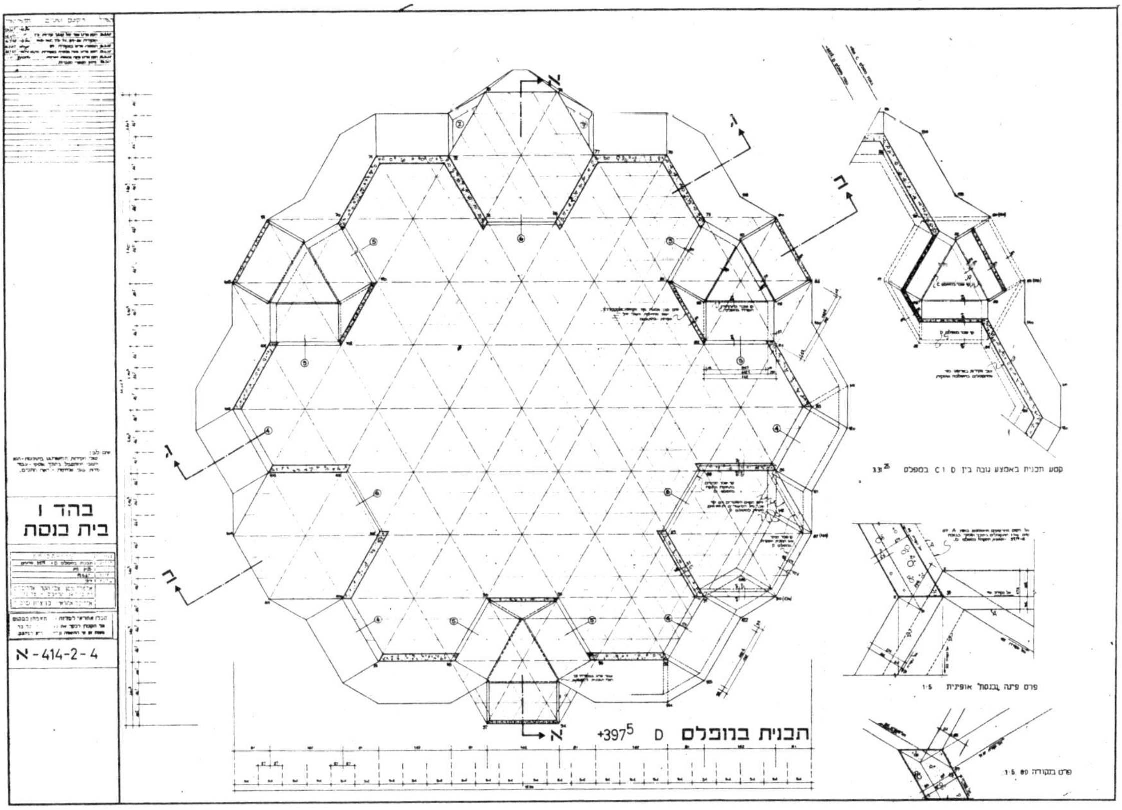

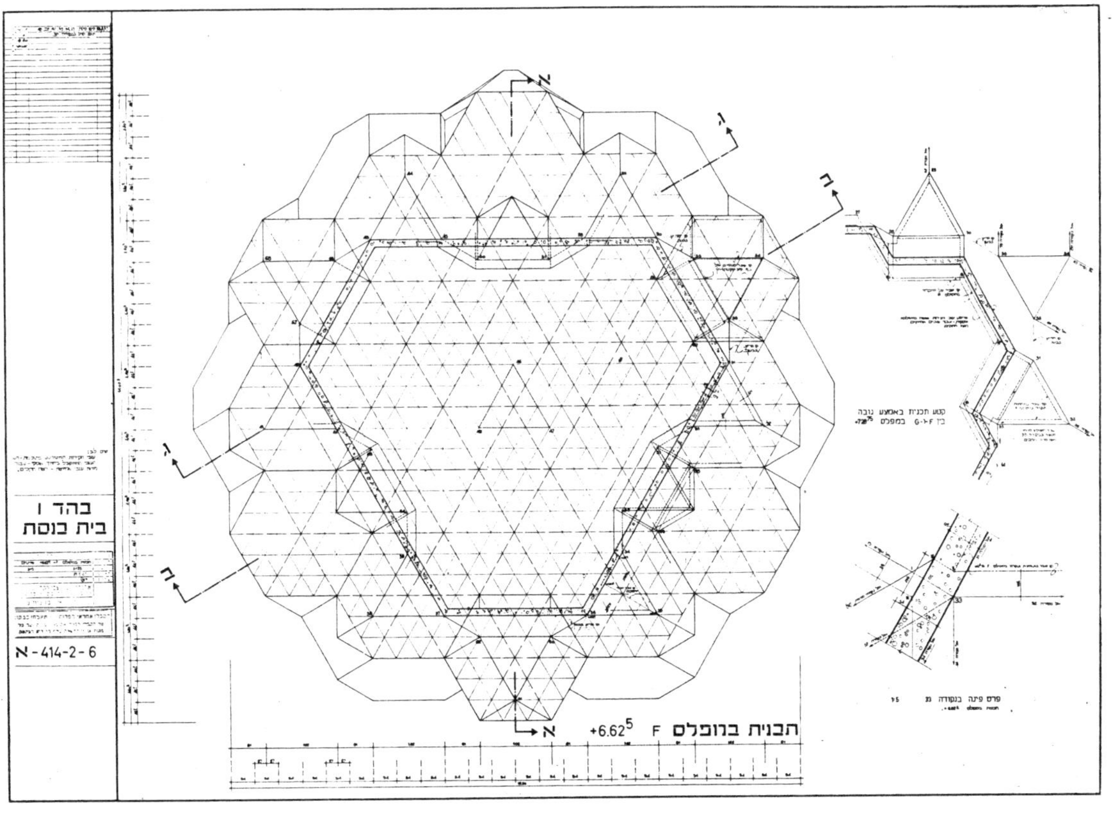

26.6 Original construction drawing: plan view at level +3.975m
26.7 Original construction drawing: plan view at level +6.625m

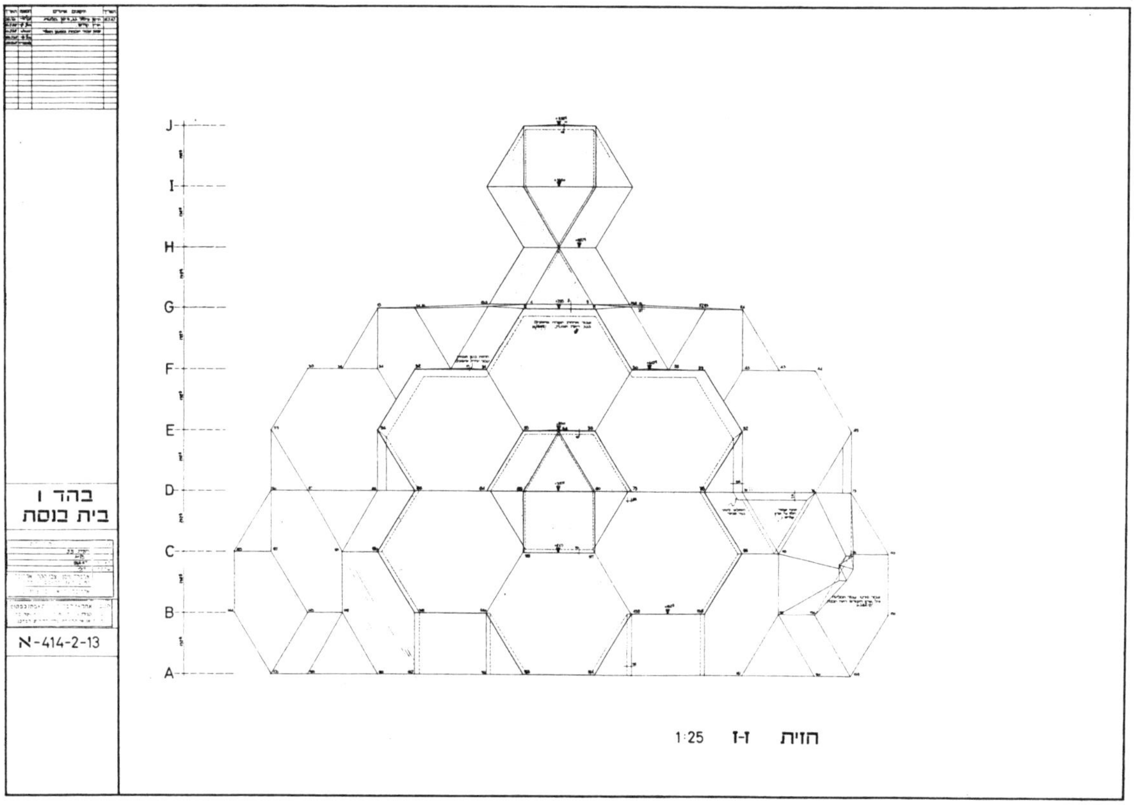

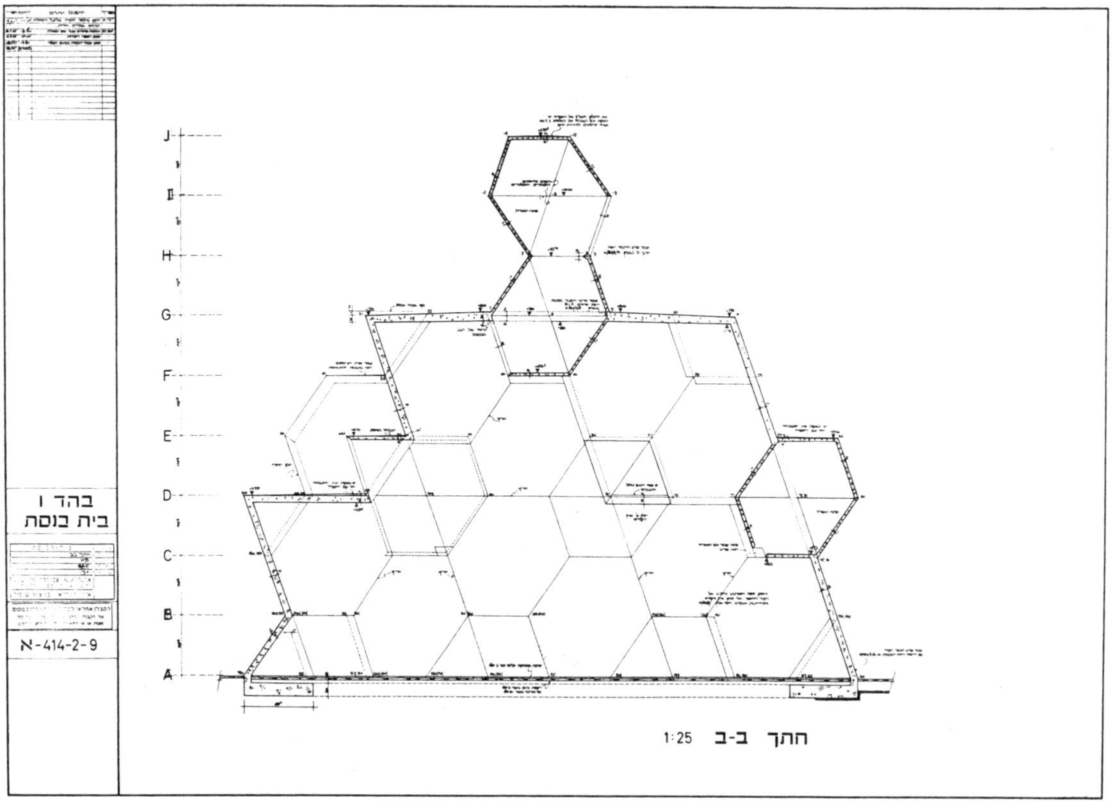

26.8 Original construction drawing: elevation
26.9 Original construction drawing: section

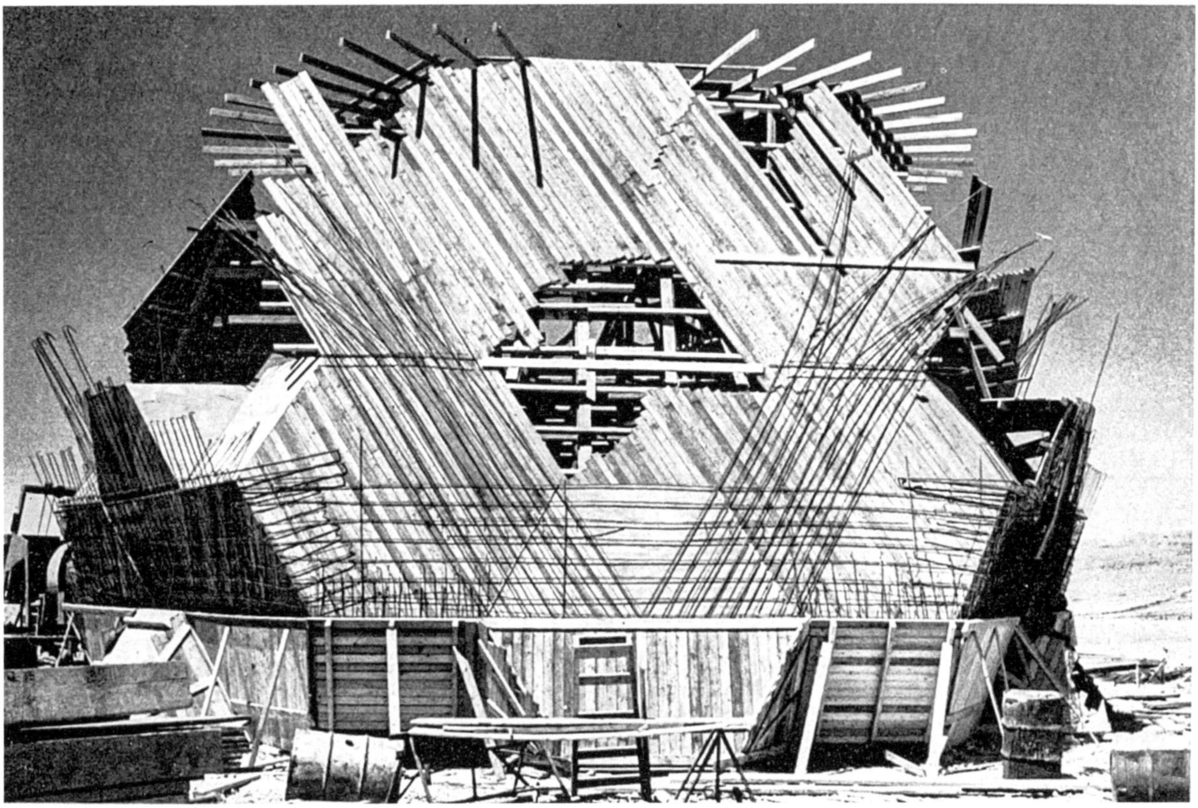

26.10 Construction: concrete case on site

9840-1

9840-2

9840-3

9840-4

9840-5

9840-6

9840-7

9840-8

9840-9

9840-10

9840-11

9840-12

26.12 View of interior with Bimah in center

Appendix

The MΦ System: The Humanization of Space 1956

Extracts from *L'Humanisation de l'espace: le système MΦ*, Editions Architecture d'Aujourd'hui, Boulogne, Seine, 1956, a booklet that includes text, mathematical equations, tables, charts, geometric drawings, and illustrations. Translated from French by Rafi Segal and Carla Georgescu.

Towards a Human Concept of Space

Facing the constant evolution of technological civilization, man, even though gifted with the most stunning ability to adapt, finds himself safeguarding his specifically human qualities.

The new modes of transportation and telecommunication have modified our sense of space: reduction and extension of space have become familiar things. The scale of dimension has been enlarged, yet the old experimental concept continues; in the existential notion of space, the different classical notions: height, length, depth, maintain all their emotional and practical meaning, while in geometrical space coordinates can be changed at will without necessarily a direction or points of preference.

We find today imaginative abstractions. The experimental notions of the past have been generalized and integrated in our contemporary spatial conceptions. The domain of our spiritual adventures is being modified according to multiple aspects of our daily environment. It seems that only contemporary man has become conscious of space; space is a modern term. Today, this term is encountered in literature, art, geography, urbanism, biology and chemistry. In previous literature we find very little trace of this concept. The modern consciousness of space is more complex than before.

For man, being a whole, a biological unity, it is extremely difficult to separate sensory perception from emotional, rational, and other elements. Evolution based on a spontaneous, prelogical and mystic experience of the environment results in differentiated appreciation. The observer takes an active part in the formation of present space. Every civilization has transformed its accessible environment and its inaccessible sphere in analogy with its habitat. Nowadays art and science have created types of spaces that are unusual and that only in exceptional cases contain ancient forms.

The history of art, supported by many documents, restored to us a sense of the space of the past. This retrospective rendered our conception of space more flexible, opening the path to a new form of space. This also contributed to the destruction of a paradoxical tradition. Scientific space was reduced to abstract structures, intelligible only through mathematical symbols, without the possibility to represent it through a concrete model. The result is that causality has been erased from our customary notions.

Indeterminate subatomic space and cosmic space-time only penetrate our daily space in the form of statistical laws. Uexkull writes about the variety of organic spaces that are determined by the physical constitution of living beings.

Man, due to his faculty of abstract thinking, is able to translate other biological spaces into the language of human space. These biological spaces are for him analogies of which the content has been reduced to an abstraction.

Ecological sciences deal with the relation between vital phenomena and their environments. Human geography is a synthesis of existing relations between man and space. There are signs indicating that science, after having explored the boundary domains of space, is currently turning towards our immediate sphere of influence.

The different current perceptions of space appear isolated without mutual relationships. It does not seem, as a matter of fact, that there are relationships between the physicist's, the geographer's, the biologist's, and the artist's concepts of space; nevertheless, they are all united by an affirmed analogy, and carry, without doubt, the imprint of our epoch. They are all implicit in our collective spatial conscience.

The elements that constitute our space have transformed, and are connected through, a new order. The space of past civilizations was based on a principle of vital organization, a principle to which we have been accustomed by millennium-long accommodation. Technological space is not inscribed into our genealogical memory—hence the aversion to technology, the escape to nature and to regressive forms of leisure.

This passive escape has to be substituted by a consciously active behavior. The technical world is constructed according to the unilateral design of the physical universe, in which the human factor has not been accounted for, and this is why our world is chaotic. The need to re-create harmony was never more urgent than today.

Paul Valéry expressed this same thought in his *Eupalinos*: "Nature is formed, and the elements are separated; but something enjoins him to consider this work as unfinished, and as requiring to be re-handled and set in motion again for the especial satisfaction of man."[1]

Man's transforming activity encompasses the physical and the organic world. Consciously or unconsciously, the human factor is always present, but it has not been taken into consideration on the scientific level and has only been treated from a strictly utilitarian point of view. The immediate task that imposes itself is that of isolating the human factor from the confused mass of elements that determine space.

The scientific landscape of the current world presents an empty space of scattered particles; the tendency of the general evolution in architecture also goes from full to empty, from mass to space. The dimensions represent the result of the correlation between man and space; the proportional unity poses a certain constant.

> But since the whole was an unlimited multitude [...] an order was needed [...] but, it is in the Decade that a balance pre-existed between the whole and its parts (elements). That is why, by his reason, God organized artistically, using the Decade as a canon for the whole [...] and that is why the whole and its parts have their relationships of concord based upon it and are to be ordered after it.[2]
> —Nicomachus of Gerasa

Pythagorean intuition has been scientifically confirmed by Ghyka and Hambridge. The Golden Number and correlated Decad are the morphological structures of man. In the same way that the different organs and different functions of the human body are correlated by an integrated system of proportion, it seems possible to link the most heterogeneous elements of our habitat by means of an analogous structure. A production method capable of connecting the organic functions should be even more appropriate for the linking of mechanical functions, which are much more simple; such a structure could become one of the most efficient means enabling us to humanize space.

Towards a synthesis of art and technology

According to some out-of-date conceptions, life appears to be a complex mechanism, yet on the other hand, broad perspectives from biology allow us to recognize the specific constitution of life. In the beginning of the technological evolution, mechanization was trying to claim vital phenomena, but as our understanding of inanimate nature broadens, biological thought penetrates more and more profoundly into the domain of technology. We are at the dawn of a biological era.

The new sciences were born about twenty years ago; they enable us to sense the coherence that exists between biological events and physical phenomena. Wherever the biological perspective dominates, the morphological structure of life appear essential. The Golden Section seems to play a role in the quantitive mechanics of life.

We could never enter into the details of this evolutionary parallelism; we can only establish that biology has put an emphasis on certain morphological structures of our life that do not exist in inanimate nature. The Golden Section is the structural scheme of these properties. This principle is not reversible. The hierarchy of nature allows the hatching of forms of inferior structures within the framework of more evolved forms, but never the other way around. Now, only in the realm of art has it been possible to realize the contrary, by communicating the structural qualities of life to inanimate nature. A Greek would have never dreamt of establishing a difference between art and technology (*tekhne* meaning both art and technology). These two activities were artificially separated in the nineteenth century. Architecture, in its larger sense, is called to suppress this separation and to utilize technology as a means to humanize space. Today it would seem possible to realize a synthesis between the abstract culture of mathematics and aesthetic emotional culture by creating a balanced frame (setting) for human life. It appears probable that the biological principle will equally play out in determining the proportions and dimensions of technology. The Golden Section has become the instrument of this synthesis.

Our culture, our science, our art are based on the principle of analogy. The mathematical expression of this principle is proportion, a factor that introduces repetition of similar forms, a return to the "same" in the eternal process of change. Out of all the proportions possible, the one named the Golden Section offers the greatest variety of analogous combinations. We will try here to reveal this structure and to present its extension.

Humanization of space

In principle, all the terms of the numerical tables can be considered through the metric system. But all the decimals can be repelled by their structure: It is therefore a broad decimal system. The terms can be either divided by two or doubled. Thus all the dimensional demands have been fulfilled without losing the fundamental proportion. The civilizations that have utilized elements of limited dimensions for their methods of construction preferred the Fibonacci series for proportions. The employment of prefabricated elements became more and more common in construction. We can thus utilize the Φ tables (grilles) to obtain a dimensional unity. We are in a period of transition, in a paradoxical situation where the majority of architects call for standardization, but once that this is accomplished, they refuse to adopt it. The architect is a coordinator. He needs those elements that will allow him to create a unified coherence. The norms proposed until now are not satisfactory for these demands. Only a science of dimension in relation with rational proportions can constitute the basis for a satisfactory normalization that takes us beyond the stage of improvisation. Only after we have clarified these problems would it be possible to create a human framework of life and to humanize space.

The ancient mystical number attempts to express biological fact through symbols. The current return of Pythagorism will lead to the renewal of ancient conceptions even within this area. It is surprising to see how many of the Fibonacci series correspond to the periodical structure of human life. Fibonacci himself discovered these series when he was trying to calculate the offspring of a pair of rabbits, supposing that each couple of rabbits produce a new couple which in turn becomes a procreator. We can therefore suppose that the system not only reflects the structural organization of human dimensional space, but also corresponds to the spatial and temporal structure of social groups and their habitat. In order to prove this fact it will be necessary to compare many statistical documents. It is apparent that the accumulation of 100–200, 1,000–2,000, 10,000–20,000, 100,000–200,000 inhabitants are the most frequent, which confirms the analogy that exists between the numbers and the dimension tables mentioned above.

Gaston Bardet has established an hierarchy of social units following the scheme of 5–15, 50–150, 500–1500 families. This corresponds to the decimal series of 0.618–1.618. Hippodamus of Miletus, the urbanist of Ancient Greece, demanded that the population of a city not exceed 10,000 inhabitants. The number of citizens of Ancient Athens was fixed, by law, at around 20,000 habitants. An investigation on this theme would enable the urbanist to conceive the ideal dimensions of accumulation.

The dimension and the proportion exercise (provoke) a strong emotional reaction. Man needs to feel himself surrounded by life. When he creates an artificial world, like in art and technology, he imposes the structural properties of life and humans onto inanimate matter, conferring more firmly the appearance of a potential energy.

1 From William McCausland Stewart's translation of Paul Valéry's *Eupalinos or the Architect*, (London: Oxford University Press, 1932).

2 Gerasa, *Introduction to Arithmetic*, translated by Martin Luther D'ooge from Frank Egleston Robbins and Louis Charles Karpinski, *Studies in Greek Arithmetic*, (New York: The Macmillan Company, 1926).

Morphologic Architecture

1963

First published in *RAIC Journal* 40, May 1963, pp. 40–47. Later republished in *Zodiac* 16, 1966

Even after long experience in teaching architectural design, one cannot get rid of the unpleasant feeling of conveying a rather subjective know-how lacking theoretical justification. There are theories about many aspects of architecture, but there is no single consistent theory of architecture. The vague term art is often evoked to cover the confusing situation. Sometimes one has the near certitude of touching the border of art. But the built human environment, seen as a whole in its geographical distribution and historical process, has almost nothing to do with art. To use an analogy—of all the spoken or written communication material, very little represents poetry. It is obvious that, in building, a certain latent potential of art can be freed, but such a case represents more the exception than the rule.

I was repeatedly asked, by interested laymen, to recommend a book which explains the essence of architecture in a general, accessible way. To my own astonishment, I was unable to do so. The inadequacy of all architectural speculation goes back to its beginning. It is a case of heredity, and it is not easy to get rid of a negative tradition. The ten books on architecture by Vitruvius are a compilation of information about building and related fields in the Mediterranean basin during the Augustan period. They do not form a coherent system but contain independent references on such topics as climatology, hydrology, building materials, proportion theories, and also recipes for conventional building types as well as for the construction of war machinery. Since the Renaissance, the expression Vitruve has become a collective term for architectural theory. All architects bowed before the authority of antiquity and pressed their own thinking into the traditional pattern.

This pluralistic approach has not changed up to the present. Under the influence of the general development of technology, the scientific methods replaced the trial and error of construction. More recently, the life process within the built structures, from the dwelling to town and region, underwent sociologic and ecologic analysis. But it remains doubtful whether there is direct interdependence between function and structure.

Without having contributed to the understanding of architecture, those studies have widened the existing gap between architecture in the narrower sense and town-planning, which tends to become a super discipline where specific shape is without importance. Another field of study, *History of Architecture*, catalogued nearly the entire building production of the past and brought it into geographical and chronological order. The so-called science of art (*Kunstwissenschaft*) has attempted an interpretation of that accumulated material. The most important outcome of that work was the awareness of architectural space and its evolution.

The research lines mentioned have hardly any relation to each other. The possibility exists to conceive the whole man-made human environment from a unifying point of view by applying morphological criteria. Scientific domains, which have been developed up to now and which are predominantly of ecological nature, can easily be integrated into a morphological system, because they possess the value of selection factors only.

A science of architecture, like any other science, should describe the different phenomena by a common lawfulness. But until now, styles and periods of style have remained isolated phenomena. There were endeavors to demonstrate mutual influences of forms and to represent the flow of motives geographically. But styles, as such, remain enigmatic in this representation. Analogies with biological phenomena might contribute to a better understanding. Morphogenesis of design is analogous to morphogenesis of biology. It also is a science at its beginning, but since it moves in the accepted tracks of scientific methods, a normal evolution can be expected. Similarly to architecture, one could follow the way from cell to cell (aggregate), the transformation of shape and dimension which the element undergoes, the laws and symmetries determining the shape of aggregations.

I do not believe that values can ever be entirely eliminated from architecture, as from any other any other human activity. As in any creative activity, whether in the domain of art, science or technology, the deciding contribution will always depend on intuition. But the mechanism of intuition works only if certain preconditions are given, the most important one being profound knowledge of the subject. Musical talent without thorough training will rarely become productive. In a certain stage of investigation the introduction of a scale of values is hampering. As known, there are, again, actual attempts to put value relations on an experimental mathematical basis, to "scientifice" them. (Hartman, New Mexico). These endeavors continue earlier trends, for instance, Fechner's experimental esthetics "Esthetics from Underneath," using statistical methods. The results were rather primitive and even when further extended one doubts if they could do justice to so complicate a phenomenon that is involved in architectural esthetics, with its intricate interpenetration of logic, sentiment, function, structure, etc. In spite of the insurmountable difficulties, architectural science has pursued this way. At the basis of architectural research stands architectural history and architectural history is conceived as a part of the history of art. That implies that under the raw material offered by building history, a division into works of art and non-art was made. The development of works of art is discussed and the others ignored.

Thinking of biology, we often encounter in nature phenomena of astonishing beauty. Naturally the professional esthetician will strictly prove that an unbridgeable rift exists between beauty in nature and beauty in art. But where would biology stand if morphological research had introduced esthetic appreciation in advance? I do not know if morphologists and biologists are less receptive to beauty than architects and art critics, but the idea of a mixture of biology and esthetics in research seems derivative.

I believe that architecture can be investigated like any other phenomena. The cumulative efforts of scientific thinking, when approaching a phenomenon, have always helped to reach a conceptual order. Architecture itself has never been attacked scientifically, although there exist a multitude of scientific investigations of side issues to architecture (climatology, light, acoustics, sociology, ecology, etc). Whenever architects devote their time to architectural research, they tackle these subject-matters; and one can rightly assume that non-architect scientists would do the job better. And as a matter of fact, they do. Tackling architecture itself is taboo. Of course, architecture is a creative activity, but so is physics, for the creative mind. There is a pronounced trend to withdraw into foggy irrationalism, with plenty of humanitarian slogans as opposed to the platitudes of common-sense, common-sense being the label which the fake mystic but wildly efficient businessmen architects stick on any attempt at creative order. It is an advertising trick relying on the 19th century popular image of the irresponsible romantic artist, and which still appeals to the provincial taste. They discredit art and they discredit science.

The present views on architecture are distilled from highly complex works of the Baroque period where space had an absolute meaning and received a perfect expression. The concept of space as known today was first discovered through the investigation of Baroque architecture. That means that it has been abstracted from the final product of a long evolution. The thus derived concepts of space do not apply to simpler, earlier or less intricate structures. Although no coherent architectural theory has emerged through the discovery of space, the recognition of space as a constituting factor of architecture, unrecognized by previous generations, remains a lasting contribution.

Architecture is a projection of space images into material form. In the development of architectural space, the known parallelism of ontogenesis and phylogenesis is equally present. Some insight into the space perception of children has been won. They go through a topological stage into a projective stage, and arrive finally at the Euclidian space of the adult. The building activity of mankind all over the world follows this evolutionary scheme. This is true not only for building alone but also for the whole man-made human environment, and particularly for containers.

The artifacts of the whole human environment can be roughly divided into two groups, tools and containers. I do not wish to enter the domain of tools, which might by itself be a subject for extensive studies. All tools are a prolongation or multiplication of the human body. Tools and arms developed on the same pattern. When the human hand developed into the gripping organ, the primary tool came into being. Next a transfer of the teeth function to the hand and from there to the primitive tools took place. All mechanical tools are a kind of mobile teeth connected to the hand. Knives, scissors, hammers, tongs, forks, shovels show this morphological relationship from the first glance. The lever bar is the prolongation of the arm. There is a third element, the handle, an adaptation to the human hand. Tools acquire artificial muscles, first, animal muscular power, then with the first industrial revolution, the mechanical muscle, the motor. A further evolutionary line prolongates the human sense-organs, prolongation of the eyes: microscope, telescope, television, X-rays; prolongation of the reach of the ear: telephone, radio, ultrasound; prolongation of the tactile sense: magnetic detectors, radar, thermometer, barometer, ionization. Recently prolongation of the brain function forms an additional range of tools: cybernetics, automation, electronic computers.

Animals cannot take off or change at will their teeth, claws, saws, tongs, scissors, as nature developed them. Tools are an extended, exchangeable, removable organ, which means a greater amount of freedom in evolution, therefore less constraint, less specialization. Man seems to be the least specialized being.

Man is a complex container with the head and the body as two conspicuous main containers, the whole equipped with tools—the limbs, for moving and grasping like a child's drawing. The containers next to man are an inexhaustible domain, which would merit a deeper investigation. Many connections lead to the neighboring domains of clothing and building.

The container nearest to man is clothing. It is a container for a container, a reinforced skin, as many animals have developed—like sea shells. The armor of a knight is built on the same principle. Clothing hardly allows movement inside the container, only the wider container of the house allows this freedom. The snail leaves its shell to a certain degree, but is still bound to it. Man's clothing represents an extension of his skin and is removable and changeable. This feature puts clothing in analogy with tools. Man is the prisoner of neither his clothing nor of his tools.

One approach is to see man as a building animal. Building of most animals is guided by instinct. It is most obvious with insects. Instinct is characterized by narrowly bound reactions which do not admit deviations. It is orientated towards certain environmental stimuli. Once those stimuli change, the instinct no longer reacts purposefully. It is too specialized. Man is a learning being. He can adapt to a great extent his reactions to environmental changes, thereby heightening his chances of survival. His buildings are richer and offer great variety. But it is submitted to lawfulness, as is instinctive building. Wasps and bees and related insects build a cylinder with a horizontal rotation axis. As social beings they group themselves and build "skyscrapers," cell aggregates, within which the cylinders are transformed into hexagonal prisms with half rhombic dodecahedra at the end. It is a very rational, but restricted, building system. The architecture is as monotonous as the business architecture of today's evolution line. The mole-hill has a vertical rotation axis. It is a complex pattern of a central space with a surrounding double ring system. The radical corridors show the numerical order of the Fibonacci series. Most birds' nests also show rotational symmetry. If I were to name a further geometric property of those buildings, I would say those structures are round and that they approach, as far as execution in different building materials allows, the form of minimal areas. Building materials are determined by the environment; it is a factor that introduces minor changes but does not influence the basic shape. If we look for analogies to animal buildings in the man-made environment, our attention is drawn towards our containers, which show the same characteristics: rotational symmetry and enclosing minimal areas. One could say that they show a stylistic affinity. The contours of those containers are so-called *plateau* figures, mainly roulettes of conics. Gravitation adds a further element, influencing the symmetry relations. Broadly speaking, one can divide our container into two subgroups of soft and stiff containers. The soft container is a suspended construction, like the tent or clothing, and its prototype are the sacks and soft containers for liquids: for example, the pockets in clothing, the rucksack of the alpinist, the saddle bag of the horse man, the lady's hand bag, the tobacco pouch, luggage, kitbags, balloons, giant petrol tankers of plastic, and also the modern big tents and inflatable structures. Those containers are essentially mobile and are put on the ground for a certain time only.

The stiff container has a different genealogy. It first sinks into the ground to lift itself out of the ground, and finally free itself into independent shapes. The first stiff containers are hollows in the ground: for example, grain storage of animals and man, water cisterns, with the typical narrow neck reminding the bottle shapes to reduce evaporation. Even after having detached itself from the ground, the stiff container sinks once more into the ground, like the Egyptian pointed vases.

The shapes of the stiff and soft containers converge towards common shapes and their origin can no more be identified.

In the containers next to man the problem of grouping or packaging had no significance in the past. For a long span of time, and in different civilizations, those shapes had hardly changed. Mass transport of containers has brought the packing shape into being. Consider only jerry cans for petrol, and, above all, our over-production of paper packaging. The evolution of containers omitted an intermediate stage which could be called the projective stage, and can be detected in the evolution of houses. Modern package containers are mostly rectangular orthogonal. Of necessity, they should have straight edges and surfaces, but not necessarily right angles. But group containers were born into a rectangular civilization and architecture therefore had to assimilate itself. Problems of transport and storage have forced it. Interpreted into geometry, this means that the densely packed containers have undergone a topological transformation. In the topological rubber geometry, a sphere can be transformed into a cube. I simplify a bit. In analogy to biology one can see the house element as a kind of container cell with a smaller or larger group of man as the nucleus. This cell can develop in two directions:

a) change its size and create large spaces like large cells. Examples: The Syrian, Roman and Byzantine cupolas, and the big modern shell vaulting. The spans grow absolutely, the amount of material used diminishes. The building dematerializes.
b) lead to differentiated container aggregates, like cell aggregates. Examples: office buildings, flat blocks, hospitals, etc.

Architecture creates containers for man. It begins with the horizontal area as man moves optimally on horizontal areas. Where horizontal areas do not occur in nature, man introduces them by terracing mountains and by creating stairs. He creates sunken and lifted horizontal areas, juxtaposes and superposes them.

The end of a linear movement is a rotation movement, creating a round area as an expression of rest. Animals like cats and dogs turn to prepare their resting place. Long after the house became rectangular, the resting place, the apses, remained round. The house, the container cell, is primarily round, a hollow space with a rotation axis like the other containers next to man. There are cupolas both cylindrical and conical. In clothing similar shapes are found in the head cover. These shapes are very independent of environmental factors like building material and climate. The igloo of the Eskimo is identical in shape with the equatorial round hut and the tent of the steppes. Excavations show the same house type in old China, India, Africa and the Near East. Like other containers, houses follow two evolutionary lines: that of soft containers, like tents, and that of stiff containers, starting with sunken floor caves, later rising out of the ground with forms lifting massive houses.

Grouping follows the same scheme. The huts are loosely arranged in a circle, sometimes enclosed by a round wall, which could either be elliptic or take any free round shape. The openings of these houses are also round.

Cell growth of containers follow the same form structure, whether covered spaces like the Atreus tomb of Mycenae or the non-covered space of Stonehenge. Incidentally, the round shapes belong mainly to the pre-agricultural civilization stage. We could call this round structure stage a topological stage. But with the emergence of agriculture round shapes do not disappear but receive a sacred character.

Under social pressure, the cells move closer to each other and undergo topological transformations. Certain transitional forms come into being. These transformations could best be visualized by a film. The round cells move closer and closer, the shapes become oblong, only the corners remain round, occasionally an apses remains, until a complete form transformation takes place. There are not yet rectangles or squares but straight lined figures with oblique angles. The Megaron type has been created. One could call this the projective stage of architecture.

Consequently this architecture transforms into a rectangular pattern. This rectangular architecture has, seen stereometrically, the advantage that area angles and dihedral angles are identical of 90 degrees. Thus the final result of the topological transformation of loose round shapes is a tightly knitted rectangular pattern. This process provides matter for thought. Geometrically, it is not self-evident that the round houses become rectangular. Remembering beehives, where the social structure formed the package into a hexagonal pattern having the advantage of being isotropic. The rectangular pattern is not isotropic but hexagonal houses are rare. It may be that the rectangular structure offers a greater degree of freedom; besides it allows the transfer of proportions of other polygons as the pentagon in the golden section.

The house as we know it from children's drawings is a synthetic form. It is a combination of the two evolutionary trends, of the soft and stiff container. Remember the drawing of a typical house section which Le Corbusier demonstrated as an obsolete example which is opposed to his new section. A typical house consists of a roof, which is a direct descendent of the ancient tent; then of a cellar, which is the descendent of the old sunken floor cave; and then the house proper, which is the central part and which is the cave lifted from earth to the sun. The image of such a house has become a kind of archetype, deeply anchored in the individual and collective subconscious. Now we understand the general popularity of this type of house and the emotional resistance against all attempts of reform.

Obsolete shapes do not disappear even after having ceased to fulfill their function. The obsolete house type covers, in a growing measure, the suburbs of highly civilized industrial countries. Inside that house remains the old fireplace, which does not serve for heating anymore, and is another instance of the inertia of form.

The grammar of space developed gradually from Euclidian to projective geometry and from there to the new discipline of topology. The evolution of architectural space took the inverse direction: at the beginning there was a topological stage tending towards space enclosure by minimal areas; for example, tholos-type round houses and clusters, absidial and round-cornered houses. Then came a projective geometric stage with undetermined angle length relations; for example, early Megaron-type houses in irregularly grown clusters. Finally architecture arrived at a Euclidian organization with straight lined rectangular shapes; for example, building and town planning in high civilizations.

Except for the rectangular prismatic patterns, the possibilities of Euclidian order in architecture are far from being fully exploited until now. The large array of space packing patterns, using the Platonic and Archimedean solids and their duals, prisms and anti-prisms, has not yet found any architectural application. These patterns are related to the problem of sphere packing, where mathematical investigations are still in development. Besides the crystallographic space structures, there is a whole range of little explored looser packing forms, some appearing in organic life. These forms could have repercussions on architecture.

The architect entering this research field would find, to his surprise, that crystallographers had preceded him. In the discovery of crystal structures, mathematical intuition anticipated later observed confirmation on the X-ray screen. The morphogenetic factors producing crystals operate on the molecular scale level, where gravitational forces are negligible. But, within the realm of container groups on the human scale, as in architecture, these forces strongly influence the configuration of space enclosure. A general science of space should reflect equally upon nature and human creation. The crystallographic discoveries remained without resonance in architecture. The cross-fertilization between art and science, which one could normally expect after an important finding in the domain of form, did not set in. The inadequate state of tectonic and massive construction methods prevented a direct impact on architecture. With the actual development of 3-dimensional construction methods, the transposition into another medium has become less possible.

Space packing patterns are a geometrical abstraction only. In chemistry, many aspects besides the crystallographic ones enter the stage to perform the drama of matter in space time. Also, in architecture, the geometric aspect covers only a part of the complex tissue. It would be naïve to believe that one could mechanically transfer shapes from crystallography to architecture. This would mean a worse formalism than the application of historical forms. What is important is *thinking* in analogies. Geometric space patterns have to be transposed into human scale and put into a visually sizeable order to be of architectural value. In traditional rectangular packing, questions of scale have found routine answers. Approved cooking recipes exist. In the non-traditional proposals they solicit new approaches. Because of the inherent difficulties a fresh awareness of scale arises.

Historic architecture was mainly concerned with the dramatization of statics. The restricted register of baroque space order soon became exhausted. We are now able to distinguish the possible elements constituting architecture. Like in crystallography, the elements are limited in number. Even so, 3-dimensional space packing offers far more possibilities than the 2-dimensional patterns, commonly called ornament (also 2-dimensional crystallography), on which architecture was mainly based until now. Different stages of civilization have different optimal population densities and use corresponding space packing. Hunting and fishing communities lived in loosely packed round houses, of the topological kind, in accordance with the low population density. Agricultural civilizations created the rectangular Euclidean pattern. Industrial civilization with its high population density is still packed into an outlined agricultural framework and has yet to create its appropriate pattern. The rotational symmetries of the new patterns which were meaningless before the space age now become the exact bearers of widely understood contemporary symbolism.

Particular design problems arise at the boundary portions of the new space packings, where different conditions prevail than in the homogeneous inside parts. One of the direct implications is the change of the shape of the openings. In the topological stage, the openings followed the general character, and were consequently rounded, as in African huts. In the rectangular space pattern, doors and windows were rectangular, their distribution tending towards certain proportional orders. In the proposed packings rectangular openings are the exceptions. This evolution was forecast by cars and planes, where no more rectangular openings occur. A parallel evolution is noticeable in newer industrial and religious buildings.

Where does architecture as an art, with all the perfection for the senses, fit into? Where Greece? Italy? Japan?

Architecture is not so much a direct art of the senses, but is like music memory. The tone of the chord which I now hear does not exist in the next moment, nevertheless the synthesis of music forms in my memory. The space through which I passed I do not see anymore; even so, it is present in my memory and directly connected to my actual perception. Architecture is interwoven with reality and the stuff that dreams are made of. This is equally true for the interior of a building as well as the exterior. The façade of the Gothic dome does not reveal the nature of its nave. This remark shows our relation to the slogan "Form Follows Function," which characterizes the actual unwinding period of architecture. Stone minarets still tower above the cupolas of the mosques. Not far from them on some missile launching site rise identical shapes, the rockets no more built of stone. These containers built of modern synthetic materials fly into outer space to destroy themselves and perhaps to spread destruction. Two identical shapes but what difference in function. The cupola might be one of the inflatable structures which blow off here today and there tomorrow. Tinguely, the Swiss sculptor, in the courtyard of the Museum of Modern Art in New York, fired his self-destructive sculpture symbolizing one aspect of architecture projected on the mind of the contemporary artists. Architecture has become aggressive and has conquered the de-divined heavens. The nostalgic longing for the stable, symbolic architecture of yesterday, and maybe of tomorrow, remains stronger than ever, the eternal polarity of all human endeavor.

Architecture as Ornament (Extracts) 1967

Extracts from a transcribed lecture delivered at Laval University, Quebec City, Canada, 1967
Published in *Zodiac* 19, 1969, pp. 90–98, a year after Alfred Neumann's death.

For the architects of the 19th century, ornament had a fatal, irresistible magic. The compilatory zeal with which artists, and particularly architects, assembled, registered, and classified ornaments of all periods and civilizations, awakens our wonder and respect. With the industrial revolution, the down-break of the preceding period and its old social order, cultural unity and artistic orientation were lost. The 19th century believed that a new orientation could be gained only by a historical retrospective. The 19th century became the period of the great historical works and historical criticism: a retrospective and history-conscious period, demonstrating an astonishing collecting activity. The great museums are nearly all a product of that period.

Every collecting activity is by necessity selective; the selection norms reflect the character of the collector. Collecting was always an attribute of wealth and the 19th century was preoccupied with economics, hypnotized by the idea of wealth. These ideas found expression in a rich literature on national economics. Primitive-minded collectors prefer richly decorated articles made of expensive materials with much invested handicraft. Public collections followed this trend and displayed particularly expensive over-decorated art and craft articles.

An aesthetic doctrine was extracted from these collections by means of historical art analysis. As a result, a distorted picture of past handicraft productions persisted for a long time. It was believed that the more decorated an object, the higher its artistic and cultural value. Abundance of ornament became an urban status symbol distinguishing the city-dweller's household from the simpler and more modest rural one. At the beginning of the 19th century, classicistic revival revolted against over-decoration but these objections were soon swept away by a growing tide of romanticism and profusion of ornament. The 19th century experienced a neurotic fear of rising technological and social changes, which expressed itself in the need for overdoses of ornament. The hippy movement showed parallel features. But the naïve attempts of the 19th century to revive and recreate ornament, the efforts of those serious utilitarians to bring a bit of visual music into their smoke-blackened daily life were accompanied by a growing awareness of a diminishing creativity.

Crystallography deals, amongst others, with the regular division of space, a feature it has in common with ornament and architecture. The possibility of 230 crystal types was independently proved by three crystallographers, Fedorov, Shoenflies, and Barlow and later confirmed by Von Laue with X-ray diffraction patterns by crystals. Fedorov also first described the two-dimensional analogy of three-dimensional crystallography, but it remained unnoticed until the twenties when Polya and Niggly rediscovered two-dimensional crystallography, commonly called ornament. These findings, like many others in the 20th century, presented a strictly bounded world. There are 230 crystal groups, there are seventeen possibilities of area-covering ornament and seven possibilities of strip ornament.

Examples for all seven strip symmetries and seventeen area-filling symmetries can be found in ornamental patterns of Antiquity, particularly Egypt. The investigation field seemed to be exhausted until after 1950 when Shubnikov and others discovered anti-symmetry, or colored symmetry, and new groups had to be added to the already known ones. Again there is a certain parallelism between the development of science and art. The painter Escher used colored symmetry intuitively before its importance in crystallography was realized.

Ornament is one manifestation of the general category of symmetry. In the course of history, the word symmetry has undergone repeated change of meaning. Originally, it meant consonance of the parts of a whole, particularly in their proportional relationships. Today the term varies from a vague use in matters of art to mathematical precision.

Wherever a number of elements occur in a certain density in space, they will tend towards an ornamental order. In time, analogous conditions produce rhythm, as a complementary phenomenon to ornament. An analogy drawn from physics of the different states of matter seems not too far fetched. In the gas the atoms are dispersed and move freely, in the liquid, while the atoms are much closer packed, they are still able to shift and their arrangement remains disordered. In the solid the atoms are densely packed and though they vibrate, they do not move freely. This property is the crystallinity of the solid.

In ornament we meet with similar structures in its evolutionary process. The shapes of separately developed signs have a sort of topological equivalence. In prehistory and in primitive painting the distribution of the form elements in the area is first irregular. Only after these elements appear in a denser packing do they enter into a symmetry-induced pattern. The form of the elements is dependent upon the density of the motives constituting the ornament. The packing system can deform these elements until they are no more recognizable.

With the additional form-restricting conditions, like the representational prohibition in Mohammedanism, the motive elements disappear completely and only the geometric scaffolding remains. We obtain the ornament in pure state.

The formation of an ornament presupposes equal constituting elements. Architectural space is discontinuous, nonhomogenous and interpenetrated by anti-space. The space bubbles surrounding every individual or group are very uncertain and elastic in size and shape. But under the pressure of tradition, those spaces become unified when they form their definite shell. So the houses of most clans or other groups are very much the same and even in Western civilization bedroom sizes are standardized by general consent. So are the shapes and sizes of offices. Thus, the general pattern of our architecture is given. The same is true for the endless rows of suburban houses which represent a very restricted number of types. The fight against monotony cannot change the form of the elements, but only their arrangements in the choice of certain town planning patterns.

In architecture the space arrangements follow the same course. First the single space element can adopt nearly any shape, generally a rounded one with a vertical rotation axis. In the early state the elements are simple revolution surfaces with varied sections. Their shapes often resemble surfaces of constant mean curvature (minimal areas with respect to the volume contained). The right-angled shapes appear as a rule in the dense packing of the space elements.

The strip ornament, and more so, the area-filling ornament, form a sort of packing system of two-dimensional containers, if the expression is permissible. The two-dimensional containers often become symbol carriers. To become contained, the symbols themselves answer symmetrical exigencies. Thus, a limited set of standard signs develops which becomes a cultural collective property of a social group, as, for example, the Classical Greek ornament. Naturally, this applies not only to architectural ornament but also to all known writing systems, musical and mathematical notation systems, etc. We are surrounded by an extended wealth of ornament of which we are hardly aware because we have become accustomed to the fact. Our symbol notation is in general two-dimensional. The plane is the man-invented symbol carrier. The straight plane is one of the most astonishing inventions demanding a great degree of abstraction power. The system of composition, the symmetrical order of the plane, has evidently also a symbolic character.

The morphology of an object has nothing to do with its use, what one calls its function. The weaving process and the resulting structural pattern are independent of the tissues used as carpet or clothing. The steel structure of a skyscraper is not determined by its use as an office building.

Technology has brought with it an abundance of ornament. Cog-wheels, turbines, tire-treads (which resemble the framing of Romanesque church portals) etc. Measuring instruments, indeed, measuring itself with its translations in length measurements and its rotations in angle measurements, are based on the principles of symmetry.

It just seems that technology, with its wealth of objective rational ornaments, has encroached upon the older ornament of emotional symbolic elements. A historical survey shows that even where we entirely lose the symbolic sense of ornament, the character of form alone retains a continuous appeal for us. As Andreas Speiser put it: "As the true continuation of discoveries of earlier art periods, appears the theory of space-groups. Here on the models of crystal-structure, as one finds them in any physical or mineralogical institute, the new art will learn. On this basis, it can again dare approach ornament."

Besides the strip-ornament and the plane-filling ornament, there exist the regular and semi-regular plane tessellations, corresponding to regular and semi-regular polyhedra in space.

The plane in this case is considered as a polyhedron of infinite radius. There are of course many more plane-filling possibilities with a lower degree of regularity. From the psychology of form (*Gestaltpsychologie*) we know the complementary relationship of figure and background, depending on whether attention is focused on the one or the other. In ornament the relationship of background to figure is not arbitrary but is determined by the laws of symmetry. In the ornaments of Escher, both aspects have a meaning. In architecture the relationship of space and volume is analogous. The introduction of symmetries as in ornamental relationships facilitated perception and orientation in architectural space.

In geometry the concept of congruence implies the movement of rigid solids. But the movement is a neglected abstraction. In perception, the ornament demands movement of the eyes to seize the symmetries and when we deal with architectural scale, the whole man has to displace himself. The dimensions at these different scale levels are rationally related to the scale of the human body and his movements.

Any surface could be indefinitely extended as could the Euclidian plane that carries it. For the mathematician, this is simply a logical conclusion of the idea of symmetry. But for most human beings, the idea of a limitless repeating pattern is simply frightening. The artist's endeavor will always be oriented towards organizing a restrictive space or time. Therefore, his first aim will be to find a limiting frame, an enclosure. Mathematically the linear or area elements of an ornament could have any possible dimension, reaching from microscopic to macroscopic scale. The artist has to introduce a dimensional frame of reference fitted to the perception requirements of man. The choice of dimension is an essential artistic act.

Although architecture deals with three-dimensional forms, the ornament which rules the relations of the volume is necessarily two-dimensional. This may have optical reasons as two-dimensional relations are directly readable. But it might also be an outcome of the graphic media. Gothic cathedrals are regulated in plan and elevation by two-dimensional ornamental grids, as illustrated in the sketch book of Villard de Honnecourt, or the often-reproduced elevation of the Duomo of Milano taken from Serlio's Vitruv edition. Many Renaissance builders still followed the same method.

In more recent times, the same analogy system was used in Berlage's stock exchange in Amsterdam. The regulating grids of F.L. Wright's architecture reveal the influence of crystallographic geometry which he was taught in kindergarten. But also Corbusier's buildings express ornamental trends by the introduction of the Modulor. The golden section system which is the basis of the Modulor, works with similitudes instead of congruencies. But this does not change its basic ornamental character. By coordinating the architectural packing by a proportional system based on the golden section, an organic form factor is introduced and the cold impression of the crystal structure avoided. Patterns like the golden section which do not strictly follow crystallographic laws convey the impression of reduced entropy. They are more elastic and give more variation possibilities than stricter patterns.

To the symmetry of ornament in the plane corresponds crystallography in space. Here again, sequences of equal or similar elements form higher units which when combined, give further groupings of still higher units. The result is a hierarchy of containers for human occupation. The constituting element is a rectangular prismatic space which, when packed, produces the next higher unit—the house. The juxtaposition can be horizontal or vertical, so we obtain the low building or multi-storey building and their numerous combinations. Rows of houses form streets and squares depending upon translational or rotational symmetry.

What is true for architectural space is just as true for the solid space-enclosing elements. It is again a question of density of the elements. The original stone walls consist of irregularly superimposed and juxtaposed stones—cyclopic masonry. Rectangular architecture requires rectangular prismatic building stones and its many packing systems, the brick bonds. There is no essential difference whether one deals with cut natural stone or with formed brick. The packing system of the wall is the primary factor which dictates the form of the single wall element. In later development, other packing systems occur like, for instance, the building stones for factory chimneys, and stone elements in oriental vaulting, etc.

The well-known aesthetics of Kant considered the object of art as liberated from any practical purpose—beauty is purposeless. Following this doctrine, architecture as a structure serving a purpose can only have a kind of adherent, accidental beauty. To us it seems that architecture is in first place the creation of patterns (regularity, order, symmetry, etc.). This feature is common to architecture, music, poetry, painting, and mathematics. To those patterns, the architectural functions have to accommodate as well as possible. The only deciding criterion for a pattern, whether in mathematics, music, or architecture, is its aesthetic quality. What one calls function may have an influence on the choice of the pattern among different equivalent possibilities. Architecture as a space cell aggregate follows necessarily the laws of symmetry. The forms of this ornament are not dictated, as was thought, by function, but by the inherent space structure.

Attempts to computerize architecture were paralyzed by the difficulties to seize and quantify so-called functions. The efforts of functionalists have lead architecture astray into the field of formal arbitrariness. Once recognized that architecture is just a more or less regular space configuration system, to which the functions adapt themselves, mechanization and computerization of design become an immediate reality, independent from whether one considers it a curse or a blessing.

The recently proposed division between a self-conscious and unself-conscious design process does not seem to fit reality. There is good or bad design on a high or low technological level. The best criterion for designs is whether artists absorb their forms and incorporate them into their form vocabulary. The bicycle, for example, has been adopted by Fernand Léger and incorporated in some of his paintings. The bicycle presents a perfect mutual adaptation of man and mechanism. Adolf Loos already pointed out its neutral form which needs no adaptation to its environment. The bicycle is an example of good anonymous, but it has nothing in common with products of a pre-industrial period. In a series of paintings entitled "Les constructeurs," Léger showed a contemporary steel construction, but he did not show the finished building. He must have felt that 100 years of architectural evolution had not solved the aesthetic problem of the exterior aspect of buildings. The best architectural solutions were those which left the construction untouched, like the side elevation of Frantz Jourdain's "La Samaritaine" department store in Paris.

In the industrial society, the artist has a deciding role in the form selection process. The artist places a form in an aesthetic value context, which is after some initial resistance, recognized by the general public. The actual form of our watch dial-plate is derived from Cézanne's still-life with the clock. Only lines show on the dial-plate instead of the usual figures.

Irrational Factors in Building Industrialization 1968

Published in *Architecture Canada*, 45 (November 1968), pp. 37–38 after Alfred Neumann's death.

The first post-war congress of CIAM (*Congres Internationaux d'Architecture Moderne*) took place in Bridgewater, England in 1947. It was mainly concerned with reconstruction problems. Modern architecture had by that time become a respectable movement, and had spread from the continent to overseas countries. With the change of generation, England had accepted the doctrines of modern architecture and was putting them diligently into practice in her reconstruction work.

During the congress, I accompanied Le Corbusier on a visit to an industrialized building plant in Bristol, in fact, a recently converted airplane plant. The plant was producing fully equipped individual houses at the rate of a couple of houses a day. Le Corbusier followed with great interest the manufacturing process and admired the ingenuity of the details. But he did not spare his criticism for the environmental implication of the product. He was shocked by the prospect of having the landscape covered by a suburban sprawl. The one family house was still the accepted standard in England. There was a discrepancy between the layout of settlements and the changing technology in the production of houses. Architects had not yet learned to converge these two independent lines of architectural thinking.

In those days, Corbusier was preoccupied with his idea of the "unité d'habitation" which was being realized in Marseille. He advocated collective housing with industrialization of the building components but with a free composition of the whole. Corbusier was, and still is, criticized for his alleged lack of humanism. But it is often overlooked that Corbusier is being criticized for other peoples' realizations. He himself never really got an opportunity to show his concept in its totality. The plan of St.-Dié, which was the most perfect presentation of his ideas, remained unrealized.

A building or a town is a structure, a system of systems. A structure is to a large extent independent of its constituting parts. Building industry deals before all with building components, not with the whole environment which is not the sum of its parts. Thus, building research has to become structural research.

At the graduate course of the School of Architecture at Laval University, we paid due attention to the ideas inherent in the various outlooks on structuralism. At the moment, this might seem highly abstract, but it is certainly directly connected to architectural practice as far as industrialization of building is concerned. Even systems research seems too narrow to embrace the highly complex phenomena of architecture with its many implications on irrational human conduct. After a long round about way one arrives again at the priority of architecture as the most general structure.

As long as those basic relationships between part and whole are not sufficiently investigated, all attempts at coordination and standardization will be in vain. The priority of the architectural whole is the key to efficient industrialization, not the summation of parts which leads to the architecture of the absurd. At present the whole field shows an irrational development, rendered even more grotesque by the rationality of the details.

Industrialization is neither a panacea far all the woes of architecture nor a devilish instrument for the destruction of traditional values. Its only criterion is whether it adapts to creativity in the human environment. We have to get rid of many economic restrictions imposed upon the process of industrialization. The key projects of our period are simply meta-economic. Architecture will never be the outcome of the cheapest production method. Its economy is only seizable in human terms and in long range projection.

Industrialization has most developed where it is least needed—in administration buildings. Housing has remained nearly untouched by it. In developing countries only an insignificant portion of buildings will be constructed with industrially produced parts. The traditional building techniques are lost and a new non-architecture has appeared using the masses of waste material which accompany the handling of industrial products. Shanty towns, bidonvilles, are today the necessary complement of industrialization of building.

Industrial elements in architecture are not chosen for their rational value but for their emotional excitement qualities. They are usually combined with outright regression forms: picturesque stone walls with wide glass windows, fire-places with air conditioned interiors. At present, industrialization means individualization of the product. The linearity of the assembly line cannot cope with the demands for human environment.

One of the problems industrial building production faces today is planning or no planning. There is obviously always a certain amount of planning involved. But the question is whether to proceed to overall planning of the whole production. The theoretical advantages are obvious: better coordination, less waste, etc...But, in practice, total planning has been braking progress and creating bureaucratic dullness. There are no more loopholes for creativity. This is too high a price to be paid. The ultimate criterion is whether the environment can be harmonized. Planning of industrial building parts is a means, not an end in itself. Building is not a rational process, although its structure is interwoven with rational elements. The super-imposition of an entirely rational structure, as it is done in planning, deforms the structural logic and produces those hybrid buildings which are a sign of housing bureaucracy all over the world. The computer or any other brain prosthesis in the hand of building bureaucracy will only strengthen their position.

Chronology

1900
Alfred Neumann is born on January 26 in Vienna to Hermina Hickl and Sigmund Neumann, a cabinetmaker.

1910
Neumann's family moves to Brno, where his father sets up a cabinetmaking workshop.

1914
Neumann begins his studies in architecture at the German Building Trades School, also attended by the architects Leopold Bauer, Josef Hoffmann, Hubert and Franz Gessner, and Adolf Loos.

1917
Neumann enlists in the Austro-Hungarian army and participates in World War I. Until the end of the war, he was stationed at a small Tyrolean town near Innsbruck.

1919
After the war, Neumann enrolls at the German Technical University of Brno to continue his architectural studies. He also works as an assistant at the school and at his father's shop designing furniture.

1922
Neumann completes his studies in Brno, and moves to Vienna. There, he enrolls at the Academy of Fine Arts to study architecture under Peter Behrens. On July 18, 1922, Neumann's first article, "Scenic picture: spatial stage," a theoretical consideration of illusive expression on the theater stage, is published in *Brünner Tagesbote*.

1923
As part of his studies, Neumann designs his *House for California* project.

1924
Neumann is awarded the Behrens Prize of the Vienna Academy.

1925
Neumann passes his state exam at the Academy, and then moves to Paris, where he works in the Art Deco atelier of Charles Siclis.

1926
Neumann joins Auguste Perret's Atelier du Palais de Bois in Paris.

1927
Neumann goes to Berlin and works in Peter Behrens' office on designs for standardized and social housing projects in Vienna and Zagreb, and for department stores in Frankfurt and Magdeburg. Neumann also works on several designs for competitions, including one for a *Department Store on Friedrichstrasse, Berlin*, a *Municipal Service Center and Fire Station in Wrocław*, and an *Addition for the Reichstag in Berlin*.

1928
Neumann returns to Paris and works once more in Auguste Perret's studio. In September of this year, Neumann and Jacques Guiauchain, his colleague from Perret's studio, travel to Algiers to collaborate on the design and construction of the *Government Palace for Agriculture and the Centenary Hall* for the Bureaux Administratifs du Palais du Gouvernement. These projects mark the arrival of modern architecture on the African continent.

1929
In May, Neumann returns to Paris and begins to work with the architects Lucien Beugnet and Pierre Forestier. Together, they submit designs for a competition for a *School in Boulogne-Billancourt* (formerly Boulogne-sur-Seine), which are never realized. Later, Neumann and Forestier collaborate on a design for a competition for a *School in the Paris suburb of Villejuif*, which is shortlisted against the winning project by André Lurcat.

1930
The designs of the two schools Neumann worked on with Beugnet and Forestier are published in the second volume of *Bibliotheque de l'Architecture Modern*, entitled *Écoles*. Neumann also reconfigures his earlier, expressionist *House for California* as a light, steel-frame building with glass walls, which is published in the third volume of the *Bibliotheque*, entitled *Villas modernes*. He also travels to Brno during a short holiday, and participates in a competition for the *Moravia Sanitorium* in Tatranská Lomnica.

1931
Neumann works in the offices of Jean Ginsberg in Paris. Here, he befriends one of his colleagues, the Russian émigré architect Berthold Lubetkin. Neumann also joins the Parisian avant-garde artists' groups Abstraction-Création and Cercle et Carré. Furthermore, he designs a *Villa* for a client in Paris, but as this project coincides with the late onset of the Great Depression in France, it is never built.

1932–1934
Neumann mostly divides his time between Paris and Brno.

1932
Neumann goes to Vienna and works in the office of Josef Frank on houses for the Werkbundsiedlung. He also works on a design for a competition for the *Justice Hall* in San Salvador, Chile.

1934
Neumann designs a *Renovation and Extension for Dr. Josef Slezak's House at 179 Viničiá Street* in Brno, which includes built-in furniture and seems to have been influenced by Adolf Loos's Raumplan approach. In December of this year, Neumann moves to Cape Town, South Africa and works for the firm Kallenbach-Kennedy-Furner on residential and commercial projects.

1936
Neumann leaves Cape Town and spends his summer in Paris before returning to Brno to practice independently.

1937
Neumann designs a *Family House in Brno*, and marries Valerie Šlampová on April 14. As Hitler's Germany becomes increasingly militant and powerful, Neumann attempts to leave Europe. He submits an immigration request to the South African Government, but it is denied.

1939–1945
Neumann spends the beginning of the Second World War in Brno, and then moves to Prague. It is unclear where, and how, Neumann survives during these years, but it is likely that someone assists in hiding him.

1945
On February 11, while in hiding in Prague, Neumann is captured and deported to the concentration camp at Terezin (Theresienstadt), Czechoslovakia, where he stays until the war ends in May. Thereafter, he returns to Brno, and befriends the photographer France Graubnerová (France Grubner).

1945
Neumann begins working at the Regional Research and Planning Institute in Brno, an organization that brings scientific and sociological studies to bear on the planning process, and is responsible for designing regional and urban plans for the entire Moravian region of Czechoslovakia. Here, Neumann works with Bohuslav Fuchs and Emanuel Hruška.

1947
In September, Neumann travels with a Czech delegation to CIAM 6 in Bridgewater, England, to present the Institute's planning studies for the Moravian-Silesian region alongside Emanuel Hruška.

1948
Following a coup by the Communist Party of Czechoslovakia, Neumann is dismissed from the Regional Research and Planning Institute and makes plans to leave the country. Shortly thereafter, the Institute is abolished entirely.

1949
Neumann immigrates to Israel and settles in Jerusalem. He works for the Jerusalem municipal planning department on *Urban Plans for the Latrun Area of Jerusalem*, which are never realized.

1949–1956
Neumann continues his research on modular and proportional systems. Throughout the 1950s, he also designs *Studies and Proposals for Various Dormitory and Housing Schemes*, which are never built.

1952
Neumann is appointed Assistant Professor in the Faculty of Architecture and Town Planning at the Technion–Israel Institute of Technology, the only school of architecture and town planning in Israel at this time.

1953
Neumann represents Israel at CIAM 9 in Aix-en-Provence, France. Later that same year, he is promoted to the position of Dean of the Faculty of Architecture and Town Planning.

1956
Neumann publishes his work on modular and proportional systems as a booklet written in French, entitled *L'Humanisation de l'éspace: le système MΦ*, which appeared as part of the *Collection Éspace* series of *Architecture d'Aujourd'hui*, arranged by Andre Bloc.

1958
Neumann's term as Dean of the Faculty of Architecture and Town Planning ends, ends, but he remains on the faculty as a professor.

1959
Neumann and two of his former Technion students, Zvi Hecker and Eldar Sharon, establish an architectural practice in Israel called Neumann-Hecker-Sharon.

1959–1963
Neumann-Hecker-Sharon design the *Bat Yam Town Hall and Civic Center* in Bat Yam.

1960–1961
Neumann-Hecker-Sharon design the *Club Méditeranée Holiday Camp* in Achziv.

1961
Neumann-Hecker-Sharon design the *Michmoret Holiday Camp* in Michmoret, and the *Kiryat Yam Holiday Camp*, Kiryat Yam.

1961–1962
Neumann-Hecker-Sharon design a *Housing Complex in Ein Rafa*.

1961–1964
Neumann-Hecker-Sharon design the *Dubiner Apartment House* in Ramat Gan.

1962
Neumann marries his former student Naomi Gottesman (1938-1988) and the couple's daughter, Eva-Marie Neumann, is born the same year.

1963
While on leave from the Technion, Neumann moves to Quebec City, Canada, and works as a visiting professor for the École d'Architecture at the Université de Laval. He teaches a third-year design studio.

1963–1966
Neumann divides his time between Israel and Canada. He designs the *Danciger Building for the Faculty of Mechanical Engineering* at the Technion's new Haifa campus. Hecker is his sole collaborator for this project, as in 1964, Sharon leaves the firm to work for his father, who is also an architect.

1964
Neumann and Hecker submit a design for the *Netanya City Hall* competition.

1965
Neumann and Hecker submit a design for the *Ashdod City Center* competition.

1966
Neumann and Hecker design *Beit Zeit Youth Camp and Restaurant* in Beit Zeit, and a synagogue, which was ultimately not built. Neumann also submits a design for a competition for the *El-Al Terminal in Tel Aviv*, and works with Hecker and Naomi Neumann on a design for the *Amsterdam City Hall* competition. A disagreement between Technion officials and the architects concerning the Danciger Building's envelope ignites into a full-blown controversy, and prompts Neumann's resignation from the Faculty of Architecture and Town Planning. He leaves Israel for Quebec City to take a permanent teaching position at the Université de Laval, leaving Hecker to oversee the completion of their joint work in Israel. At Laval, Neumann establishes a graduate architecture program.

1967
Neumann and Hecker continue to collaborate on the research project, *Studies in Polyhedral Geometries*.

1966–1969
Neumann and Hecker design a *Synagogue at the Officers' School, Training Base 1*, Mitzpeh Ramon.

1968
Neumann dies of lung cancer on October 23. He is buried as a Christian, as per his request, at Notre-Dame de Belmont in Quebec City, Canada.

Above: Neumann (center) in late 1920s, probably in Algiers
Below: Portrait in late 1940s

Opposite Above: Neumann (right) presenting the Czech contribution to CIAM 6 in Bridgewater, England 1947. This photograph also appears in Sigfried Giedion, *A Decade of Contemporary Architecture* (New York: George Wittenborning, 1954)
Opposite Below: Neumann (center in light gray) with large-scale plan of Czech regional planning department, 1947–48

Above: Le Corbusier (left) with Neumann (right) at CIAM 6, Bridgewater, 1947

Below: Neumann (pictured right) in Israel, 1950s

Above: Neumann (left) with Max Bill (right) at CIAM 6, Bridgewater, 1947 *Below*: Neumann in Israel, 1950s

Above: Neumann at Technion, Haifa, 1950s

Below: With Eldar Sharon (left) and Zvi Hecker (right) in their Tel Aviv office, 1960s

Above: Neumann (left) teaching a class at the Technion, Haifa, 1953, Zvi Hecker (center)

Below: Eldar Sharon (left) with Neumann at their Tel Aviv office, 1960s

Neumann on a visit to Achziv, site of Club Med Holiday Camp, 1960

Naomi Neumann, 1960s

Self portrait
Charcoal drawing of France Grubner

Portrait, date unknown
Pencil sketch, 1920

Watercolor, 1952
Watercolor, date unknown

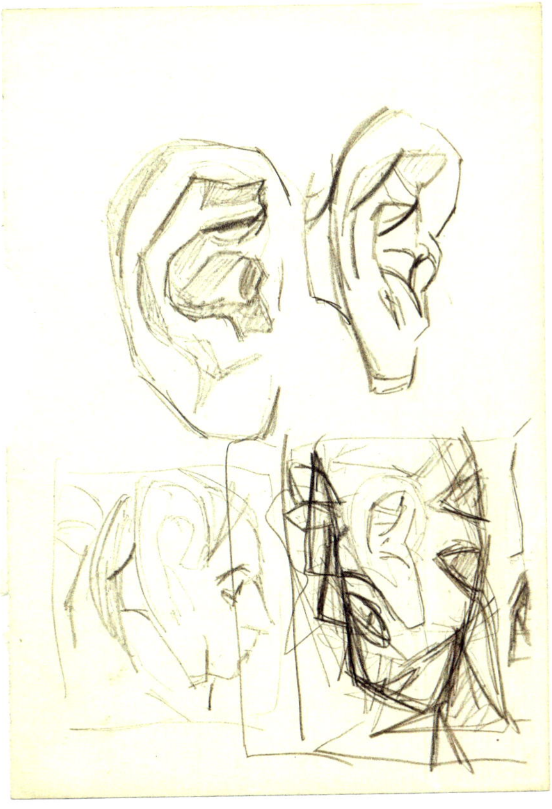

Pen sketch, date unknown
Brown pencil sketch, date unknown

Sketches drawn while in Terezin (Theresienstadt) concentration camp, both dated March 20, 1945

Sketches drawn while in Terezin (Theresienstadt) concentration camp, dated March 19 and May 9, 1945

Watercolor paintings (likely in Jerusalem), dates unknown

Brown pencil sketch, date unknown
Brown pencil sketch, date unknown

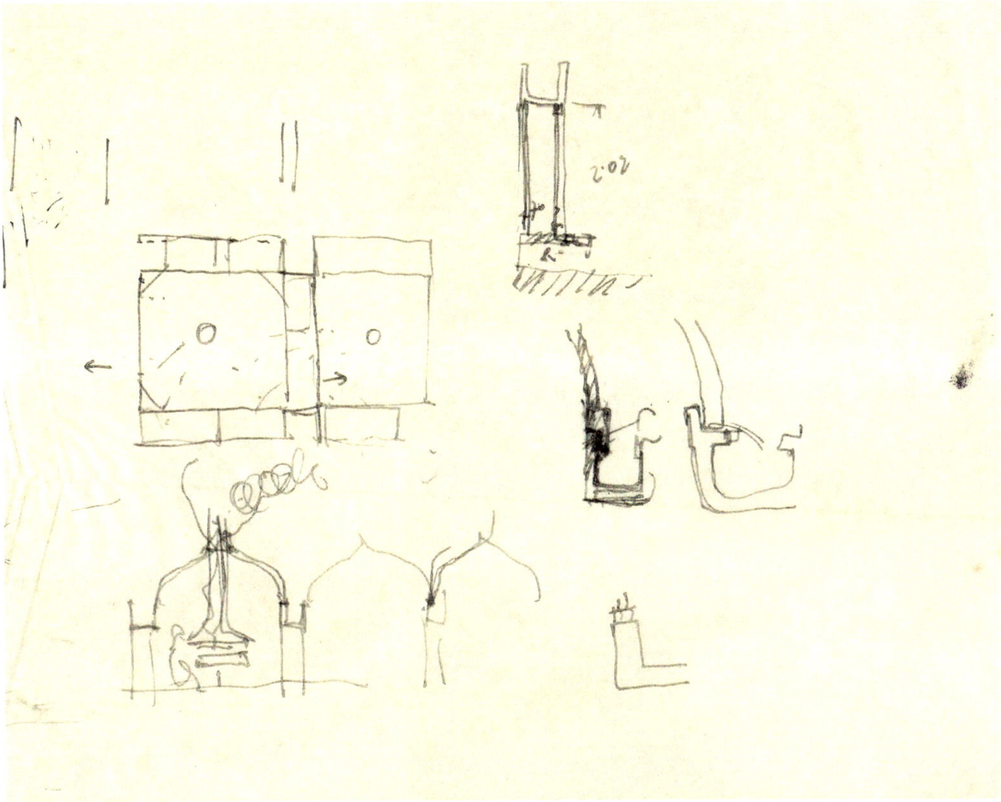

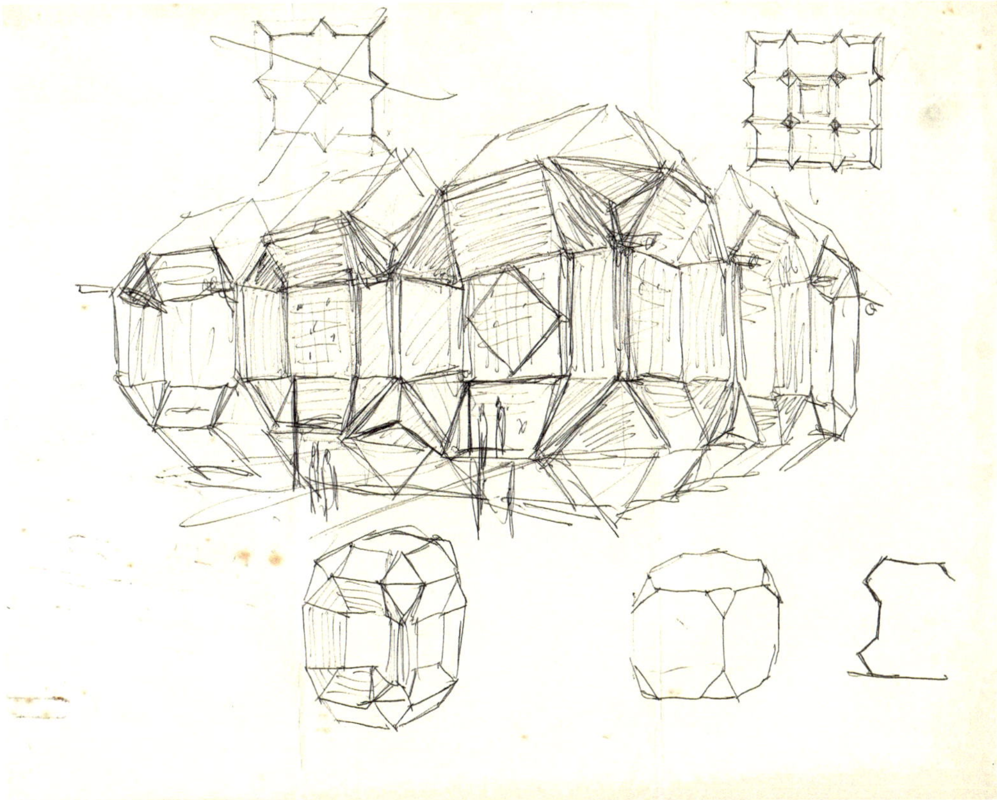

Study sketch
Sketch for unknown project

RAIC JOURNAL

domus
411

11 ARCHITECTURAL DESIGN
November 1964
Price 4/-

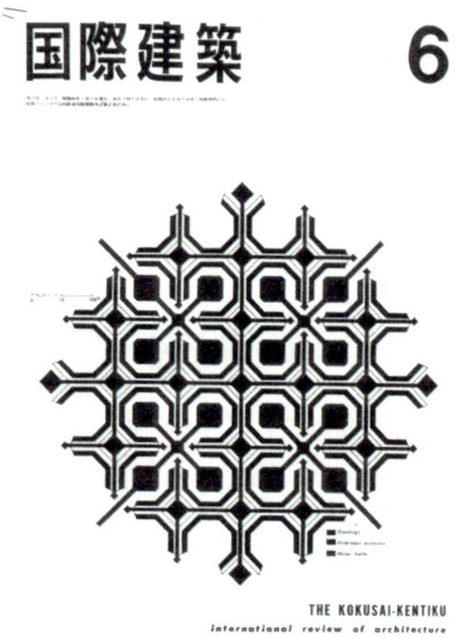
国際建築
6
THE KOKUSAI-KENTIKU
international review of architecture

ארכיטקטורה
ARCHITECTURE IN ISRAEL

arts & architecture

Selected covers of journals that featured Neumann's work (left to right)

RAIC Journal, May 1963
Domus, February 1964
Architectural Design, November 1964
L'Industria Italiana del Cemento, 8, 1965
Domus, front and back, June 1965
Kokousai Kentiku, June 6, 1966
Architectura in Israel, January 1966
Arts and Architecture, July 6, 1966
The Architect 51, December 1966
L'Industria Italiana del Cemento, 1971
L'Industria Italiana del Cemento, 1981

Index

Abram, Rehoven, 38
Achziv Holiday Camp, 83, 166–167, 182, 188, 304, 345
Alberti, 22, 25
Alexander, Christopher, 61–63, 67, 68, 81n37
Algebra, 28
Amsterdam Town Hall, 302–303
Anti-prisms, 334
Apon, Orek, 66
Arabs, 11, 40, 82, 92–95
Arab Village, 51, 192–203
Archimedean solids, 304, 334
Architectural Composition and Building Typology: Interpreting Basic Building (Caniggia and Maffei), 78–79
Architectural Design magazine, 83
"Architectural Morphology" (Neumann course), 77–78
Architectural Principles in the Age of Humanism (Wittkower), 20–21
Architectural Review, 26
"Architecture as Ornament" (Neumann), 35, 54, 336–340
Architecture as Space (Zevi), 33–34
Architecture Canada journal, 6, 342
Aristotle, 32
Arnheim, Rudolf, 24
Arts and Crafts movement, 54
A. Sharon-Idelson Architects, 166
Ashdod City Center, 270–277
Asplund, Gunnar, 13
ATBAT project, 47
Atelier du Palais de Bois, 10, 13, 17n13, 49, 344
Athens Charter, 19
Atomic warfare, 18
Avant-garde movement, 10, 13, 43, 54, 83, 345

Bakema, Jaap, 66
Banham, Reyner, 25–26
Bardet, Gaston, 327
Barlow, 336
Bat Yam Town Hall and Civic Center, 137–165
  competition for, 42
  EM-PHI system and, 136–137
  examining design of, 11
  Neumann-Hecker-Sharon and, 43–51, 71, 136, 304, 345
Bauhaus style, 40, 42
Behrens, Peter, 10, 13, 104, 344
Beit Zeit Youth Camp and Restaurant, 292–302, 345
Ben-Gurion, David, 42
Berkeley School, 61
Berlage, 339
Béton brut, 48
Beugnet, Lucian, 112, 345
"Biological Form and Pattern" (Waddington), 60
Biology
  ancient symbolism and, 327
  building as container cell and, 332
  humanization of space and, 26, 31, 324–327
  Le Corbusier and, 26
  morphology and, 15, 329
  pattern thinking and, 59–60, 65, 78
  spatiality and, 31, 325
  technology and, 326–327
Bochner, Mel, 80n10
Bonfanti, Ezio, 78
Boon, Gert, 66
Bottero, Maria, 7, 17n6, 84
Boyer, Christine, 8
Brise-soleil (sun-break), 47
British Mandate, 40, 82, 92
Brno, Czechoslovakia, 9–10, 13, 17, 19, 27, 53, 344–345
Bronowski, Jacob, 18, 32
Brutalism, 37n22, 48–49
Buber, Martin, 34
Building as assembly, 71–72
Building as filter, 74
Building as object, 11–12, 59, 63, 70–71
Building as pattern, 11–12, 58, 63–70
Burckhardt, Jacob, 33
Byzantine style, 35, 50, 95, 332

Cambridge School of Architecture, 79
Canada, 6, 50, 88–90, 128, 204, 308, 345
Candilis, George, 47, 68
Caniggia, Gianfranco, 78–79, 81n36
Cassirer, Ernst, 19
Centenary Hall, Algiers, 108, 111
Centre for Configurational Studies, 79
Cercle et Carre, 10, 345
Cézanne, 340
Chemistry, 31, 324, 334
CIAM (Congres Internationaux d'Architecture Moderne), 7, 10, 17n7, 19, 36n7, 58, 69, 81n23, 342, 345
"Closest Packing Systems" (Fuller), 60–61
Club Med, Achziv, 83, 166–167, 182, 188, 304, 345
Coates, Wells, 11, 31
Collin, Peter, 23
Colquhoun, Alan, 59
Communists, 10, 38, 345
Concrete, 45
  Brutalism and, 48–49
  building as filter and, 74
  Danciger Building and, 87, 240
  Dubiner Apartment House and, 205
  Israeli culture and, 48–50
  Kiryat Yam Holiday Camp and, 188
  modernism and, 93
  Netanya City Hall and, 230
  Perret and, 10, 13
  reinforced, 10, 48, 308
  synagogues and, 286, 308
  White City and, 42
Conzen, Michael Robert Gunter, 78
Cook, Peter, 7, 83–84
Crystals, 48, 56, 60, 334, 336–339

Danciger Building (Mechanical Engineering laboratory), 50, 242–269
  controversies over, 12, 86–91, 240–241
  façade complaints of, 241
  functionalism and, 86–90, 240
  geometric design for, 241
  Hecker and, 86, 88–91, 240–241
  lawsuit over, 89
  naming of, 240
  Saunders Committee and, 86–88
  Sharon and, 96n10
  windows of, 241
Darwin, Charles, 55
Da Vinci, Leonardo, 27
"Design for Growth, Change, and Uncertainty" (Mansfeld), 64
Deutsche Baugewerbeschule (German Building Trades School), 9, 53, 344
Deutsche Technische Hochschule (German Technical University), 10, 344
Dori, Yaakov, 86, 240
Dormitory and Housing Schemes, 128–135
Dr. Josef Slezak House, 122–125
Dubiner, Sam, 50, 204
Dubiner Apartment House, 11, 50–52, 57n16, 204–229, 345
Duomo of Milano, 339
Dutch Forum group, 53, 64, 66–72, 75, 81n29, 85

Eames, Charles, 37n22
Ein Rafa project, 192–203, 345
Einstein, Albert, 32
El Al Terminal, 47, 72, 278–285
EM-PHI system
  Bat Yam Town Hall and Civic Center and, 136–137
  cultural space and, 27
  Da Vinci and, 27
  factors of, 28
  Giorgione and, 27
  Golden Section and, 7, 28
  Gropius and, 7, 11, 27
  humanization of space and, 324–327
  impact of, 26–27
  Le Corbusier and, 7, 11, 27–30, 37n25, 75
  patterns and, 52
  physiognomic qualities of decimal system and, 35
  poetry and, 14
  polyhedral geometry and, 45–46, 52
  space packing and, 30, 45, 136–137
  symmetry and, 35
EM-PHI System, The: The Humanization of Space (Neumann), 11, 14, 26–27, 323–327
Escher, 337–338
Essay on Man, An: An Introduction to a Philosophy of Human Culture (Cassirer), 19
Euclidean geometry, 330, 333–334, 339
Eupalinos, The Architect (Valéry), 14
Existentialism Is a Humanism (Sartre), 19, 39

Experimental approaches, 7, 43, 80n4, 83–84, 86, 329
Expressionism, 104, 345

Family Houses, Brno, 126–127
Fedorov, 336
Fibonacci sequence, 23–24, 28–29, 326–327, 331
Field theory, 66
Forestier, Pierre, 10, 17n13, 112, 345
Forum magazine, 64, 66–67
French Enlightenment, 30
Fuller, Buckminster, 56–57, 60–61
"Function, Structure and Symbol" (Tange), 65
Functionalism
  Ashdod City Center and, 270
  Athens Charter and, 19
  beauty and, 89
  Brno and, 9–10, 13, 17, 19
  CIAM and, 19
  Danciger Building and, 86–90, 240
  Dutch Forum group and, 69
  formal arbitrariness and, 340
  Hertzberger and, 69–70
  International Style and, 11, 13, 39–40, 73–75
  Jaschke and, 67
  modernism and, 14, 40, 58–59, 65, 70, 93
  new architecture of Jerusalem and, 93
  pattern thinking and, 58–59, 65, 67, 69–70
  Sabra architects and, 82
  Safdie and, 84
  Saunders Committee and, 88
  symbolic vs. practical, 24, 40
  Tange and, 65
  typologies and, 67, 74
  utilitarianism and, 16, 36n7, 87, 90, 325, 336
  Valéry and, 14

Geometry
  Archimedean solids and, 304, 334
  brise-soleil (sun break) and, 47
  crystals and, 48, 56, 60, 334, 336–339
  energetic, 60–61
  Euclidean, 330, 333–334, 339
  field theory and, 66
  Fuller and, 60–61
  hexagons, 51–53, 128, 166–167, 182, 205, 230, 270, 278, 286, 292, 302, 304, 308, 310, 331, 333
  humanization of space and, 21–31, 35
  Islamic, 11
  modernism and, 13
  morphological architecture and, 77
  orthogonal, 11, 42, 44–46, 52, 55, 72–74, 77, 87, 332
  pattern thinking and, 72–73 (*see also* Pattern thinking)
  Platonic solids and, 304, 334
  polyhedral, 11, 45, 49, 52, 57, 72–74, 77, 80, 84, 188, 304–308
  prisms and, 51–52, 331, 334, 339–340
  ratios and, 21–24, 28–29, 37n26, 50
  rectangles, 23, 80, 333
  Renaissance and, 21
  space packing and, 11, 84 (*see also* Space packing)
  squares, 46, 77, 192, 304, 310, 333
  stacking and, 12, 30, 46, 49, 85, 136, 278
  tetrahedrons, 60, 166–167, 182, 230, 278, 286, 292, 302, 304, 310
  triangles, 48–49, 87, 166, 182, 230, 240–241, 278, 286, 304, 308, 310
  typologies and, 15
  Vitruvian man and, 22–23
  volumetric units and, 30, 46–47, 52, 74, 136
Geometry of Art and Life, The (Ghyka), 24
Germany, 9–10, 53, 78, 83–84, 106, 344–345
Gerstel, Leopold, 71
Ghyka, Matila C., 11, 24, 325
Giedion, Sigfried, 11, 19–20, 32–35, 36n8, 37n38, 81n37
Ginsberg, Jean, 10, 345
Giorgione, 27
God, 24, 36n16, 39, 80n4, 325
Goldberg, Alexander, 88–89
Golden Mean, 28, 37n26
Golden Number, 28, 325
Golden Ratio, 28–29, 37n26
Golden Section
  ancient Greeks and, 28
  EM-PHI system and, 7, 28
  Fibonacci sequence and, 23–24, 28–29, 326–327, 331
  Le Corbusier and, 7, 23–24, 28, 30, 37n25, 54, 333, 339
  mechanics of life and, 326
  proportion and, 7
  Pythagorean intuition and, 325
Goodovitch, Israel, 8, 39, 71
Government Palace of Agriculture, 108–110
Grassi, Giorgio, 78
Greeks, 28, 326, 338
Gropius, Walter, 7, 11, 27, 36n7
"Group Form" (Maki and Ohtaka), 64–65
Growth and Form (Thompson), 60
Guiauchain, Jacques, 10, 108, 344–345

Ha'aretz newspaper, 89
Habitat 67, 6, 74–75, 84–85
Hambridge, 325
Harely, Joop, 66
Hecker, Zvi
  Achziv Holiday Camp and, 83, 166–167, 182, 188, 304, 345
  Amsterdam Town Hall and, 302
  as apprentice to Neumann, 6
  Ashdod City Center and, 270
  Bat Yam Town Hall and Civic Center and, 43–51, 71, 136, 304, 345
  Beit Zeit Youth Camp and Restaurant and, 292, 345
  Bottero on, 84
  challenging conventions of architecture and, 43
  Danciger Building and, 86, 88–91, 240–241
  death of Neumann and, 6, 17n1
  Dormitory and Housing Schemes and, 128
  Dubiner Apartment House and, 11, 50–52, 57n16, 204, 345
  Ein Rafa project and, 192, 345
  El-Al Terminal and, 278
  influence of, 8
  Kiryat Yam Holiday Camp and, 188, 345
  Michmoret Holiday Camp and, 182, 188, 345
  Netanya proposals and, 204
  Neumann-Hecker-Sharon and, 11, 42–44,50, 83, 96n10, 166–167, 182, 188, 204, 345
  on Neumann's move to Israel, 38
  "Polyhedric Architecture" and, 304
  Sharon and, 11, 43–46, 50, 71, 83, 136, 166
  student days of, 6, 11, 38–39, 43
  Synagogue at the Officer's School and, 308
  synagogue competition and, 286
  Technion-Israel Institute of Technology and, 6, 11, 38–39, 42, 240
Hertzberger, Herman, 37n22, 66, 69–71
Hiroshima, 18
Honnecourt, Villard de, 339
House for California, 104–107
Humanism, 18–20, 34–35, 80n4, 342
Humanity of Man, The (Perry), 19
Humanization of space
  architecture as theory of space and, 31–33
  biology and, 26, 31, 324–327
  cities and, 18–20
  Da Vinci and, 27
  EM-PHI system and, 7, 11, 14, 26–30, 35–36, 45–46, 52, 73–75, 85, 136–137, 205, 324–327
  experience and, 35
  Fibonacci sequence and, 23–24, 28–29
  geometry and, 21–31, 35
  Le Corbusier and, 22–30, 54, 69, 342
  planar method and, 25
  polyhedral geometries and, 72–73
  prefabricated construction and, 326
  proportion and, 20–26
  psychology and, 14, 31–32, 34, 36n8, 78, 83, 338
  ratios and, 22–23
  Renaissance and, 20–22, 26–30, 35, 36n8, 12, 16, 328
  symbolism and, 21, 24, 27, 31–32, 36n7, 37n22

symmetry and, 35
synthesis of art and technology for, 326
towards a concept of, 324–326
Unité d'habitation and, 25, 54, 69, 342
Vitruvian man and, 22–23
war atrocities and, 18
Huxtable, Ada Louise, 7, 84

I-beams, 52, 128
Industrialization, 6, 26, 93, 342–343
International Style, 11, 13, 39–40, 73–75
Intuition
act of creation and, 15
Bronowski on, 32
mathematical, 325, 334
mechanistic preconditions and, 329
Pythogorean, 325
spatial, 31
"Investigation into Collective Form" (Maki), 64–65
"Irrational Factors in Building Industrialization" (Neumann), 6, 342–343
Islam, 11, 50, 67, 73, 75, 95
Israel
See also Specific projects
Arab-Israeli war and, 82
architectural context of, 8, 12, 16, 39–43, 47–48, 51, 64, 71, 73, 80–95
art scene of, 50
Bauhaus style and, 42
brise-soleil (sun-break) and, 47
British Mandate and, 40, 82, 92
building boom of, 11, 86
building materials of, 48–49
CIAM and, 7
climate of, 47, 52
Haira, 10, 39, 50, 86, 188, 240, 345
International Style and, 39–40
Jaffa, 42, 50, 84
Jerusalem, 7, 10, 12, 34, 38, 64, 91–95, 96n22, 192, 292, 308, 345
Likud party and, 94
modernism and, 40, 42, 47–48, 91–94
Mount Carmel, 86, 240
natural environment of, 47–48
Neumann's emigration to, 10–11, 38
postmodernism and, 13, 91–95
prefabricated construction and, 26, 93, 96n21, 286
Sabra generation and, 82, 94, 96n23
Six Day War and, 12, 91
Technion-Israel Institute of Technology and, 6
(*see also* Technion-Israel Institute of Technology)
Tel Aviv, 8, 11, 40–45, 50, 182, 204, 230, 278, 345
War of Independence and, 82
White City and, 40–42
Zionist movement and, 41, 50
Israeli Ministry of Housing, 192
Italian school of morphology, 78–80

Jaffa, 42, 50, 84
Jaschke, Karin, 67
Jerusalem Planning Department, 38
Jourdain, Frantz, 340
Justice Hall, 120–121

Kahler, Erich, 19
Kalenbach, Kennedy, and Furnes, 10
Kant, Immanuel, 340
Karmi, Ram, 48, 94
Kepes, Gyorgy, 60, 65–66
Kibbutzim, 41, 57n6
Kiryat Yam Holiday Camp, 188–191, 345
Kunstwissenschaft (science of art), 328
Kurokawa, Noriaki, 65

L'architecture d'aujourd'hui journal, 7
Larochelle, Pierre, 78
Lavi, Rafi, 82–83
Le Corbusier
biology and, 26
brise-soleil (sun break) and, 47
EM-PHI system and, 7, 11, 27–30, 37n25, 75
Fibonacci sequence and, 23–24
Golden Section and, 7, 23–24, 28, 30, 37n25, 54, 333, 339
humanization of space and, 22–30, 54, 69, 342
Modulor and, 7, 20–25, 27, 29–30, 37n22, 75, 339
planar method and, 25
proportion and, 7, 27
regulating lines and, 25, 30
symbolism and, 24, 27
Unité d'habitation and, 25, 54, 69, 342
Universal Man and, 26
Léger, Fernand, 340
Levant, 41
L'Humanisation de l'espace, le système mΦ (Neumann), 27
Liggett, Robin, 79
Likud party, 94
Loos, Adolf, 13, 49, 54–55, 122, 340, 344–345

Maffei, Luigi Gian, 78–79
Maki, Fumihiko, 64–65
Man Ray, 10
Mansfeld, Alfred, 64, 71, 88
Man the Measure: A New Approach to History (Kahler), 19
Martin Centre, 79
Mat buildings, 12, 66
Mathematics
algebra, 28
Archimedean solids and, 304, 334
Fibonacci sequence and, 23–24, 28–29, 326–327, 331
geometry, 11 (*see also* Geometry)
Golden Section and, 28 (*see also* Golden Section)
intuition and, 334
Platonic solids and, 304, 334
Pythagorean school and, 21, 325, 327
ratios and, 21–24, 28–29, 37n26, 50
Vitruvian man and, 22–23
Metabolism in Architecture (Kurokawa), 65
Metabolists, 64, 70, 72, 75
Michmoret Holiday Camp, 182–188, 345
Mitchell, William, 79
Modernism
avant-garde, 10, 13, 43, 54, 83, 345
Behrens and, 10
brise-soleil (sun break) and, 47
building as object and, 11–12
challenging conventions of, 9, 13
European influence on, 11, 47
functionalism and, 14, 40, 58–59, 65, 70, 93
independent façade and, 74
International Style and, 11, 13, 39–40, 73–75
Israeli, 40, 42, 47–48, 91–94
Le Corbusier and, 55 (*see also* Le Corbusier)
North African, 108
pattern as spatial operation and, 73–74
Perret and, 10, 13–14, 48–49, 108, 344
planar surfaces and, 15
polyhedral geometries and, 72–73
postmodernism and, 13, 91–95
scale and, 59
settlement typologies and, 36
slabs and, 11, 87
Van Eyck and, 67
Zevi and, 33–35, 37n44
Modern Movement, 19
Modulor (Le Corbusier), 7, 20–25, 27, 29–30, 37n22, 75, 339
Montreal Expo, 84
Morocco, 47
Morphological architecture, 6
cell growth and, 333
changes in form and, 12
courses on, 8, 77–78
pattern thinking and, 75–80
polyhedral geometries and, 77, 80
space packing and, 12
spatiality and, 57
Steadman on, 79–80
Technion-Israel Institute of Technology and, 77, 80
"Morphologic Architecture" (Neumann), 14, 35, 75, 77, 80, 81n28, 328–335
Morphology
biology and, 15, 329
Conzenian School and, 78
definition of, 76
function and, 338
Italian school of, 78–80
space packing and, 12 (*see also* Space packing)
spatiality and, 57
typologies and, 78–80
urban, 36

Mount Carmel, 86, 240
Muratori, Saverio, 78
Museum of Modern Art, New York, 335

Nazis, 10
Negev synagogue, 47, 49, 71–72, 308
Netanya City Hall, 72, 230–239
Netsch, Walter, 65–66
Neumann, Alfred
- Achziv Holiday Camp and, 83, 166–167, 182, 188, 304, 345
- "Architectural Morphology" and, 77–78
- "Architecture as Ornament" and, 35, 54, 336–340
- background of, 9–11, 53
- Bat Yam Town Hall and Civic Center and, 43–51, 71, 136, 304, 345
- Behrens Award and, 10
- Beit Zeit Youth Camp and Restaurant and, 292, 345
- challenging conventions of architecture and, 43
- death of, 6
- dual teaching/designer roles of, 7–8
- Dubiner Apartment House and, 11, 50–52, 57n16, 204, 345
- Ein Rafa project and, 192, 345
- EM-PHI system and, 7, 11, 14, 26–30, 35–36, 45–46, 52, 73–75, 85, 136–137, 205
- as experimental architect, 7, 43, 83–84, 86
- Golden Section and, 7
- influence on Safdie, 6–7
- "Irrational Factors in Building Industrialization" and, 6, 342–343
- Kiryat Yam Holiday Camp and, 188, 345
- *L'Humanisation de l'espace, le système mΦ* and, 27
- "Morphologic Architecture" and, 14, 35, 75, 77, 80, 81n28, 328–335
- Michmoret Holiday Camp and, 182, 188, 345
- Netanya proposals and, 204
- Neumann-Hecker-Sharon and, 11, 42–44, 50, 83, 96n10, 166–167, 182, 188, 204, 345
- pedagogical style of, 39
- "Space-Packing Patterns" and, 52 (*see also* Space packing)
- Technion-Israel Institute of Technology and, 6, 8, 10, 38–39, 42, 77, 84, 86–90, 345
- theory of design of, 9
- volumetric units and, 30, 46–47, 52, 74, 136
- World War I and, 10

Neumann, Eva-Marie, 91
Neumann, Naomi, 6–7, 91, 128, 302
Neumann-Hecker-Sharon, 166–167, 182, 188, 204, 345
- See also Specific project
- beginnings of, 11, 42–44
- Danziger and, 50
- international recognition of, 43
- radical reputation of, 43, 83
- Sharon's departure from, 96n10

New Landscape in Art and Science, The (Kepes), 60, 65–66
Newton, Isaac, 32
New York Times, 7, 84
Nicomachus of Gerasa, 325
Niggly, 336
Nitzan-Shiftan, Alona, 92
Notes on the Synthesis of Form (Alexander), 62–63

Ofrat, Gideon, 48
Ohtaka, Masato, 64–65
Open University, 79
Organic perspective, 28, 31, 33, 37n41, 85, 324–325, 334, 339
Ornament
- "Architecture as Ornament" and, 35, 54, 336–340
- elimination of, 13, 42
- Islamic, 95
- Larochelle and, 78
- Loos and, 54–55
- Renaissance and, 339
- space packing and, 334
- symbolism and, 336, 338
- three-dimensional, 55, 334
- two-dimensional, 55, 334

"Ornament and Crime" (Loos), 54
Ottomans, 11, 75, 95

Palestine, 40–41, 57n6, 92–96, 166–167, 192
Palladio, 21–22, 25
Patterned-object approach, 12, 57, 71–72, 75, 205, 286
Pattern Language, A (Alexander), 62–63, 68
Pattern thinking
- architectural form and, 63–71
- architecture as creation of, 58–80
- Bat Yam and, 46–47
- biology and, 59–60, 65, 78
- building as assembly and, 71–72
- building as filter and, 74
- building as object and, 11–12, 59, 63, 70–71
- building as patterns and, 11–12, 58, 63–70
- color and, 49
- crystals and, 48, 56, 60, 334, 336–339
- Dubiner Apartment House and, 51–52
- emergence of, 58–61
- EM-PHI system and, 52
- functionalism and, 58–59, 65, 67, 69–70
- geometric specificity and, 72–73 (*see also* Geometry)
- kit of parts and, 61–63
- as language, 61–63
- morphologic architecture and, 75–80
- non-programmatic unit function and, 74–75
- patterned-object approach and, 71–75
- space packing and, 8–12, 30, 45–46, 49, 52–57, 70–74, 84–85, 87, 93, 136, 230, 286, 304, 334–335
- spatiality and, 14, 30, 46, 55, 60–62, 65–68, 70–75, 81n37, 83, 128, 136
- stacking and, 52, 71–72, 74, 85, 128–129
- symbolism and, 65, 72, 334–335
- symmetry and, 15 (*see also* Symmetry)
- types of, 61–71

Payne, Alina, 22, 24
Perret, Auguste, 10, 13–14, 48–49, 108, 344
Perry, Ralph Barton, 19
Persians, 11, 95
Phi. *See* Golden Section
Piazza San Marco, 44
Platonic solids, 334
Poincaré, Henri, 32
Polya, 336
Polyhedral geometries, 305–308
- Bottero on, 84
- EM-PHI system and, 45–46, 52
- floor area and, 188
- humanization of space and, 72–73
- Islamic traditions and, 11
- modernism and, 72–73
- morphological architecture and, 77, 80
- non-programmatic unit function and, 74
- space packing and, 11, 45, 49, 52–57, 84
- unique approach of Neumann to, 304

"Polyhedric Architecture", 80, 304
Pompeii, 44–45
Postmodernism, 13, 91–95
Prefabricated construction, 26, 93, 96n21, 286, 326
Prisms, 51–52, 331, 334, 339–340
Proportion
- Da Vinci and, 27
- EM-PHI system and, 7, 11, 14, 26–30, 35–36, 45–46, 52, 73–75, 85, 136–137, 205
- geometry and, 24 (*see also* Geometry)
- Golden Section and, 7
- humanization of space and, 24 (*see also* Humanization of space)
- Modulor and, 7, 20–25, 27, 29–30, 37n22, 75, 339
- planar method and, 25
- polyhedral geometries and, 11, 45, 49, 52–57, 84
- post-World War II discourse on, 20–26
- ratios and, 21–24, 28–29, 37n26, 50
- Renaissance and, 20–22, 26–30, 35, 36n8,12,16, 328, 339
- space packing and, 136 (*see also* Space packing)
- spatiality and, 30 (*see also* Spatiality)
- symbolic role of, 24
- symbolism and, 21, 24

theories of, 7–8, 11, 20–21, 5–30, 34–35, 36n16, 37n32, 328
Universal Man and, 26
Provincial Research Institute, 10
Psychology, 14, 31–32, 34, 36n8, 78, 83, 338
Pythagorean school, 21, 325, 327

Ramat Gan, 50, 204, 345
Ratios, 50
Fibonacci sequence and, 23–24, 28–29, 326–327, 331
Golden Ratio and, 28–29, 37n26
harmony and, 21–22
Renaissance and, 21
Vitruvian man and, 22–23
whole number, 21–22
Raumgestaltung, 31
Raumplan, 54, 122
Renaissance
architecture as science and, 21
geometry and, 21
hierarchical order and, 21
humanization of space and, 20–22, 26–30, 35, 36n8,12,16, 328
ornament and, 339
tradition and, 21
whole number ratios and, 21–22
Rossi, Aldo, 78
Rotbard, Sharon, 42

Sabra generation, 82, 94, 96n23
Safdie, Moshe, 6–7, 71, 74–75, 84–85
Samaritaine, La, 340
Sartre, Jean Paul, 19, 39
Saunders Committee, 86–88
Schmarsow, August, 31–33, 35, 37n47
School, Boulogne-Billancourt, 112–117
School of Architecture, Laval University, 77–78, 342
School of Architecture and Urban Planning, UCLA, 79
Schrödinger, Erwin, 18–19
Schrofer, Jurriaan, 66
Schwarzer, Mitchell W., 37n47
"Science and Humanism" (Schrödinger), 18
"Science and Human Values" (Bronowski), 18
Scolari, Massimo, 78
Serlio, 339
Settlements
Dutch Forum group and, 67
Ein Rafa project and, 192
grouping and, 332
housing technology and, 342
individual cells and, 12
kibbutzim and, 41, 57n6
non-grouped, 55
old Holy city and, 92, 94
primitive forms of, 12, 55, 67, 77
pseudo-anthropological analysis of, 35
rotational movement and, 332
typologies for, 35–36, 44
Sharon, Arieh, 42, 166
Sharon, Eldar
Achziv Holiday Camp and, 83, 166–167, 182, 188, 304, 345
Bat Yam Town Hall and Civic Center and, 43–51, 71, 136, 304, 345
Beit Zeit Youth Camp and Restaurant and, 292, 345
challenging conventions of architecture and, 43
Danciger Building and, 96n10
Dubiner Apartment House and, 11, 50–52, 57n16, 203–204, 345
easy-going nature of, 42
Ein Rafa project and, 192, 345
father's firm and, 96n10, 166
Kiryat Yam Holiday Camp and, 188, 345
Michmoret Holiday Camp and, 182, 188, 345
Neumann-Hecker-Sharon and, 11, 42–44, 50, 83, 96n10, 166–167, 182, 188, 204, 345
Shklarsky, 89
Shoenflies, 336
Shubnikov, 337
Siclis, Charles, 10, 344
Six Day War, 12, 91
Slapeta, Vladimir, 38
Smithson, Alison, 37n22, 66
Smithson, Peter, 37n22
SOM (Skidmore, Owings and Merrill Architects), 66
Space, Time, and Architecture (Giedion), 32–33
Space packing
Archimedean solids and, 334
Bat Yam Town Hall and Civic Center and, 136–137, 304
building as assembly and, 71–72
building as filter and, 74
crystals and, 48, 56, 60, 334, 336–339
Dutch Forum and, 70
efficiency and, 56
EM-PHI system and, 30, 45, 136–137
Fuller and, 56–57
generative device and, 73
Habitat and, 6, 74–75, 84–85
homogeneity and, 334–335
Huxtable on, 84
Jerusalem architecture and, 93
morphological architecture and, 12
Neumann as father of, 7–9, 12, 52–57, 84
new Jerusalem architecture and, 93
ornament and, 334
pattern thinking and, 8–12, 30, 45–46, 49, 52–57, 70–74, 84–85, 87, 93, 136, 230, 286, 304, 334–335
Platonic solids and, 304, 334
polyhedral geometries and, 11, 45, 49, 52–57, 84
settlement aggregation and, 12
stacking and, 12, 30, 46, 49, 52, 71–72, 74, 85, 128–129, 136, 278
system description of, 52–57
theory of design and, 9
triangular units and, 87
unit of repetition and, 72
volumetric units and, 30, 46–47, 52–53, 74, 136
"Space-Packing Patterns" (Neumann), 52
Spatiality, 37n35, 47
abstract concept of, 31
architecture as theory of space and, 31–33
biology and, 31, 325
constructional approach and, 30
contemporary concepts for, 324–325
crystals and, 48, 56, 60, 334, 336–339
efficiency and, 53, 56
enclosure elements and, 304
Fuller and, 56, 60–61
Giedion on, 32–35
grids and, 45–46
humanization of space and, 14
(*see also* Humanization of space)
morphological architecture and, 57
movement routes and, 15
nature and, 56
new languages for, 84
pattern thinking and, 14, 30, 46, 55, 60–62, 65–68, 70–75, 81n37, 83, 128, 136
polyhederal geometries and, 11, 45, 49, 52, 57, 72–74, 77, 80, 84, 188, 304–308
positive, 68
psychology and, 14, 31–32, 34, 36n8, 78, 83, 338
scale and, 9
Schmarsow and, 31, 33, 35, 37n47
settlement organization and, 77, 327
space packing and, 7–9
(*see also* Space packing)
stacking and, 12, 30, 46, 49, 52, 71–72, 74, 85, 128–129, 136, 278
symmetry and, 35, 340
(*see also* Symmetry)
three-dimensional expression and, 55
typologies and, 77
unified objects and, 53
Vitruvian man and, 22–23
volumetric units and, 30, 46–47, 52, 74, 136
Speiser, Andreas, 338
Stacking geometry and, 12, 30, 46, 49, 85, 136, 278
pattern thinking and, 52, 71–72, 74, 85, 128–129
volumetric units and, 30, 46–47, 52, 74, 136
State Ministry of Housing, 91–92
Steadman, J. P., 79–80
Steel, 104, 292, 338, 340, 345
Stonehenge, 333
Structuralism, 64, 71, 81n30,34, 342

Structuralism in Architecture, Selected Works of Al Mansfeld and his Team (exhibition), 64
Studies in Polyhedral Geometries, 304–307
Switzerland, 83
Symbolism
ancient, 327
color and, 49–50
concrete and, 48
Danciger Building and, 90
humanization of space and, 21, 24, 27, 31–32, 36n7, 3n22
Israeli postmodernism and, 91–93
Le Corbusier and, 24, 27
ornament and, 336, 338
pattern thinking and, 65, 72, 334–335
proportion and, 21, 24
Tange and, 65
White City and, 42
Wittkower and, 24, 27
Symmetry
Amsterdam Town Hall and, 302
color and, 49, 337
crystals and, 48, 56, 60, 334, 336–339
EM-PHI system and, 35
Escher and, 337–338
human body and, 22–23
humanization of space and, 35
laws of, 338, 340
ornament and, 337–339
pattern repetition and, 60, 85
rotational, 331, 334, 339
scale and, 75
Schmarsow and, 37n47
shape of aggregations and, 329
Shubnikov and, 337
space packing and, 56
(*see also* Space packing)
Synagogue at the Officer's School and, 308
Vitruvian man and, 22–23
Synagogue, *Competition*, 286–291
Synagogue at the Officers' School, 308–321
"Systems of Generating Systems" (Alexander), 62

Tange, Kenzo, 65
Team 10, 64, 67–68
Technion-Israel Institute of Technology
Danciger Building and, 50
(*see also* Danciger Building)
Dori and, 86, 240
Faculty of Architecture and Town Planning and, 8, 10, 38–39, 86, 345
Goldberg and, 88–89
Hecker and, 6, 11, 38–39, 42, 89, 240
lawsuit against, 89
Mansfeld and, 64, 88
morphological architecture and, 77, 80
Neumann and, 6, 8, 10, 38–39, 42, 77, 84, 86–90, 345
Tendenza group, 78
Thereisenstadt concentration camp, 10, 345
Thompson, D'Arcy, 60
Tinguely, 335
Typologies
art and, 9
functionalism and, 67, 74
geometry and, 15
mat buildings and, 12, 66
morphology and, 78–80
Muratori and, 78
orthogonal, 77
positive space and, 68
settlements and, 35, 36, 44
spatial cell and, 77

Unité d'habitation, 25, 54, 69, 342
Universal Man, 26
University of Birmingham, 78
University of California, Los Angeles (UCLA), 79
Utilitarianism, 16, 36n7, 87, 90, 325, 336

Valéry, Paul, 14, 325
Van Eyck, Aldo, 66–69, 81n20,23
Van Stigt, Joop, 53
Venice, 44
Vienna Academy of Fine Arts, 10, 104, 344
Villa, Paris, France, 118–119
Vitruvian man, 22–23
Vitruvius, 21–24, 36n16, 328, 339
Volumetric units, 30, 46–47, 52, 74, 136
Von Laue, 336

Waddington, C. H., 60
Waiting for Godot (Beckett), 39
Weizman, Eyal, 93
Weltanschauung, 24
West Bank, 92–94
White City, 40–42
Wittgenstein, 39
Wittkower, Rudolf, 20–22, 24–27, 36n8, 37n22
Wolfflin, Heinrich, 33
Woods, Shadrach, 47
World War I era, 10, 344
World War II era, 18–20, 25, 34, 58–60, 68, 78, 82, 345
Wright, F. L., 339

Yishuv, 40

Zeitgeist, 33
Zevi, Bruno, 33–35, 37n44
Zionist movement, 41, 50

Photographic Acknowledgments

Materials on Alfred Neumann by kind permission of Eva-Marie Neumann and Zvi Hecker.
Reference images that accompany chapters 1 to 4 to be credited to the following:

Rudolf Wittkower, Architecture Principles in the Age of Humanism (New York: W. W. Norton, 1971): p. 22

Le Corbusier, *The Modulor—A Harmonious Measure to the Human Scale, Universally Applicable to Architecture and Mechanics* (Cambridge, MA: Harvard University Press, 1954, second edition): p. 23

Le Corbusier, *Modulor 2* (Cambridge, MA: Harvard University Press, 1958): p. 25

Nitza Metzger-Shemuk, *Batim min ha'col (Houses from the Sand)—Architecture of the International Style in Tel Aviv 1931–1948* (Tel Aviv: The Tel Aviv Foundation, 1994): p. 41

Hassan Fathy, *Natural Energy and Vernacular Architecture* (Chicago, London: The University of Chicago Press, 1986): p. 49 (left)

Elisabeth Beazley and Michael Harverson, *Living with the Desert* (England: Aris and Phillips Ltd, 1982): p. 49 (right)

Arnulf Lüchinger, *Structuralism in Architecture and Urban Planning* (Stuttgart: Karl Kramer Verlag, 1981): pp. 68 (right), 69, 85

Wim J. van Heuvel, *Structuralism in Dutch Architecture* (Rotterdam: Uitgeverij 010 Publishers, 1992): p. 64, 66, 70

Christopher Alexander, Sara Ishikawa, Murray Silverstein, *A Pattern Language Which Generates Multi-Service* Centers (Berkeley, CA: Center for Environmental Structure, 1968): p. 62

Christopher Alexander, Sara Ishikawa, Murray Silverstein, with Max Jacobson, Ingrid Fiksdahl-King, Shlomo Angel, A Pattern Language (New York: Oxford University Press,1977): p. 68 (left)

Sabrina van der Ley and Markus Richter, eds., *Megastructure Reloaded* (Berlin: Hatje Cantz, 2008): p. 65

Robert W. Marks, *The Dymaxion World of Buckminster Fuller* (New York: Reinhold Publishing, 1960): pp. 56, 61

Zvi Efrat, *The Israeli Project: Building and Architecture, 1948-1973* (Tel Aviv: Tel Aviv Museum of Art, 2004): pp. 43, 47.

Amiram Harlap, *New Israeli Architecture* (London: Associated University Press, 1982): pp. 92, 94.

Courtesy of Eva-Marie Neumann: p. 76

Author's Acknowledgments

First and foremost to thank are Eva-Marie Neumann, Alfred Neumann's daughter, and Zvi Hecker, both of whom generously enabled me to access materials and provided invaluable insights into Alfred Neumann's life and work. This book is based on my PhD dissertation at Princeton University's School of Architecture and I am grateful both to the university, for the exceptional support that I received, and to my dissertation committee, namely to Christine Boyer, Beatriz Colomina, Stan Allen, and Kenneth Frampton, for their guidance, insight, and belief in the importance of this book. Several teachers, colleagues and friends from my time at Princeton generously supported this project: Mario Gandelsonas, Hal Foster, Sarah Whiting, Alysa Nahmias, Noam Elcott, Joaquim Moreno, Els Verbakel, Daniel Lopez-Perez, Alicia Imperiale, Romy Hecht, Leonardo Diaz, Craig Buckley, Lydia Kallipoliti, Maya Galbis, Ari Kardasis, Landry Smith, Simone Brasky, Carolyn Guile, Ingeborg Rocker, and Stephen Phillips. I would like to express special gratitude to the people whom I interviewed for this project: Zvi Hecker, Pierre Larochelle, Eytan Kaufman, Moshe Safdie, Ariella and Israel Goodovitch, and Dan Eytan, who all knew Neumann personally, and Vladimir Šlapeta, who studied Neumann's early years in Czechoslovakia. In 2013 a renewed interest arose in Neumann's work when I collaborated with Tadeás Goryczka, Jaroslav Nemec, and the Czech "Cabinet of Architecture" team to launch a series of exhibitions on Neumann's work. A fantastic group of students, colleagues and friends, mostly from MIT, played a critical role in making these exhibitions possible. I would like to thank Yonatan Cohen, Ariel Noyman, Caroline Murphy, Grisha Enikolopov, Josh Eager, Benjamin Albrecht, and graphic designer Ben Fehrman-Lee. Ben first became involved in the graphic design of the exhibitions and later continued whole-heartedly to design this beautiful book. Caroline Murphy also extended her help beyond the exhibition and offered extremely valuable edits to the entire text. I am thankful to those who invited me to lecture on this project: Ines Weizman at the Bauhaus in Weimar, Arindam Dutta and Alexander D'hoodge at MIT, Kevin Bone at the Cooper Union, Kerem Halbrecht of the Spaceship Gallery in Tel Aviv, Mark Wigley at Columbia University, and Beatriz Colomina at Princeton University. Eyal Weizman offered valuable advice in the early stages of the work when I was debating how to approach the materials. My thanks also go to Cornelia Mechler of the publisher Park Books for her commitment and understanding of the project's contribution to architecture history and theory and to Bronwen Saunders for her careful and sensitive editing work.

This publication was supported by a grant from the Graham Foundation for Advanced Studies in the Fine Arts, in part by the Barr Ferree Foundation Fund for Publications, Department of Art and Archaeology, Princeton University, and by the Council of the Arts at MIT.

Most importantly, I am thankful to my family, my parents Nurit and Itzhik, my wife Sara, and children Raz, Ben, and Boaz, who provided many a blessed distraction that kept me from sidetracking into minute details. People, places, and the relationships between them cannot be disconnected from the study of architecture. While writing on Neumann's work several questions arose as to what determined some of his choices or approaches and what shaped his ideas and attitudes. Faced with these questions, I have not attempted to single out the motivation behind these decisions. My concern has rather been to unfold and place the various events, thoughts, and notions both in relation to each other and independently, and, as they occur in parallel, to describe the setting in which things happen rather than focusing on the actions themselves. The picture painted will at best be a landscape view, to which each viewer can find his or her own point of entry.